A Remarkable Woman

A BIOGRAPHY OF
KATHARINE HEPBURN

Anne Edwards

POCKET BOOKS

New York   London   Toronto   Sydney   Tokyo   Singapore

Portions of this book appeared originally in *Ladies' Home Journal*.

POCKET BOOKS, a division of Simon & Schuster Inc.
1230 Avenue of the Americas, New York, NY 10020

ISBN: 0-671-72756-7

First Pocket Books printing October 1986

10 9 8 7 6

POCKET and colophon are registered trademarks of
Simon & Schuster Inc.

Printed in the U.S.A.

MIKE (low): "There's magnificence in you, Tracy. I'm telling you. . . . A magnificence that comes out of your eyes, that's in your voice, in the way you stand there, in the way you walk. You're lit from within, bright, bright, bright. There are fires banked down in you, hearth-fires and holocausts—"

TRACY: "You—I don't seem to you—made of bronze, then—"

MIKE: "You're made of flesh and blood—that's the blank, unholy surprise of it. You're the golden girl, Tracy, full of love and warmth and delight—"

—Act 2, Scene 2, *The Philadelphia Story,* Philip Barry

CONTENTS

CONTENTS

1938:
The
Turning
Point

CHAPTER
1

The Hollywood columnists crowed that she had got "just what she deserved." Katharine Hepburn, after six years of film stardom and seven straight flops, had bought out her R.K.O. contract for $220,000, packed her bags and headed for her beloved family summer home, Fenwick, at Old Saybrook, Connecticut. Guarding her privacy with her usual ferocity toward the press, she refused to talk about her departure from Hollywood or her headlined romance with millionaire aviator and film producer Howard Hughes.*

At Fenwick, warm May breezes and a close family circle greeted her arrival that spring of 1938. The Hepburns were a clannish group. Their Kate had been publicly chastised as rude ("Katharine of Arrogance" one newspaper called her), "the Czarina," and "Box Office Poison." Overbearing at times, her moods chameleon, Kate's behavior was still con-

---

* Howard Hughes (1905–1976). At eighteen, Hughes inherited a large fortune; at twenty, he began investing in Hollywood films. In 1932, after winning great success with his film Hell's Angels, Hughes left Hollywood to pursue his love of aviation. In 1935, he broke the world's speed record in an airplane of his own design. In 1937, he bettered his own mark, and in 1938, he flew around the world in the record-breaking time of a little more than ninety-one hours. This last was during the time of his romance with Katharine Hepburn. In addition to Hell's Angels, which he also directed, his four major Hollywood films were: The Front Page, Scarface, Bombshell and The Outlaw (also directed).

sidered more "true to herself" than outrageous among her family. All her life (she had celebrated her thirtieth birthday that previous autumn) she had openly fought for what she wanted and believed in and thought that everyone else did the same. She had never experienced financial hard times. Home and Hepburn money were always there if she needed them. That anyone had to kowtow to anyone else, in the paralyzing fear that otherwise job and security might be lost, had never dawned upon her. Yet, she had been wise enough to see that R.K.O. was forcing her hand when they cast her in a modest programmer called *Mother Carey's Chickens.** The studio had wanted to get rid of her. They had counted on her pride and won. Kate, however, viewed her high-priced freedom from R.K.O. as a victory. She refused to work in second-rate films or to concede that her departure from Hollywood might be professional suicide.

Once she was home at Fenwick, her confidence soared. She swam and played golf and tennis. Tall, slim, leggy, dressed in baggy trousers, white tennis dress or conservative bathing suit, bronzed, her fly-away red hair caught up and pinned in a careless fashion (as though no mirror had been consulted), her keen gray-blue eyes defiant, Kate charged through the summer months with her usual amazing energy. She glowed with a golden radiance and looked more like a woman in love than one whose career had just collapsed.

Kate had been seeing Howard Hughes since November, 1936. Hughes bridged the worlds of film and society in which she moved. He was a mover and a shaker, a man of adventure and daring, and they shared many of the same interests: golf (Kate played near championship level), flying (he had had a stretch of beach adjacent to Fenwick prepared for a landing field and taught her to be a fine pilot), and films (as a producer, he had launched the career of Jean Harlow in *Hell's Angels*). Both Kate and Hughes were tall, angular, handsome young people with the self-assurance old money gives. Both were individualists who loved fame and would have expired without attention. Yet, perversely, they loathed publicity and

---

* *Mother Carey's Chickens* was made and released by R.K.O. in July, 1938, with Anne Shirley in the role originally offered Katharine Hepburn. The film drew good reviews and was moderately successful.

the press and enjoyed nothing better than dodging and outwitting reporters and autograph hunters.

Howard Hughes remained in California when Kate left for Connecticut. He was preparing his plane, the *New York World's Fair 1939*, for a record-setting flight around the world. Nonetheless, he secretly managed to fly to see Kate several times in May, June, and July, 1938. Few people impressed Kate, but Hughes—already a hero having broken the transcontinental speed record—had an aura of excitement about him. He believed in her talent and held an ardent and sincere interest in her career. At Fenwick on July Fourth he told her that he wanted to star her in a film, *The Amelia Earhart Story*, about the aviatrix whose mysterious disappearance in the South Pacific near the end of her around-the-world flight the previous year had been haunting him.* He admired Amelia Earhart enormously and thought Kate would be magnificent in the role. Kate agreed, but for the time being they kept the planned project to themselves.

Other film offers—each smaller and more demeaning than the one before—were refused by Kate without indignation. Hollywood's interest, however belittling, meant the industry had not given her up entirely and the studios knew Katharine Hepburn's unique contribution to films could not easily be dismissed.

In fact, everything about Kate and the Hepburns was extraordinary. On weekends, when the family—Dr. and Mrs. Hepburn, their sons, Robert and Richard, their three daughters, Katharine, Peggy and Marion, and Marion's husband, Ellsworth Grant—were all in residence, their impact on one another was explosive. Kate's ex-husband, Ludlow Ogden Smith (introduced by Mrs. Hepburn as "our dear, sweet ex") had his own room at Fenwick. "Luddy" and Kate remained good friends despite their divorce four years earlier.

The Hepburn life-style at Fenwick and at their West Hartford home was organized chaos. "The Doctor says he

---

* Amelia Earhart (1898–1937), first woman to cross the Atlantic by airplane (1928), first woman to make solo flight across the Atlantic (1932), and first person to fly alone from Honolulu to California (1935). In 1937, she attempted with a co-pilot, Frederick J. Noonan, to fly around the world, but her plane was lost on the flight between New Guinea and Howland Island.

runs the family, Mrs. Hepburn thinks she does and Kate *knows* she does," an observer once said. All the Hepburns functioned on sheer nervous energy. There were no schedules. Breakfast could well be served at noon, lunch at four and dinner at nine. Visitors always seemed to arrive in the middle of a meal, and there was a great deal of walking about the dining room, plate in hand, as one Hepburn found the distance to another inhibiting to a lively conversation that could have had as a topic anything from the atomic bomb to birth control. The only note of formality about dinner was the carving of the roast, done by Dr. Hepburn with surgical expertise.

"How do you stand politically?" was Mrs. Hepburn's first question to a visitor. If the reply was in any way conservative, the far-Left Mrs. Hepburn's usual retort was, "How dull, how *awfully* dull." After such a pronouncement the guest might be ignored completely.

The Hepburns could be charming or intolerant, but were always outspoken. The "untouchables," the "dumb," the "complacent" and the "conservative" were immediately labeled to their faces "hopeless" and quickly dispensed with. On the other hand, the family was instantly and intensely excited about "anybody doing something interesting or eager to talk about something interesting." Writers, artists, actors, directors, political and social activists, inventors, and any other intellectually stimulating exhibits were thus frequent guests at the Hepburn table. Though Howard Hughes certainly fit into this category, Mrs. Hepburn was not too pleased with his visits to Fenwick. For one thing, he refused to eat when the family did, and for another, his slight deafness kept him from joining into the family's lively discussions. Hughes found the Hepburns' nonchalant attitude and their disordered life irritating and was not silent in his criticism.

Indeed, if not for Dr. Hepburn, a bill would never have been paid, a mechanical device repaired, nor any of the Hepburn cars filled with gas. Marion and Peggy were apt to drive off with no gas and fifty cents borrowed from a maid. When a canopy was put over part of the lawn for Marion's wedding, no one ever got around to having it taken down. Kate had been on her own for nearly a decade, yet not only did her father take care of all her finances, she still considered

Fenwick home and presented any serious beau for her father's approval. Dr. Hepburn reserved judgment at this time on Howard Hughes. Therefore, so did Kate.

The five Hepburn offspring had inherited brains, looks and money. A progressive upbringing had contributed much to their uniqueness. Kate's brothers and sisters were every bit as much a maverick as she. Partly responsible was the elder Hepburns' fierce dedication to independent ideas and the fact that they set a careful intellectual stage upon which their children were allowed full expression. Since the death of an older brother when she was thirteen, Kate had been the eldest of the siblings. This could have accounted in part for her being their leader. Certainly her adult fame might have also contributed. Still, Kate had had an imperious personality since childhood, a take-command attitude; bossy, outspoken to an eccentric degree, she wore what she wanted (boys' clothes and shaved head at nine), did what she wanted, and said what she wanted, discounting the censure of either of her parents.

"I find it droll that Kate, who is not a democrat but a Democrat, should create such a royalist atmosphere," one of her closest friends was to say.

The cut-through nasal voice, the proud posture, the self-possession, along with a "beguiling femininity," became Kate's trademarks. She thought for herself. If she gave the impression that her determination was "to remold this man's world," at the same time she made it quite plausible that it *could* be a woman's world. There had been many serious beaux besides Howard Hughes. Most remained as loyal a friend to her as her ex-husband did. At Fenwick in the summer of 1938, these old flames came and went, as did Luddy and Hughes. Some were celebrities. Others were relationships that went back to her girlhood days in West Hartford and her college years at Bryn Mawr. Kate was irreplaceable, an original. Her curious but dynamic personality could not be easily exorcised. Kate's friendship was addictive, and once won not easily forfeited.

The Hollywood pundits wrongly believed Katharine Hepburn had retreated to her family's summer cottage to nurse her wounds. Throughout May and June, the "fallen" star was happier than she had been for years and was certain that in no time at all she would make those Hollywood dolts eat every last nasty word they had said of her.

At seven-twenty P.M., July 10, 1938, Howard Hughes's plane thundered along the thirty-five-hundred-foot runway at Floyd Bennett Airfield in New York. The evening was insufferably hot and some five thousand spectators who waited to witness Hughes's take-off on his flight to break Lindbergh's record welcomed the momentary breeze created when the plane lifted off the ground, banked to the left over Jamaica Bay and started across Long Island. A few minutes later, the plane's wings dipped over Fenwick as Kate stood on the pier and enthusiastically waved Hughes on. Sixteen hours and thirty-eight minutes after leaving New York, he arrived at Le Bourget Airfield in Paris, cutting Lindbergh's time in half. Before he left the cockpit, he asked that Kate be notified of his safe arrival. Eight hours later, with a telegram from her in his pocket agreeing to meet him in New York on his return, Hughes got back into the plane to continue his flight to Moscow, across Russia, through northern Siberia, to Fairbanks, Alaska, and then on to New York. Three days, nineteen hours and seventeen minutes after take-off, he arrived back at Floyd Bennett Airfield with a new record for flying around the world. Immediately he was one of the most famous men in America. Crowds that met him were so dense that he could not be reached by a messenger who had a note for him from Kate.

Several hours passed before he could slip away from his fans and the welcoming committee, headed by wealthy merchant Grover Whalen* and the city's mayor, Fiorello H. LaGuardia, and direct a taxi to take him to Kate's New York address. Unfortunately, the street in front of her house was mobbed with fans hoping to outguess the hero, and so he went on to his suite at the Drake Hotel. The next evening, traveling in separate cars, Kate and Hughes met at the home of Grover Whalen in Short Hills, New Jersey. Rumors now circulated that they were to marry.

---

* Grover Whalen (1886–1962) was a man of many and diverse careers. He was at various times general manager of John Wanamaker department store (1924–1934), chairman of Schenley Products (1934–1937), president of the New York World's Fair (1939–1940) and police commissioner of New York (1928–1930).

Kate was in a terrible dilemma, not at all sure that marriage to Hughes was what she wanted. Hughes, with gentlemanly diplomacy, flew to Houston for a few weeks to give her time to think. He joined Kate at Fenwick on August 15, and the two of them went to look at a million-dollar yacht with an eye for purchase. The newspapers reported that the boat, *The Viking,* was to take them on their honeymoon. A week later, when Hughes left Fenwick, Kate had not yet made a decision.

Monday, September 19, after a particularly festive and crowded weekend, Dr. Hepburn, all the Hepburn guests and most of the family departed Fenwick, leaving Kate and Mrs. Hepburn behind. Around two P.M. on Wednesday, September 21, a northeast wind began to blow. Even when the wind rose and the rain came in horizontal sheets, inhabitants of the area did not believe the hurricane that had been reported as turning away from Florida and moving northward could be approaching them. With New England rationality, they were certain that since there had never been a hurricane in their latitude, there could never be one.

The day darkened early. Great black clouds rolled across the sky. Kate remained as unsuspecting as her neighbors. She liked the excitement, the challenge of storms. Shortly after lunch, alone, a scarf across her face, she walked out onto the pier. Waves slapped viciously against the pilings. A severe storm watch had been issued, but no mention had been made of an approaching hurricane. Kate braced herself, fighting the wind. Then, gale winds pushing her from behind, she turned back to warn her mother of the force of the storm.

Fenwick was situated on an open promontory, with the Long Island Sound on one side and the Connecticut River on the other. Built as a summer cottage, the structure was not capable of withstanding the raging hurricane winds. Slashing rain made it difficult to see more than a few feet beyond the windows, which Kate and Mrs. Hepburn had fastened as tightly as they could. One by one the shingles on the roof tore off and whirled away. Trees thundered as they fell, windows smashed, and the floor began waving like a shaken carpet. Clinging together, Kate, Mrs. Hepburn and the maid deserted the cottage and managed to reach a neighbor's more protected house. They were safe, but Fenwick was lost, along with many other summer homes and the lives of two neighbors. Telephone and power lines were down over the entire area. Knowing her father would be worried, Kate left her mother and walked, fighting the winds, to the main street of town, a good distance in any weather. "My God," she recalled, "it was something *devastating*—and unreal—like the beginning of the world—or the end of it—and I slogged and sloshed, crawled through ditches and hung on to keep going somehow—got drenched and bruised and scratched—*completely* bedraggled—finally got to where there was a working phone and called Dad. The minute he heard my voice he said, 'How's your mother?'—And I said—I mean shouted—the storm was screaming so—'She's all right. All *right*, Dad! But listen, the house—it's gone—blown away into the sea!' And he said, 'I don't suppose you had brains enough to throw a match into it before it went, did you? It's insured against fire, but not against blowing away!—and how are you?'"

Upon hearing the news of the disaster the next morning (about 300 dead and 230 missing on southern New England's coastline), Howard Hughes, who was now in California, sent a rescue plane into the area where the Hepburn cottage had been located. The pilot found Kate surrounded by the devastation of the storm, "undistressed, even gay, as she sifted sand with an army of small boys, hunting for the family silver."

The role Kate had most desperately wanted when she left Hollywood had been Scarlett O'Hara in Margaret Mitchell's *Gone With the Wind*. Almost no one except Kate thought she was right for it. She had worked with director George Cukor* in four films. Cukor was scheduled to direct David O. Selznick's† production of *Gone With the Wind* as soon as

---

* George Cukor (1899–1983) had directed Katharine Hepburn in her first film, *A Bill of Divorcement*, as well as in *Little Women, Sylvia Scarlett* and *Holiday*. One of the pantheon of Hollywood directors, Cukor was known as a "woman's director," and most of his finest films have memorable performances by great women stars, i.e., Greta Garbo, Katharine Hepburn, Joan Crawford, Audrey Hepburn and Judy Garland.

† David O(liver) Selznick (1902–1965), the son of film magnate Lewis J. Selznick (1870–1933), had produced Katharine Hepburn's debut film, *A Bill of Divorcement*, in 1932. Selznick went on to make many film classics—*Gone With the Wind, Rebecca, Spellbound* and *The Third Man* among them.

Scarlett O'Hara was cast, and both he and Kate had tried to convince Selznick that she would be an admirable Scarlett. Selznick had not wanted to commit himself. A nationwide search for an unknown girl to play the role was in progress, with the kind of press coverage a Hollywood producer dreams about. To cast a familiar face at this stage would have disappointed film audiences. But as Selznick wanted to leave himself as many options as possible, he did not say a final no to Kate.

Summer passed with no call from Selznick. Hughes, meanwhile, was still talking about filming *The Amelia Earhart Story*. In September, Kate told the *New York Herald Tribune*, "Motion pictures *could* be one of our greatest mediums of education today. However, let a movie try to depict situations in which we are all involved now, let a movie try to wake people up to their own plight, let a movie try to present a moral, economic problem of today honestly and simply, and they are advised to hear nothing, say nothing, do nothing."

The frank interview was not one that would cause the Hollywood studios to change their minds about her. Nor did the recent release of *Holiday* (the film she had made just before her departure).* Decades later *Holiday* would be called "one of the best-acted comedies in cinema annals" and viewed by critics as a classic. In 1938, the wit and nonconformity of the script and the tomboy beauty of Kate as Linda Seton, the heroine of *Holiday,* were too off-center to be appealing to the general public. Though reviews lauded Kate's lively and winning performance, her critical success in the film was a pyrrhic victory.

But why think about Hollywood ("smog patch," as she often called the place)? The stage was her first true love. Just before the hurricane, Philip Barry† had visited Fenwick. Barry was the author of the play *Holiday,* in which Kate, years before, had been the understudy to the role she eventually played on the screen. Wealthy, of a good social background, a man of impeccable taste and grooming, Barry had become famous for his portraits of the ultrarich (although

---

* Originally titled *Free to Live* in Great Britain; rereleased as *Holiday*.
† Philip Barry (1896–1949), American playwright, best known for *The Animal Kingdom*, *The Philadelphia Story*, *Without Love* and *Holiday*.

most of his plays eschewed strong social themes). He had come to tell Kate about an idea for a new play that he considered ideal for her. His timing could not have been better.

"Let's go on the pier and talk about it," she said, and they walked off in the stiff Atlantic breeze—Kate in her baggy pants and man's windbreaker, Barry in a finely tailored suit and a silk cravat. The heroine in Barry's story was a Philadelphia society girl named Tracy Lord, who at the outset is to be married in twenty-four hours to a stuffy Philadelphia blueblood. Not only does the appearance of her ex-husband, also well born but something of a drunk, confuse her, but she finds herself attracted to a reporter from a scandal magazine. Even in the play's early conception, there were similarities between Katharine Hepburn and Tracy Lord. The fictional character's voice patterns and language were distinctly Kate's, as were Tracy Lord's arrogance and aristocratic aloofness. The Lord family were, like the Hepburns, rugged individuals (although the Lords owed more to George Kaufman and Moss Hart's Sycamore family in *You Can't Take It with You** than to the Hepburns). Other parallels existed: Kate's hatred of the press, her demands for privacy, her regard for the artist, her love of swimming and the sea, her dedication to her family and its good name, and—perhaps even more pointedly—her inability to make up her mind to marry. And, of course, Luddy, her ex-husband, was a Philadelphia blueblood who had remained close to her family. Perversely unconcerned by these similarities, Kate told Barry to go ahead and work on it. They had more conversations at Barry's summer house in Maine. For a time, the playwright was working with Kate over his shoulder.

Howard Hughes offered to finance the new play for her even before he read it. Kate asked her father what he thought, not only of her returning to the stage in *The Philadelphia Story* but of buying a part interest in the production herself.

Dr. Hepburn told her, "The most precarious of all investments is a theatrical venture. As your advisor I could never

---

* *You Can't Take It with You* (1936), written by George S. Kaufman (1889–1961) and Moss Hart (1904–1961) won the Pulitzer Prize in 1936.

recommend one." After a moment, he tapped the playscript. "But this one might be it."

Kate put up a quarter of the production costs for an equal interest in the stage profits. She also bought the screen rights from Barry, agreeing that a sizable bonus be paid him based on the Broadway run of the play.

Her personal situation began more and more to imitate the fictional play Philip Barry had written for her, and she had no clearer answer to her predicament than the playwright's heroine had at the end of act one. Hughes was now beginning to insist upon an answer to his proposal of marriage. The press dogged Kate's every step. And, in January, 1939, Vivien Leigh* was signed for the role of Scarlett O'Hara. In the short hiatus that existed before Kate was to go into rehearsals on *The Philadelphia Story*, she decided to rebuild Fenwick. With her beloved home once again there to shelter and comfort her, life would not be so confusing.

At F.A.O. Schwarz, a toy store in New York City, she bought a large set of children's blocks. Then, in the living room of the Hepburn home in West Hartford, where she had lived as a young woman, she gathered the family on the floor about her and with their help constructed a model of what the new Fenwick would be like. Each Hepburn had a hand in the plans and not always did they agree. One thing, however, was certain. Fenwick would remain the place where Hepburns could come for sustenance and protection, always.

---

* Vivien Leigh (1913–1967) starred in many English films before coming to Hollywood in 1938 and her appearance in *Gone With the Wind*. While in Hollywood, she married Laurence Olivier. They appeared together in numerous stage productions. Leigh made many films after *Gone With the Wind*, the most noteworthy probably being *A Streetcar Named Desire*, for which she won an Academy Award.

The
Hepburns

CHAPTER 2

Katharine Martha Houghton, Katharine Hepburn's mother, had been orphaned along with her two younger sisters when she was thirteen.* The Houghtons, a rich and socially prominent family, had founded the Corning Glass Works. The girls were assured a certain income and the home and protection of their wealthy uncle, Amory Bigelow Houghton. This meant moving from Buffalo, New York, to Boston, Massachusetts, and to a home very much at odds with their former life. The sisters, with Kit, as Katharine Houghton was known, as their leader, were inseparable renegades, bringing considerable chaos into their uncle's home.

Kit grew into a tall, startling, dark-haired beauty, strong willed, haughty, an aristocratic young woman of such independent ideas that she constantly puzzled and shocked her conservative uncle. Kit believed that tradition was numbing, liked nothing better than a good argument on politics (considered a taboo subject for women in the 1890s) and insisted she and her sisters, Edith and Mary, be allowed to fulfill their mother's wish and attend Bryn Mawr College. At Bryn Mawr, her wild chestnut hair swept up in a high pompadour,

---

* Katharine Martha Houghton's two younger sisters were Edith Houghton (Mrs. Stevens Mason) and the youngest, a half-sister, Mary Houghton.

17

her nasal voice strident, Kit presided at a salon in her sitting room and, to her Uncle Amory's constant agitation, spent far more than her generous allowance. Uncle Amory's oldest son, Alanson,* had taken his post-graduate courses in Paris before entering the family glass business in Corning, New York, in 1889, and Kit had set him as an example.

Upon her graduation in June, 1898, she sailed for Paris over Uncle Amory's strong objection and despite the fact that he refused to advance her the next installment of her allowance (not due for another six months). Determined to see a bit of the world before marriage and children took up her life, she landed in Paris with just ten dollars. A bistro owner near the Gare du Nord rented her clean rooms over his establishment on credit, obviously believing her story that she was from a well-to-do family and that he would be reimbursed.

Fundless, Kit haunted libraries and museums during the day and spent most of her evenings under the watchful, somewhat paternal eye of the bistro patron. Her French grew fluent and her naïveté worked to protect her. The following January her allowance arrived, and with it an additional sizable check (meant to be used as her return fare) that more than paid up all her debts and allowed her to purchase a first-class train ticket to the Riviera. At Monte Carlo, she won two hundred dollars at the tables and promptly sailed home. Boredom, not homesickness, had suddenly overcome her. She went directly to visit her sister Edith, who was studying medicine at Johns Hopkins University in Baltimore, Maryland.

Norval Thomas Hepburn was born in 1879 in Hanover County, Virginia, seventeen miles from Richmond near the Civil War battlefield of Cold Harbor, where his father, the Reverend Sewell S. Hepburn, originally from Missouri, had come to be an Episcopal clergyman. Of Scottish descent, the Hepburns could trace their ancestry back to James Hepburn,

---

* Alanson Bigelow Houghton (1863–1941), vice-president of Corning Glass in 1903, president from 1910 to 1918. He was a member of the House of Representatives from 1919 to 1922; appointed ambassador to Germany on February 10, 1922; and ambassador to Britain from 1925 to 1928.

Earl of Bothwell, third husband of Mary, Queen of Scots. "Tom" Hepburn had graduated from Randolph-Macon College in Ashland, Virginia, and, in 1901 when he met Kit Houghton, was a graduate student at Johns Hopkins Medical School in Baltimore. A big, brawny, red-headed young man with a booming Southern voice that made one think of generals on a field of battle, Tom Hepburn was so much an original that Kit told her sister just after having been introduced to him—"That's the one!" Edith, being more practical, pointed out that the gentleman didn't have a penny. "I'd marry him even if I knew it meant I'd die in a year—*and* go to hell!" Kit replied.

In June, only a few months after their first meeting, the new Dr. Hepburn (without declaring himself) left for Heidelberg, Germany, as a special exchange scholar in surgery. Letters made their way back and forth across the Atlantic, Kit's provocative, Tom's merely informative. After four months had passed, in desperation Kit wrote, "The best thing about our relationship is that whenever one of us marries, it won't hurt that relationship at all."

"How can you say such a thing?" he replied, and added, to her great delight, "If I don't marry you, I'll never marry anyone!"

Uncle Amory was never keen on the idea of a marriage between his niece and Tom Hepburn, the profession of medicine being considered only a mite more respectable than being in trade. True, the Hepburns were a genteel family, but they were not an old rich, influential family. The Reverend Sewell S. Hepburn was a country preacher, and his wife, Selina Lloyd Powell Hepburn, had had to augment their meager income by taking in boarders. Furthermore, their son was radical and too free speaking for his own good. Nonetheless, in 1904, after Kit had earned a master's degree in art at Radcliffe and Tom had returned from Germany to take up an internship at Hartford Hospital, they were wed, the young doctor thus becoming the hospital's first married intern. For thirty dollars a month (a good share of his income) they rented one half of a small "ugly" red house opposite the doctors' entrance of Hartford Hospital. Within a year, their first child, Thomas Houghton Hepburn, was born. The following year, having completed his internship, Tom senior opened an office on High Street for the practice of surgery. The formerly unheard of idea of surgical specialization was considered too radical by the standards of Hartford Hospital. The daring move, therefore, delayed Dr. Hepburn's appointment to the staff for several years.

None of this bothered Dr. Hepburn. He believed that if a man spent all his time on surgery, he would become better at it and survive economically by a good reputation that would lead to referrals. His theory proved correct, and when their second child, a girl, named (on Kit's insistence) Katharine Houghton Hepburn, was born on November 8, 1907, the Hepburns moved to the slightly more affluent address of 133 Hawthorne Street.*

The story goes that right after her daughter's birth, Kit—who had hoped for a red-haired child (young Tom had been a brunet)—asked the nurse to "hold her up to the window" so she could see, and then exclaimed, "Yes, it's red!" Her father called her "Redtop," the rest of the family, "Kathy."

The house on Hawthorne Street was the former home of Charles Dudley Warner,† publisher of *The Hartford Courant*, who had collaborated with Mark Twain on *The Gilded Age*. Mrs. Charles Dudley Warner** was a fine pianist and a famous hostess, and, to Kit Hepburn's delight, the house on Hawthorne Street had once been a meeting place for such authors and artists as Samuel Clemens (Mark Twain), William Dean Howells and Thomas Bailey Aldrich, and such performers as Madame Modjeska, the Polish tragedienne, and her famous compatriot—pianist Ignace Paderewski. Warner had written a critically well-received book of essays, *My Summer in a Garden*, which included descriptions of the two acres that backed 133 Hawthorne Street, a wild, natural garden, "thick with rambler roses, vines and shrubs." Shaded by one of the eight giant cedars on the property, small Kathy

---

* For years Katharine Hepburn's birthdate was given as November 8, 1909. No birth certificate survives to support this. However, her brother Thomas was born in 1905, and she was listed as two years his junior in all statistics. Therefore, November 8, 1907, would be correct.
† Charles Dudley Warner (1829–1900) also edited the *American Men of Letters* series and wrote a life of Washington Irving.
** Susan Lee Warner (?–1921) gave frequent local piano recitals and one well-received concert at Carnegie Hall in February, 1911.

played by the brook that ran through her parents' land. Because of the peace and sanctity of that tiny part of nature that then formed her world, the child was always to feel most secure with a garden—indeed—a world of her own.

In the early 1900s, Hartford was a small city served by the New Haven Railroad, two New York steamers and a number of trolley lines. The city had established itself on the solid foundation of three insurance companies, Aetna, Phoenix and Travelers, and was guided by the conservative tradition of the men who ran these companies as well as those who ran Royal and Underwood (typewriters), Pratt & Whitney (machine parts) and Colt (guns). The wives of these businessmen struggled to bring beauty and culture to Hartford. But it could not escape the label of being an industrial city.

Just south of the Hepburn house on Hawthorne Street were two factories—Hart & Hegeman and the Arrow Electric Company.* Workers brought their lunches in tin boxes or in paper bags. No such thing as a union existed in those days to ensure cafeterias or lunch rooms to factory employees, so the workers sat out on the sidewalks or on the fences to eat. "Mother was outraged," Katharine Hepburn later recalled. "One day she walked over and told them they were welcome to use our place—the lawns or the porches or anything they wanted . . . you can imagine what happened. They tore the place up—left all their garbage around—broke things, ruined the lawn. Dad said to her, 'Well, my dear, now you've learned something about the difference between having principles and acting on them.'"

The Hepburns at this time were not considered rich by Hartford's standards. Still, they owned their home, had servants, and were one of the first families in their new neighborhood (which had fallen from its glittering past into middle-classdom) to possess a car. Since young Dr. Hepburn could not have earned enough as a new doctor in private practice to support his current style of living, family money was correctly suspected to be responsible, though something about "Dr. Tom's" authoritative manner gave the false

---

* These companies merged c. 1920–1928 to form Arrow-Hart, an electrical company. This factory still stands close to the location of the Hepburn house.

impression of a Hepburn, rather than a Houghton, inheritance.

By nature and tradition, the native New Englander of this period was frequently suspicious of strangers and inclined toward clannishness. Yet, along with these characteristics came a great respect for individual opinion. All of these marks of her New England background were inherent in Kit Hepburn's personality. But, also, as a young girl in Boston, she had viewed daily the relics of the American Revolution that had changed the trend of history. Since she was a rebel at heart, a believer in change, and a woman dedicated to her own emancipation, the role of wife and mother would soon prove too limiting to her.

Shortly after Kathy's birth, she attended a suffrage lecture given by Emmeline Pankhurst.* That Dr. Hepburn, seeing his wife bored and restless, had persuaded her to go, gives a good picture of the respect these two people had for each other and the extent of their common interest. Dr. Hepburn was fond of saying that "perhaps all young women should have their children when they're twelve or thirteen, and then when they'd be rid of them still be young enough to get an education and live their own lives."

Mrs. Hepburn was much impressed with the diminutive, dynamic Mrs. Pankhurst (they were later to become good friends). A few days after her attendance at the suffragist meeting, Mrs. Hepburn came to the decision that there had to be more to life than pushing a baby carriage. That evening she told her husband that she wanted to go into the suffragist movement and asked him if he thought it would be a handicap to him. His reply was in the affirmative, but he added, "If I haven't enough brains to succeed in spite of it, why, we'll take the penalty."

Kit Hepburn went at her new cause with an astounding dedication and ferocity. She marched and carried banners on

---

* Emmeline Goulden Pankhurst (1858–1928), British woman suffragist, founded her own movement, the Woman's Social and Political Union, in 1903. Arrested many times for the militant means by which she furthered her cause, she turned her powers of leadership from the suffragist movement to the war effort in 1914. After the war she moved to Canada, returning to England in 1926. She died there two years later while standing for election to Parliament as a Conservative candidate.

which Dr. Hepburn had painted for her: EQUALN.
WOMEN. She mounted the lectern after Mrs. Pankhurst n.
moved on to other arenas and carried on the suffragist battle
with flaming oratory and fiery enthusiasm. So shocked were
Dr. Hepburn's associates that they spoke to him only in the
line of duty. Editorial criticism in *The Hartford Courant* was
vociferous enough that a friend urged Mrs. Hepburn to sue
for libel. Kit Houghton Hepburn was unconcerned. "Silly,
isn't it? They must have needed something to print," she
replied.

Katharine Hepburn was to remember that if, when she was
a child, she and her mother met a neighbor, her mother
would say good morning and the neighbor "would look right
through us as if nobody was there. My mother didn't mind.
She kept on saying good morning the next time and the next.
Sooner or later the neighbor could no longer sustain her
rudeness. Faced with my mother's good manners, she'd feel
compelled to return my mother's greeting."

Until she was four years old, Kathy was the baby of the
family. Following Mrs. Pankhurst's example, Mrs. Hepburn
took Kathy to suffragist meetings and lectures. Seated either
on the platform or in the front row, the child listened with
awe to her mother's booming voice as she rallied audiences to
her cause, unaware that Mrs. Hepburn's public appearances
at the time of an advanced pregnancy were scandalizing
conservative Hartford. The third Hepburn offspring, Richard
Houghton Hepburn (he, and all future Hepburns, were to
carry their mother's maiden name), was born in 1911, in the
midst of a new campaign his mother was spearheading for the
practice of birth control. Six weeks after Richard's birth, and
accompanied by a nurse who held him for her, she took him
to her meetings, excusing herself to nurse him at the appropriate times in a fairly private anteroom.

The growing business of prostitution and the plight of its
female victims now occupied Kit Hepburn's attention, and
she became one of the most outspoken women in the
campaign to rid Hartford of this vice.

When Tom junior was six, he developed St. Vitus's dance,
a form of rheumatic fever in which frequent and involuntary
movement is accompanied by high temperatures and bouts of
confusion and depression. He suffered a noticeable facial tic

about which the neighborhood children taunted him. More and more, Kathy and Tom played together, almost to the exclusion of other children. A tutor was brought in to help Tom with his schoolwork and Kathy studied with him as well. The two elder Hepburn children were conspirators in childhood adventures, but Kathy led the way. Because Dr. Hepburn firmly believed that exercise was the sure road to health, Tom junior attempted valiantly to overcome his illness with a rigorous athletic regime. Any small achievement in this area brought him instant approval from his father. But Kathy remained the natural athlete and by the age of eight was an expert wrestler, tumbler, and trapeze performer.

Athletic equipment littered the house and yard. Dr. Hepburn's obsession with sports extended to his daughter as well as to her older brother. Every day he led them in calisthenics, taught them wrestling holds (Kathy complained her long hair was a disadvantage) and had them join his male friends in team matches of touch football. Winning was important to Kathy, for it brought the highest praise from her father.

Mrs. Hepburn, who did not share her husband's enthusiasm for sports, never joined in these activities. Her objective was to get her children to exercise their minds. Meals became a time for lively debate. The children were expected to discuss the day's happenings intelligently. Young, eager minds excited Kit Hepburn. She had no patience for slovenly habits or lazy thinking. Not demonstrative outwardly, she bestowed her affection in a manner of pride or approval of what Tom or Kathy did. Being clean won points with her, as did knowing some bit of information that could add to the general interest of a conversation.

Kathy collected stuffed animals and dolls and privately made up little plays in which they and she were the characters. Dr. Hepburn thought the toys a waste of time and money—a foolish, empty entertainment. But in this, Kathy refused to submit. Her animals and dolls became her charges, and she protected them fiercely.

In the next eight years, there were to be three more Houghton Hepburns: Robert (Bob), Marion and Margaret (Peggy). The growing size of her family did not deter Mrs. Hepburn from the militancy of her causes, nor did she recognize anything inconsistent about fighting for birth control while raising a large family. Limited families obviously meant for the poor or for those women lacking sense of personal independence. Kathy continued to attend meetings with her mother and to pass out pamphlets at the neighboring factory gates on everything from planned parenthood to venereal disease.

Freethinkers though they were, both Dr. and Mrs. Hepburn believed naughty or thoughtless children should be spanked. Katharine Hepburn, the woman, was later to recall Kathy, the child, "being cuffed around a good deal" by her father. By nine, she had learned enough about her parents' reactions not to cry. The spanking stopped, but not Kathy's outlandish behavior and general bullheadedness. Once when a friend of her mother's remarked on Kathy's "frailness," the child, running at full speed, butted her head into the trunk of a tree to exhibit her strength. Miraculously, she was unhurt.

Her mother was courageous and dedicated, but her father was an intellectual: "I mean a real intellectual—a thinker—not just a memorizer," Dr. Hepburn's "Redtop" later declared. "He was mad about [George] Bernard Shaw—most people in Hartford hadn't even *heard* of Shaw—must have been because Dad was such a fan of Shaw's that he got to read that play by [Eugène] Brieux, *Damaged Goods*—you know, the one about syphilis that caused such a scandal—and because Dad was a urologist,* the play had a special appeal for him—and he wrote to the Shaws—Mrs. Shaw had translated the play [from the French] and George Bernard Shaw had done the introduction. Dad thought it superb—a great way to get this notion of what to do about it [venereal disease] into the open."

Dr. Hepburn requested permission from the Shaws to reprint and distribute the play through the Connecticut Social Hygiene Association, which he had founded. When the Shaws agreed, he drove to Boston to speak with Dr. Charles Eliot, president emeritus of Harvard,† and convinced him to help form the American Social Hygiene Association to fight

---

* Dr. Hepburn became a specialist in urological surgery early in his career.
† Dr. Charles W. Eliot (1834–1924) was also known as an author and wrote numerous books on subjects varying from *Educational Reform* (1900) to *Charles Eliot, Landscape Architect* (1903). He was a member of the International Health Board from 1913 to 1917.

venereal disease. He brought mounds of statistics and a sheaf of photographs, X rays and personal statements of victims to prove to Dr. Eliot the severity of the problem in America. So eloquent had been his plea, that Dr. Eliot turned down an ambassadorship to Great Britain to become the new association's president.

"There are men of action," Katharine Hepburn said, "and men of thought, and if you ever get a combination of the two—well—that's the top—you've got someone like Dad."

Despite Mrs. Hepburn's work for women's equality, her rebellious nature, and her dominant personality, the Hepburn household was a classic patriarchy. Dr. Hepburn believed in cold baths, the colder the better, and all the children had to get used to them. Cold baths stimulated the brain and the body and they kept you from getting soft. With a cry of "Here I go!" Kathy, at five, would jump into the filled bathtub of icy water with a splash, laughing and shrieking as she darted up and down in it before she bounced out, streaking nude to the fireplace where her mother would wrap her in a big red Navaho blanket. ("That gave me the impression that the bitterer the medicine, the better it was for you," Katharine Hepburn later said.)

Kathy read books that her father recommended, joined in the wrestling and boxing matches he initiated for Tom and the neighbors' boys, and damn well held her own. Dr. Hepburn's license plates for his Maxwell were 3405. On snowy days the call would go up from one end of Hawthorne Street to the other, "Here comes 3405!" While the factory workers cheered them on, the neighborhood children (mostly boys) would throw their sled ropes over the Maxwell's bumper to hook a ride. Dr. Hepburn never slowed the car even when Kathy hooked on for a spin. If a sled was whip-snapped into a ditch or drift, Dr. Hepburn kept right on going.

One morning when Kathy was about seven, her father opened the door to a policeman. "Sir," the officer reported, "your little girl is in the top of that tallest cedar. I can see her red hair sticking out above the green."

"For heaven's sake don't call to her," Dr. Hepburn scowled. "You might make her fall." He then shut the door and returned to his reading.

CHAPTER 3

The Hepburn children were never asked to leave a room no matter what the topic of conversation. Kathy sat in the parlor and listened to Mrs. Pankhurst, Charlotte Perkins Gilman and Emma Goldman—women of radical ideas—in ardent discussions on venereal disease, prostitution and the use of contraceptives, as well as heated political debates and medical specifics of Dr. Hepburn's cases. Mrs. Hepburn, now president of the Connecticut Women's Suffrage Association, believed that if you weren't forthright with your children about sex, they would not confide in you. When Kathy asked her mother about her own birth, Mrs. Hepburn explained it to her "scientifically and specifically."

"Oh, then I can have a baby without getting married," Kathy replied. "That's what I shall do!"

Nudism and fake modesty were among the topics the Hepburns discussed often and openly. Their oldest daughter listened to these conversations and thought, "Some day nobody is going to wear any clothes." What bothered her most was her overabundance of freckles that covered her from head to toe. Fearing that because of them no one would want her, she confessed this worry to her father. "I want to tell you something, Kathy, and you must never forget it," he replied. "Jesus Christ, Alexander the Great and Leonardo da Vinci all had red hair and freckles, and they did all right."

On April 6, 1917, the United States declared war on Germany. The Hepburns were only indirectly affected. They contributed to various committees working for the war effort, bought Liberty Bonds and War Savings Stamps, and Dr. Hepburn gave free time and treatment to returning Hartford war veterans. But Tom was only twelve at the outbreak of war, and it was over long before there would be any chance that he could enlist or be drafted.

Having long outgrown the house on Hawthorne Street, in 1917, the Hepburn family moved to a larger home at 352 North Laurel Street. Dr. Hepburn had prospered greatly. The Hepburns now had five servants and, in the same year that they moved to Laurel Street, built Fenwick, their rambling wooden summer cottage on the waterfront in Old Saybrook.* At Fenwick, Mrs. Hepburn took a respite from the demands of her various campaigns and her contributions to the war effort and concentrated on her children. The Hepburn house soon became a gathering place for the youth of Old Saybrook. By the end of the first summer at the cottage, Tom junior's health had improved greatly, and upon his return to West Hartford he was entered into the Kingswood School, which occupied the old Mark Twain House and had been founded by a Mr. Bissell "in the English tradition."† Dr. Hepburn already spoke of the boy following in his oversized footsteps in medicine.

Kathy was enrolled in the co-educational Oxford School the next year, 1918, when she was not quite eleven. The school, a gray-shingled house at 232 Oxford Street, was the home of the founder, Miss Mary Martin. By 1918, the small

---

* Fenwick was named after Colonel George Fenwick, whose wife, Lady Anne Butler, was the daughter of an English nobleman. In 1639, during the perils of Indian warfare and the privations of the wilderness, Lady Anne left behind the comforts of the English upper class to join her husband in the New World, where he was to act as governor of the town of Saybrook. Nine years later, she died and was buried in the village cemetery beneath a rudely carved red sandstone monument bearing no inscription. This section of Saybrook became known as Fenwick, and a large summer hotel built nearby in 1871 was called Fenwick Hall.

† Kingswood School was founded in 1916. According to drama critic and author Brendan Gill, who attended Kingswood School in the 1920s, "To the middle-class Hartford families who had furnished the money with which to establish the school, Kingswood gave off just the right aristocratic ring."

house was crowded with about ninety pupils. The kitchen was used for sewing and cooking classes. Sitting-up exercises were conducted on the porch, the girls wearing skirts to their ankles. Kathy was in awe of Miss Martin, a neat, tightly corseted and full-bosomed woman, with her hair "à la concierge," but Catherine Watson, the gym teacher, had the greater effect upon her. "Oh she was so very, very pretty," Katharine Hepburn recalled six decades later, "a soft and gentle face—soft sandy hair—it was long and she did it in a knot and a velvet ribbon she wore about her head. She was medium sized and I literally adored and worshipped her.

"Why—why Cathy Watson—I don't know—I just remember that I thought about her and watched her and waited for her and brought her presents. Just love it was—first crush."

"I was never a member of the club," she later confessed. "I never knew what other girls were talking about." She made few attempts at Oxford School to become part of the social scheme. For companionship, she depended upon Tom and upon the hours she spent in athletic endeavors with her father. With four younger children and the growing importance in her life of her work, Kit Hepburn devoted less time to her oldest daughter. The girl possessed an independent nature and an inquiring mind, which Dr. Hepburn encouraged. The spanking stopped as soon as Kathy had begun to look like a young woman. Still, Dr. Hepburn treated her like one of the boys and she seemed content with this arrangement.

She bicycled to school: "Niles to Woodland to Asylum to Scarborough then left on Oxford Street." The next year the school moved to the elegant old Ensworth House on Farmington Avenue, and her bike route changed and she went "straight out Farmington." She had at last made a few friends, Elsie and Louise Field and Lucy Goodwin, but her relationship with her peers remained unsatisfying and her sense of competition was keen. One Oxford schoolmate, a tall girl, Oisey Taylor, always beat her in the high jump. "I still remember," she said years later, "yes she beat me—oh my dreams of floating over that bar—but no, she beat me—she just did." She never could bear losing.

Behind Ensworth House was a big garage where a Mrs.

A REMARKABLE WOMAN

Godfrey taught a class called "aesthetic dancing," which Kathy hated. She merely existed from one summer to the next to run barefoot along the waterfront at Fenwick, dive off the pier, and dig for clams. A strong swimmer, she would lead Tom junior two to three miles down the channel from the house. One rough day they were saved from being swept out into the ocean by fisherman William Ingham,* whose shed was nearby. From that day, Ingham's fish shed became Kathy's hideaway. Ingham taught her not only how to fish and fillet her catch but also how to row a boat. She talked her father into buying her a small craft, swiftly christened *Tiger,* which was wrecked that same season in a storm. So determined had Kathy been to save the boat, that she had hung on to the board with the boat's name painted on it as she gasped her way to shore.

Theater and films interested her, and she idolized the cowboy star William S. Hart. In order to go to his movies and purchase fan magazines with his photographs in it, she cut lawns and shoveled snow. At eight years of age, she dramatized *Uncle Tom's Cabin,* cast it with neighborhood children and presented it in the tiny theater Dr. Hepburn had had built for her in the backyard of the Laurel Street house. "I wouldn't play Eva because Eva was too good," she later recalled. "I played Topsy—and as there was a little girl in the neighborhood who I wanted to get even with—I chose her for Eva—as Topsy played all the mean tricks on her." Another time she said, "I never was willing to watch any other girl being wonderful."

At Fenwick with Tom, their friend Robinson Smith (who later became a theater producer), and her two younger brothers, she established a repertory company in the dining room. Fruit boxes, pillows, and miscellaneous furniture were used for props. The group's prime achievement was their fund-raising presentation of *Beauty and the Beast.* The plight

---

* William Ingham's family owned the riparian rights to the waters near Fenwick. The summer colony was later to unite to revoke these rights. Ingham lost the case but received a cash settlement. He soon went into the ice business. When Fenwick was being rebuilt after the 1938 hurricane, Katharine Hepburn insisted an old-fashioned ice box be repurchased instead of an electric refrigerator. Not until Ingham retired years later did she allow a modern machine to be brought into the house.

30

of the Navaho Indians in New Mexico had long been an object of Mrs. Hepburn's compassion and she was responsible for bringing Bishop Howden of New Mexico as a guest speaker to a local church in Old Saybrook. The bishop's description of poverty among the Navahos was so moving that Kathy decided her group should stage a benefit performance. A box-office top of fifty cents was fixed. Kathy played the beast and wore a blue Fauntleroy suit with silver stripes and a donkey's head. The benefit was a huge success, sixty dollars being collected. To Kathy's disappointment the Navahos bought themselves a phonograph that had a horn and was the envy of all New Mexico.

Another effort of the Fenwick Repertory Company was *Blue Beard,* with Kathy as Blue Beard and Robinson Smith dressed in female attire as the leading lady.

Tom junior joined Kathy in all her theatrical adventures. He played the banjo, loved to sing, and wrote some songs of his own. A good athlete, by the time he was fifteen he had won his letter on Kingswood School's football team. Since he was a senior and an honor student with fine scholastic potential, his father was making plans for him to enter Yale as a medical student that next autumn. But in the spring of 1921, with the need to decide his future a pressing issue, Tom junior was not at all sure he wanted a career in medicine, and, despite the combative, freethinking, crusading tradition of the Hepburn household, Dr. Hepburn was not an easy man to sway from a decision.

On Tuesday, March 29, two days after Easter Sunday, Mrs. Hepburn boarded a train to New York with Tom junior and Kathy. The two older children still had a week left of their Easter school holiday. The three of them were to visit for a few days at the home of Mary Towle, an old Bryn Mawr friend of Kit's and a successful lawyer. Tom and Kathy (now thirteen) immediately took to the dynamic Miss Towle and loved New York, the theater, the films, the people—so much that they implored Mrs. Hepburn to let them stay on until Sunday morning, although she was returning to Hartford on Thursday. She agreed.

Brother and sister saw Pavlova dance and explored the Village, Fifth Avenue and Central Park together. Friday night, April 1, they attended a movie at the Selwyn Theater,

William Fox's presentation of *A Connecticut Yankee in King Arthur's Court,* billed as a "faithful picturization of [Mark] Twain's most popular story. All the laughs, satire—contrast —humor—comedy have been heightened," the advertisements promised.* On Saturday evening, Tom played his banjo for Mary Towle, Kathy and some of "Aunt Mary's" young friends, who, without malice, teased the young man about his romanticism. He remained somewhat removed the rest of the evening. The small gathering in Mary Towle's living room broke up at around ten P.M. Kathy and Tom went directly to their rooms, Kathy's on the first floor, Tom's on the floor above. The Hepburn brother and sister were scheduled to leave the next morning, Sunday, April 3, on the train for Hartford. Their bags were packed and Tom had purchased two parlor-car seats.

The Towle maid had left for church early on Sunday morning. Kathy and her mother's friend ate breakfast alone. When the dining-room clock struck half past eight, Mary Towle suggested Kathy go up and fetch Tom or they would have a problem making the ten-twenty train from Grand Central to Hartford. Kathy ran up the stairs calling out, "Tom!" No reply was forthcoming and the door to his room was closed.

"Tom!" Still no reply. She knocked and then pushed the door open. The bed had been slept in, but the room—which was under a pitched part of the roof—appeared to be unoccupied. One curtain was hanging askew, the cotton tieback missing from it. Tom's good trousers were stretched out flat on a table, but she could not immediately see his suitcase. Where could her brother be? She had passed the one bathroom in the house on her way upstairs and its door had been open. An elongated shadow caught her eye. "Tom?" she called again. She entered to explore further and her shoulder brushed against something heavy hanging in the dark angle between the doorway and the corner of the room. She screamed for help even as she turned to see her brother's body suspended from a noose made of the curtain tie, which had been placed around a beam in the ceiling. The room was

* Appearing live on Broadway at the same time were Marilyn Miller in *Sally,* and Laurette Taylor in *Peg O' My Heart.*

not high and though he had obviously mounted his suitcase, which was on the floor just behind the hanging body, the boy's knees were drawn up. Yet, his feet almost touched the floor.

Mary Towle arrived in a matter of moments. Frantically, the woman and girl tried to undo the noose. When this was unsuccessful, Mary Towle ran to call help while Kathy, knowing that her brother was dead, nonetheless grabbed the lower part of his cold, stiff, pajama-clad body and lifted the dead boy as high as she could so that the noose would not pull at his neck. According to the police report, Kathy was still holding him clear of the floor when Dr. Condy of nearby St. Vincent's Hospital arrived fifteen minutes later. Tom, he said, had been dead about five hours.

A telegram was dispatched to the Hepburns in Hartford. That night Mrs. Hepburn returned to New York with her husband. Newspaper reporters waited for a statement on Mary Towle's front steps. "My son was normal in mind and body," Dr. Hepburn insisted. "The taking of his own life can be accounted for only from a medical point, that he was suddenly afflicted with adolescent insanity."

The next day Dr. Hepburn returned to Hartford. Mrs. Hepburn and Kathy stayed behind to take care of the grim details. The body would not be released until a coroner's report had been filed. Monday morning *The New York Times* ran the story on page six with the lead: MYSTERY IN SUICIDE OF SURGEON'S SON. *The Hartford Courant* featured the tragedy on the front page—DR. HEPBURN'S SON, 15, HANGS HIMSELF WHILE VISITING IN NEW YORK—DEAD BODY SWINGING FROM CURTAIN. FOUND BY SISTER IN HOME OF AUNT—DESPONDENCY SUSPECTED. The Hepburns' united war against the press had begun.

Kathy became obsessed with the need to absolve her brother from the taint of suicide. Perhaps, too, the questions that remained if Tom had taken his own life were too painful for her to probe. Grasping for an explanation that could label his death an accident, she reminded Dr. Hepburn of a story he had once told her brother and herself.

During Dr. Hepburn's undergraduate days at Randolph-Macon, his school was scheduled to compete on home ground against a northern college's football team. The northern visitors asked if lynchings still occurred. As a prank, some of Dr. Hepburn's classmates hired a black man who was famous in the area for being able to constrict the muscles of his neck so that he could not be choked. Tom had been intrigued by this story and had experimented with the tightening of his neck muscles, but he gave it up in a few days.

On Tuesday, after frantic calls back and forth between Kathy, Mrs. Hepburn and Dr. Hepburn, the latter gave the newspapers a new statement: "I am now convinced that the boy was the victim of an accident as the result of a foolish stunt," he told *The New York Times*. "I had entirely forgotten that he considered himself an expert in hanging by the neck in such a way as to look as if he were dying, to the entertainment of his brothers and sisters. . . . Friday night he saw a moving picture [a reference to *A Connecticut Yankee in King Arthur's Court*] in which I am told there is the picture [scene] of a hanging. That must have recalled his old stunt, and when he arose next morning he decided to rehearse it for a performance when he got home. This accident theory would explain all the findings. Tom's sister [Kathy] called me up today to recall to my mind his hanging stunt of a year ago and volunteered the same explanation at which I had arrived. In view that I have given the world my opinion that the boy committed suicide, and have thereby cast a blot upon his memory, I feel anxious to repair this damage insofar as I am able."

That Tom would have awakened somewhere between three and three-thirty in the morning (the approximate time the coroner set for his death) to practice a rope trick seems improbable. But whatever the true reasons behind Tom's premature death, the tragedy had severe and long-lasting aftereffects on Kathy. A depression set in, her schoolwork suffered and she found the company of her peers even more difficult. Her parents seldom left her alone. "Whenever I needed them they were there," she later recalled. "They weren't out, they didn't have other dates—they were *there*. They showed a deep interest in anything I did. They were a source of infinite strength. And I needed that strength." Then she adds that her brother's death "threw my mother and father and me very close together. Very close."

At the time of the tragedy, Kathy was still attending the

Oxford School. By June, with her grades off and her nerves on edge, the Hepburns decided to return their children, including Kathy, to the tutorial system. The Hepburns were now a self-contained unit with Kathy, the eldest, taking much of the responsibility for her two brothers and two sisters. Mrs. Hepburn was actively working with Margaret Sanger, crusading for liberalization of birth-control legislation, while Dr. Hepburn prospered in his profession. Like her parents, Kathy was scornful of pretense and reactionary attitudes, and like her father, she was a lover of the outdoors. She became an ardent golfer, for golf was Dr. Hepburn's favorite recreation. Knowing how much Tom's athletic prowess had meant to him, she worked hard to compensate; at fifteen she entered the Connecticut Women's Open to take second place and then went on to win a junior ice-skating championship. Nothing pleased her more than to walk beside Dr. Hepburn on a wintry day, battling the elements to keep up with his brisk stride, both father and daughter dressed in casual clothes and wrapped in mufflers, wearing gloves but disdaining all other outside garments. And with her even closer attachment to her father, the pain of Tom's death began to ease.

CHAPTER
4

The Hepburns moved from North Laurel Street into an impressive twenty-two-room house at 201 Bloomfield Avenue, West Hartford, in the autumn of 1921. Over the fireplace was hung a plaque engraved with the words "Listen to the song of life." Built at the turn of the century, the rambling rooms were filled with bright flower chintzes, rich earth tones and fine early American antiques—cherry-wood chests and gleaming brass fireplace screens, candlesticks, and drawer pulls. Chairs were large and sturdy, cushions abounded and books crammed shelves and were piled high on tables and bureau tops. Their neighbors thought the Hepburns were a curious lot, inbred, aloof, obviously rich. People knew that Kit Hepburn was a Bigelow Houghton of the Corning Glass Houghtons. This made the Hepburns' flamboyant life-style even more incomprehensible. With the appointment of Kit's cousin, Alanson B. Houghton, as the first ambassador to Germany since before the war, newspaper society columns printed with much frequency Alanson and his wife Adelaide's social achievements.

"Reddy," as Dr. Hepburn now called his teenage daughter, had become a beauty of uncommon looks and somewhat unfeminine characteristics. Her wispy brick-red hair framed a haughty, sharp-boned face. Tall and lanky, with a loping gait and broomstick posture, she also possessed an overgenerous mouth, widely spaced, piercing gray-blue eyes, flaring nostrils, high cheekbones, and a strange voice—nasal, part Bostonian (learned from her mother), part affectation, part Virginia belle (learned from her father). Yet, these curious characteristics came together with startling effect.

By her fifteenth birthday, young men were queuing at the Hepburn door, and the doctor would glare down reprovingly at each from the top of the wide, curving staircase in the house on Bloomfield Avenue. About this time, Kathy brought a Catholic boy home. "Oh, with what chill politeness my father made him welcome," she later recalled. "Some days I'd go with him to mass—not that I'd go inside his church—I wasn't that brave. I'd sit on the steps outside and wait for him. Somehow my father would just happen to drive by every time I was sitting on those Catholic steps waiting and he'd smile at me and keep on driving. Pretty soon that boy and I just seemed to drift apart."

"Your beaux are the dullest I have ever known!" he informed his daughter, avoiding a direct reply after she had accused him backhandedly of possible prejudice toward Catholicism. And to his wife, he added, "If she marries any of them, it's going to be hell!"

Marriage was the farthest thing from Kathy's mind. She still felt much the little girl. With no female school friends with whom to associate, she spent the majority of her time either in the company of her younger siblings, tending to their needs and arranging games for them, or with her parents as an active participant in their running political battles (the usually dignified Mrs. Hepburn once hurled a full coffeepot at Dr. Hepburn when he adamantly disagreed with her political opinion).

As in the past, Kathy's summers at Fenwick allowed her to endure life the rest of the year in West Hartford. Suntanned and freckled within a few days of her arrival each summer, she swam and fished and boated up the glinting river and to the Sound. The summer of 1924 took on special meaning; for in September she would leave for college, to live away from home and her family for the first time.

She arrived at Bryn Mawr College, in Bryn Mawr, Pennsylvania, a suburb of Philadelphia, seventeen years old, totally undisciplined scholastically, used to being the focal point both of her family's attention and their unwavering acceptance as well. The other girls in the college found it impossible to identify with this strange, aloof young woman who took her showers after midnight when the rest of her dormitory was asleep and who had not only waded barelegged in the fountain of the library cloister and then rolled herself dry on the grass, but allowed herself to be photographed in the nude in her dormitory room and then mocked the outraged druggist who refused to print the films.

Perversely, the first time she entered the dormitory dining hall, she wore one of her most elegant dresses, flame colored and form fitting. "Ah! Conscious beauty," an upperclasswoman called out. Backs were immediately turned to her and she sat through her dinner alone. Seven months were to pass before she would enter the dining hall again. Even then, no one sat with her, and after that she ate all of her meals in local tea rooms and restaurants.*

In her freshman and sophomore years, she would have nothing to do with college activities and exerted no effort to make friends. Classmates claimed she called no one by name. She dressed eccentrically in rumpled clothes most of the time and seemed "exhaustingly intense." Her marks grew worse with each passing term. Told by the dean that his daughter might do better elsewhere, Dr. Hepburn replied, "If I had a patient in the hospital, and the patient grew worse, I should not discharge him, but try to work out a more efficacious treatment."

What kept her going was a dream. At some point during her first two years at Bryn Mawr, she had decided she would be an actress. History had been her original major. When she returned to school for her junior term, she changed to English, aware that she could not be eligible for campus dramatics unless her grades were greatly improved. Setting her mind on this goal, she studied night and day. Her grades took a dramatic upswing. Before the year was over, she had appeared in lead roles in two plays—A. A. Milne's *The Truth*

---

* Years later, Hepburn developed a phobia about eating in restaurants. In 1924, women did not eat in restaurants alone as a rule. A woman who did, particularly a young woman, would quite naturally be stared at.

About Bladys and *The Cradle Song*. No one thought she showed any special talent. She had finally made a quartet of friends, however, who called themselves, inexplicably, The Tenement.

The summer following her junior year, Kate and a member of The Tenement traveled together to Europe. Kate's school friend had accumulated $500 by picking potato buds. Kate said she'd hock her bedroom furniture to go, but in the end Dr. Hepburn matched her friend's $500. The fare was $210 round-trip steerage to Plymouth, England. When they arrived they hired bicycles, but they hadn't figured on England being so hilly. They did not get far from the dock when they decided they must get hold of a car. They turned in their bicycles and trained to London, where they found "a very nice man called Mr. Seymour, in Great Portland Street" who let them have a Morris for £95 ($475 at that time). Living proved very expensive. Lodging was 2s. 7d. a night, and with food and the car expenses, their outlay was over $5 a day. They quickly realized they were running out of funds, and so after a week they sold the car back to Mr. Seymour for only £5 less than they had paid for it and took a train for Paris.

In February, 1927, in the previous year, Kate had attended a Yale prom with one of her Saybrook friends and had met a good-looking senior, Robert J. "Bob" McKnight. McKnight came from Springfield, Ohio, and was related to J.S.A. Ward, one of America's best-known nineteenth-century sculptors.

While they were dancing, Kathy asked McKnight, "What are you going to be?"

"I'm going to be the greatest sculptor in the world," he replied. "What about you?"

"I'm going to be the greatest actress in the world."

McKnight spent that Easter break in West Hartford, sharing a room with the much younger Dick and Bob Hepburn, then in their early teens. A gentle man, somewhat a dreamer, from a conservative though artistic family, Bob McKnight had never seen anything quite like the Hepburns, and was amazed at the table conversation dominated by the younger children, who asked questions on sex and their parents' current work and preoccupations and received full answers. He got along well with Dr. Hepburn, who convinced him he should go to a medical school to study anatomy if he really wanted to be a sculptor. Though she had invited him, Kathy left McKnight to his own devices for most of the visit. Early one morning she woke him up with a fairly passionate kiss and then dashed out of the bedroom he shared with her brothers. McKnight considered this impulsive act a statement and was certain that not only was he in love with Kathy but she with him.

For nearly forty years, Bryn Mawr College had sponsored a quadrennial Elizabethan May Day. With the school's English setting—rolling hills and well-tilled fields, gray-stone, ivy-covered buildings of Elizabethan architecture—nothing could have been more apt. Kathy won the lead role of Pandora ("sometime sullen, sometime vain, and sometime martial") in John Lyly's *The Woman in the Moon*, first performed for Queen Elizabeth I in 1597. May Day (actually two days—May 4 and 5) consisted of revels and six plays presented simultaneously on various parts of Bryn Mawr's sprawling campus.

Dressed in a white flowing gown, her hair loose and blowing madly in the brisk spring winds, Kathy walked barefooted (as Pandora would have) on the graveled path during the procession of the players. A teacher pressed her to put on sandals to avoid injury to her feet. "You can take them off for the performance," the teacher assured her. Kathy firmly refused.

Her wild, militant Pandora startled students and faculty at Bryn Mawr. Her performance was overblown and lacked a sense of ensemble playing. But from the moment she walked barefooted and bare-armed down the library stairs and onto the lawns of the Cloister Garden, head defiant, her hair a red flag of independence, her audience was aware of a powerful presence. A man named John S. Clark, whose home abutted the grounds of the college, saw one of her performances and gave her a letter of introduction to Edwin H. Knopf, a young theatrical producer who was preparing a season of summer stock in Baltimore.

Without funds at the time and fearing her father would never approve, Kathy called Bob McKnight in New Haven and asked him to send her ten dollars so that she could drive her car (a recent acquisition) down to see Knopf. McKnight dispatched the money immediately.

Kathy wasted no time after her arrival in Baltimore. To Edwin Knopf's fury, she entered his office above the Auditorium Theatre without an appointment and over an assistant's refusal to grant her time. Her hair was drawn back tight into a bun, her freckled skin blotched magenta with excitement. "Her forehead was wet. Her nose shone," Knopf later recalled. "She was tremendously sincere, but awkward, green, freaky-looking. I told her that my plans for the season were already made and there was no place for her, especially since I only hired professional actors. Then I rose in the hope this would indicate to her that the interview was over. Her parting shot from the door was, 'Thanks Mr. Knopf, I'll be back as soon as school is finished.'"

She returned a month later, four days before her graduation. This time she managed to enter a rehearsal in the theater unseen, and sat in the dark directly behind Knopf.

"You see I've kept my promise," she leaned forward to say.

"What promise?" he asked, after turning to look hard at her.

"To come back as soon as school was finished."

"There is nothing for you," he insisted, having finally recognized her. "I never use amateurs."

"Oh, that's all right," she said calmly. "I'll just stay here and watch." Three days later she still haunted the rehearsals. Finally, Knopf gave in.

"There are four ladies-in-waiting in *The Czarina*," he called down to her from the stage. "Report [next] Monday morning for rehearsal." This was on a Wednesday and her graduation from Bryn Mawr was that Saturday. Somehow her family had to be told, for the plans were for her to drive her parents back to Hartford after the commencement exercises (they had taken the train down). Fearing her father would disapprove of an actress in the family, she lost her nerve initially and got into her car without a word. Some thirty miles from Bryn Mawr she blurted out the news that she had accepted a job in a stock company in Baltimore and was due to begin work two days hence. Dr. Hepburn was in turn stunned and furious.

"You want to be an actress only because it is the easiest and most conspicuous way to show off!" he scoffed.

She protested loudly and her father shouted at her to stop the car and let him out. "I don't want to hear anything about it!" he threatened. "I'll go the rest of the way on the train!"

The atmosphere in the vehicle had become explosive. Mrs. Hepburn reminded her husband of the hundreds of public appearances she had made. Dr. Hepburn thundered back that she had done so in the public interest while what Kathy planned was nothing but vanity. The argument kept up all the way to Hartford. Finally, the next day, a Sunday, Dr. Hepburn gave in.

"All right," he said wearily. "I'll give you fifty dollars to help pay your expenses for a couple of weeks, until you recover from this madness, but that's the last penny you'll get from me until you do something respectable."

She took the money and packed a suitcase in a matter of minutes. All the Hepburns stood out on the front porch waving to her as she drove away. The trip to Baltimore was a day's journey. But no matter what happened after she arrived, she would not give up or return home beaten. A Hepburn might be many things—an intellectual snob, bull-headed, self-motivated—but never a quitter.

Kate:
A
Malady
of
Madness

CHAPTER 5

In Baltimore Kathy was renamed "Kate." No declaration was made to this effect. The members of Edwin H. Knopf's stock company simply adopted the Shakespearean diminutive of Katharine, which seemed to fit the determined, shrewish newcomer to their company.

Eddie Knopf—urbane, literate, young (only twenty-nine in 1928), most attractive and possessing a tremendous enthusiasm—made a strong impression upon Kate. He had begun his career as an editor at his brother Alfred Knopf's publishing house, but he soon switched to acting and had played leads in New York and abroad before joining with William Farnsworth to form the Auditorium Theatre Players in Baltimore. Unhappily married at the time to Mary Ellis, the lovely singing star of the musical *Rose Marie*, and discontented with the critical acceptance of his stock company, Knopf had one eye on Hollywood and the possibility of becoming a film director.* He, therefore, had little patience with an amateur who bristled each time she was corrected. He

---

* Edwin H. Knopf (1899–1981) went on to Hollywood as a writer, director and producer in December, 1928, remaining to make nearly thirty films, the most notable being *The Santa Fe Trail* (1940), *The Trial of Mary Dugan* (1941), *Cry Havoc* (1944), *The Valley of Decision* (1945) and *Lili* (1953). He made two films with Spencer Tracy—*Edward My Son* (1949) and *Malaya* (1949), which brought him once again in contact with Hepburn.

gave her a walk-on, nonspeaking role in Melchior Lengyel and Lajos Biró's *The Czarina* (about Catherine the Great) and figured Kate would give up and go home in short order.

Both Knopf and the company, which included the future film star Robert Montgomery, were overwhelmed at the transformation that took place when Kate, as a lady-in-waiting to Mary Boland's Catherine the Great, walked onstage dressed in her Russian Court costume and curtsied deeply.* The girl with the bunched hair, sloppy clothes and mannish golf-stride step had disappeared, and for that moment Kate commanded the stage. During the first two days of rehearsals, Knopf's star, Mary Boland, found her terribly disconcerting and complained that she sat in the wings staring at her and making her feel very uneasy. But she also confessed that she had "never seen anyone more beautiful than that eager girl, so proud to walk across a stage that she and the costume seemed borne up by light."

The Hepburns did not travel to Baltimore for their daughter's stage debut. Kate's Aunt Edith attended a performance of *The Czarina*, as did some old Johns Hopkins associates of Dr. Hepburn, and the word went back to West Hartford that Kate had made a good show of herself. During the third week of her Baltimore engagement a letter arrived from Dr. Hepburn. "I won fifteen dollars at bridge last week. Here it is—a present." The next week a larger check arrived.

A small role as a flapper in Russell Medcraft and Norma Mitchell's *The Cradle Snatchers* followed her brief appearance in *The Czarina*. The male lead was Kenneth MacKenna,† an actor who had already made a name for himself in silent

---

* Mary Boland (1880–1965) made her Broadway debut in 1905 and was a successful tragedienne, but her fame as an actress came as a comedienne onstage in the 1920s and in film during the 1930s and 1940s portraying scatterbrained wives and mothers. A few of her best films were *Ruggles of Red Gap* (1936), *The Women* (1939) and *Pride and Prejudice* (1940). She never again appeared with Hepburn.

† Kenneth MacKenna, born Leo Mielziner (1899–1962), brother of noted stage designer Jo Mielziner. MacKenna had an early film career as an actor and director in silents and sounds. In the mid-thirties he turned to script editing, at one time heading the M.G.M. story department and teaching theater arts at U.C.L.A. He returned to films in 1960 and played a small part in *Judgment at Nuremberg* (1961).

films. Self-conscious because of the transition he would have to make to adapt his voice to the new talking pictures, MacKenna was also fearful that Kate's high-pitched nasal voice would be a future hindrance and gave her a letter to Frances Robinson-Duff, one of New York's finest voice coaches. (Before this he had convinced Knopf that Kate could play a small part in an upcoming Broadway production, *The Big Pond,* to which Knopf owned the rights.)

During Kate's last year at Bryn Mawr, Bob McKnight had proposed. She had avoided an answer with maddening charm. Kate had visited him at Yale and walked with him to a spot that commanded a magnificent view of New Haven. This is where, he told her, he always came to make decisions. He sat down with her on a rock. The sun made a fiery circle of her hair. Her long legs were caught up under her chin and as he waited for an answer Kate began a breathless dissertation on her dream of becoming an actress. An hour was to pass before she finished, stood, grabbed his hand and, running, led the way back to the campus. McKnight took this as indecision on her part, but not necessarily rejection, and he remained an ardent admirer. He did not know that another young man whom Kate had met at a Bryn Mawr dance was also pursuing her and that she found him more intriguing for reasons McKnight could not have understood.

Ludlow Ogden Smith believed unequivocally in Kate's ability to succeed as an actress. Indeed, he found the idea of her being an actress exhilarating. Luddy's mother was the beautiful Gertrude Clemson Smith, wife of Lewis L. Smith, of Strafford, Pennsylvania, where the Smiths' estate, Sherraden, on Deepdale Road, was the scene of many lavish weekend parties. The son of wealthy parents, educated at exclusive boarding schools and having graduated the University of Grenoble in France, Luddy possessed a quality of sophistication that Kate found attractive. He had a degree in industrial engineering that he never used. Charming, socially oriented, he preferred to pursue a career as an insurance broker.

Twenty-nine in 1928, tall and lean with a profile that could have belonged to a matinee idol, Luddy dressed elegantly and impeccably, handkerchief just so in his breast pocket, imported silk tie for evening, paisley silk ascot and blazer for the country. He spoke perfect French and colored his speech with short Gallic phrases, skied, boated, was wonderfully amusing, knew all the right people and small bits of information on the most esoteric subjects, and seemed to have a quotation for every occasion.

In Luddy, Kate had found an attentive escort, an amusing companion, a sympathetic friend, and a man who would never stand in the way of her career. She saw a good deal of him while she prepared for her role in *The Big Pond*, and every weekend they went up to West Hartford together. Kate was always busy, but Luddy did not object to trailing after her.

In a townhouse at 235 East Sixty-second Street between the Second and Third Avenue Els in New York, Frances Robinson-Duff taught actors and actresses how to breathe and then how to act. David Belasco had called her the greatest acting teacher in the world. Now a grande dame in her fifties, Frances Robinson-Duff had studied voice in Germany, been a Wagnerian soprano, acted in France, then for eleven years was a member of actress Julia Marlowe's theater company and played all over America with the best-known artists of the time. Miss Robinson-Duff's mother was also a teacher of voice and drama in Paris, where the two women became famous in the theater world for their stellar list of students and the exuberance of their Sunday afternoon salons. Miss Robinson-Duff knew every theater personality of consequence in Paris: Sarah Bernhardt, Mount-Sully, André Bacque of the Comédie Française, Réjane. She had studied a method of breathing control and voice projection with Sarah Bernhardt's teacher, and that method was the one she had embellished, refined and now taught. Mother and daughter had returned to the United States at the outbreak of World War I, bought a townhouse and created in New York the same aura of celebrity as they had had in Paris. Clark Gable,* Mary Pickford, Mary Garden, Helen Hayes, Mar-

---

* Clark Gable (1901–1960) had played occasional extra roles in films and appeared with touring stage companies before he worked with Miss Robinson-Duff in 1928. His first lead on Broadway in *Machinal* (1928) was the direct result. He then costarred with the well-known actress Alice Brady in *Love, Honor and Obey* (1930), which led to his going to Hollywood.

galo Gillmore, Billie Burke, Mary Boland, Dorothy Gish, Corinne Griffith, Hope Hampton, Kenneth MacKenna, Libby Holman, Ilka Chase and Ina Claire were only a few of the performers who had been coached by her. Kate was awed by "the Great Teacher's" credentials and was certain the association would lead to stardom. She had sent in a two-hundred-dollar check in advance to cover two lessons a week for a period of three months.

September skies delivered a thundery cloudburst on the morning of Kate's first drama lesson with Miss Robinson-Duff. Not able to find a taxi, Kate ran nearly the entire distance from her small midtown hotel to Miss Robinson-Duff's studio and home. A French butler, fully liveried, opened the door to her and stood back from the bedraggled young woman he faced. She removed, but held on to, her dripping raincoat and assured the man that she had an appointment. He directed her to a stairway although there was a hand-pulley elevator (later she learned this was for the personal use of the occupants of the house and their private guests), and informed her that Miss Robinson-Duff's studio was three flights up on the top floor.

Louis XVI decor dominated the house. Ornate gold-gilt framed portraits of costumed performers lined the narrow staircase. Kate took the steps at breakneck speed. On the second floor Miss Robinson-Duff's elderly mother taught singing, and a soprano voice could be heard going through some vocal exercises to the thumping beat of the hard tip of a cane against a wooden floor.

Kate burst into Miss Robinson-Duff's fourth-floor studio without knocking, flung herself against a black-laquered chest and, staring at the amazed, portly drama coach (who sat on a red velvet and gilt throne chair on a dais with a reading stand in front of her), said between great breaths, "I want to be an actress. I want to learn everything."

Miss Robinson-Duff silently studied her new student. Rain ran from Kate's untidy hair, down her nose and onto the floor from the coat she held. "Sometimes we have an inward vision, a flash," Miss Robinson-Duff said later of that first meeting. "I looked at her, huddled there, bedraggled and wet—at the terrific intensity of that face—

49

and something inside whispered, 'Duse. She looks like Duse.'"*

"Darling," (she always called her students, male or female, "darling") she said aloud, "we will begin immediately. First you must learn the proper use of your diaphragm and the control of your breathing. Before learning to act, one must first learn to breathe . . . put down your coat and come nearer."

Kate approached the raised platform.

"Now pant as hard as you can so you can find your diaphragm and then exhale in three strokes to empty surplus air."

Kate obliged. Her drama course had begun.

For weeks, Miss Robinson-Duff worked on breathing exercises that Kate had also to study at home. Then the drama coach turned to the elements of acting. "You hold your hands like a soldier at attention," she reprimanded. "And you must never stand with your feet so far apart." Once, she told Kate, she had taken an Italian actor to an American play. The ingenue, during a touching scene, stood in what she called the "spread base" position. Not understanding English and knowing only his continental pantomime, the Italian naïvely inquired, "They are discussing whether she will sleep with him, no?"

Kate immediately warmed to Miss Robinson-Duff. She coaxed her to retell stories of her experiences in the theater. She brought Luddy up to meet her and he was equally impressed. Because Kate's lessons were private, she had little chance to meet Miss Robinson-Duff's many other students. She did meet one, who had her class directly after Kate, Laura Harding, an athletic blond girl from New Jersey, heiress to the American Express fortune, who had hopes of a stage career but had never yet appeared in a play. "I thought—'She's not my type,'" Laura Harding remembered. "She had long hair pulled back in a knot, a man's sweater pinned at the back with a big safety pin—what we called a Brooks sweater—and a tweed skirt."

Laura Harding wasn't the only one to be put off by Kate's

---

* Eleanora Duse (1859–1924), the Italian actress, was considered to be Sarah Bernhardt's equal.

attire. The way in which Kate dressed drove Miss Robinson-Duff to despair, for she appeared more "bedraggled" at each lesson. One day Miss Robinson-Duff could take no more.

"You won't wear clothes fit for a decent scarecrow but will you do me a favor?"

"What?" Kate asked.

"Throw away that old felt hat and get one without a hole in it."

"Good Lord!" Kate replied with astonishment. "What's the matter with people? Can't their imaginations supply enough cloth for that little hole?"

Kate's arrogance worked as a cover-up for her growing fears and insecurities. The profession of acting had not turned out to be what she had imagined. Auditions for parts were torture and she would arrive at them bathed in perspiration, disheveled, her hair in disarray, and breathlessly late. She relied (as she had all her life) on bizarre dress and behavior to get her through and to command attention. Other hopeful actresses trying for roles did not wear torn clothes held together by safety pins. They dressed neatly and as fashionably as their pocketbooks allowed. They also looked very much alike. Kate, on the other hand, stood out. She was five feet seven inches tall, and her à la concierge hairdo added even more to her height. Her wardrobe consisted mainly of men's expensive sweaters and pants that were too large for her. She gave the appearance not so much of being dressed carelessly, poorly or sloppily, but of being costumed for a role she had cast herself in.* And the device worked as it always had; she was noticed. The impression given was of a most attractive eccentric; for no matter how curious her attire, Kate chose flattering lines and colors and, by concealing her feminine form, caused the beholder's eye to concentrate on her striking face.

Theresa Helburn of the Theatre Guild recalled that when Kate came into her office for her first Guild audition, "she was carelessly groomed . . . an odd looking child. But when

---

* Hepburn always said that she chose to wear pants to avoid such uncomfortable female accoutrements as garter belts and high-heeled shoes. But she had worn boys' clothes as a young girl when such things were not necessary.

she opened the office door it was as though someone had turned on a dynamo. The air vibrated with the electric force of her personality."

Nine days before the opening of *The Big Pond* and only three weeks from the time Kate had commenced lessons with Miss Robinson-Duff, the leading lady quit and Kate was suddenly shifted from a supporting role to appear opposite Kenneth MacKenna. She worked frantically to memorize her lines. On opening night, she arrived only fifteen minutes before curtain, and, rushing to apply her makeup, got mascara painfully in her eye. Then, as she slipped into her costume, she realized the elastic on her lace panties was loose. An instant before her entrance, in fear that they might fall off onstage in full view of the audience, she stepped out of them and stuffed them in the hand of an astonished stage-hand. She claims she was terrified, at wit's end, certain she would fail. Then, after an amusing opening scene, the audience applauded a humorous line. Her timing was thrown and she speeded up her delivery.

Her performance was so appalling—rushed lines, voice higher and higher, body stiff—that by the final curtain the audience was laughing *at* her, not with her, but she was not aware of it.

Knopf could not bring himself to tell her that Lee Shubert, part owner of the play, had ordered "that Park Avenue amateur" to be fired and replaced with "a real actress." Knopf delegated the unpleasant task to Miss Robinson-Duff, who, when she saw Kate in her studio the next day, was surprised to hear the young woman ask, "Aren't you proud of me, Miss Duff, aren't you proud?"

Miss Robinson-Duff ran her hand over her marcelled gray head and took a deep breath.

"You don't mean I'm fired?" Kate asked.

"Yes, you're fired," was the instant reply.

Kate drew herself up to her full height and threw her head back. "Look how I'm taking it. Not a tear! I know you're proud of me now."

"I'd have some hope if you wept," Miss Robinson-Duff answered. "How can I ever make an actress of you, if you keep that shell over your emotions?"

The Hepburn pride could not be quashed. She returned to

Knopf's company and said good-bye to the rest of the cast. Then she and Luddy drove up to West Hartford to show her family how she could take it on the chin. To her astonishment, she received a call from producer Arthur Hopkins, who had been in the audience on the night of Kate's opening. Hopkins had seen a quality beneath her poor performance that struck him as unique. He offered, and she accepted, a small part in a play, *These Days,** which he currently had in rehearsal. The story was about a group of mostly upper-crust young women at a finishing school. While rehearsing, she hardly saw Luddy, or anyone else for that matter. She was not only working daily with Miss Robinson-Duff but also taking dance lessons from the renowned Mikhail Mordkin (whom she had seen dance with Pavlova two days before her brother's suicide). *These Days* opened at the Cort Theatre on Thursday night, November 12, 1928, and closed after eight performances. *The New York Times* did not single Kate out, but John Anderson of the *New York Evening Journal* noted that "a perfect passage of repressed deviltry is done gorgeously by Miss Katharine Hepburn." This comment referred to a scene Kate had with the overpowering Helen Freeman, who played the finishing school's head mistress. Kate had only two lines that she repeated in this scene—*"Yes,* Miss Van Alstyne" and *"No,* Miss Van Alstyne"—but she used them to good effect.

The torturous rounds of producers began again. Her courage was flagging. Arthur Hopkins rehired her as understudy to Hope Williams in Philip Barry's *Holiday,* which had just opened successfully in New Haven and was on its way to New York. Kate watched rehearsals from atop a thirty-foot ladder used by the stagehands to reach upper ropes and pulleys. Arthur Hopkins, unable to bear seeing her teeter back and forth precariously, finally ordered her down with the threat of firing her. When the show opened, she stood in the wings every night and made Hope Williams extremely nervous. At the end of the first week she and Luddy went to West Hartford together and applied for a marriage license.

---

* *These Days* was written by Katharine Clugston and filmed by R.K.O. in 1934, retitled *Finishing School* and starring Frances Dee and Ginger Rogers. Ironically, Katharine Hepburn's stand-in, Adylyn Davis, appeared in the film in a small role but Hepburn did not.

The Hepburns were surprised, but they wanted her to have a proper wedding. Staunchly, she refused to agree to more than the most intimate family members in attendance.

Recognizing the hopelessness of understudying a star who would never miss a performance, Kate went straight to Hopkins on her return to New York that Monday and handed him her uncashed salary checks for the two weeks, announcing, "I'm getting married." Hopkins asked to whom. When she told him it was Luddy, he was surprised. He had assumed they were just good friends, as had other members of the cast and Miss Robinson-Duff.

On December 12, 1928, she and Luddy were married with a good deal of unexplained secrecy by her grandfather Hepburn, the oldest Episcopalian minister in the state of Virginia,* at the West Hartford home of her parents. ("If you want to sacrifice the admiration of many men for the criticism of one, go ahead, get married," Mrs. Hepburn told her.) Because no marriage announcement was printed in Hartford, Philadelphia or New York—Kate's circle of association—the question of whether she planned to give up her career in the theater would not be asked.†

Marriage, Kate frequently said (and continued to say), was not a natural state. While in her teens she had insisted she would never have children; her early dedication to her younger brothers and sisters satisfied any need she might have had for mothering, and the preponderance of children, all under ten years of age, who filled Fenwick every summer (first cousins from Baltimore and Detroit, besides the cook's son and the children of the visiting governess) turned her "off kids." Many "oldest daughters" never married, never had children. And, anyway, marriage would interfere with the pursuit of her career. Since Kate did not appear to be so in

---

* "We've had some nuts in the family," Hepburn later recalled. "My grandfather was one. He never owned a toothbrush. He'd say he didn't want to become dependent upon anything. So he cleaned his teeth with the same soap and washcloth he used for the rest of his toilet."

† Hepburn later said of this marriage, "I wasn't fit to be married. He [Ludlow Ogden Smith] was a nice man and no nice man should marry an actress or anyone else whose mind is always on herself—I know if I were a man I wouldn't be dumb enough to marry someone who couldn't pass a mirror without looking into it."

love with Luddy that her heart might overcome reason, why would she marry when he did not seem to be head over heels in love with her either? They were wonderfully good friends. And Kate showed more of a protective interest in him than he did in her; Luddy was coming to terms with his relationship with his mother, his own sexuality, his lack of enthusiasm for a career, and his lack of need to earn a living. Perhaps he filled her brother Tom's place in her life and she anticipated being able to help him surmount problems similar to those that had overwhelmed Tom.

According to Kate, after their secret wedding in West Hartford on December 12 (a Tuesday), she and Luddy went to Bermuda for a short honeymoon. Then they looked at houses on the Main Line in Philadelphia while they stayed with Mrs. Smith at Sherraden. Kate later admitted asking herself, "What am I doing? I couldn't live here!" Luddy, she claimed, "was swell about it," and they moved into a small walk-up apartment on East Thirty-ninth Street, where he joined her on weekends. Very few people in New York had even heard that Kate had been married.

It has been written that Kate's marriage to Luddy was a platonic arrangement. Her contracts, as in the past, were signed Katharine Houghton Hepburn (that is the name she has used throughout her life on all legal documents as well as on her personal printed stationery). She seems not to have been known as Mrs. Smith, but the knowledge of Luddy's presence—however platonic—in Kate's life meant that she did not have to play either the flirt or the cool virgin or listen to any proposals of marriage. Luddy, or rather the knowledge that she had a husband, had liberated her from all that.

CHAPTER
6

The Broadway production of *Holiday* closed in June, 1929, without Kate ever appearing in the role of Linda Seton. A month later, she and Luddy crossed to France for their own holiday. Luddy intended to show her the scenes of his youth and Kate wanted to share with him some of the Left Bank locations of her previous visit. But the crossing (first class at Luddy's insistence) had been difficult. Despite Kate's love of boats, she had been ill most of the time. Once they were on land, other difficulties arose between them. The vacation was cut short and they returned to New York within two weeks. In the time of her absence, *Holiday* had reopened in the Riviera Theatre at Ninety-seventh Street and Broadway in preparation for a cross-country tour. Kate finally had her chance to step in for Hope Williams when the star took sick one night. Arthur Hopkins watched her from the back of the theater, and he thought her performance was "even more compelling" than any he had seen his leading lady give.

On Hopkins's recommendation, Theresa Helburn of the Theatre Guild offered Kate $225 a week to appear in the ingenue's role in S. N. Behrman's *Meteor*, with Alfred Lunt and Lynn Fontanne. Kate accepted, then backed out just before the play went into rehearsals. She had been offered the lead in the fantasy-drama *Death Takes a Holiday* by Alfredo Casella, which Walter Ferris had adapted from the Italian.

Throughout rehearsals and for the five weeks out of town, Kate and the play's director, Lawrence Marston, were battling. Kate wanted to play the role of Grazia as a gamin, a tomboy, and Marston felt her interpretation made the story implausible. Three days before the opening, Lee Shubert, the play's producer, sent word asking for her resignation.

"Resign hell!" Kate claimed she told Lawrence Marston. "If he wants me out of the cast he can fire me." Shubert obliged, firing Marston along with her. Dr. and Mrs. Hepburn drove all the way from West Hartford to Philadelphia to catch her last performance.

Right after the final curtain, Dr. Hepburn came "storming" backstage. "They're absolutely right!" he shouted. "You are carrying on on that stage. You are galumphing there like a maniac. Who's going to believe that my daughter, a big healthy girl like you, could fall in love with death. With death, for God's sakes!"*

Kate spent Christmas with Luddy and her family in West Hartford. The country had been in an economic depression since October. Wall Street had suffered paralyzing losses. Luddy's new career as an insurance broker was in serious jeopardy. Dr. Hepburn's money was invested in the manufacture of medical equipment and the Hepburns' financial security seemed unthreatened. Nonetheless, a pall existed throughout the Christmas season. The competition for roles would be keener, fewer plays would be produced. Dr. Hepburn stressed the need for even greater excellence during hard times and Kate agreed with him. Her decision was to return to her studies with Miss Robinson-Duff upon the New Year.

Back in New York, she swallowed her pride and re-approached the Theatre Guild with the possibility of taking on their original offer for *Meteor,* which was only now going into rehearsals. They refused to reconsider her, but suggested she see Rouben Mamoulian,† the director, who had adapted

---

* *Death Takes a Holiday* played 180 performances and then was filmed with Fredric March in the Philip Merivale role of Death and Evelyn Venable as Grazia. Rose Hobart replaced Kate as Grazia when *Death Takes a Holiday* opened at the Ethel Barrymore Theatre on December 26.
† Rouben Mamoulian (1898–   ). Born in Russia, he had just recently made his first film, *Applause.* An innovative film director, he went on to direct many

Ivan Turgenev's *A Month in the Country* for a Theatre Guild production in early spring. Alla Nazimova was to star. Kate went to audition for the ingenue role. Mamoulian had already seen about fifty young women when Kate, shaking, hair askew, perspiring profusely, entered his office.

"I tried to put her at ease," Mamoulian later remembered. "I asked her to sit down, and I said to her, 'This is going to be difficult because it's a very big part.* Have you ever done anything?' She said, 'No.'" (Untrue, of course, but Kate could easily have considered her past experience too inadequate to qualify.)

Rouben Mamoulian gave her a scene to read and told her to go into the next room to study it for ten minutes or so and to return. Her reading reflected her inexperience and Mamoulian told her he did not think she was ready for such a large part. "However," he confided in his soft, rolling Russian accent, "if I have a chance for you, an opening for a smaller part, I would like to call you." After she left he went in to speak to Cheryl Crawford, the casting director.† "Cheryl," he said, "I want you to take this girl's name down because the kid has something. Whenever I have an opening remind me." Later he recalled, "There was something about her—it's very difficult to describe in words. You can't describe music. There was—is—a kind of luminosity . . . there are some faces that project the light; hers does."

Cheryl Crawford offered her a job as understudy to the ingenue at a salary of $30 a week, a humble comedown from

classics, the Fredric March version of *Dr. Jekyll and Mr. Hyde, Song of Songs* (Marlene Dietrich), *Queen Christina* (Greta Garbo), *Becky Sharp* (Miriam Hopkins), and the musicals *Summer Holiday* and *Silk Stockings*, among others. But he never abandoned the theater and staged the original productions of *A Farewell to Arms* (1930), *Porgy and Bess* (1935), *Oklahoma* (1943), *Carousel* (1945) and *Lost in the Stars* (1949). Rouben Mamoulian and Kate Hepburn were never to work together again.

* The role (played in the Theatre Guild production by Eunice Stoddart) was that of Viera Aleksandrovna, a young woman whose girlish love succumbs to a jealous woman's treachery.

† Cheryl Crawford (1902–   ) was casting director for the Theatre Guild from 1926 to 1930. In 1931 she helped found the Group Theatre and remained with that organization for eight years before she became an independent producer. Some of her many productions were: *One Touch of Venus* (1943), *Brigadoon* (1947), *The Rose Tattoo* (1951), *Paint Your Wagon* (1951) and *Sweet Bird of Youth* (1959).

the $225 a week the Guild had previously offered her. Even so, Kate accepted. *A Month in the Country* opened to fair reviews on March 17, 1930. Five weeks later, Kate replaced Hortense Alden* as Katia, the maid, maintaining her duties as understudy to Eunice Stoddart. Kate asked for a five-dollar raise in salary but the Guild refused, saying that they could get plenty of girls at thirty dollars to handle both jobs and that she could quit if dissatisfied. She stuck but harbored harsh feelings toward the Guild. (Miss Stoddart failed to miss even one performance.)

Kate by now had become great friends with Laura Harding, and the two young women decided to put in a summer of stock with the Berkshire Playhouse in Stockbridge, Massachusetts, where Laura had apprenticed the previous year. Luddy planned to join Kate on weekends and he seemed to have no objection to his wife's arrangement to share a room with Laura in the home of a minister named Bradley, his Southern wife and their three teenaged daughters. Nineteen other members of the company were also established at the minister's huge old eighteen-room house—all of whom shared one bathroom, which was next to Kate and Laura's room. Kate infuriated everyone in the house by taking "endless baths"—eight, nine and even ten baths a day into the late night, shouting out French poetry as she bathed. On the weekends, Luddy washed her hair for her in the bathtub and brought her ice cream from the village where he had a room in the local hotel, the Red Lion Inn.

The company was a diverse group with extreme and conflicting political and artistic opinions. Kate fought violently with almost everyone but Laura. The two women got to know each other very well over the summer and, according to Laura, "laughed an awful lot." Laura had a strong personality, a talent for easy persuasion. She could get Kate to agree to small adventures, rather childish pranks to play on fellow company members. With Laura, Kate seemed to regain some of the sense of camaraderie she had experienced with her brother Tom, and she reacted warmly to it.

---

* Hortense Alden years later appeared as Mrs. Violet Venable in the off-Broadway production of Tennessee Williams's short play *Suddenly Last Summer*, the same role Katharine Hepburn portrayed on the screen.

Richard Hale,* a well-known actor and concert singer, and Kate were constantly battling. Hale's mother was a violent anti-feminist and an adversary of Mrs. Hepburn's; his brother-in-law was the arch-conservative Heywood Broun and Kate and Laura hated him categorically. Osgood Perkins was a member of the company, as were Mary Wickes, Leo Carroll, Aline MacMahon, Walter Connolly and George Coulouris.† Coulouris immediately took a dislike to this "skinny red-haired girl [who] ran in saying, 'I've come all the way from Hartford with a golf tee between my teeth!' in a high, squeaky voice." She had driven to Stockbridge in her new and luxurious LaSalle convertible and though she dressed in trousers and ate her meals with her knees almost up to her face, "she played the prima donna from the time of her arrival."

Kate took tremendous pleasure in baiting Coulouris, and their arguments usually reached a crescendo over Rev. Bradley's meal table. During one dinner Coulouris rose from the table indignant at something Kate had said and she got up and pursued him at a mad clip through the house, both of them holding their cutlery midair in a threatening gesture. Finally Coulouris, much winded, turned on his heel and wagged his fork at her.

---

* Richard Hale (1893–1981) sang with the Metropolitan Opera. He also narrated the Boston Symphony Orchestra's first United States concert of *Peter and the Wolf* under the direction of Serge Prokoviev and repeated the role in the popular recording. He went on to Hollywood in the 1940s, appearing in character roles in numerous films, but never was to work with Katharine Hepburn again.

† Osgood Perkins (1892–1937), a star of numerous silent films, father of Tony Perkins. Mary Wickes (1912–   ) went on to play wisecracking busybodies; her most famous role was as the nurse in *The Man Who Came to Dinner* (1942). Leo Carroll (1892–1972), born in Weedon, England, became known to American television audiences as Cosmo Topper in TV's *Topper* series and Mr. Waverly in *The Man from U.N.C.L.E.* Aline MacMahon (1899–   ) later appeared with Katharine Hepburn in *Dragon Seed* and was nominated for an Oscar for her supporting role. George Coulouris (1903–   ), born in England, had made his stage debut in 1929, the year before he came to the Berkshire Playhouse. He went to Hollywood in 1933, appearing as a villain in several dozen character roles. He became a member of Orson Welles's Mercury Theatre and appeared in *Citizen Kane*. He returned to England following the war and pursued a successful career as a character actor. Walter Connolly (1887–1940) went to Hollywood the following year (1932) and remained there until his death only eight years later. During that time he made nearly fifty films, playing supporting roles in all but one—*The Great Victor Herbert*—in which he played the title role.

"You're a fool, Katharine Hepburn! You're a fool!" he shouted. "You'll never be a star. You'll never be important in the theatre. You don't make any sense at all."

Kate yelled back, "You're the fool! I will be a star before you're ever heard of!"

Becoming a star meant a great deal to Kate. Good reviews and love of the theater were all well and good, but she wanted to be recognized. This meant maintaining her own strong personality even while becoming the character she played—a difficult task. To some her voice was irritating, the aggressive tone containing a certain kind of violence. ("Well I like that. And I feel good, so I'm violent. I come by that naturally," she replied to such allegations.) Her voice was a challenge, the edge she put on words seemed to say, "What the hell are you going to do about this?"

She had been hired for a five-week engagement with an option on her services for an additional five weeks if she did well. Piqued at being cast in a role no larger than Laura Harding's in the first play of the season, Sir James Barrie's *The Admirable Crichton,* she ignored the director's instructions and treated him with rude disdain. Portraying Lady Agatha and Lady Catherine (two rather silly young women), Kate and Laura were generally onstage together. Onstage alone in only one scene, Kate was to step to the wings and call out, "Catherine? Lady Catherine?" Throughout rehearsal week she yelled, instead, "Lau-au-ra! Lau-au-ra Ha-a-rding!" Alexander Kirkland,* who was directing, lost his temper.

"Miss Hepburn, you just can't do that!"

"No?" Kate asked. "Who's going to stop me?"

The Admirable Crichton opened on June 30 starring June Walker (who had gained wide recognition on Broadway as Lorelei Lee in *Gentlemen Prefer Blondes*) and Richard Hale. The play, and especially Miss Walker, received good reviews in local and neighboring papers, but neither Kate nor Laura gained so much as a mention, or an "also in the cast."

Kate champed at the bit and fought fiercely to be given the lead in the Berkshire Playhouse's second production, *The*

---

* Alexander Kirkland (1908–   ). His third wife was Gypsy Rose Lee; went on to films but not too successfully; retired as an art dealer in the 1950s.

Romantic Young Lady. Biographical profiles usually state that she played the lead in the Martínez Sierra comedy,* but Edith Barrett,† the star of *Michael and Mary* (a Broadway hit the previous season), performed the role of Rosario. And while Kate did everything to command attention (including wearing her dress backward one night and her hat reversed another), once again the reviews made no mention of her appearance.

George Kelly's** farce, *The Torch Bearers*, followed on July 21, starring Aline MacMahon. The day before the opening, the drama editor of *The Hartford Courant* wrote: "I do not know whether or not Kath[a]rine Hepburn is to have a part in *The Torch Bearers*. She had played in the three plays already given [Kate had a minor role in the third production, *Romeo and Juliet*] and I understood was to be in the company five weeks. I have never seen Mr. Kelly's play and I hope to be able to get to Stockbridge next week to enjoy it. I also am inclined to hope that I may see Miss Hepburn in the cast for I belong to the I-knew-her-when Club—when she was a very small child indeed!"

Mr. Brown was disappointed; for Kate, in a huff, and with Laura in the front seat beside her, had left Stockbridge in her "marvelous LaSalle convertible" the night that *Romeo and Juliet* closed, after completing three weeks of her five-week contract. "I asked for decent parts and they gave me strictly mediocre," she later explained.

Other company members claimed that her "disruptive perverseness" had become so great by the end of the three plays that Alexander Kirkland would never have picked up her option for the second five weeks and that Kate quit to have the last word. Their opinions reinforced by the unprofessionalism of her action, most of the stock company

---

* Martinez Sierra was the pen name of the husband and wife writing team—Don Gregorio Martínez Sierra and Marie Lejárrago.

† Edith Barrett (1907–1977) married actor Vincent Price while they were both appearing in a Broadway production of *The Shoemaker's Holiday* (1938) and left the stage for Hollywood that same year. She appeared in numerous films in supporting roles in the forties and fifties but did not fulfill her early stage brilliance.

** George Kelly (1887–1974), author of *The Show-Off* and the Pulitzer Prize-winning *Craig's Wife*. Grace Kelly was his niece.

were glad to see her leave; certainly, her contribution and Laura's had been so small they were not missed.

Kate has said, "I just don't like to be half good. It drives me insane. And I'm willing to do anything to try to be really good. I'm very aware when I'm very good—and I like to be very, very good. Oh, I think perfection is the only standard for people who are stars."

But in the fall of 1930, Kate Hepburn was not a star and her idea of perfection seldom corresponded with the views of her directors and the actual stars of the plays she appeared in. Ensemble playing was not something she ascribed to. She had to stand out from the crowd, be noticed. Her dedication and commitment—which were awesome—were not so much to the theater as to fulfilling her ambition to become a star.

By now her parents and Luddy believed in Kate almost as much as she believed in herself. Backing would be no problem. Her already ample self-confidence increased. Theatrical agents whose offices she haunted said she was too aristocratic looking to play anything but a society girl. She answered haughtily that they were stupid, and she called on producers herself. She heard that British playwright Benn W. Levy had arrived in New York to supervise the casting of his forthcoming Broadway production of *Art and Mrs. Bottle*.* Jane Cowl† was to play the lead and a young woman was needed for the small but showy role of her daughter.

In her usual bizarre audition clothes, Kate burst into Benn Levy's office, in the same way she had done in Baltimore with Edwin Knopf, and announced brusquely that she would consent to take the part. Unlike Knopf, the British dramatist was amused. This girl was so lanky, bony and freckled that her air of assurance struck him as absurd. However, most of the applicants had been too attractive to please the aging Miss Cowl. Kate was "homely enough," and her reading, if not exactly right, did show promise. Jane Cowl approved her and Kate was hired. As soon as rehearsals began, Levy's enthusi-

---

* Benn W. Levy (1900–1973), married to actress Constance Cummings, was best known for his later plays, *Springtime for Henry* (1931) and *Skylark* (1942).
† Jane Cowl (1887–1950). Besides starring in many plays and films, she co-authored a number of plays. One, *Smilin' Through*, was filmed twice (1932 and 1941).

asm collapsed. She came dressed in men's faded silk pajamas, a Chinese coat and scruffy slippers, wore no makeup, was rude, and refused to listen to his direction. Levy fired her but, after unsuccessful interviews with fourteen other applicants, rehired her at Jane Cowl's insistence.

"What does she use to get that shine?" Levy demanded to know, when Kate appeared each day with glittering cheeks and nose. Kate carried a concealed flask of alcohol and doused her face from it. She still took eight, nine or ten baths a day and at night wrapped her feet in wet cloths when she was unable to sleep. Whether her obsession with cleanliness and her need to feel cool were at the root of her splashing her face with alcohol could be debated. The gleam on her face was visible halfway back into the auditorium and picked up the light from overhead spots.

When the play opened on November 18, Miss Cowl insisted Kate submit to makeup. Kate agreed grudgingly, but continued to splash the alcohol on her face, which streaked the makeup and made her look garish. To add to this, on her initial entrance early in the first act, she had to kiss Miss Cowl on the cheek. Opening night, Miss Cowl heard a murmur in the audience from that point. When the first-act curtain came down she learned why. Kate had left a vivid lipstick print on her cheek. Miss Cowl demanded Kate use indelible lipstick.

The incident repeated itself the following night. Jane Cowl was furious. "Didn't I ask you to get some indelible lipstick?" she asked Kate.

To which Kate replied, "Well, I just thought I mightn't like it."

"An uncommonly refreshing performance was given by Katharine Hepburn as the young daughter," said Alison Smith of the *New York World* of her performance as Judy Bottle. Despite the fact that she had been outrageously rude to Jane Cowl, the leading lady, who had a reputation for gentility, was so impressed with Kate's "promise of power" that she commented later, "I don't think anything that child could have done could have turned me against her."

By the summer of 1931, Kate and Laura Harding were inseparable friends. Since her marriage to Luddy was in name only, Kate had no hesitation in pursuing her own aims in life. In fact, never during their marriage did they act the part of a married couple. Nonetheless, a great loyalty existed between them.

When Kate contracted for the season of summer stock at Ivoryton, Connecticut, Laura, who had given up all thoughts of an acting career, went with her. Because great wealth had deprived her of the need to work, Laura could afford to follow Kate around; and she was willing to live vicariously through her friend's achievements, becoming a catalyst for Kate, cheering her, pushing her on. At Ivoryton, Kate got her opportunity to play major roles in three plays—*Just Married, The Man Who Came Back* (opposite Henry Hull*) and *The Cat and the Canary*.

Theater producer Gilbert Miller caught her in one of her performances at Ivoryton and offered her a choice role in a play that he and British actor Leslie Howard† (who was also to star) were bringing into New York that fall. The play was *The Animal Kingdom* by Philip Barry. Kate was to appear as Daisy Sage, a character who bore a kinship to his Linda Seton in *Holiday*. Kate was ecstatic. After Ivoryton, Luddy joined her and Laura at the Hardings' Pennsylvania mountain retreat, the Lodge. Every day for three weeks Kate ran through her part with her husband and close friend.

Rehearsals began in Boston at the end of August. From the moment Kate and Leslie Howard faced each other onstage, war was declared. Howard hated her "outrageous posturings" and her "insufferable bossiness." Philip Barry, on the other hand, was quite taken with her and on the second day of rehearsal added some lines to her part that she herself had inspired. Leslie Howard began to apply pressure on Gilbert Miller to remove her immediately from the cast. Actors Equity ruled that if an actor rehearsed with a show for six days, he or she was entitled to two weeks' notice with pay.

---

* Henry Hull (1890–1977). Best known on the stage for his role as Jeeter Lester in Erskine Caldwell's *Tobacco Road*. He made several dozen films, playing the title role in *The Werewolf of London* (1934) and Emperor Franz Josef in *The Great Waltz* (1938). In July, 1932, he appeared in summer stock at the Croton Playhouse in Ossining, New York, with Hepburn in *The Bride the Sun Shines On*.

† Leslie Howard (1893–1943) went on to star and co-star in many films, and to play Ashley Wilkes in Margaret Mitchell's *Gone With the Wind*. Howard was a passenger on a plane that was lost on a Lisbon-U.K. flight during World War II. His body was never found.

The fifth day was a Friday and Kate drove home to West Hartford afterward to spend the weekend, as she almost always did, usually without Luddy.

Mrs. Hepburn had recently mounted the rostrum at Carnegie Hall and picketed the White House on behalf of birth control. A *Life* magazine article reported that "The Hepburn house is a piquant compound of Margaret Sanger's emporium —Madame Recamier's salon and the Roman Coliseum." In West Hartford, the Hepburns were considered "pink, arty and Godless" and those who dared come close were either stimulated or incensed by their forcible and contentious natures.

Kate's intense energy and austere intellectuality combined with a rare facial beauty and physical gaucherie caused her to stand out from the crowd. And she wore her "strangeness" with panache. Pleased that she struck others as peculiar, she was quick to admit, "I have an angular face and body and I suppose an angular personality that jabs into people." She never considered herself in the same category as those young actors who sat around in Sardi's or the Penn-Astor Drugstore, or stood in the hallways outside producers' offices waiting for auditions. Those hopefuls thought of her as a "high-class broad who was going to make it." So did Kate. And the role of Daisy Sage could have been the vehicle to catapult her into stardom.

If Kate believed her mother would be impressed with the size of her new role, she was quickly disappointed. Mrs. Hepburn glanced at the playscript, judged it "la-de-da commercial" and did not think it had "enough to do with what really mattered in the world." Despite her mother's lack of enthusiasm, Kate was thrilled to be cast in *The Animal Kingdom* and her spirits were high.

The usual turmoil and excitement greeted her arrival in West Hartford. She talked a blue streak, the words tumbling over each other in her enthusiasm. Her brother Dick, several of his Harvard friends, her brother Bob, and her sisters, Marion and Peggy, sat cross-legged with her on the living-room floor as she told them all about the week's rehearsal. Later she went up to her room (still—and always—as she had left it), unpacked and went to bed. She rose before anyone else the next morning and breakfasted by herself while she read a book. The sun poured in through the two sets of French doors of the dining room. The day would be good for tennis (which she played on a nearby court). The doorbell rang just as Dick and his college friends appeared for breakfast. A registered letter had been sent from Gilbert Miller: "Pursuant to clause C-1 in your contract, you are hereby given notice of the termination thereof." She had been fired again. This time, the shock and the disappointment were tremendous.

First she blamed Leslie Howard, who she said hated her because she was taller than he. She ranted and raged through the house and finally reached Philip Barry by phone in Mount Kisco, New York, where he was then living. Barry claimed she then went into "a fish wife tirade." After he had listened to her abuse for a few minutes he shouted back, "They're right about you! Nobody with your vicious disposition could possibly play light comedy! You're totally unsuited to the part! I'm glad they threw you out!"

"I think Leslie Howard didn't like me," Kate later rationalized. "It's agony to be fired. And it's nice to be able to make up a lot of reasons proving you're the hero. That firing was a big blow to me and I thought, 'I'll never survive this.'"

Kate was certain that the play would fail without her. A young woman named Frances Fuller replaced her and the show was a great hit when it opened on Broadway, January 12, 1932. A few weeks later, Kate was hired to play an Amazon queen in Julien Thompson's farce, *The Warrior's Husband*, loosely based on Aristophanes' *Lysistrata*. All of her past athletic training, her vivid coloring, her statuesque carriage and her volatile personality combined to make Antiope a perfect role for her. She also displayed to great advantage her extremely shapely legs in the short costumes designed for the character. Nonetheless, her usual perverseness got Kate fired and rehired twice before the play opened at the Morosco Theatre on March 11, 1932.

From the moment on opening night when Kate entered in her short-skirted Greek costume, a prop stag wrapped around her shoulders, and "bounded down a treacherous forty-step stairway three steps at a time, threw the stag down and wrestled with her leading man," Colin Keith-Johnston,* her claim to stardom was staked. The role called for her to display a facet of her personality that was infallibly appealing; seemingly indomitable strength made vulnerable by a man stronger than she. Kate represented the distilled essence of the battle between the sexes.

"Miss Katharine Hepburn comes into her own as Antiope," wrote Richard Garland† of *The New York World-Telegram*. "Ever since she supported Miss Jane Cowl in *Art and Mrs. Bottle* I've been waiting for Miss Hepburn to fall heir to a role worthy of her talent and her beauty. Antiope is that role and Miss Hepburn makes the most of it, bringing out its tenderness, its humor, its bite. It's been many a night since so glowing a performance has brightened the Broadway scene."

The play ran for eighty-three performances and during that time Laura helped her fend off reporters and Hollywood talent scouts ("They didn't like me until I got into a leg show," was Kate's comment). Her salary was seventy-six dollars a week, a good living wage in the Depression years. Nonetheless, the Hepburns contributed additional assistance. Kate rented a townhouse at 244 East Forty-ninth Street for one hundred dollars a month so that she would have a proper home to return to each night after the show. Laura, whose taste she trusted, decorated the house for her, turning the basement rooms into a comfortable and charming apartment for Luddy with his own private entrance. Mrs. Hepburn had approved the house with one proviso: that a bathroom be constructed on the ground floor in consideration of any elderly visitors. Kate obliged.

Directly after each Saturday night performance, Kate would head up to West Hartford (a three-hour drive) and return on Monday morning. Laura and Luddy, as well as members of the cast, often came with her.

"Hello, everybody! Here I am!" she would shout as she

* Colin Keith-Johnston (1896–   ), an English actor who made his debut on the stage at the Drury Lane Theatre in 1919. Well known for his Shakespearean and classic roles.
† Mr. Garland was the same critic from whom the great entertainer Judy Garland (née Frances Gumm) took her professional name when she was a child appearing at the Chicago World's Fair.

threw open the door. Despite the hour, in a few moments the entire family would gather around her and gifts would be exchanged by all, as if months instead of days had passed since they had last seen each other. Colin Keith-Johnston says of his first visit: "Kate had some little present for everybody, and everybody had a present for her. I remember that two presents were made by the givers' hands. The children [Marion and Peggy were only thirteen and eleven, respectively, at the time] stood around. We grownups sat where we could—the room was her mother's combination bathroom and dressing room. We all ate bananas and milk, and all talked at once, and it was all bewildering and warming."

Kate's West Hartford bedroom was a large one with two French windows that allowed sunshine and air to flood the area. The walls were a terra cotta color and the furniture was maple. Her stuffed animals and dolls still littered the bed. Books were scattered about and a Victrola sat upon a small table made for her by Luddy. Everyone met for lunch and tea (an important rite in the Hepburn household) and dinner, but otherwise each member went his or her own way. Monday mornings were always painful departures for Kate.

Popularity among her peers had completely escaped her grasp. Mostly her friends were loyal subjects caught up in her uniqueness, unable to fulfill their own expectations, living vicariously through her. Her rarefied background had developed her into a hybrid, never at peace with the performers with whom she worked or with the social world that Luddy and Laura inhabited when away from her. Home was where she felt the most complete, accepted, comfortable. She never liked to stay awake late at night. Yet, after her Saturday night performance, she drove at breakneck speed to West Hartford to her father's house.

Halfway through the run of *The Warrior's Husband*, a Hollywood agent named Leland Hayward* began to court Kate as a client. Kate thought he was "rather horrible and rather awful" and confided to Laura, "I'm just sort of making

---

* Leland Hayward (1902–1971) began his career in the publicity department of United Artists and in the scenario department of First National. Next he became a talent agent, and then a highly successful stage and film producer. *Mister Roberts* (stage and screen) was one of his greatest hits. His second wife was actress Margaret Sullavan.

it difficult for him." Laura had known Hayward during her debutante days when he had been in the stag lines of several society dances, and she remembered him as "sort of a John Held type with sideburns." Kate's unflattering comments notwithstanding, Leland Hayward had a great deal of charm and inordinate good looks.

Leland Hayward thought Kate's kinetic personality and striking appearance would best be displayed on film, and he saw in her star potential. He talked to Paramount Studios about her and they made a small offer for her services. Kate turned them down.

From childhood she had loved films. But to go to Hollywood as a mere starlet, a contract player, would never do. She insisted Leland Hayward set fifteen hundred dollars a week as her price, believing a studio would not be likely to pay such a price for a relative beginner unless they intended to make that person an important player. R.K.O. picked up the bait and asked her to take a screen test in New York under the direction of R.K.O. talent scout Lillie Messenger. She chose a scene from *Holiday* and asked Alan Campbell* (who was in the cast of *The Warrior's Husband*) to play opposite her. Against Hayward's advice and pleas, she perversely kept her back to the camera during most of the test. The scene was one where the very rich maverick Linda Seton, slightly inebriated from champagne, tells her sister's fiancé to run off before the wedding. Kate put the champagne glass on the floor beside her and had to swoop down to retrieve it for a drink to emphasize her statement. Then, for a long moment, she turned to the camera, eyes misty but defiant, to announce if she were her sister she would run away with him.

As fate would have it, at R.K.O., David O. Selznick was struggling with the casting of the film version of Clemence Dane's *A Bill of Divorcement*. John Barrymore was set to star as the father, and George Cukor to direct. Norma Shearer, Irene Dunne, Anita Louise and Jill Esmond were all being considered for the pivotal daughter's role. To Cukor's shock, Selznick suddenly decided to cast his current lady friend, "a pretty little blonde ingenue." Cukor was ready to quit. "It's

---

* Alan Campbell (1905–1963), actor and author, future husband of author Dorothy Parker.

too terrible! It's fantastic! Nothing on earth could make me do it now!" he told screenwriter Adela Rogers St. Johns. "She's a lovely girl [Selznick's choice]. She'd make a great Little Eva, but if she plays Sydney, one of us will never live through the picture."

Leland Hayward got word of the problem at R.K.O. and convinced Cukor to see Kate's test. Cukor was stunned by that electric moment when Kate bent down, retrieved the glass of champagne and then turned with it full face to the camera. "She had this very definite knowledge and feeling [of the camera]," Cukor recalled. "She was quite unlike anybody I'd ever seen. . . . I thought, I suppose right away, 'She's too odd. It won't work.' But at one moment in a very emotional scene, she picked up a glass. The camera focused on her back. There was an *enormous* feeling, a *weight* about the manner in which she picked up the glass."*

Cukor had a terrible time even getting Selznick to look at the test. He burst into St. Johns' office a few days after Hayward had brought it to him and enlisted her help to get the studio to okay the casting of Kate in *A Bill of Divorcement.* "She's too marvelous," he crowed. "She'll be greater than Garbo. Nobody wants her but me so come and help me fight for her. You don't need to see the test. It's a foul test anyway. She looks like a boa constrictor on a fast, but she's great." Cukor grabbed St. Johns' arm, propelled her out of her office, and pulled her across the studio lawn toward Selznick's office, talking all the while. "Take my word for it, darling. Just say you think she's great. Start raving. Don't go too strong. Just say she'll be better in the part than Katharine Cornell."

Meanwhile, *The Warrior's Husband* had closed and Kate had taken on a summer-stock engagement at the Croton Playhouse in Ossining, New York, where she was appearing in the role of Psyche Marbury in Will Cotton's *The Bride the Sun Shines On,* which Dorothy Gish had done on Broadway.

---

* Hepburn saw this test for the first time in 1938 at a party at the end of shooting of the film version of *Holiday,* in which she starred. "The company laughed themselves sick," Hepburn recalled in 1948 to an interviewer for *The New York Times.* "I didn't think it was so awfully funny. It's true, I looked terrible in it. But there was something awfully heartbreaking about the girl I was in those days. I was trying so hard—too hard. I was so eager—too eager."

On June 30, during the Thursday night performance, she received a telegram from Leland Hayward telling her that not only would R.K.O. meet her fifteen-hundred-dollar-a-week demand, she was to leave for California on Sunday to appear opposite John Barrymore in *A Bill of Divorcement*. The *Ossining Citizen Register* carried the story that "the break that Katharine Hepburn got last night—a telegram from Hollywood, offering Miss Hepburn a lead in Clemence Dane's 'A Bill of Divorcement,' playing opposite John Barrymore—nearly broke up the performance of 'The Bride the Sun Shines On' in which Miss Hepburn is appearing . . . the young actress was so excited that her exultation was manifest in her performance, much to the amusement of the audience—which was tolerant and understanding." Henry Hull, her co-star, was not nearly so indulgent. Kate had spoken her lines at such a pace that he had trouble keeping up with her.

A picnic supper was served on the terrace of the playhouse preceding Kate's last performance and in honor of her departure for Hollywood. Kate, bronzed and glowing in a white sundress, her hair falling gently on her bare shoulders, was nervously accepting congratulations when a short, wiry man with dynamic dark-brown eyes and a kind of snide smile approached her. She smiled back uneasily. The man was the legendary theater producer Jed Harris, whom she had once read for and been turned down by at an audition.

He gestured at the fawning group nearby. "Not bad for an amateur," he said grinning, and then walked away before she could reply.

Early
Stardom

CHAPTER 7

"The very rich are different from you and me," F. Scott Fitzgerald wrote about Kate's generation of monied families. "They think, deep in their hearts, that they are better than we are because we had to discover the compensations and refuges of life for ourselves. Even when they enter deep into our world or sink below us, they still think that they are better than we are. They are different."

Kate most certainly was different, "a queer fish" in the jargon of the 1930s. So preposterously different was she from the people with whom her work brought her in contact that she might as well have been a foreigner. Not only did she have an accent that was peculiarly high-toned, but her habits and attitudes displayed a distinct disdain for almost everyone except her few intimates, like Luddy, Laura, Bob McKnight and the close members of her family. Yet, even in these circles, she was not happy unless she was the center, a position she had the ability to achieve. Upon meeting her or simply seeing her enter a room or walk down a street, people recognized her not as an actress but as a rich young woman who had attended one of the nation's best schools.

Kate was a stranger to compromise. She wanted it all and on her terms. Their marriage offered very little for Luddy other than the knowledge that he had a beautiful and extraordinary wife. Her refusal to accept what most of the world considered proper marital behavior seemed irreverent rather than unconventional. Her confident manner, brusque speech and air of superiority when paired with her Yankee independence, her impatience with others and her attitude of self-righteousness, alienated almost everyone who crossed her path while at the same time endowing her with a distinctiveness that made a lasting impression. In any walk of life other than the acting profession, Kate's personality might have done her in, as it had at Bryn Mawr. But she had *looked* a star for a very long time. Now, she was on her way to being one.

That July in 1932 when Luddy saw Kate and Laura off to Hollywood on the Super Chief, the Depression had settled into an American way of life. Straggling, sullen breadlines and soup kitchens appeared in most major cities. Newspapers reported that an estimated fifteen million people were out of work and another estimated thirty million were living on public welfare or private charity. Millions more survived by depleting the savings that were meant to see them through retirement and old age. But the Hepburns, the Hardings and the Smiths had not been seriously affected. Perhaps this was the reason that Kate, Laura and Luddy could hang on so securely to their ideals of independence and good times. They all shared one dream—Kate's future stardom, a curious dream on Luddy's part, since he had to know it would place a distance between Kate and him.

When Kate met the Super Chief on Sunday morning in Harmon, New York, during the train's brief three-minute stop to connect with its dining car before starting its cross-country journey, Laura was already onboard. Kate was in high spirits, first because she believed she had outfoxed the press, who would have expected her to depart for Hollywood from Grand Central Station, and second, she had made the cover of *Vanity Fair* magazine and was waving the issue in the air as she looked for Laura. The two women were to share a compartment and Laura stuck her head out the window and shouted to Kate, who was surrounded by luggage on the small platform. A mad dash followed to get Kate and all her baggage onto the train in so short a time. Their laughter co-mingled and was nearly drowned by the churning of the train's engine as it ground its way out of the station where Luddy stood futilely shouting, "Good luck!"

Kate and Laura had embarked upon what they called their "Hollywood adventure" unaware that Adolph Zukor, head of Paramount Pictures, the ebullient Miss Billie Burke, one of the stars of the film Kate was to make for R.K.O., and her husband, the great impresario Florenz Ziegfeld, were on the same train, having boarded, like Laura, in New York. The train trip did not prove to be as pleasant as the friends had expected, for the Midwest was in the grips of a heat wave. Without any air-cooling system, their compartment was insufferably hot and the two young women spent considerable time on the train's sooty observation platform. Just past Albuquerque, a fleck of steel flew into Kate's eye. When she tried to remove it she forced it to go in deeper and caused it to scratch the retina. Within a short time, the pain was considerable and the eye swollen shut.

Despite the condition, Kate was determined to make a good impression upon her arrival; and for the occasion Laura had purchased for her a gray silk suit with a matching pancake hat designed by New York couturière Elizabeth Hawes. Kate stepped off the train in Pasadena, California (once again to avoid the press), believing she looked quite elegant, if a bit puffy in the eye. To Leland Hayward and his partner, Myron Selznick,* who had driven out from Los Angeles to collect her, Kate's outfit appeared more bizarre than stylish. Their new star, with her swollen eye and her hair drawn tightly back and tucked under the band of the flat-topped hat she wore, looked like a cross between a nun and a college graduate who had mixed it up a bit the night before. "*This* is what David's paying $1,500 a week for?" David Selznick's older brother, Myron, gasped.

They delivered the baggage to the then very chic Chateau Marmont Hotel above Sunset Boulevard, where the two women would be staying until other arrangements were made. Then Kate and Laura were driven to R.K.O. Studios

---

* Myron Selznick (1898–1944) had been a producer early in his career. In 1928, he became a talent agent with swift success. Selznick's clients were among the most prestigious in Hollywood, giving him great leverage with the studios.

to meet David O. Selznick and George Cukor. Smaller than the major studios, R.K.O. nonetheless presented a strange and fantastic sight to the newcomers. The streets and pathways were filled with a most extraordinary mixed population of Old West gunmen and their blowsy ladies, gypsies in dark makeup, men in tuxedos and women in gala ball gowns. Many of the buildings were mere façades. The vast sound stages festooned with ropes, chains and other "haphazard impediments, were as lofty and awe-inspiring as cathedrals." The buildings were mere shells that had been constructed so that they could be used when necessary as backgrounds in more than one film. Her first glimpse of the studio was enough to alert Kate to the unreal world she was about to enter. Yet, Hollywood possessed no mystery for her. Films were to be a game and most games bored her unless she knew she could win. She would have to put her considerable energy into that endeavor.

Cukor's reaction on seeing his "boa constrictor on a fast" for the first time was even worse than Myron Selznick's. Cukor felt literally faint, believing he had made the most terrible mistake and not knowing what in the world David Selznick would say or do when he set eyes on this bizarre-looking creature. Kate had arrived at the studio just in time for lunch and Cukor had no alternative but to ask her to join him.

Adela Rogers St. Johns recalled, "As long as I live I will never forget the first day she appeared on the lot. Everybody was in the commissary at lunch when she walked in with Mr. Cukor. Several executives nearly fainted. Mr. Selznick swallowed a chicken wing whole. We beheld a tall, skinny girl entirely covered with freckles and wearing the most appalling and incredible clothes I have ever seen in my life. They looked like something Lee Tracy [an actor] would design for the Mexican army to go ski-jumping in—yet you could tell they were supposed to be the last word. George Cukor looked across at us. He was a little pale but still in the ring."

After lunch, Kate was escorted to David Selznick's office. Selznick, a bespectacled bear of a man, greeted his new star with apprehension. Kate's appearance had so seriously unnerved him that he even considered sending this bizarre-looking creature and her society friend straight back to New York on the next train. Cukor, trying to ease the difficult situation, brought up the wonders that makeup and wardrobe could accomplish and quickly escorted her out of Selznick's office and down to his own to show her the costume designs she would wear in the film in her role as an upper-class English girl. If Selznick's obvious disapproval could be overcome, she was to be on the set for the first scene the next morning. Getting her wardrobe immediately approved and in order was all important, for Cukor's first reaction had now dissolved into fascination. The girl had a unique quality, Garboesque as he had originally thought. Even her imperious attitude added a dimension of interest to her. To his amazement, Kate rejected one dress after another, declaring them inappropriate, and far too garden-party girly-girly.

"I'm sure Miss De Lima [Josette De Lima, the designer] is very talented," she conceded as she wiped the tears from her inflamed eye, "but I want my clothes designed by someone like Chanel or Schiaparelli."

"Considering the way you look, I can hardly take your judgment seriously," Cukor replied.

Kate was stunned at his retort. "I thought these clothes were pretty fancy. I paid a great deal for them," she answered, head back, voice arched, never revealing the fact that the outfit had been purchased for her.

"Well, they're terrible. You look ghastly. I think any woman who would wear such an outfit outside a bathroom wouldn't know what clothes are. Now, what do you think of that?"

An awkward moment passed. Kate appraised the solid, stocky man whose dark eyes held her steady in their gaze. About the same height as she, Cukor was a man who would never easily back down. Only seven years her senior, he gave the impression of also being a person of infinite wisdom. When he spoke, his thick-lipped mouth opened and closed with steely precision. His handshake was hard and sure and his gestures like semaphores. "You win!" she finally said. "Pick out the clothes you want." Kate extended her hand and Cukor took it, convinced for the first time since her arrival at the studio that he had made the right choice in hiring her.

Leland Hayward then drove Kate and Laura to an eye specialist in downtown Los Angeles. The cinder was removed from Kate's eye, but since the retina had been scratched, she was asked to wear a patch for a few days, which would delay her first scene before the camera.

The motion-picture production company that brought Kate to Hollywood had a highly complex corporate history. After near bankruptcy and numerous mergers and acquisitions, in 1928, under a group led by Joseph P. Kennedy,* it had become Radio-Keith-Orpheum, or R.K.O. The studio's financial position had remained shaky despite the recent success (1931) of its Academy Award–winning western, *Cimarron*.† As it struggled for its survival, the studio changed its top brass yearly. When Kate and David Selznick (considered a thirty-two-year-old "boy wonder" at the time) met, he had just joined R.K.O. as head of production at a large salary with the hope that he would bring the studio out of its $5.5 million deficit. Selznick was a compulsive gambler to whom winning meant a great deal. Meeting the arrogant, unconventional young woman he had hired at the crunching weekly salary of $1,500 was not reassuring. Kate's actions the next few days made him increasingly dubious.

The first thing Kate did upon returning to her hotel the day of her arrival was to call an agency to hire a "distinctive" car and a chauffeur. She had always loved stylish cars and was delighted when an enormous imported Hispano-Suiza that had been used by Greta Garbo in *Grand Hotel* was delivered to the Chateau Marmont. The next morning, she had the liveried chauffeur park the limousine directly under Cukor's office window, then honk loudly as she emerged dressed in her old pinned-together sweater and baggy pants (she disregarded doctor's orders and had not worn her eye patch). She thought the incident would amuse Cukor, but she had miscalculated. Cukor was once again beginning to become as

---

* Joseph P. Kennedy (1888–1969), father of President John F. Kennedy, financier and one-time ambassador to Britain. In 1928, he became chairman of the Keith-Albee-Orpheum Corporation. When the company merged with R.K.O., Kennedy became executive producer for the films starring his mistress, Gloria Swanson.

† Based on the Edna Ferber best-selling novel of the same name, the film starred Irene Dunne and Richard Dix and was directed by Wesley Ruggles.

insecure as Selznick about R.K.O.'s new "star." As the day progressed, his nervousness increased.

Kate's first studio appointment was with the press department. It lasted no more than five minutes, during which time she announced that her private life was her own and that she did not believe in publicity. (The R.K.O. publicity department did not learn until much later that she was married.) Meetings with the makeup and hairdressing department heads proved equally difficult. Kate was certain she could groom herself better than they could. Cukor, who felt Kate had a special quality that should not be lost, backed up some of her arguments. Her natural, intelligent good looks were to be preserved; the freckles and frizzy hair were to go. (For years heavy makeup blotted out her freckles on screen and an air brush was used to remove them from stills.)

A story circulated about Kate's first meeting with her co-star, the notorious womanizer and former matinee idol John Barrymore.* Supposedly, the man of the magnificently carved profile and the dissolute reputation studied her puffy eye for a moment and then offered her a vial of eye drops he kept in his pocket, with the comment, "I also hit the bottle occasionally, my dear."

At lunch a studio photographer took some shots of Kate with Billie Burke and Barrymore. Later that same day several copies of the stills were presented to Kate for her to autograph for some visiting out-of-town executives. Although her co-stars had already obliged, she refused to sign them. Cukor was furious and turned on her. "You! Do you really think anyone would want your autograph alongside Barrymore's and Miss Burke's? Those two are actors! If you study for twenty-five years, maybe your signature will be worthy to go with theirs!"

Cukor's sharp words spurred Kate to immerse herself in the script of *A Bill of Divorcement* as soon as she and Laura had moved from the Chateau Marmont to a small cottage in Franklin Canyon, found for them by a friend of Laura's. They

---

* John Barrymore (1882–1942). The youngest of the famous Barrymore theater family, son of Georgiana Drew and Maurice Barrymore, brother of Lionel and Ethel Barrymore. Star of stage and screen. Famous for his role as a great lover, he preferred playing grotesque, tortured roles, such as *Dr. Jekyll and Mr. Hyde* (1920), *Svengali* (1931) and *Rasputin and the Empress* (1933).

kept the glittering Hispano-Suiza and embarked upon a kind of unorthodox behavior that alienated most of Hollywood. When not before the cameras, Kate would dress in overalls, a fireman's shirt and torn canvas tennis shoes. Invited to a formal tea at the home of one of the studio executives, Kate sent the properly dressed Laura inside while she paraded on the front lawn of the mansion in her usual, eccentric attire. No one in Hollywood knew quite what to think about Kate. On one hand she demanded privacy, while on the other she created public scenes that invited censure and created gossip and secret speculation. Most people felt her demands for privacy were all an act. Others called attention to her odd, masculine dress, her imperviousness toward men (her marriage to Luddy was still not known) and her symbiotic relationship with Laura.

Filming of *A Bill of Divorcement* began less than two weeks after Kate had arrived in Hollywood. Generally, Laura was right on the set with her. In the evenings, however, Kate remained at home while Laura made the rounds with her West Coast friends. A day seldom passed without Kate calling her parents. On one of these calls, after Laura and Kate had been in California for several weeks, Dr. Hepburn inquired as to what Kate had done with her salary. She replied that she had spent it all. Dr. Hepburn was furious and insisted she direct her checks to him and he would in turn send her an allowance sufficient for her needs. She obliged, an odd action for a woman not only independent financially but married.

During the filming of *A Bill of Divorcement*, with Cukor's and Barrymore's help and her own dedication, Kate started to become a competent film actress. Ten years later, Barrymore remembered "every hour" of their working together. "Something about her recalled my mother, Georgiana Drew,* the best actress who ever lived. Miss Hepburn's talent was so clearly perceptible, and she was so intelligent in learning, that working with her was all pleasure. But Lord,

---

* Georgiana Drew (1856–1893), sister of John Drew, the foremost actor of the nineteenth century in America. She married matinee idol Maurice Barrymore (Hubert Blythe). Their three children, Lionel, Ethel and John Barrymore, all became famous actors. The play and film *The Royal Family of Broadway* parodied this famous theatrical family.

she was innocent! I'd have to punch her black and blue to force her upstage in front of the camera. You have to knock most actresses practically unconscious before you can get yourself into the picture."

And about the same time Kate replied, "I learned a tremendous lot from Barrymore. One thing in particular has been invaluable to me—when you're in the same cast with people who know nothing about acting, you can't criticize them, because they go to pieces. He never criticized me. He just shoved me into what I ought to do. He taught me all that he could pour into one greenhorn in that short time." Some time later, she remembered watching Barrymore's first scene and thinking, "'You're not much good . . . hmmmmm . . . phony.' That's what I thought. But later, I changed my opinion when we had the scene together in which I said, 'I think you are my father,' and he came over to me and took my face in his hands. He looked long at me, and he was absolutely shattering."

Barrymore was an aging matinee idol in 1932, his dark, handsome face marked by years of drinking and a fast, hard life. His debauchery was legend, and few of his leading ladies escaped his lustful overtures. In an interview about a decade later he recalled that he gave Kate the eye a few times, "Then I stopped till she gave me the eye. After a few more days we gave each other the eye. So I knew the time was ready. I'm *never* wrong about such things. I never *have* been." Kate claimed he suggested they run over the scene "we were going to shoot after lunch—imagine how I leaped at *that* chance—to be coached by John Barrymore. I was absolutely fascinated by him. What an actor! I went over to his dressing room. . . . We ran the scene and he did help me enormously. Then as I was getting ready to go, he suddenly took off his dressing gown—one of those ridiculous flannel ones, the kind we used to wear when we were children. His was absolutely repulsive, filthy, food-stained, and caked with makeup on the collar— simply *revolting*. Anyway, he slipped it off and stood there stark naked. My first thought was to get out, but I simply couldn't move. I was petrified—couldn't speak."

Barrymore corroborated her memory. "She just stood there looking at me, and finally, I said, 'Well, come on.

What're you *waiting* for? We don't have all day. Cukor's one of those finickers who goes into a *spin* if you're five minutes late.' She didn't move, so I did and started to grab her, but she backed away and practically plastered herself against the wall, by God! I said, 'What's the *matter?*' and she said, 'I cahn't.' I said, 'Never mind, I'll show you how.' She started babbling, 'No! No! Please. It's impossible. I *cahn't.*' I've never been so damn flabbergasted. I said to her, 'Why not?' and what do you think she said? 'My father doesn't want me to have any babies!' and she edged over to the door and made a quick exit."

Barrymore's fury lasted for some days, but he was an artist who greatly admired talent and he felt that Kate possessed a special spark—although he considered her "a creature *most* strange. A nut. She must come from Brazil 'where the nuts come from.'"*

Once Kate moved before the camera, all of George Cukor's fears dissolved.† Her impatience and directness, her quality of cutting through the extraneous, made her ideal for the role of Sydney Fairfield. She lacked the tenderness Katharine Cornell had brought to the part on the stage, but this gave reality to the melodramatic nature of the story (which bore a strong likeness to Ibsen's *Ghosts*). A shell-shocked victim of World War I (Barrymore) escapes from an asylum, returning home on the very day his wife (Billie Burke), who has divorced him, is to marry again. His daughter (Kate), who also has plans to be married, gives up her own future (once she realizes that his affliction is not from the war and might be inherited) to care for her father.

Cukor was hard on her. One time during the shooting she turned to him and said, "Just because you don't know what you're doing don't take it out on me!" He quickly grew to respect her instincts. She looked at things with "the cold eye of youth," as he called it, and made her own evaluation. In the scene where Hillary Fairfield (Barrymore) returns home, Sydney (Kate), his daughter, is concealed halfway up a flight of stairs as he wanders around the room, gazing at mementos

---

* A quote from *Charley's Aunt* by Brandon Thomas.
† Because of her eye, Katharine Hepburn's first scene in *A Bill of Divorcement* was moved up to the third day of shooting.

of his former life. Kate played the scene with the attitude "I never knew my father, how can I necessarily be expected to love him?" Cukor felt another actress might have found it necessary to indicate "of course I'd never *really* be mean to my own father."

Because Kate had always been a day person, rising and retiring early whenever she could, the ten- and twelve-hour days required in filming well suited her. She and Laura rose at six-thirty and were at the studio an hour later. Kate still took numerous showers and baths each day and claimed she brushed her teeth with Ivory soap almost as frequently (an eccentricity which, if true, she might have stolen from her grandfather). She set up her dressing room as home and ate a hearty lunch there (usually steak and salad and some fresh fruit and milk), seldom joining her fellow workers in the studio commissary. Her strict regime impressed everyone on the set. She endeared herself to the crew, who shared jokes with her and ate the candy she passed around at four P.M. when she liked to stop for tea and a sweet. To them, she quickly became one of the gang, although remaining a bit aloof with the cast and executives in the front office. All of the artifices and strange behavior that had marked her stage work disappeared. Cukor has said he saw immediately that Kate had a quality "made for the screen." Her face had a light, a radiance, and it moved correctly. All her "odd awkwardness, her odd shifts of emphasis" worked to bring her alive on screen. "She wasn't too smooth, she was *fresh*."

Kate found it easier to communicate with Barrymore than with Billie Burke.* In her youth, Miss Burke, a great beauty, had been the toast of Broadway and had married the flamboyant Florenz Ziegfeld. When her husband left for work, he left to work with the most beautiful women of the day—the Ziegfeld Follies girls. For years, her life had been geared to holding on to a man who found monogamy almost impossible. Now, at forty-seven and still married to the suave but

---

* Billie Burke (1885–1970) made her debut on the London stage in 1903. She came to New York in 1907 to star opposite John Drew in *My Wife*. She appeared in many silent films and more than seventy-five sound productions, her most memorable performance probably being Glinda the Good Witch of the North in *The Wizard of Oz* (1939). She and Hepburn made one more film together, *Christopher Strong*.

ailing impresario, she considered herself an expert in affairs of the heart. She advised script girls, makeup women and wardrobe ladies alike, "It's your job to creep out of bed early—ten minutes early will do, five in a pinch—brush your hair and your teeth, put on something crisp, use some scent, and—no matter how tired you are, no matter how your head aches, no matter how late you were up last night—*look kissable!*"

Kate was understandably unsympathetic toward a woman with such an antifeminist attitude. But Flo Ziegfeld died midway through the shooting of *A Bill of Divorcement* and his widow coped with her bereavement with such maturity and professionalism that Kate altered her first opinion. Three days after her husband's death, on the morning following the funeral, Billie Burke returned to the sound stage, giving a fine performance in a difficult character part and keeping her grief to herself.

By the end of Kate's first week on the film, the press got on to the news that a new star might be rising on Hollywood's horizon. Reporters visiting the set became a daily occurrence. To the publicity department's chagrin and the news photographers' delight, Kate would appear between scenes in her old dungarees. The studio threatened to steal the objectionable piece of clothing unless she stopped wearing it. She refused their ultimatum. One day she returned to her dressing room to find the trousers gone, and she threatened to walk "practically naked through the R.K.O. lot" if they did not immediately give them back.

The decision was not an easy one for the studio. In 1932, well-born, well-educated young ladies (the image of Kate the publicity department had decided upon) did not expose themselves in public, and the studio already was aware that Kate was rebellious enough to carry through her threat. Nonetheless, they refused to return the dungarees.

"So I did it," Kate recalls. "Of course I did it. I walked through the lot in my underpants."

Barrymore thought this was uproarious, but the studio did not laugh. They immediately confiscated all pictures taken of Kate in her stroll and, to her delight, gave her back her dungarees.

The film was shot in four weeks (not unusual for those

preunion days). Kate's contract called for her to be available for any retakes, but she and Laura trained back to New York the following week, only to have to return within two weeks for Kate to reshoot two brief scenes.

David O. Selznick was to remember that "Everybody was shocked silly [when I signed Hepburn]. The world knows that startling Hepburn face now, but when she first appeared on the R.K.O. lot there was consternation. 'Ye Gods, that horse face!' they cried, and when the first rushes were shown, the gloom around the studio was so heavy you could cut it with a knife. Not until the preview was the [executive] staff convinced we had a great screen personality. During the first few feet you could feel the audience's bewilderment at this completely new type, and also feel they weren't quite used to this kind of a face. But very early in the picture there was a scene in which Hepburn just walked across the room, stretched her arms, and then lay out on the floor before the fireplace. It sounds very simple, but you could almost feel, and you could definitely hear, the excitement in the audience. It was one of the greatest experiences I've ever had. In those few simple feet of film a new star was born."*

Selznick decided R.K.O. would pick up Kate's option. Whether or not Kate was a fine actress had not been a decisive factor. Movie audiences do not require their favorite performers to be great actors. They want idols, personalities, glamour. In the early thirties times were hard and going to a movie was one of the few inexpensive escapes. Films with content had to be sugar-coated and spoon-fed to sell tickets. Crime films, such as *Public Enemy* and *Little Caesar,* featured stars the public loved to hate (James Cagney, Edward G. Robinson). Occasionally such films contained a spurious social consciousness, but even so they were clearly designed as escapist entertainment. Audiences grew to know exactly what to expect from a film's star once they had purchased a movie ticket. Joan Crawford would more than likely be a

---

* Selznick claims that immediately after the preview of *A Bill of Divorcement* he decided to do *Little Women* with Hepburn as Jo March, and started making production plans for it. Then he left R.K.O. to return to M.G.M. just before the actual filming began.

fallen woman; Garbo, a woman of mystery; Irene Dunne, a charming, well-bred, always lovable lady. Kate represented a new category: the independent woman of money and breeding.

A meeting was held at David Selznick's beach house with David's battery of lawyers present, as well as his brother Myron, Leland Hayward, Laura and Kate. Kate wanted, and was promised, star billing, approval of parts and the right to return to the stage between films. The contract that was delivered to her the following week did not contain these points. Kate refused to sign until Selznick's verbal concessions were put in writing. While Leland Hayward entered into negotiations with Selznick, Laura and Kate headed back to New York, where Luddy met them. Nothing was as it had once been with Kate and Luddy. The great camaraderie they had shared had somehow diminished as the depth of Kate's friendship with Laura had grown. Kate was uneasy about herself and her marriage, and—since she had not yet seen the final cut of *A Bill of Divorcement*—fearful as well that she might have made a fool of herself on screen. Laura retreated to her family home in New Jersey when Kate and Luddy decided they should go to Europe before the film was previewed to see if they could make something viable of their marriage. They sailed on steerage tickets because, as Kate explained, "There's no reason why I should get sick on a first class ticket." But the discomfort of the voyage and Luddy's resentment of the irrelevancy of such travel arrangements in their circumstances placed more stress upon their already strained relationship.

Shortly after Kate and Luddy departed for Europe, *A Bill of Divorcement* premiered at the Mayfair Theatre in New York. The film was generally well received, but Kate's personal reviews were marvelous. Richard Watts of the *New York Herald Tribune* wrote that "Katharine Hepburn . . . seems definitely established for an important cinema career." Thornton Delehanty of the *New York Post* commented on her "dignity and an instinct for underplaying an emotion. . . . Miss Hepburn has the makings of a star. . . ." *The New Yorker* called her "half Botticelli page and half bobbed-hair bandit, [who] might well be the daughter of one of the old English families." A more florid press (the *Journal-*

American) claimed that she had "flamed like an opal, half-demon and half-madonna."

Kate possessed that intangible something the movies call star quality." Mae West, who entered films at the same time as Kate, had it. So did Garbo and Dietrich. A contemporary legend persisted that the role of the daughter in *A Bill of Divorcement* was actress proof, that any comparatively inexperienced young actress would seem miraculous in it and would be hailed as a possible star. Critics insisted the role genuinely touched audiences irrespective of the actress playing it. However, the three young women besides Kate who had portrayed the tragic daughter in *A Bill of Divorcement* also happened to have that incandescent quality that differentiated a star from an actor.*

The number of technically brilliant stage performers that Hollywood could have cast in lead roles was enormous. The stars of a film, however, had to possess an elusive power of personality and a physical magnetism that could stand up to the greatly enlarged close-up of a movie screen, where bone structure that gives off planes of light is often crucial. The fact that Garbo, Dietrich, and Mae West, as well as Katharine Hepburn, had high cheekbones, wide-apart eyes and broad jaw lines, could be a coincidence. But too many film stars, male and female, have had these similarities to discount the fascination this facial type has for movie audiences.

Kate had much more than an intriguing face. Her powerful, authentic personality never became restricted by the camera. She later claimed she loved the camera, its warmth, its familiarity. She responded to its naked glare, its slavish attention to every expression of her face and body, with the kind of immediacy a trusted lover could expect; and she seldom rejected a studio request for posed still-camera sessions despite the work and hours these entailed.

Kate and Luddy were in Vienna when she received a telegram from Leland Hayward urging her to return to New York. The new R.K.O. contract—with even better terms than either she or Hayward had anticipated—was ready for her

---

* The three actresses who had portrayed Sydney Fairfield and became stars thereafter were Katharine Cornell (Broadway), Edna Best (London stage) and Maureen O'Hara (films).

signature, and the studio had a film planned for her, entitled *Three Came Unarmed*, that he felt she would approve. The trip had been an exercise in futility where she and Luddy were concerned. With Kate's decision to return to New York prematurely, even the most tenuous bindings of the marriage were now severed.

She stood on the deck of the French liner that had brought her back to New York, dressed in pants and surrounded by a gaggle of reporters snapping photographs that showed her lean figure etched against the Statue of Liberty (looking no more regal or unbending than she). Luddy had "discreetly" disappeared, disembarking later, unrecognized and alone. But Kate had been registered on the ship as Mrs. Ludlow Smith (a rare acknowledgment of her legal name) and the press scented a story. She denied she was married, an unfortunate lie that she later made worse by answering a fan magazine writer's query, "Have you any children?" with, "Yes, two white and three colored."

Hollywood fan magazines then had a tremendous circulation and a strong hold on the film-going public. The star system was well established. A growth of intimacy between stars and their fans was necessary to make the latter loyal to their favorites' films. Garbo's silence was intriguing, but no other film star had been able to succeed using such tactics. True biographical information was seldom given. Studios employed armies of publicity people to create an aura of glamour about their players, and Hollywood reporters were looking for good copy not true stories. Kate's major miscalculation in her treatment of the press would later prove extremely costly.

She returned to Hollywood with Laura, where the two women rented an isolated, dismal house in the hills above Hollywood and near the Los Angeles Reservoir.* What strikes one here is the collegiate behavior of both women who, after all, were in their mid-twenties at the time. Under the guise of revolting against Hollywood's nouveau riche pretentions, they bribed the servants at the home of film

---

* Once Cukor took Greta Garbo to visit Kate in this house. "God, what a dreary place!" Cukor reported Garbo commented. "But then, I always loved dreary places."

producer Walter Wanger (whom they knew only slightly).* Before being found out they dressed in uniforms and served one course at a dinner party at which film stars Charles Boyer† and Madeleine Carroll** were present. Mrs. Wanger was *not* amused, but she recovered enough to ask Kate and Laura to join her guests. "No, no! Thanks all the same," Kate replied as she and Laura retreated to the kitchen, changed back into their own clothes, "and rushed out to fall on the grass and laugh hysterically."

On another occasion, they hid in the trunk of director William Wellman's imported limousine and "didn't emerge until he reached home, jumping out and making funny faces." They made several nocturnal invasions of Hollywood's most elaborate homes, usually entering in and out of windows while the owners were away, somehow avoiding guards, dogs, alarms and detectors, and leaving unsigned notes in obvious places so the occupants would know they had had uninvited guests. "I could look over a place and get in faster than any teenager in Juvenile Court," Kate admitted. "But, of course, being naturally timid, I could never do it alone. I had to have [Laura] going along with me. She'd say, 'We're going in here,' and I'd say, 'Oh, do you think we ought to?' and she'd say, 'Yes, you go up and drop through that skylight.' I would throw a rope down to her and lug her up. I don't have too much nerve on my own, but I have great ability when I am prodded."

---

* Walter Wanger (1894–1968) made his first film, *The Cocoanuts*, in 1929. In 1934, after producing Garbo's *Queen Christina*, he became one of Hollywood's most prestigious producers. Some of his finest films were *History Is Made at Night* (1937), *Stagecoach* (1939) and *The Long Journey Home* (1940). In the early 1950s, after shooting and injuring his second wife Joan Bennett's lover, Jennings Lang, he served time in prison. He returned to Hollywood but was never as successful again.
† Charles Boyer (1899–1978) had only recently arrived in Hollywood from France to star in *The Magnificent Lie* (1931). An immediate success, he went on to appear opposite the films' most glamorous stars. Hepburn co-starred with him four years later in *Break of Hearts* and again thirty-eight years later in *The Madwoman of Chaillot*. They were on friendly terms and Hepburn once rented his former home.
** Madeleine Carroll (1906–) made her London stage debut in 1927. In 1936, after playing the lead in two of director Alfred Hitchcock's films, *The 39 Steps* (1935) and *The Secret Agent* (1936), she came to Hollywood where she appeared as leading lady until 1942, when she left the United States.

None of these escapades did the press report, although stories of Kate's "eccentricity" were inevitable when she was seen walking with her new acquisition, a pet monkey, on her shoulder. Off the set Kate now wore pants almost exclusively. She claimed bad indigestion was responsible. "If my feet are as high as my seat, I digest my dinner, if they aren't, I don't," she told George Cukor when he complained about her mode of dress and her insistence at refusing all dinner invitations.

She did, however, attend Cukor's very private Sunday afternoon salons where Hollywood's more intellectual residents gathered. Cukor called her "the tigress" and warned friends to put on their boxing gloves to meet her. But her great charm was her uncompromising individuality and the fact that she could talk on anything from atomic energy to how to grow beans in your backyard. Cukor's Sunday guest list often included such luminaries as author Hugh Walpole, Tallulah Bankhead, opera singer Mary Garden, silent-screen star Tilly Loesch, and, on occasion, Greta Garbo. The day Garbo and Kate were both to be guests at Cukor's house, Kate arrived early and Garbo late. Cukor had a well-protected pool and Kate decided to go swimming in the nude. Just as she came out of the water, Cukor appeared with Garbo. Kate quickly grabbed a towel to wrap around herself and stammered a greeting to the impeccably groomed Swedish star. The experience truly distressed Kate. Garbo was one of the few performers Kate revered.

The phone calls home continued. Kate listened to her father's advice and welcomed his grudging approval of her new status as a high-salaried member of the Hepburn clan. In view of her mother's continuing accomplishments in the field of birth control, her own success seemed inconsequential. Dr. Hepburn had less respect for films than for theater and was of the mind that his daughter was grossly overpaid for what she was doing. His main concern was that Kate might spend her money in an irresponsible manner. Her salary, she agreed, would continue to be sent to him for care and cautious investment while she lived on the allowance he doled out to her weekly.

Kate was now part of a world where, as F. Scott Fitzgerald (who had just arrived in Hollywood) said, "Everybody watches for everybody else's blunders, or tries to make sure they're with people that'll do them credit." Kate was the exception. She no longer needed Hollywood as much as Hollywood needed her. Not until 1930, when sound-on-film systems replaced the awkward use of disc synchronization, were "talkies" exclusively made. The voices of a large percentage of Hollywood's silent-screen stars proved inadequate to the requirements of a microphone, and their careers ended. Desperate for performers who could speak distinctly, studios had turned to the theater for recruits.

As the hard years of the Depression threw women out into the work market, the need for education was obvious, and Kate's was one of the first college-educated women's voices to be heard on film.

CHAPTER
8

Kate's union with Luddy was never a marriage, but Luddy
had been her confidant, her one close good friend. Now she
had Laura.

"I think men and women are more shut off from each other
than a woman and a woman," Kate was to comment. "I think
women are more interested in the same things. Two women
can live together as friends. It's more difficult for a man and a
woman to be friends and not leap into bed. Of course, it
depends on the individual but I've always thought that men
and women are not too well suited to each other. It's
inevitable that they should come together, but, again, how
well suited are they to live together in the same house?"

She and Laura *were* well suited to cohabit. Laura had
enthusiasm, *zing*, plus an openness, an honesty. Kate found
complicated people "disturbing" and "tiring." Despite her
great wealth, Laura was quite a simple person whose one
main concern and interest was Kate and her career. Life in
their "dreary" Canyon house was unpressured, almost austere. Kate accepted few invitations. Immediately after a day
at the studio she would rush home, eat an early supper, study
her lines for the next day, wrap her feet in cold cloths and,
about nine, retire. Weekends she and Laura would embark
on their "sub-collegiate idiotic" adventures. Men, the dating

kind that is, had no part in Kate's life. She refused to attend premieres with a studio escort or be photographed with any man. Her private life, she maintained, was her own, and her "secret" marriage kept her from appearing in public with a man. Kate greatly respected the vows she had taken (although they were subject to her own interpretation). Cukor, who had become a good friend, was known to be a confirmed bachelor; and her visits to his house provoked no interest on the part of the press.

Kate's upbringing was in a good measure responsible for her antisocial leanings. Fury still rankled within her for the snubs she had suffered in West Hartford as a young girl, a fact she also held responsible for her success since it had given her the impetus to get up and do something. Her parents' beliefs had allowed her to be a nonconformist. Her self-indulgence was never condemned. But her desire to be accepted, though sublimated, remained.

Shortly after Kate's return to Hollywood, the proposed film, *Three Came Unarmed,* which was to have paired her with Joel McCrea, was abandoned because of script problems with the adaptation of the E. Arnot Robertson novel. David Selznick also rejected the idea that Kate, who represented the upper-class young woman to her new audiences, play the unglamorous role of a missionary's daughter in Borneo. On the other hand, Gilbert Frankau's novel *Christopher Strong* had just been purchased by R.K.O., and the role of the aristocratic daredevil aviatrix Lady Cynthia Darrington seemed tailor-made.

David Selznick thought he had a winning combination when he hired one of America's few women directors, Dorothy Arzner, to direct *Christopher Strong.* Arzner, still in her thirties at this time, had once waited on tables in her father's small Hollywood café and had worked her way up in films from a secretary in the story department of Famous Players to script clerk, film cutter and then to film editor. She had been responsible for the editing of the dramatic bullfight scenes in Rudolph Valentino's *Blood and Sand* and for the magnificent editing on the silent-screen classic *The Covered Wagon* before she became a script writer and finally, in 1927 at the age of twenty-seven, a director, one of the few who had successfully made the transition from silent films to sound-motion pictures. Arzner's films all had featured independent women. However, from their very first meeting, a competitive rivalry existed between Kate and Arzner.

Selznick, working a three-way hunch, hired a third woman, author and playwright Zoë Akins,* to script *Christopher Strong*. An unproduced Akins play, *Morning Glory,* had just been purchased by Selznick with an eye to casting Kate as the stage-struck lead. Selznick's hunch proved to be a real clanger. Kate and Arzner never made it on a first-name basis; but as *Miss Hepburn* and *Miss Arzner,* they developed a mutual respect (cold, distant and competitive though it was). Arzner remained proud of her roots and had few pretentions. On the other hand, Zoë Akins represented everything nouveau riche that Kate hated. Story conferences with the three women were held in Akins's palatial pink stucco home in society-oriented Pasadena. Because her husband was terminally ill, she refused to leave him to travel into the studio. Akins was naturally distracted; and Kate, who never believed in exposing one's personal tragedies to outsiders, was offended by the experience and not at all surprised when the author delivered a pedestrian script.

From its inception, *Christopher Strong* was fraught with problems. Kate took seriously ill with influenza during the production and had to be hospitalized for several days. Dr. Hepburn was set to fly her home to West Hartford, but Kate refused to allow it. Another impasse occurred when Arzner warned David Selznick that she would quit unless Miss Hepburn stopped interfering with her direction. Perhaps Kate wished that would occur and George Cukor be brought in to replace her. But Selznick held fast and all three of the women stayed to the end of the film.

Christopher Strong was, not surprisingly, a disappointment, though it was handsomely produced. The sets were in perfect taste; and the costumes—including one tight-fitting glittering gold lamé moth costume designed by Walter Plunkett and worn by Kate in the costume-ball opening—were

---

* Zoë Akins (1886–1958). In addition to the play that was the basis for Hepburn's next film, *Morning Glory,* Akins's plays—*Her Private Life, The Old Maid* and *How to Marry a Millionaire*—were all adapted for the screen.

striking. The cast, which once again included Billie Burke, was impeccable. Kate, looking the fresh, well-to-do young woman, seemed sprinkled with the same obvious star dust—but Zoë Akins's dull, desultory script and Dorothy Arzner's heavy-handed directing could not be overcome.

Film reviews were still being printed under a heading of "The New Talkies" when Kate's second talkie opened on March 10, 1933, at Radio City Music Hall during the same week in which *Forty-second Street* premiered nearby. Jack S. Cohen, Jr., of the *New York Sun* said of Kate, "She resembles somewhat an aristocratic American Garbo save that she hasn't got Garbo's warmth . . . whoever spotted her for the screen after her brief appearance on the stage in 'The Warrior's Husband' knew the camera's power. Her personality is far more interesting and alluring on the screen than it ever was on the stage."

In *Christopher Strong*, Kate (as the adventurous titled aviatrix, in love with a married man, who—while breaking the world's record for altitude—crashes her plane rather than tell her lover she is pregnant) stalked around in aviatrix garb in a labored imitation of the lanky air hero Charles Lindbergh. *Christopher Strong* did contain one postcoital bedroom sequence that was highly effective. But a steamy portrayal of sexual passion is not what Kate's audience wanted from her film performances; her first film had given them "a woman of breeding and intelligence, spirit and strength, who had more on her mind than bed, babies, and the beauty parlor." From the time of *Christopher Strong*, Kate was to approach sex in future films "with a certain fastidious reluctance, nostrils flaring."

Leland Hayward included her in his list of the world's ten most beautiful women—"right up there with Garbo and Dietrich—definitely the best. God yes." Hayward had fallen in love with Kate. He saw in her what the world now saw—"A certain look in her eyes, a style—an awareness of her effect on people—the way she holds herself, moves, a sense of her own mystery." Leland Hayward was a man who loved and respected intelligent women. He had married, divorced and remarried Lola Gibbs, a startling Texas beauty and debutante who was also an aviatrix and had taught

Hayward how to fly. His knowledge of and passion for planes brought him and Kate closer together during the filming of *Christopher Strong*. Kate now reversed her original feelings about Hayward, or perhaps (and more likely) her first "loathing" of the man was a cover-up for a sexual attraction to him that had unnerved her. Kate never liked the dizzying feelings brought on by liquor either. She had to feel "in control."

Lola and Leland Hayward had been remarried for two years (they had first been married eleven years earlier) when Leland fell deeply in love with Kate. Leland still looked like a character from a Fitzgerald novel: handsome, charming, hair parted debonairly in the middle, "an air both haggard and elegant." He made his way through the executive offices of the major Hollywood studios dressed in white flannels and yachting sneakers. The majority of Hollywood agents either had strong ethnic backgrounds—Russian-Jewish, Italian—or had served an apprenticeship handling vaudeville or burlesque acts. Leland Hayward was a breed apart, the scion of a well-to-do Nebraska family who had spent his youth in eastern prep schools and attended Princeton. Almost courtly with women, he was nonetheless a buccaneer, asking outrageous salaries for his clients, always daring the impossible. Within a matter of a few years he had become an enormous success. "The wives of the moguls were crazy about him," George Cukor later reminded Hayward's daughter Brooke. "Mrs. Goldwyn was just crazy about him. So was Mrs. Warner. *All* the wives were crazy about him and kept talking about him, because he was a very attractive, handsome, dashing man. He should have been a captain in the Austro-Hungarian Army—something like that. He was certainly miscast as an agent. If I were to make a picture about an agent, a very successful agent, and my casting director brought in Leland Hayward, I would say, 'You're out of your mind! This is not the way an agent looks.' That was part of his success. Just charmed the birds off the trees, the money out of the coffers, and ladies into their beds."

Still, Leland Hayward was married and so was Kate, and they could not be seen in public together. He invaded Kate's Cold Water Canyon house, lounging on the couch, his long legs hanging over the end, and constantly talking on the telephone while Kate cooked away in the kitchen, apparently loving both attending to him and the enforced privacy their relationship demanded. She held him in great esteem; he was bright, successful, strong, and—most important—quick and decisive. Like her father, he encouraged her idiosyncrasies and her independent mind. His plans for her stardom became her ambition. He negotiated a new contract for her with R.K.O. with an unprecedented percentage of the gross, approval of co-stars and director, and a guarantee that she would have time between films (a minimum of two a year) to appear on the stage.

Shortly thereafter, while waiting for a meeting with Pandro Berman* in his office, she picked up a script off his desk and began to read it. "I thought, 'Oh—my—God—that's the most wonderful part ever written for anyone,'" she remembered of her first glance of *Morning Glory*. She slipped it in her bag and took it home, finished it, and returned to announce to Berman, "This is what I'd like to do."

"It's not for you."

"Who's it for?"

"Connie Bennett."†

"Has she read it?"

"No."

"Me, me, me!"

Akins had modeled the role of Eva Lovelace on Tallulah Bankhead.** Kate disliked Bankhead (whom she referred to as "your friend, Miss Bankhead" to Cukor), finding her rude and foul-mouthed. The character in the first version of *Morning Glory* was neither of these things, but she did have a

---

* Pandro S. Berman (1905–   ) produced at R.K.O. from 1931 to 1940, where he was responsible not only for several of Katharine Hepburn's films, but for many of the Ginger Rogers–Fred Astaire musicals. In 1940, he went to M.G.M., where he and Hepburn were once again to team together on three more films, *Dragon Seed* (1944), *Undercurrent* (1946) and *The Sea of Grass* (1947).

† Constance Bennett (1904–1965), sister of Joan Bennett. Sophisticated comedy was her specialty, but she often played teary-eyed heroines. Except for *Topper*, none of her films was especially memorable. In the 1950s she returned to the stage, appearing mostly in road-show revivals.

** Bankhead was to say that Kate was "one of the most stimulating women I know. She's unfeminine in that she scorns gossip, back biting, and log rolling. . . . She spits out her opinions no matter how unpopular they may be. . . . She's a gal I'd like to have on my side."

strong sense of sarcasm. Kate wanted changes and they were supposedly made by scenarist Howard J. Green (although it is likely that Akins, without Kate's knowledge, had some hand in it). The script, even when rewritten, had great limitations. But the role of Eva Lovelace was ideally suited to Kate's talents.*

Using the unusual technique of rehearsing and filming in continuity, Lowell Sherman,† the director of *Morning Glory*, shot the film in an unprecedented eighteen days, during which time Laura (who did not approve of the Hayward-Hepburn relationship) was in New Jersey and Kate spent almost every evening surreptitiously with Leland. Douglas Fairbanks, Jr. (along with Adolphe Menjou), was cast in the film with her. Fairbanks tried unsuccessfully for days to get Kate to go out with him. Finally, she accepted. Halfway through dinner, she complained of a headache. Fairbanks drove her home but didn't drive off, watching as she entered the house. "Suddenly," he recalls, "the front door flew open and Kate came running out. Another car I hadn't noticed was hidden further up the driveway under some trees. She hopped in, and I saw a man at the wheel [Leland Hayward]. They drove right past me without noticing me. She was laughing happily, her hair blowing over her face."

Within a week of the opening of *Morning Glory*, Kate knew that her performance had been a grand success. More than 130,000 people had paid to see her in the first week of the film's run at Radio City Music Hall, an attendance closely approximating that of its then greatest box-office triumph, *Cavalcade*. It had to be Kate the public came to see because *Morning Glory* was a slim film with a familiar plot that contained no surprises. But Kate, as a bookish, art-for-art's-sake girl from a small town in New England who goes to New York to conquer the stage and does, was not only fresh and

---

* Hepburn was later to say (upon seeing *Morning Glory* forty years later), "I should have stopped then. I haven't grown since."
† Lowell Sherman (1885–1934) also directed Mae West in *She Done Him Wrong*. Film critic Andrew Sarris wrote of Sherman (who also had a brief early career as an actor), "Sherman was gifted with the ability to express the poignancy of male lechery when confronted with female longing. His civilized sensibility was ahead of its time, and the sophistication of his sexual humor singularly lacking in malice."

earnest in the role, her performance was riveting. All of Selznick's previous efforts to implant her on the public's mind as a sort of American exotic, an American Garbo (a paradoxical figure of the imagination to say the least), had been dispelled by her appearance in *Morning Glory*.*

"Miss Hepburn shines," wrote one critic, "as a stage-struck girl named Eva Lovelace, whose curious nature is a mixture of ingenuousness and cleverness, and persistence and pride. There are even moments when she does not appear quite rational, particularly when she declares that possibly when she reaches her zenith she will end her life. But let it be said here that she attains success and does not intend to be a morning glory, a flower that fades before the sun is very high."

The role of Eva Lovelace came as close as Kate would come to self-parody. After two films, she settled into her lifelong love affair with the camera. "I can remember thinking," she later recalled, "Oh, this is great! Oh, the camera! That's a friend. This is all very easy. Warm! Cozy!" and admits being "madly anxious to succeed."

Along with Kate's newfound celebrity and her sudden multitude of fans came the Hepburn detractors who would complain from film to film that she reduced them in no time at all to a state of galloping twitches. *Morning Glory* and Eva Lovelace did, indeed, cast the first mold for the Hepburn cinema mannerisms that were so distinctive they led almost instantly to burlesque impersonations of her by radio amateurs and nightclub professionals. Frank S. Nugent of *The New York Times* was one critic to whom Kate gave "the jitters," and he listed in the *Times* the many reasons for this: "The way she walks—those little scurrying steps, with her body inclined forward like a student roller-skater who hopes desperately to reach a catch-hold before falling on his face. The way she talks—the breathless, broad A'd style, with meaningless breaks and catches, the so-soulfully brave, husky tones with the pipe of hysteria beneath them. The way she plucks at this and that, and drapes her throat with tulle, and flutters and is so fearfully feminine that almost any normal

---

* *Morning Glory* was remade unsuccessfully in 1958 as *Stage Struck* starring Susan Strasberg and Henry Fonda in the lead roles.

woman would seem a Tarzan in comparison." Yet even her dissenters would have to admit that Katharine Hepburn was an "original"—as much so as Garbo and Dietrich and no less mannered than either of these ladies.

Kate was ecstatic when Selznick told her George Cukor would direct her next film, *Little Women,* adapted from the classic by Louisa May Alcott. Since *A Bill of Divorcement,* Cukor had directed the highly acclaimed *What Price Hollywood* and *Dinner at Eight,* and Kate was convinced he was a genuine artist. Like her father, he treated her with a certain indulgent affection while at the same time not allowing her to get away with anything.

Little Women had always been a personal favorite of Kate's; but Cukor, who had thought of the book as "a story that little girls read" was startled when he read it for the first time. Louisa May Alcott had written "a very strong-minded story, full of character, and a wonderful picture of New England family life." At the time he would not have known how close the theme and substance of *Little Women* were to Kate's own life, which was filled with the same "admirable New England sternness." Kate and Cukor pitched into the preproduction work on the film with a fervor and togetherness that would bind them irretrievably from that time as creative artists and friends.

The concentration required on her new film and her delight in working on a project she so endorsed kept Kate from having to dwell on the confusion in her personal life. The schoolgirl pranks suddenly ended. Laura returned from the East more subdued. Kate had to deal with her feelings for Leland, the responsibility of perhaps causing him to divorce his wife to marry her, and the issue of her own probable divorce from Luddy.

George Cukor has said that Kate was born to play the part of Jo March in *Little Women.* Tender and funny, fiercely loyal, inclined to play the fool when she felt like it, Kate also had a purity about her, a Yankee conservatism—all the qualities that were the essence of Jo March as well. Kate was to say the role was the most autobiographical she ever undertook. She had never known her maternal grandmother, but from the stories her mother had told her she felt a close kinship. Jo March would have been Grandmother Houghton's contemporary, and Kate played her with this in mind. She even had wardrobe designer Walter Plunkett copy one costume exactly from a tintype she had of Mrs. Houghton.

Cukor claims Kate cast "a spell of magic [over the film], a kind of power that dominated even those scenes she's not in." *Little Women* appeared deceptively simple; "no obvious effects, no big scenes." The film's adaptors, Victor Heerman and his wife, Sarah Y. Mason, had constructed a loose, episodic script very true to the novel, no plottiness, no false or contrived tying-up-of-ends. Hobe Irwin's sets were designed without chichi. The Louisa May Alcott house was reproduced with great taste and detail. Walter Plunkett's costumes retained a sense of New England frugality, and the four March sisters wore clothes that they borrowed from each other from time to time—very real.

Problems occurred. Joan Bennett, who played young Amy March, had not informed the studio she was pregnant, hoping she would complete the film before her condition was noticed.* But midway through the production it became evident. Walter Plunkett did a masterful job of camouflage by reworking Bennett's costumes, and Cukor reblocked the scenes that included the character Amy so that she was shot from the waist up.

"Once," Cukor admitted, "I actually hit Kate. (Not hard enough, probably.) She had to run up a flight of steps carrying some ice cream, and I told her to be very careful because we didn't have a spare of the dress she was wearing, so she *mustn't* spill that ice cream. But she did and ruined the dress, and then she laughed—and I hit her and called her an amateur.

"You can think what you want," she snapped back.

Cukor later admitted he had been wrong, she was immensely professional. They had their tiffs; but after each

---

* Joan Bennett (1910–   ) was married to her second husband, writer-producer Gene Markey, at the time. She divorced him in 1937 and married Walter Wanger in 1940. Her best films, *Man Hunt, The Woman in the Window, Scarlet Street* and *The Secret Beyond the Door,* were all directed by Fritz Lang and produced by Wanger in the 1940s. She never made another film with Hepburn, but both of them were strong contenders for the role of Scarlett O'Hara.

apologized their relationship seemed all the stronger for it, and Cukor and the crew all respected Kate greatly. In the scene in which she wore the copy of her grandmother's dress, she twirled around in a conceited manner and spoke extravagantly of becoming a great author or opera singer. On that line, to everyone's delight, including Kate's, from a crane overhead the crew lowered a large ham at the end of a rope, which they dangled before her.

There had been a lot of Kate in *A Bill of Divorcement*, the impatient and antiestablishment young woman, and in *Little Women*, the independent idealist. George Cukor recognized the depth of her own self that Kate gave to each role, and he admired her intensely for never flinching from that reality. Also, during the shooting of *Little Women*, a strike of sound men was called. Cukor was forced to hire a makeshift, inexperienced crew.

"Kate [who had not felt well] had to do take after take of a very emotional scene simply because the sound men kept messing it up," Cukor later recalled. "After the fifteenth take, or whatever, they got it—and Kate was so exhausted and agonized by all that weeping she threw up. But not *until* we'd got the take."

Even in rough cut, *Little Women* was an exquisite screen drama skillfully made, and Kate's Jo March was a memorable performance. Billboards were soon to banner: "Again she weaves her Magic Spell! Katharine Hepburn in *Little Women*." And full-page newspaper advertisements were to proclaim under romantic head shots of her: "The radiant Star of *Morning Glory* marches still deeper into your heart as the best loved heroine ever born in a book. . . . See her . . . *living* . . . the immortal Jo."

Little Women was the last film David Selznick was to supervise at R.K.O.,* but the studio's executives immediately lined up numerous projects for Kate, among them Edith Wharton's *Age of Innocence*, a film based on the life of Sarah Bernhardt; a biography of Nell Gwyn, *The Tudor Wench*, that took Queen Elizabeth I from age fifteen to old age; an

---

* David O. Selznick had actually left R.K.O. for M.G.M. prior to the making of *Little Women* but had returned to do it as the one film left in his contractual agreement with R.K.O.

original screenplay, *Without Sin,* by Melville Baker and Jack Kirkland; and a script based on the play *Trigger* by Lula Vollmer, about a young, uneducated tomboy faith healer in the Ozark Mountains.

None of these film ideas inspired enthusiasm in Kate. Leland Hayward was no longer persistent in his wooing. A friendship that Kate had struck up with Elissa Landi* had greatly irritated Laura upon her return to Hollywood. Kate's life had hit a bit of a snag. Hollywood had not taken her to its glittering breast, nor did she care to belong there. New York and Old Saybrook remained home to her and the stage the only exalted career.

Besides that brief meeting with Jed Harris in Ossining, New York, Kate had once auditioned unsuccessfully for him.† The rejection had hurt more than most and she had never been able to forget him. Lean, dark and hungry-looking despite his meteoric success as Broadway's most newsworthy producer, Harris had "a genius for making enemies" and a reputation for wooing, winning and victimizing the women who came into his orbit. His intelligence was neither predictable nor commonplace. His wit was acid, his behavior truculent. Convinced that he was the greatest man on Broadway, he had little trouble convincing others as well. Jed Harris was and remained the wizard of the Broadway theater.

Wizards by nature possess a power over people. Harris proved no exception. A contemporary wrote that "he had the grin of a sorcerer. . . . He purred when he spoke. His skinny jaw jutted. His eyes were dark and slightly up-turned as if listening to some inner music." Women found his style, "his athletic use of language, the fresh routes of his nimble mind"

---

* Elissa Landi (1904–1948) claimed to be the stepdaughter of an Italian nobleman and a descendant of Emperor Franz Josef of Austria. She starred in Cecil De Mille's *The Sign of the Cross* in 1932. *The Warrior's Husband* proved a mistake for she was miscast in the role of Antiope, which R.K.O. had refused to buy for Hepburn.

† Jed Harris (1900–1979). Born Jacob Horowitz, he never legalized his professional name. He attended Yale University and became one of Broadway's most successful producers at the age of twenty-five. By 1934, he had already produced *Broadway* (1926), *The Royal Family* (1928), *Front Page* (1928), *Wonder Boy* (1932) and *The Green Bay Tree* (1933). Subsequently, his best-known works were *Our Town* (1938), *The Heiress* (1945) and *The Crucible* (1953).

seductive, and the sense of menace he exuded contributed to his sexual appeal. Jed Harris had seldom had a problem winning any woman he wanted.

To Kate's surprise, upon her return to Hartford, Harris called and offered her the lead in a play, *The Lake*, by Dorothy Massingham and Murray MacDonald, that he planned to produce. Kate suggested he send her the script. During the course of the conversation, she managed to convey to him the information that her parents were away and she had time alone on her hands.

Harris took this as an outright invitation and, with playwright Edward Chodorov,* set off for West Hartford in a borrowed convertible. Wise enough to realize that *The Lake* (a brooding spook of a play) could not succeed without a star of Kate's caliber, Harris wasted no time in pursuing her, convinced that under his direction she could pull off the difficult soap-opera role. He recalled the teary look she so often affected on the screen, the vulnerable tilt of the proud chin.

As soon as he and Chodorov checked into a hotel in Hartford, Harris rang Kate at home. At her suggestion, he left the playwright and drove directly to Bloomfield Avenue. Harris had the instincts of a true gambler but he liked to hedge his bets. Though in a financial slump, he was financing *The Lake* himself and had sold his last solid asset, his beloved 150-foot sloop, *Señorita*, to do so. Kate's present box-office popularity would help secure his investment.

With her marriage at an impasse, her relationship with Leland Hayward threatened, and her friendship with Laura in troubled waters, Kate was especially susceptible to Harris's charm. His energy and intelligence stimulated her own. An undeniable spark passed between them. To Harris, Kate was the forbidden gentile girl: rich, beautiful, a part of a society that excluded Jews. He obviously made overtures to her as a woman, for later that night he grumbled to Chodorov that "her parents had *most* unexpectedly returned." To Kate,

---

* Edward Chodorov (1904–   ). Jed Harris had directed and produced Chodorov's first Broadway play, *Wonder Boy* (1932). His best-known play was *Oh Men! Oh Women!* (1953). He also wrote and directed for films. *Craig's Wife*, *Yellow Jack* and *The Hucksters* are among his credits.

Harris's bullying attitude had the touch of authority she needed at the time.

During her stay in West Hartford, Kate and Harris saw a good deal of each other and Harris was invited to the Hepburn home. He qualified as the kind of guest Mrs. Hepburn adored, for Jed Harris could always be counted on to spark an intriguing and off-beat conversation. Chodorov, his closest friend at this time, could not understand Kate's great attraction to the acerbic and often ill-kempt Broadway producer who thought nothing of appearing at the Hepburn house unshaven. That Kate was "smitten" with Harris, he had no doubts. Before she returned to Hollywood to film *Trigger* (almost immediately retitled *Spitfire*), Kate signed to do *The Lake*. Her enthusiasm was enormous.

The film was shot mainly in the San Jacinto Mountains in California near the Mexican border, under the direction of John Cromwell.* This backwoods melodrama was completely different from any of Kate's previous movies and was a curious choice to follow *Little Women*. The drama centered entirely on Kate's characterization of a mountain girl with a religious fervor who is feared, cursed, stoned and almost lynched by her neighbors, as well as deceived by the one man she turns to for love. Kate managed to inject Trigger, the spitfire, ". . . with a free and dynamic spirit." But her natural elegance could not be buried, and perhaps, as *The New Yorker* was to comment, "her artistry does not extend to the interpretation of the primitive or the uncouth."

Spitfire ran into delays caused by the location work required. Originally the film was due to be completed by five P.M. on November 15, when Kate was to take a night plane to begin rehearsals on *The Lake* the following day. By six-fifteen P.M, two scenes remained to be shot. Kate rescheduled her flight for the next night but agreed to work only five hours and forty-five minutes (the studio's definition of the time she

---

* John Cromwell (1888–1979) came into his own on his next film, *Of Human Bondage*. Among other films, he also directed *Little Lord Fauntleroy, The Prisoner of Zenda, Algiers, Abe Lincoln in Illinois, Since You Went Away, The Enchanted Cottage, Anna and the King of Siam* and *The Goddess*.

owed them). When the last of the two scenes had not been shot by the afternoon of the sixteenth, Kate confronted producer Pandro Berman. "You make other people live up to conditions you write into contracts. It's time you learned to do so too," she said.

"How much do you want to finish the scene?" Berman asked.

"Ten thousand dollars," she replied, later explaining, "I wanted to show them [R.K.O.] that if I set a definite date, I meant to keep it, but they didn't. Time means a lot to me."

Berman had no choice but to pay Kate the exorbitant overtime (her pay for the film—four weeks shooting—had been fifty thousand dollars).

Wand thin (105 pounds), her fine-spun hair still bobbed for the role she had just completed, Kate boarded a plane for the East on the night of November 16, 1933. At Cleveland she transferred to a train when she found out hordes of fans were waiting for her at Newark Airport. She had made three demanding films in less than a year and had been under unusual stress. Much of her natural gaiety was subdued. Her high cheekbones loomed higher, her blue eyes were more intense than they had been when she first arrived in Hollywood. The idea of seeing Jed Harris again was a stimulating thought, especially with Leland Hayward so involved with the new young star Margaret Sullavan, who seemed determined to out-Hepburn Kate.

BOW-GAYNOR-DIETRICH-GARBO-HEPBURN-NOW IT'S MARGARET SULLAVAN bannered a movie-page headline in the *Los Angeles Times* only a few days after Kate had left Hollywood to join the company of *The Lake*.

Margaret Sullavan* had been signed to films by Leland Hayward six months earlier. Sullavan had an image of herself as a femme fatale. Originally from Virginia and the perennial

---

* Margaret Sullavan's (1909–1960) temperament and disdain of Hollywood kept returning her to Broadway. She won the Drama Critics' Award for *Voice of the Turtle* in 1943. She will probably be best remembered in films for *Three Comrades* (1938) and *The Shop Around the Corner* (1940).

Southern belle, she was outrageously flirtatious and seemingly irresistible to men. Petite, lithe, fun-loving, with a "kind of
off-beat and naughty" sense of humor, Margaret Sullavan
also possessed Kate's rebellious individuality. Kate's pride
was hurt by Leland Hayward's affection for his twenty-four-
year-old protégée. Hayward had fought hard to keep Kate
from signing Jed Harris's contract. But Kate's perversity was
a reflex action, as was her penchant for running away from
difficult personal situations. That Jed Harris was to direct as
well as to produce *The Lake* was an added arrow she could
sling at Hayward. Kate had no idea at the time that Sullavan
had also had an affair with Jed Harris and that it had ended
her marriage to the yet-to-be-discovered Henry Fonda.* In
fact, the Harris-Sullavan affair was not yet over, Leland
Hayward notwithstanding. The two women were competitors
on more than one level. Displaying a Hepburnian quirk-
iness, she wore blue jeans (definitely not "in" at the time)
and rode a motorcycle back and forth to the studio. She
refused to make personal appearances, would not show
up on opening nights, and "when in New York [spent] most
of her evenings barging up and down on a Third Avenue
streetcar, dressed in something which [looked] as if it had
been discarded by the Salvation Army." Leland Hayward
thought she was a brilliant actress. So did Jed Harris,
who had originally acquired the American production rights
of *The Lake* for her just before she had left for Hollywood. The lead role in *The Lake* had to be played by what
Jed Harris called "a classy broad." Margaret Sullavan fell
into that category, as did Katharine Hepburn. In fact,
Harris referred to Sullavan as a Southern Katharine
Hepburn.

---

* In *Fonda, My Life*, Henry Fonda (1905–1983) recalled: "I'd wait until night,
and then I'd go . . . down from the sidewalk and into the garden. I'd lean against
the fence and I'd stare up at our apartment with the lighted windows on the
second floor. I knew Jed Harris was inside with her and I'd wait for him to leave.
But instead the lights would go out. . . . I couldn't believe my wife and that
son-of-a-bitch were in bed together. But I knew they were. And that just
destroyed me, completely destroyed me. Never in my life have I felt so betrayed,
so rejected, so alone." Fonda's last performance was to be opposite Hepburn in
the film *On Golden Pond*, for which he won the Academy Award for Best Actor
(1982).

A REMARKABLE WOMAN

Kate arrived in New York with only three weeks for rehearsal, believing she was Harris's first and only choice for *The Lake* and that he would dedicate himself to her success in the play because of his respect for her as a stage actress. Nothing could have been farther from the truth.

CHAPTER
9

With Kate on the West Coast, Harris's interest in her had paled. Margaret Sullavan had joined her family in Virginia while Leland Hayward ironed out some contractual problems for her in California. Harris spent so much time in the succeeding weeks in Virginia that New York newspaper columnists printed the rumor that he was negotiating "a play with some Southern playwright and one of the Broadway games is to guess which." Harris now not only resented the fact that Kate, not Sullavan, was playing the role of Stella Surrege in *The Lake*, he thought he had made a grievous error in casting her.

Despite its melodramatic content (a blighted young society woman whose husband drowns in a lake the first day of their marriage suffers tremendous guilt because she loved a married man instead of him), *The Lake* had been a tremendous success in London, where it had been directed "in high-toned English drawing room" style by Tyrone Guthrie with an unusually large cast of twenty-seven.* Noël Coward had

---

* *The Lake* opened at The Arts Theatre Club in London on March 1, 1933, and transferred on March 15, 1933, to the Westminister. (Sir) Tyrone Guthrie (1900–1971) had previously made his name with productions of James Bridie's *The Anatomist* and J. B. Priestley's *Dangerous Corner*. In London, Marie Ney (1895–1981), well known for her classical work at the Old Vic, played Stella Surrege and (Dame) May Whitty (1865–1948) her mother.

warned Harris that the play would not travel well. American audiences liked their heroines to be rebels and did not subscribe to stories of young women dominated by their mothers and living their lives by the laws set down by high society. Stella Surrege was anything but the rebel. To succeed, the actress playing the role had to exude great pathos and a brooding sense of implacable tragedy.

Harris's first instincts had been right. Onstage, Margaret Sullavan's piquant personality inspired great sympathy. Kate's appeal was her strength. The teary eye and flashing vulnerability moved her audiences only because they knew the character she portrayed would fight valiantly to overcome such moments of weakness.

Kate reported for rehearsals directly upon her arrival in New York. Within forty-eight hours, she and Jed Harris had reached an impasse.

Jed Harris claimed that Kate came to that first day of rehearsal without the slightest doubt that she could play the role. "I could see she was hopeless. I fought with her—I begged her to stop posing, striking attitudes, leaning against doorways, putting a limp hand to her forehead, to stop being a big movie star and *feel* the lines, *feel* the character. I was trying the impossible, to make an artificial showcase of an artificial star, and she couldn't handle it. Tremendous artificiality! It's as though she had seen her own performance and liked her own rather charming babbling at everything, and she had decided that was acting."

Other members of the company, which included distinguished theater performers of the caliber and long experience of Colin Clive (who had played with her in *Christopher Strong*), Blanche Bates and Frances Starr, disagreed with Harris's first impression of Kate.* They found her unsure and they all agreed that Harris drove her unmercifully. One witness confessed, "If she turned her head to the left, he didn't like it. If she turned it to the right, he liked it still less."

Kate's confusion was as noticeable as her infatuation with

---

* Colin Clive (1898–1937) is best remembered for his title role in *Frankenstein* (1931), in which he played Dr. Frankenstein and Boris Karloff the monster, and as Rochester in the 1934 film production of *Jane Eyre*. He had previously been a leading man on the British stage. Blanche Bates (1873–1941). Frances Starr (1881–1973).

Harris. Within a week he had undermined Kate's belief in herself so thoroughly that she was reduced to weeping in his presence. During one of these emotional confrontations Harris said that to his shock Kate threw her arms around his neck and clinging to him cried, "I could have loved you so.'

"I never thought of loving her or being loved by her. I was intensely embarrassed. . . . She clearly felt she could have been in love with me." Kate had never met a man she wanted whom she had not been able to win over. Harris's rejection was not only brutal, but he also walked away as director, turning this duty over to his stage manager, Worthington (Tony) Miner.* Miner had to beg her to go with the company to Washington, D.C., for the final week of rehearsals. He recalled, ". . . she was totally demoralized. She cried helplessly. . . ."

The situation grew worse. Harris disapproved of Kate's original costumes, which left her only a week to substitute others. Kate borrowed some clothes she thought appropriate from Laura, who had been coming to the theater to watch the rehearsals. Harris insisted she be barred, and Kate left for Washington alone but with faith in Tony Miner's untried talents. To Kate's distress and the dismay of the cast, Harris fired Tony Miner when they arrived in Washington. Geoffrey Kerr, who had been the star of Kate's debacle with the Berkshire Players, replaced him.

Jed Harris had a reputation for brutalizing the actresses who worked for him. But, his treatment of Kate was inordinately cruel, even for him, and foolhardy considering the high stakes that rode on her success or failure. He had put all his money into *The Lake*. No more assets existed, yet almost immediately he had seen the handwriting on the wall. *The Lake* was a second-rate play and Kate Hepburn would never be able to make it anything else. He wanted to abandon the project during rehearsal but contractual commitments prevented him. He desperately needed money to finance a vehicle for Margaret Sullavan, something intriguing enough to lure her back from Hollywood and the arms of Leland Hayward, "an agent, My God!" By all appearances Harris

---

* Worthington (Tony) Miner (1900–1982) was to work with Hepburn some years later on the Theatre Guild production of *Jane Eyre* (1937).

believed that if he pushed Kate far enough she would be forced to buy out her contract.

The Lake opened in Washington, D.C., on December 17, 1933, at the National Theatre. A crowd filled every seat and stood rows deep in the rear. Washington had made this evening a glittering social event. Preceding the play, dozens of dinner parties were given throughout the capital city by prominent hostesses. The audience (including alumnae of Bryn Mawr who turned out in force) were dazzling in their jewels and dress. Kate received an ovation when she stepped out on the stage looking very much the college debutante in Laura's tan jodhpurs. Her confidence returned and remained with her through the entire performance, even when an audible gasp was heard from the audience on her entrance in the second act costumed in a bizarre bridal outfit of brightest red beneath a full black velvet cloak. At final curtain Kate, now dressed in a long, trailing spectral gown of gray crepe, spoke her last lines: "There are ghosts who are friendly ghosts. I shall be back." Fervent applause rang out.

The reviews were kinder than Kate had expected, for she sensed that her voice had not been in control. The critic for *The Washington Post* did comment on her "staccato" speech pattern and her timing, but he also noted that "there was never an instant when she failed to command attention, hold the audience's undivided interest and win its unstinted acclaim." But the performances Kate gave for the remainder of the week in Washington were not on a par with her first. Jed Harris, his cash supply badly depleted, went to Kate and begged her to agree to tour the show for a month or so before coming into New York. When begging didn't help, he turned to bullying. She was not ready was his simple verdict. With time, "yes," but if she went into New York the following week as planned, she would be butchered by the critics. Of course, he also knew that out-of-town audiences would fill houses to see a movie star of Kate's magnitude, but such exposure before New York would also have given Kate time to work on her performance and her voice. Kate stubbornly refused. Harris then rang her later on the telephone to tell her that his decision was final: He would take the play on the road to Boston or Chicago, or he would close it in Washington. Kate's version of this conversation is that after she spoke calmly to him about the detrimental effect on her career, he had replied, "My dear, the only interest I have in you is the money I can make out of you."

Stunned, Kate stammered, "How much?" meaning what would it take for him to open in New York.*

"How much have you got?" he asked.

"Wait a minute." She put down the telephone and opened her checkbook. "I've got exactly fifteen thousand, four hundred and sixty-one dollars and sixty-seven cents."

"O.K.," Harris replied, "I'll take that."

Kate wrote out a check for the full amount and the next day the company left for New York.

Opening night, December 26, the entire Hepburn family, as well as Laura Harding, Frances Robinson-Duff and Leland Hayward, were out front for support. A light snow had fallen. People arrived a little late and Kate sat nervously in her dressing room being told every few moments which celebrity had arrived—Noël Coward, George S. Kaufman, Amelia Earhart, Dorothy Parker, Kay Francis, Judith Anderson were all present. Leland Hayward came backstage to wish her well, a painfully awkward moment for Kate, still hurt by his affair with Margaret Sullavan and knowing as well that he had heard about her failed romance with Jed Harris.

A replay of what had happened to Kate years before in Baltimore occurred during the New York opening of *The Lake*. She started at such a fast pace that her timing was thrown off and her voice grew steadily more frenzied in decibel and pitch. The next day a New York critic was to write pungently, "Miss Hepburn began the first act in hysteria." At intermission, her maid put a Bible in her hands to help her get herself into a properly solemn mood for the second act. She carried it onstage at curtain's rise, but the high emotion demanded by the drama of the second-act climax never was achieved.

Noël Coward came backstage. "Don't let it get your goat,"

---

* This story has been quoted as occurring *after* the close of *The Lake* in New York. But Edward Chodorov, who was with Harris at the time, claims it occurred in Washington, and that Katharine Hepburn's contract did not evoke a clause that would hold her to touring with the show *after* it completed its New York run, but it did state that she would be available for a longer out-of-town run *before* the New York opening if required.

he told her. "It happens to everyone." But Kate could not be so easily placated. The next day Dorothy Parker's* famous barbed quote appeared in the press: "She ran the gamut of emotion from A to B." Parker was not a theater critic, and the cruel remark was not an excerpt from a review that might have also said some flattering things to offset it. Yet this quote (because of Dorothy Parker's celebrity and its obvious humor) was printed in almost every major newspaper in the United States and England. The effect on both Kate's stage career and the fate of *The Lake* was devastating.

Kate returned to the studio of Frances Robinson-Duff, and her performance did improve. No critics returned, however, to see the improvement. Advance sales kept the show going —but *just*. Kate, with a run-of-the-play contract, assumed that a closing notice would be posted momentarily and managed to cope on a day-to-day basis as she did with her personal life, now at its nadir. Margaret Sullavan had shocked everyone by marrying director William Wyler, whom she had only known a few weeks, and Kate sensed that Leland had taken this news harder than she might have wished. Jed Harris had been incensed by it and irrationally blamed Kate. Luddy spoke of a divorce, and Laura had been cool to her ever since Kate had encouraged a friendship with a woman named Suzanne Steele. To add to these tensions, the Hepburn tribe were all involved in Mrs. Hepburn's current national notoriety after appearing on the stand of the House Caucus Room in Washington in passionate argument on behalf of the Pierce Bill to permit dissemination of birth control information by physicians.

Amid the flashing of news cameras, Mrs. Hepburn spoke out against the Pierce Bill's arch opponent, Father Charles E Kaufman, who had argued that birth control was a step toward communism and that "100 years from now Washington will be Washingtonsky and you'll foster it if you un criminalize contraceptives."

"Ridiculous!" Mrs. Hepburn had disdainfully exclaimed. When her opponent brought up the declining birthrate

---

* Dorothy Parker (1893–1967), celebrated short-story writer, satirist, poet screenwriter (co-author of the original *A Star Is Born*) and lyricist ("Paris in the Spring," "Hands Across the Table").

Mrs. Hepburn retorted, "With twelve million on public support [welfare] I would think that was the last thing one had to worry about now!"

An interview in *The New York Times* carried the headline STAR'S MOTHER FIRM IN STAND and a prominent photograph of Mrs. Hepburn with her hand raised in some emotional response. The caption identified "the women's rights leader fighting for birth control" as "Mrs. Thomas N. Hepburn, mother of 6 children, including Katharine Hepburn, the actress."* To the question of people's reaction to her controversial stand, Mrs. Hepburn came back, "I have ceased to worry about people being shocked—they're shocked already and I want to get it over with—humans have always done so many stupid things and under such righteous terms that it is very difficult for us really to use our intelligence about anything."

Reminded that her opponents had called birth control "the suicide of the species," Mrs. Hepburn's eyes flashed with indignation. "Nonsense! Women want children but they want them when they can afford them physically and economically."

Kate still managed to go home on those days when the theater was dark, but she kept her problems to herself. Finally, to Kate's relief, on February 10, 1934, after fifty-five New York performances, *The Lake* closed.

After more than fifty years the enigma of Suzanne Steele remains. The story that has appeared in two previous biographies of Katharine Hepburn presents Miss Steele as a mature, "plump" former opera singer who had been giving Kate private coaching during the weekends for the run of *The Lake*. In fact, Suzanne Steele was an attractive woman, amusing and exceptionally clever and well educated. Not only had she never sung in opera, her Broadway debut had occurred at the Little Theatre as a protean actor eight months before *The Lake* opened at the Martin Beck. Having been schooled in France, Miss Steele chose for her first public appearance her own English translation of the Molière classic

---

* The article obviously included Hepburn's deceased older brother. Mrs. Hepburn had only five living children at the time.

The School for Wives, portraying in dramatic reading all the characters, male and female. "Miss Steele," wrote the critic for the *New York Sun,* ". . . has two kinds of voices, one for male characters and the other for female characters. But her ability to differentiate her characterizations is rather limited. . . . Let me suggest that Miss Steele confine her work for the present to women's clubs and to other audiences in which she will not be judged by too high a standard."

Kate later said that Miss Steele, a complete stranger, appeared in her dressing room one night after a particularly bad performance and offered to privately coach her on weekends. Although Kate was already working with Miss Robinson-Duff at the time, she accepted the offer. Perhaps she was grasping for straws, a way to approach the role with new insight. Suzanne Steele did possess certain intriguing qualities. Her French was impeccable. She had, after all, translated Molière, and she had presented a series of three Sunday evening programs of "Literature Across the Footlights" in April, 1933, with the Little Theatre.

Shortly after *The Lake* closed and just a few days before Kate learned that she had won the Academy Award for Best Actress in 1933 for her role in *Morning Glory,** she booked passage for the two of them under the names of K. Smith and S. Steele on the *Paris,* leaving for France on March 18. Kate's intention was to continue to Cannes, where she had won a Cannes Film Festival Award for *Little Women,*† and then spend several weeks on the Riviera and touring France, learning the language and venturing beyond the tourist spots with Suzanne's linguistic help.

Kate came aboard the *Paris* a few steps in front of Suzanne at eleven-thirty A.M. via the lower level of the pier and the third-class gangway, scrambling through a group of reporters and photographers. Refusing to pose for the news camera-

---

* Other nominees for Best Actress, 1933, were May Robson, *Lady for a Day,* and Diana Wynyard, *Cavalcade.* Best Actor was won by Charles Laughton for *The Private Life of Henry VIII.* Katharine Hepburn's award was accepted for her by B. B. Kohane, president of R.K.O.

† *Little Women* was nominated for Best Picture, 1933, but lost to Noël Coward's *Cavalcade.* Victor Heerman and Sarah Y. Mason won for Best Adaptation for *Little Women,* the only award the film was to win.

men, she shouted over her shoulder as the cameras clicked despite her warnings, "The pictures will be lousy!" (One paper ran a photograph with the notation "Katy Was Right".) Once they reached their state-room, Kate and Suzanne locked themselves in. Members of the press do not easily go away, and they pounded insistently on the door. Suzanne finally stepped out to say that she was "an old friend of Miss Hepburn's" and that they would be "abroad for four or five weeks, visiting Paris and the Riviera."

The *Paris* made the Atlantic crossing in six days, landing in Le Havre on March 24, 1933. The weather was rough and Kate was not a good sailor. Suzanne had expected a more festive crossing than Kate could manage. Meals were served in their state-room, constitutional walks were taken at six A.M. and eight P.M. (when the majority of the first-class passengers were inside dining). The women began to bicker, Suzanne to drink. By the time they reached Le Havre they hardly spoke. (United Press snidely reported, "Miss Hepburn sought to elude admirers when she landed at 5 A.M. and hurried to a motor car . . . the fact that she wore men's trousers somewhat thwarted her efforts to avoid attention. Miss Hepburn wore men's garb during the entire voyage aboard the liner Paris.") After four days in Paris, Kate decided to return to the United States.

Rumors had it that Kate had come to Paris to arrange a divorce. Suzanne's last statement as "official spokesman" for Kate was, "Kate has no intention of getting a divorce. She wants to stay married." The Associated Press dispatch reported that "Miss Suzanne Steele, concert singer, traveling companion and official spokesman for Katharine Hepburn, motion picture actress, sailed with Miss Hepburn." Suzanne Steele's name, however, did not appear on the passenger list of the return voyage of the *Paris*.

The passenger list on the homebound journey included Kate Hepburn, Marlene Dietrich (traveling with her eight-year-old daughter, Maria) *and* Ernest Hemingway. Upon hearing Kate was aboard, Hemingway sought a meeting. Greatly admiring the famous author, Kate agreed. Hemingway worked wonders on her. They strolled the windy decks together, dined together and argued enthusiastically. When the ship docked in New York on April 4 (just seventeen days after Kate had first embarked), they sat together as reporters clambered aboard.

"Don't be a mug!" the rugged Hemingway was heard to say to her.

Her long, thin face was very pale except for a crimson slash of lipstick.

"I'm not a mug," she snapped back, and then turned on her best screen smile. "Really, I'm not disagreeable. How many reporters are there?"

She was told there were twelve.

"Well—steward," she said, "bring champagne for twelve gentlemen of the press."

She smiled again at the reporters.

"I never meant to cause you any inconvenience," she told them. "The only reason I didn't see you when I went away was that I had nothing to say. I talk so little for publication because I'm so indiscreet."

Then she proceeded to talk volubly about everything from her penchant for wearing men's trousers (the chic, tailored, blue-wool suit and matching beret, shoes and gloves she wore notwithstanding) to her desire to return to the stage in the face of *The Lake*'s poor notices. She denied emphatically that she had gone to Paris to arrange a divorce. "I just needed a vacation and took it—that's good enough reason, isn't it? And I came back because I got homesick."

"For what?" a reporter asked.

"I'm sure I don't know. I just didn't see anything in Paris, so I came back on the same boat."

Hemingway grinned mischievously. "Obviously, Miss Hepburn needed a guide," he quipped.

Hemingway told the reporters that he was "going to Key West for a season of intensive writing in order to go back to Africa." Hemingway later claimed that Kate had invited him to tea the next day at her house in Turtle Bay and informed him he "need not wait to earn enough for another safari. She would provide the necessary money and go along with Pauline [Mrs. Hemingway] on the trip." Hemingway said he considered Kate's offer and politely declined.

One week later, Kate's difficulties with Laura having been

overcome, the two women booked passage from Miami on one of America's few cruise ships, the S.S. *Morro Castle*,* for a long sea voyage that would stop at Morro Castle (the fort at the entrance to the harbor of Havana, Cuba) before continuing on through the Panama Canal and up the coast of Mexico, where Kate intended to file suit for divorce. (Her seasickness did not disturb her as much as she claimed, obviously.) Hemingway often fished for giant marlin in the ocean off this harbor. The previous year he had even written an article for *Esquire* magazine about an hour-and-a-half fight he had had there with a 750-pound giant marlin.

From Miami, Kate telephoned Hemingway in Key West. He told her truthfully that he was hard at work on a new book.

Kate and Laura registered at the Hotel Itza in Mérida, Yucatan, Mexico, on April 24. The first thing they did was to reserve two airplane seats to Miami for the evening of the day the Mexican lawyer had scheduled Kate's plea for divorce. Then they went to look at Mayan ruins with Lady Edwina Mountbatten, who was touring Mexico at the time. On April 26, the lawyer filed divorce papers in the Second Civil Court on Kate's behalf. And, on the thirtieth, with Laura as her only principal witness, the hearing was held, without Luddy, who was represented by an attorney he had instructed to help Kate in any way possible. "Deep disagreement as to life, incompatibility of character and separation for more than 300 days at a time" formed the basis of the divorce decree. When the "secret" divorce finally became public two days later, much was made of the fact that the court had also ruled that

---

* The *Morro Castle*, a Ward liner, built in the United States with government funds, was to have a dramatic end a little more than a year later when on the night of September 8, 1934, it exploded in flames and sank off the Atlantic seaboard on a return cruise from Havana claiming 125 lives. The sinking of the *Morro Castle* was one of the most famous sea disasters of the first half of the century. The ship's captain, R. Wilmott, was taken mysteriously ill at dinner that night and died shortly thereafter. Not much later a fire was discovered in the writing room on B Deck. In the eighteen minutes that had elapsed before the new captain ordered a call for assistance, the fire had made too much headway to control. Publicized erroneously as "the safest ship afloat," the *Morro Castle* had very little fire-detection apparatus. Its sinking became an American sea scandal.

the usual thirty-day restriction on remarriage would not be imposed.

Since Luddy had no plans to remarry and had even expressed the hope to an interviewer that Kate would come back to him, the press speculated that Kate must have a quick remarriage in her future. Laura, now the official spokesman, told the reporters, "Miss Hepburn has no plans to remarry." Arrangements were quickly altered; and instead of going down to Key West as Kate thought they would, she and Laura boarded a train for New York and barricaded themselves in the house at Turtle Bay while the press camped on the doorstep.

Her silence was abruptly broken when a small, newly acquired Persian kitten escaped onto the street from a momentarily opened door off the basement kitchen. Kate shouted to a reporter to stop the cat that was crossing his path and the man scooped the small animal up and met Kate at the basement door, where she let him in, cat in his arms. Her wall of reserve broken down, she granted him an interview right there.

"You pay a terrible price for fame," she told him. "The most precious thing you have is your life and it's almost impossible to enjoy life after you have success in pictures. . . . I suppose the newspapers hate me but I'm not being rude in refusing to discuss my affairs. I always tried to be helpful to newspapermen but they go away dissatisfied and perhaps prejudiced. I fear this prejudice will affect my career and shorten it. . . . Success and fame are all too fleeting. . . . I don't know how long I will last. . . . Somehow I wish I could paint pictures, play music or write books. Alas, I am not talented at all."

Asked about her feelings toward her mother's work in birth control, Kate replied, "Mother has accomplished a great deal. I detest the newspaper references to her as Katharine Hepburn's mother. My mother is important. I am not."

The reporter, who had not gained entry into the house past the basement corridor, now asked about a report that Leland Hayward was rushing to New York by plane, having just obtained his own divorce decree, to be married to her.

Kate backed off. "I will never have anything to say about

Mr. Hayward or Mr. Smith. You see I won't discuss my personal affairs ever. They wouldn't be personal if I made them public."

She turned, closed a door between them, and could be heard mounting the stairs beyond. The reporter let himself out and went to write up his story.

Mr. Hayward or Mr. Smith. You see I won't discuss my personal affairs ever. They wouldn't be personal if I made them public.

She turned, closed a door between them, and could be heard mounting the stairs beyond. The reporter let himself out and went to wr...

CHAPTER
10

Few actors can become stars without possessing charm. Some performers acquire it as they grow older; Kate's co-stars Adolphe Menjou and Billie Burke were fine examples. Good looks are not essential; consider James Cagney and Charles Laughton. Nor is sophistication; the naïve Mary Pickford and the bumbling Harold Lloyd both had it. Charm both pleases and seduces audiences. Eccentricities, foibles and affectations can be acceptable when a person radiates great charm. Since most people do not, they find idols onstage, in films and in the political arena either to admire or to model themselves after.

Kate not only had charm, she had an abundance of that other indefinable quality, class. The combination of charm, class and a photogenic appearance had made her a star in her first film, held her audience in her second *(Christopher Strong)* despite its poor reviews, and given a distinction to her role in *Morning Glory*, which had won her an Academy Award. Like many performers of her day who had entered films by way of theater and for love of money and immediate fame rather than love of the medium, Kate, despite her infatuation with the camera, had only small regard for the art of film. Later, as her respect for films grew, so did the depth of her performances. But in 1934, receiving the Academy Award for *Morning Glory* and being partly responsible for the critical and commercial success of *Little Women** did not compensate for her terrible failure in *The Lake,* for the latter was *theater* and the former only *talking pictures.*

She had agreed to make *Spitfire* only so that she could return to the Broadway stage in *The Lake;* R.K.O. would not have allowed her to do so otherwise. *Spitfire* was to fail almost as disastrously as her stage venture and for many of the same reasons. Kate had been able to overcome second-rate material in *Morning Glory,* where her role had permitted her personality to shine through. Trigger Hicks, in *Spitfire,* is an uneducated, primitive, relatively uncouth mountain girl. Kate attempted a dialect and tomboy gait that almost obliterated her own qualities. Only in her one love scene with her leading man, Robert Young,† was her talent evident. Unfortunately, she lost her mountain speech in this scene, so that the moment jars rather than highlights the performance.

Free now from even the loose strings of her marriage to Luddy, Kate had no obligations toward any individual. Her contract to R.K.O. would shortly come up for renewal and since she was financially independent, she could do as she pleased where her film career was concerned. She planned to return to the stage, and was considering a dramatization of Jane Austen's *Pride and Prejudice*** for producer Arthur Hopkins for the following Broadway season. It would have been ridiculous for her to go about pretending that the debacle of *The Lake* would not make this difficult. Nor did she take the view that "criticism was a sort of envious tribute." The harsh reactions of her peers in the theater had meant she remained an outsider to the select and current theater greats.

---

* The *Time* critic wrote, ". . . superb acting by Katharine Hepburn. An actress of so much vitality that she can wear balloon skirts and address her mother as 'Marmee' without suggesting quaintness, she makes Jo March one of the most memorable heroines of the year. . . ."

† Robert Young (1907–   ) co-starred in more than one hundred films, cast first as an amiable, reliable leading man, then charming husband and finally benevolent father. His popularity reached its apex in television, however, when he co-starred in the mid-fifties in *Father Knows Best* and a decade later in *Marcus Welby, M.D.* He never worked with Hepburn again.

** *Pride and Prejudice* had been adapted for the stage by Helen Jerome, who also adapted the production of *Jane Eyre* that Hepburn was to tour with in 1936–37.

With the box-office success of *Little Women*, R.K.O. pressed for another costume role—Joan of Arc (based on George Bernard Shaw's *Saint Joan*) or a biographical film on George Sand. Both proposals called for her to depart as far as possible from the natural charm she was able to contribute to the role of Jo March. Sensibly, she turned them down and returned to the East Coast in early June to walk the beach at Old Saybrook and think about what she should do. She certainly had not proved to be a very great success as a stage actress or as a wife. The standards she set for herself were perhaps too high for her to live up to. Another woman might have rested quite smugly on her film triumphs, but not Kate. Even discounting Dorothy Parker's vitriol, her theater reviews had been painful. Brooks Atkinson at *The New York Times* had sighted "her limitations as a dramatic actress . . . and a voice that has unpleasant timbre." Another critic had called her "too young and too shy, in the presence of an audience to seem as commanding a personality on the stage as on the screen." Robert Benchley at *The New Yorker* had said, "Not a great actress by any manner of means, but one with a certain distinction which, with training, might possibly take the place of great acting in an emergency." That one took a bit of extra pondering. Everyone had accused her of affecting a voice that was too high and flat. But it was her *natural* voice, adding to her special charm. To affect another voice would make her self-conscious. Perhaps Broadway audiences had to get used to her voice in the same way that film audiences had to—by constant exposure to it.

Curiously, once she was divorced from Luddy, she missed him. He had retained the apartment in the house in New York. Now he came to join her at Fenwick to help placate her fears and restore her pride, moving into an upstairs room and a place in Kate's life for as long as he lived. Luddy was one person who could always be counted on to take her side. No pretensions need ever exist between them. They were not man and woman but two close buddies apathetic to each other's gender. Their unusual postdivorce relationship led to stories in the press about a possible reconciliation, to which neither of them responded.

With Luddy's encouragement, in June, 1934, she agreed to return to the Ivoryton Playhouse as Judith Traherne, the

dying heroine in George Brewer's tragedy, *Dark Victory*.*
The hope was that *Dark Victory* would move on to New York
with Kate in it. Her co-star was to be Stanley Ridges, a solid
English character actor.† *Dark Victory* was to be the first play
of the summer season and Kate's appearance was a great
plum for the theater's directors, Milton Steifel and Julian
Anhalt. Rehearsals did not go well. Kate blamed the casting
of Ridges, who made her uncomfortable. A few days before
the opening, she decided she could not continue. Ridges
gallantly withdrew from the production, citing an illness in
the family, and a cancellation notice was posted. The theater
offered to present her in *Holiday* as the last play of their
season, but Kate refused. The management at the Ivoryton
Summer Theatre threatened to take action with the Actors
Equity Association but never did.

Joined by Laura, Kate boarded a train for Hollywood,
where they rented another house.

Not long after Kate and Laura had returned to Hollywood,
Theresa Helburn of the Theatre Guild arrived with the intent
of selling Eugene O'Neill's *Mourning Becomes Electra* to the
movies. She had the idea of Garbo and Kate appearing in the
roles of mother and daughter created on the stage by Alice
Brady and Alla Nazimova. Kate became terribly excited
about the possibility and even went so far as to approach
Louis B. Mayer at Metro with the suggestion that he buy the
play and borrow her from R.K.O. to co-star with Garbo in a
film adaptation.** "Louis B. said only over his dead body,"
Helburn stated. "Surprisingly Kate didn't shoot him on the
spot."‡

Disappointed that she could not appear in the O'Neill

---

* The role was played on Broadway in the fall of 1934 by Tallulah Bankhead, and in films by Bette Davis in 1939.

† Stanley Ridges (1892–1951) played many pivotal roles in such major films as *Winterset*, *Yellow Jack*, *If I Were King*, *Each Dawn I Die*, *The Sea Wolf*, *Sergeant York* and *To Be or Not to Be*.

** Hepburn's current contract was at R.K.O. but Garbo was signed to Metro.

‡ Eugene O'Neill wrote Theresa Helburn, "About *Mourning Becomes Electra*, I am sure Hepburn would be splendid as Lavinia. The rest I'm afraid would be a dreadful hash of attempted condensation and idiotic censorship. . . ." Rosalind Russell played Lavinia in the 1947 film adaptation of *Mourning Becomes Electra*.

drama, Kate turned down numerous scripts that R.K.O. sent her, including an adaptation of J. M. Barrie's *The Little Minister*. R.K.O. then approached Margaret Sullavan to play the role of Lady Babbie. As soon as Kate heard Sullavan was in negotiation with R.K.O. she changed her mind. "I really didn't want to play it until I heard another actress was desperate for the role," she later admitted. "Then, of course, it became the most important thing in the world for me that I should get it." Ungraciously, she added, "Several of my parts in those days I fought for just to take them from someone who needed them." But that kind of avarice seems foreign to Kate's personality. Except for her tenacious battle for the role of Scarlett O'Hara (won by Vivien Leigh), and another to be cast by M.G.M. in *The Gorgeous Hussy* (finally portrayed by Joan Crawford), she seldom displayed a competitive nature. And even in those two cases, the two actresses finally cast had not been involved when she originally went after the roles. A sense of true rivalry did, however, exist between Kate and Margaret Sullavan.

The Little Minister was as unsuitable a vehicle for Kate as *The Lake* had been. R.K.O. reasoned that her success in one period drama (*Little Women*) would engender success in a second. *The Little Minister* might be defined as a bit of whimsy, and though two silent film versions had been made,* they had not transposed well to the screen. Maude Adams,† the American stage star, had twice played the role on Broadway and her magnetic personality and tremendous box-office appeal had made both productions successful. Kate had always admired Miss Adams and was most flattered when told (as she often was) that there was a resemblance, although the older woman's diminutive size and gamine looks made the comparison difficult to understand. But the role of Lady

---

* In 1921, Vitagraph released *The Little Minister* starring Alice Calhoun and Jimmy Morrison, and Paramount released a more elaborate production starring Betty Compson and George Hackathorne the same year.

† Maude Adams (1872–1953) began acting at an early age. *The Little Minister* was her first starring role. Other Barrie plays in which she starred were *Quality Street* (1901), *Peter Pan* (1905) (the role for which she is most loved), and *What Every Woman Knows* (1908). Hepburn also repeated Adams's role in the film version of *Quality Street* (1937).

Babbie in *The Little Minister*—itself a dated story—was too ill-defined to have real substance.*

Both Laura and Leland Hayward urged her not to accept the part, but Kate's willfulness excluded all outside influence. Reviewers already called her "the incomparable Katharine Hepburn." Her legend was in the making. Still, despite her "unconquerable gift for turning lavender and old lace into something possessing dramatic vitality and conviction" and her fame as "one of the major wonder workers of Hollywood," she could not overcome the lack of appeal of *The Little Minister* to film audiences. It now became clear that, unlike many other stars, Kate could not bring audiences to movie houses in an inferior film.

She had alienated the press from the time of her arrival in California to make *A Bill of Divorcement.* The result was that they did not present intelligent, earnest portraits of Kate or sympathetic analyses or insights into the worthwhile sides of her character, just her pranks and the eccentricities—the things about her that made readers mutter, "Why doesn't she grow up?" and pass by theater marquees with her name with disinterest unless the film itself was sufficiently intriguing.

The Little Minister was a dismal failure. The studio wanted to counteract any effect this would have on Kate's popularity by having her win over the press, be cordial, give more interviews. Kate refused to cooperate, citing her right to privacy. Certainly fame should not deny a performer the right of privacy. But fame in films, where one becomes a public figure recognizable on sight by millions of people, makes protecting that right to an extreme a contradiction in terms. Why become a film star if you seek total privacy?

Kate began once again to see Leland Hayward. Both free and single now, they no longer needed the cloak of secrecy they continued to hide behind. Never did they dine in public or attend parties or premieres. The ground rules were Kate's.

---

* The script of *The Little Minister* was as fusty as its subject. A conservative new minister (well played by John Beal) is ostracized by his parish of the Auld Licht Kirk in 1840 when he falls in love with a gypsy wench who is the spokeswoman for the poor weavers of the county. Just when he is about to be expelled from his pulpit because he has been seen walking with the gypsy girl, it becomes known that she is in reality Lady Babbie, ward of the richest man in the county, and all is forgiven.

"When I'm asked if I take a shower or tub then I have a right to take to the tall timbers," she claimed. But being seen and getting about were important in the career of an agent. Hayward had negotiated a six-picture deal for her at R.K.O. for fifty thousand dollars a film. Considering that at that time the average major Hollywood film had a four- to six-week production schedule* and that in 1934 banks and businesses were failing in frightening numbers and the median weekly income of a family of four was fifty dollars, Kate's salary, which was higher than that of President Roosevelt, was astronomic. Still, Hayward was not strong enough either to convert her to his preferred life-style or to influence her choice of material.

In one of her few garrulous periods, she told an interviewer, "For the independent woman the marriage problem is very great. If she falls in love with a strong man she loses him because she has to concentrate too much on her job. If she falls in love with a weakling, who[m] she can push around, she always falls out of love with him. A woman just has to have sense enough to handle a man well enough so he'll want to stay with her. How to keep him on the string is almost a full time job. . . ." If Kate really believed this, she did not follow her convictions; she hardly devoted full time to Leland Hayward, although she did convey the impression that she wanted to marry him.

Upon the completion of *The Little Minister,* she and Leland flew to New York, where Kate was plagued by reporters. The day after she arrived, she boarded the Europe-bound *Majestic* to wish David and Irene Selznick bon voyage and let it slip that she and Leland would be married within a month, after which she would "join them in Paris and bring him along too."

The *New York Herald Tribune* pondered: "How she got on the boat [the *Majestic*] is as much a mystery as where she and Hayward went yesterday.

"News gatherers who talked to her early Friday night through an inhospitable crack in the front door of her house at No. 244 E. 49th St. kept watch until after midnight and would take an oath that she never left the house.

---

* In 1985, the average period of shooting was eight to twelve weeks.

"But, sad to recall, Katie's mythical husband Ludlow Ogden Smith maintains an apartment on the back side of Katharine's four-story brownstone. She may have gone out the back way.

"She may have gone to Hartford to visit her family. Or she and Hayward might have gone to be married. One thing only is certain. She is gone."

In fact, she had returned to West Hartford with Leland so that he could meet her family. Whatever his expectations, the Hepburns managed to overwhelm him. He flew back to Hollywood, leaving Kate behind.

The press now speculated that they were married, and neither of them bothered to deny the rumors despite the fact that Leland was photographed several times in the company of beautiful women. Within a few weeks Kate and Laura were back in California and Kate was set to begin a new film, *Break of Hearts*, originally entitled *The Music Man* and intended as a vehicle for Kate and John Barrymore.

From the start, nothing went right with *Break of Hearts*. Kate and Barrymore's first replacement, the continental star Francis Lederer,* played poorly together. Charles Boyer then stepped in and two weeks of work had to be reshot. The director, Philip Moeller,† a theater director of fine reputation, could not adapt his talent to the screen and the film grew more static with each scene. Still, nothing could have overcome this inept love story of an eminent musical conductor (Boyer) who falls in love with an unknown composer (Hepburn). *He* becomes an alcoholic and *she* gives up a promising career of her own to help him out of his alcoholic stupor.

It should have broken the filmgoers' hearts, but "labored and palpably fabricated writing" kept any emotion at all from occurring. The *Time* critic warned, "Miss Hepburn makes it clear that unless her employers see fit to return her to roles in keeping with her mannerisms (*Little Women*), these will

---

* Francis Lederer (1906–   ), born in Prague, was a matinee idol in Germany. In 1934, he came to Hollywood and starred in three films after making a sensational American stage debut in *Autumn Crocus* in 1932. His two most popular American films were *Confessions of a Nazi Spy* (1939) and *The Man I Married* (1940).

† Philip Moeller (1880–1958) had directed several plays for the Theatre Guild.

presently annoy cinema addicts into forgetting that she is really an actress of great promise and considerable style."

Break of Hearts failed at the box office almost as badly as *The Little Minister* had, and its release endangered Kate's reputation. Something had to be done quickly to repair the damage. R.K.O. had a $200,000 commitment to her for four more films, and unless her next appearance was a box-office success, they stood to lose considerable money. Finally, Pandro Berman, who had produced *Morning Glory,* came up with a script, adapted by Jane Murfin (who had also worked on *The Little Minister* and *Spitfire*), of Booth Tarkington's *Alice Adams*.

Kate's new contract had given her final choice of director and she vowed not to repeat the kind of costly error of judgment she had made with *Break of Hearts,* where Philip Moeller's association with the Theatre Guild had influenced her decision. Had George Cukor not been engaged in the filming of *David Copperfield,* Kate would have asked for him. She did, however, turn to him for advice on the two directors R.K.O. considered right for the assignment, William Wyler* and George Stevens,† neither of whom had made a large name for himself yet. Cukor chose Wyler, who, of the two, had had more experience. Although his early films had been uninspired western potboilers, two of Wyler's more recent efforts, *A House Divided* and *Counsellor at Law,* did exhibit a meticulous craftsmanship. George Stevens had served his apprenticeship with Laurel and Hardy two-reelers and had not yet made a film of any scope.

Kate discussed Cukor's preference with Pandro Berman, who disagreed. Alice Adams's world was workaday, her ambitions pretentious, her life a fiction. *Alice Adams* re-

---

* William Wyler (1902–1983) in 1934 had not yet reached the point in his career where he was critically acclaimed. *Dodsworth* (1936) began his ascent as a top director. *Dead End* (1937), *Jezebel* (1938), *Wuthering Heights* (1939), *The Letter* (1940), *The Little Foxes* (1941), *The Best Years of Our Lives* (1946), *Detective Story* (1951), *Roman Holiday* (1953) and *The Friendly Persuasion* (1956) were among his best films.

† George Stevens (1904–1975) directed surprisingly few films. He did *Swing Time* (1936) with Fred Astaire and Ginger Rogers, *Quality Street* (1937) and *Woman of the Year* (1942), the latter two reuniting him with Hepburn. *A Place in the Sun* (1951), *Shane* (1953) and *Giant* (1956) were his most notable subsequent films.

quired a director who could re-create the middle-class society
of small-town America and who could apply bits of humor to
the overall pathos of Alice's situation. William Wyler's
Alsatian background and his Swiss-German education
seemed ill suited to such a task. Wyler, in fact, possessed very
little humor. Kate had another reason for rejecting Wyler: his
marriage to Margaret Sullavan. Pandro Berman states that on
meeting George Stevens Kate was terribly attracted to him.
Yet the first day on the set, she was certain she had made a
mistake in not going with Wyler.

A disagreement arose between her and Stevens as to the
treatment of the opening shot. Stevens refused to back down,
and Kate returned to her dressing room in a huff. She
reappeared on the set hours later, and the disagreement
began anew. In all, only thirty seconds of film were shot the
first day. For three weeks, the tension between them remained and they were still calling each other "Mr. Stevens"
and "Miss Hepburn." Nonetheless, Kate sensed that her performance was the better for Stevens's stubborn resistance.

The scene to be shot on the twenty-first day of shooting
called for Alice (who had just lost her first real sweetheart) to
enter her bedroom, throw herself on the bed and burst into
tears. Kate had rehearsed the scene numerous times when
Stevens decided a more moving effect would be for Alice to
enter, slowly walk to the window, look beyond, and then
cry.*

Kate refused to play the scene other than the way she had
rehearsed it and she stood firm for half a day. Stevens also
remained intractable.

"It's ridiculous!" Kate finally erupted. "There's a limit to
stupidity. I've put up with all of it I can. You dumb bastard,
I'm going to cry on the bed!"

Stevens shouted back that he would return to his two-
reelers before he'd give in to her.

"A quitter!" Kate mocked. "If I ever had any respect for
you, it's gone now! You don't get your way, so you quit!
You're yellow!"

---

* Hepburn always used glycerine to cry, maintaining that the development of a
mental attitude that would make her cry normally would also affect her ability to
apply intelligence to the scene.

Stevens answered, in a cold, quiet voice, "Miss Hepburn, just walk to the window, please, and stand there awhile. You needn't weep. I'll dub someone in, in a long shot and we can fake the sound track."

For a moment everyone on the set held their breath as their eyes were riveted on star and director. Then Kate began to walk toward the scene. Stevens gave the signal for the cameras to turn. Kate entered, hesitated, went to the window, looked out beyond. The lines in her face quivered, broke and then she wept. Finally, when the action ended, she turned toward her director. "How was that *George?*" she asked as she wiped the tears from her face.

Alice Adams was extremely well received and Kate won a second Academy Award nomination for her portrayal. But for Kate, *Alice Adams* was a period of personal crisis. Her romance with Leland Hayward contained great highs and lows. She still demanded a veil of secrecy. The possibility that they might marry as indicated in her statement to the Selznicks appeared to have diminished. Kate wanted him on her terms. But Leland Hayward could not be converted into becoming a replacement for Luddy.

To add to her personal conflicts, Laura (whom fan magazines now bannered as "The Power Behind Katharine Hepburn"), after three close years with Kate, had decided to return to the East and "to stop living Kate's life for her." She later commented, " . . . it became clear to me that my presence in Hollywood was increasingly inessential to myself, to Kate, and to pictures. I had no interest in going into the industry, Kate was firmly established as a huge star and was no longer dependent on me, and I was tired of the rather meaningless, sterile life of Southern California.

" . . . I came from a totally different social milieu from either Hollywood *or* Kate. Our family was in railroads and the travel business [American Express], our friends were East Coast old money people, and I never even approved of Kate's bohemian ways. I adored her and still do, but in 1935 it had become obvious that I did not belong at the center of her life."

Laura's place as confidante and companion in Kate's life had been usurped by another young woman, named Jane Loring. Loring and Kate had met on *Break of Hearts* when the attractive film technician was hired as an assistant film editor to William Hamilton. Three months later, she had progressed to editor on *Alice Adams*. Loring, a sensitive film cutter with an understanding of Kate's best cinematic qualities, could talk a language that was foreign to Laura. Loring edited Kate's next three films, during which time she became her close adviser.

At Christmas, 1934, Leland Hayward had suddenly taken ill. Cancer of the prostate was suspected and Kate insisted they fly to West Hartford so that Dr. Hepburn could perform the operation required. In attempting to avoid newsmen at Idlewild Airport, Kate came within inches of being struck by a propeller in motion, a near accident that made headlines (HEPBURN DARES DEATH TO ELUDE THE PRESS). Reporters followed the couple to Hartford, where Hayward checked immediately into Hartford Hospital. The press sat vigil in the hospital lobby. The story was the stuff that the popular papers doted upon: a film star's father operating on the man who the press was certain *must* be his son-in-law (or, at the very least, his *future* son-in-law). For the first few days, Kate managed to avoid photographers by entering the hospital through the basement. Finally, they secreted themselves behind the garage of the Hepburn house. Kate and Mrs. Hepburn drove in, unsuspecting. Kate stepped out of the garage first. Flashbulbs exploded in her face. "I was in a blind, towering rage," she says of her succeeding actions. Bolting toward the nearest photographer, she leaped up, grabbed the camera and tearing it from the man's hand tossed it hard to the ground. Then she turned and ran into the house where she was met by her sister Peggy.

"Where's a shotgun?" she shouted. "Get it! Get it!"

Peggy tried to calm her sister, while Mrs. Hepburn beat off the photographers outside with a wire basket she had found in the garage. She put them to flight, but not before they had taken one shot of her "swinging the basket like a mace."

The photograph was featured in out-of-town newspapers but never printed locally. Dr. Hepburn was asked if this surprised him.

"Not at all," he replied grimly. "I've operated on half the newspapermen in Hartford already, and I expect to operate on the other half."

Leland Hayward's operation was a success and, after a brief recuperation at the Hepburns' home, he returned to the Coast. Kate followed, but she now became more Garboesque than ever about her marital status. When confronted by a friend who suggested that Kate's impulsive action toward the photographer and her quarrel with the press might have been improvident, costing her a great deal in good relations, Kate replied, "What does it matter how much that quarrel cost me? I think this invasion of people's private lives is rotten and wrong, and I've fought it in protest. I protest because I feel that way. I can live better with myself for doing it, and that's the most important thing in the world to me."

CHAPTER

11

Kate sat feet up on the cocktail table, dressed in a scarlet sweater and white slacks as though specially costumed to match the white walled, red carpeted living room of the house in Turtle Bay. She smiled enchantingly and carefully balanced a cup of tea in her hand as she shook her shaggy bobbed hair back from her face. She had consented to a rare interview under extreme pressure from the studio, but with one proviso: Leland Hayward's name was not to be mentioned. Filming had just ended on *Sylvia Scarlett** and the front office knew Hepburn's latest would need all the good press they could muster. Kate, realizing how bad the situation was, finally had promised she would cooperate.

The interviewer (perhaps because he had attended a press showing of *Sylvia Scarlett*) also stayed clear of any reference to her new film.

"What about your *future* plans?" he asked.

"Not altogether set," she replied. "I should like to do about two, maybe three pictures every year and appear in one play a year. That would be plenty of work."

"Who do you like especially as a motion picture director?"

---

* The film was adapted from Compton Mackenzie's novel *Early Life and Adventures of Sylvia Scarlett.*

"George Cukor," she came back in a flash. "A grand fellow, understanding, imaginative."

"And your favorite screen actress?"

"Miss Garbo. Who can touch her?"

"And your first lady of the stage?"

"I adore Katharine Cornell. . . . Now, before you get around to it, I don't mind confessing a few other tastes or whims or what have you. I am crazy about Siamese cats, English bull terriers and English history.* I am fond of golfing, horseback riding, skating, swimming and motoring. I'll tackle my bacon and eggs with any longshoreman, for I have a perfectly unladylike appetite."

She leaned forward, slid her tea cup and saucer onto the table and snatched up a fudge brownie. "I adore these," she said as she took a bite with tremendous relish.

"What part would you like best to have a go at in a stage production?"

Kate thought a moment.

"Juliet; I'd love it and I believe, on my soul, I could do a nifty Juliet!"†

"How do you feel about Hollywood?"

"I like every damned thing about the place. Palms and brown hills and boulevards and geraniums six feet tall and flowers running riot everywhere and the grand roads and the golfing and the picture people and even the work, grinding as it is. I like it! Why in hell shouldn't I?"

From that point her voice took on an edge. So much for charming the press. Anyway, her general you-be-damned reaction to the world, that take-me-as-I-am-or-go-to-hell attitude that marked her more determined moments made the best copy for an interviewer. This particular interviewer noted that "she can swear like the troops in Flanders" and that "head up, chin stuck out, [she is] a hundred and ten pounds or so of cold steel nerve . . . a lady of many angles, with a good deal of useful ego in her cosmos; but intellectually honest if ever there was such a creature. . . ."

That might not have been exactly the kind of "good" press R.K.O. had had in mind, but they were at least appreciative

---

* Hepburn was planning *Mary of Scotland* as her next film.
† Hepburn never played Juliet.

of her efforts. During this trip to New York, Kate sat through numerous such interrogations, answering the same questions over and over with considerable grace—for Kate. One thing was clear. Kate's determination, her "intellectual honesty," was in the process of replacing her early disdain and arrogance. She no longer threw obvious lies at the press, or mocked them. Kate had begun to mature.

Part of this growth had been a new interest in the film roles she chose to play. George Cukor had wanted to do *Sylvia Scarlett* for a number of years and gave Kate the book to read believing her special *garçonne* quality made her perfect for the part. Kate agreed and she and Cukor finally (after much resistance) convinced Pandro Berman to produce the film.

Sylvia Scarlett was a daring choice for Kate; an eccentric story of a girl who disguises herself as a boy to help her father who is a thief and a con man. In the 1930 film *Morocco*, Dietrich had dressed like a man; in 1931, Mary Pickford appeared in several sequences of *Kiki* dressed as a boy; and in *Queen Christina*, in 1933, Garbo had donned male attire as a disguise; and all three films had been unconditionally successful. But the approach to these impersonations had been more mocking or satirical than sexual. On the other hand, Sylvia Scarlett's former fiancé (Brian Aherne) is more aroused by her as a young man than as a young woman, and another woman finds her so attractive that she plants a passionate kiss on her mouth, which does not shock Sylvia Scarlett.*

---

* Transvestism in films had been confined mostly to men dressed as women for comedic purposes until 1935. Wallace Beery (1886–1949) had appeared as Sweedie in a series of silent comedies, Julian Eltinge (1882–1941), an American female impersonator, had made a silent version of the perennial favorite, *Charley's Aunt*, and Stan Laurel had appeared in *That's My Wife* and *Jitterbugs*. Other films with situations where men dressed as women followed: Lon Chaney (1883–1930) in *The Unholy Three*, Lionel Barrymore (1878–1954) in *The Devil Doll*, William Powell (1892–1984) in *Love Crazy*, Cary Grant (1904–   ) in *I Was a Male War Bride*, Joe E. Brown (1892–1973) in *The Daring Young Man*, Dudley Moore (1935–   ) and Peter Cook (1937–   ) in *Bedazzled*, Alec Guinness (1914–   ) in *Kind Hearts and Coronets*, Peter Sellers (1925–1980) in *The Mouse That Roared*, Tony Curtis (1925–   ) and Jack Lemmon (1925–   ) in *Some Like It Hot*, Tony Perkins (1932–   ) in *Psycho*, Phil Silvers (1912–   ) and Jack Gilford (1917–   ) in *A Funny Thing Happened on the Way to the Forum*, Bing Crosby (1904–1977) and Bob Hope (1903–   ) in several of their *Road* comedies, and, more recently, Rex Reed (1940–   ) as *Myra Breckinridge* and Dustin Hoffman (1937–   ) as *Tootsie*. In *Turnabout*

The British writer John Collier* was signed to do the script, a fact that in itself showed that Kate and Cukor thought *Sylvia Scarlett* would be a breakthrough film—because Collier (who had never before worked for films) had a literary reputation for the sophisticated and bizarre. Collier, in fact, had just won critical acclaim for a brilliant, satirical novel, *His Monkey Wife*, about a man who marries a monkey.†

"We got John Collier for the script," Cukor later admitted, "so I *must* have been thinking in that way [a daring film]."

But *Sylvia Scarlett* failed (and it appeared at the time to be a *spectacular* failure) not when it attempted to be daring but when Cukor and Kate tried to play it safe. Collier wrote a sensitive and probing script of a woman forced by circumstances before the opening of the film to don men's clothes. Because of her impersonation she begins to examine her own sexuality and her response to men.

Fearful that the audience would not react well to seeing Kate straightaway dressed as a man, Cukor hired Gladys Unger and Mortimer Offner to tone down Collier's script and to tack on a ten-minute prologue and a fifteen-minute end that would show Sylvia Scarlett first as a bereaved daughter whose mother has just died, and then as a dazzling young woman. To do this, the film became caught up in a tangled and superficial plot. (Kate wrote at the time, "This picture makes no sense and I wonder whether George Cukor is aware of the fact, because I don't know what the hell I'm doing.")

(1940), John Hubbard (1914–   ) exchanged bodies with his wife, Carole Landis (1919–1948), and even had a baby. But women disguised as men have been much rarer. After the failure of *Sylvia Scarlett* (although it had become a minor cult film by the 1960s) studios were opposed to stories involving such a changeover and M.G.M. would not agree to Garbo playing Hamlet. Annabella (1909–   ) made *Wings of the Morning* in 1937 with no more success than Hepburn's *Sylvia Scarlett*. Debbie Reynolds (1932–   ) starred in *Goodbye Charlie*, Julie Andrews (1935–   ) in *Victor/Victoria*, and Barbra Streisand (1942–   ) in *Yentl*. To judge by the failure of these films audiences are better able to accept transvestism in men than in women in both comedy and drama.
* John Collier (1901–1982), British writer famed for his polished macabre stories. *Sylvia Scarlett* was his first screen work. He also wrote the screenplays of *Her Cardboard Lover* (1942), *I Am a Camera* (1955) and *The War Lord* (1965).
† This same theme was used to the same startling effect in a musical production number in the film *Cabaret* (1972) underscoring the brutal extent of anti-Semitism in Germany in the 1930s.

Despite its convoluted plot, *Sylvia Scarlett* was beautifully made; Kate gave a superb performance and Cary Grant as a Cockney con man was a revelation, exhibiting the kind of insolent humor that made him a star.*

Cukor had attended the sneak preview of the film in Pasadena and the experience had been a nightmare. People rushed out up the aisles at the point of Kate and Bunny Beatty's ardent kiss. Kate, of course, was dressed as a man and Miss Beatty in her role as a maid did not know she was kissing a woman. (This same dramatic scene was replayed by Barbra Streisand and Amy Irving in *Yentl* with a similarly uncomfortable result.) Nonetheless, Kate had been seen as a sympathetic, lovely young woman in that ten-minute prologue and the audience could not accept the situation.

At the preview Kate sat next to Natalie Paley, who had a supporting role in the film. Both of the women thought that several scenes were meant to be—and were—hilariously funny, but the audience didn't laugh. Finally, Natalie whispered, "Oh, Kate, why don't they laugh?" And Kate replied, "Natalie, they don't think it's funny." During a climactic scene that showed Kate in a full-face close-up reciting an entire Edna St. Vincent Millay poem, the audience began leaving in droves. "It's a disaster," Kate sighed as she slouched down in her seat.

Kate and Cukor found Pandro Berman, their producer, waiting for them at Cukor's house after the preview, nervously cleaning one fingernail with another as he often did in times of tension.

"Pandro, scrap the picture," star and director concurred. "We'll do another picture for you for nothing!"

Berman replied, absolutely serious, "I never want to see either of you again!"†

R.K.O. held back the film for many months, first thinking

---

* Cukor was to say, "Up to then [*Sylvia Scarlett*] Cary [Grant] had been a conventional leading man. This part was extremely well written and he knew this kind of raffish life, he'd been a stilt walker in a circus. And he'd had enough experience by this time to know what he was up to, and suddenly this part hit him, and he felt the ground under his feet."

† Hepburn and Berman were to make four more films together at R.K.O. and two at M.G.M.

they might shelve it and then having Jane Loring edit the "offensive" scenes so that they would be less obvious. Kate had come East and she and Leland Hayward spent time together at Fenwick and in West Hartford. Margaret Sullavan's marriage to William Wyler had ended abruptly; and Kate could hardly have not known that Hayward was once again seeing her, for the gossip mongers had gone immediately to work. Luddy remained a confidant, as did Jane Loring on the West Coast and Laura on the East Coast. And one day during the filming of *Sylvia Scarlett*, a biplane had settled on a landing strip on the film's Malibu location and out stepped R.K.O.'s backer, Howard Hughes. He had come over to where Kate and Cukor sat eating during their lunch break and, in the strained, high-pitched voice that the hard of hearing sometimes possess, he introduced himself. Kate found him somewhat laughable—a stiff, off-center outsider—and displayed her old arrogance. He walked off and flew away, but returned often. Kate gave him no chance for personal conversation. Yet once she had left Hollywood, he began sending her flowers and she saw him a few times, considerably revising her first impression.

The reviews of *Sylvia Scarlett* upon its release in early 1936 were exactly what Kate had expected. All the major critics found the film ineffective, offensive, or not to their liking. Kate's personal reviews, on the other hand, were extremely good. "The dynamic Miss Hepburn is the handsomest boy of the season," wrote Richard Watts, Jr., of the *New York Herald Tribune*, adding, "I don't care for *Sylvia Scarlett* a bit, but I do think Miss Hepburn is much better in it than she was as the small-town wallflower in *Alice Adams*."

Time declared: "*Sylvia Scarlett* reveals the interesting fact that Katharine Hepburn is better looking as a boy than a woman. . . . Miss Hepburn plays with her best intuition, a scene in which a woman who has played a man so long that she has abdicated her sex tries to become a woman for the man she loves." Thornton Delehanty of the *New York Post* concluded, "And [*Sylvia Scarlett*] is a tour de force, made possible by [Miss Hepburn's] physical resemblance to the adolescent male [but] there is no justification for Miss Hepburn's throwing herself away on a part that demands little more than a studied imitation of gesture and intonation. Cary

Grant comes near to stealing the picture with his bitingly humorous portrait of a Cockney ne'er-do-well."

Grant was paid $15,000 for the six weeks of filming *Sylvia Scarlett*, considerably less than Hepburn's $50,000 fee.* Grant recalls their first meeting: "She was this slip of a woman, skinny, and I never liked skinny women. But she had this thing, this air, you might call it, the most totally magnetic woman I'd ever seen, and probably have ever seen since. You had to look at her, you had to listen to her, there was no escaping her. But it wasn't just the beauty, it was the style. She's incredibly down to earth. She can see right through the nonsense in life. She cares, but about things that really matter."

Viewed today, *Sylvia Scarlett* can be seen as amazingly ahead of its time, and Kate's androgyne a remarkable portrait of a sensitive, vital, straightforward woman facing her own sexuality in an engaging and often enlightening manner. But the film's release in 1936 was damaging to Kate's popularity. Her choices of *Mary of Scotland*, *A Woman Rebels* and *Quality Street*, all heavy period dramas, as her next three films, almost finished her career entirely.

Maxwell Anderson's† *Mary of Scotland,* starring Helen Hayes as Mary Stuart and Fredric March as the Earl of Bothwell, had been the *succès d'estime* of the 1933–34 theater season. Dudley Nichols's adaptation eliminated the blank verse of the original, but otherwise it remained faithful. As with Elizabeth and Essex and Henry VIII, the heroic proportions of Mary Stuart's life have a fascination and validity that even a poor or faulty** retelling cannot destroy.

From the moment Kate had seen the play she had been convinced she should portray Mary Stuart on screen and had been equally certain that Cukor should direct her in it. But after the disaster of *Sylvia Scarlett*, Pandro Berman refused to team them together again. Berman wanted—and got—John

---

* Hepburn also had a large percentage of the profits, but by 1984 the film had not yet recouped its original cost of one million dollars.

† Maxwell Anderson (1888–1959) won the Pulitzer Prize in 1933 for *Both Your Houses*, which was on Broadway the same year as his *Mary of Scotland*.

** Both play and film include a dramatic confrontation between Mary Stuart and Elizabeth I, but history does not record a meeting between the two queens.

Ford,* considered at the time to be the greatest American film director since D. W. Griffith. Ford was a masterful storyteller and his images had a sense of poetry to them. But his own patently male chauvinist feelings were reflected in the film, and *Mary of Scotland* failed because of them. None of Kate's or Mary Stuart's strength was allowed to show through. Instead, Mary became "a soft-focused unfairly slandered Madonna of the Scottish moors."

At the start of shooting, Kate and Ford "fought, bickered, and fussed." Except for Cukor, she had never encouraged camaraderie during filming with her directors or, for that matter, with any of her leading men or the cast members. Her buddies continued to be the technicians; and on *Mary of Scotland*, Jane Loring acted as film editor and the two women were almost inseparable. The choice of Loring as editor, whomever's choice it might have been, was a serious error in judgment. Loring, albeit a talented woman, lacked the kind of vision the film needed. Nor did she have an understanding or perception of history. She cut the film to best frame Kate and highlight her performance, which did not heighten the film's dramatic impact. But perhaps the most serious error on Kate's part was falling hard for her director midway through the film and subduing her views to his autocratic control.

"Pappy" Ford was a powerful personality, a strong Irish Catholic, a hard drinker, and a man's man. He possessed a magnetic charm and a gift for storytelling. Within a short time, he had won Kate over and members of the cast and crew suspected that they were having an affair. Ford, married and the father of two children, was twelve years Kate's senior. His age and accomplishments made Kate look up to him. He had an authoritarian quality not unlike Dr. Hepburn's and would take only so much of her bossiness before

___

* John Ford (1895–1973), born Sean Aloysius O'Fearna. Ford changed his name to become an actor and appeared in small roles in some films of his older brother, film producer Francis Ford (1883–1953). John Ford directed his first feature film, *Straight Shooting*, in 1917. By 1936, with *Arrowsmith*, *The Lost Patrol*, *The Whole Town's Talking*, *The Informer* and *Steamboat 'Round the Bend* to his credit, his reputation was thought to be at its peak. But *Stagecoach*, *The Grapes of Wrath*, *The Long Voyage Home*, *How Green Was My Valley*, *She Wore a Yellow Ribbon*, *The Quiet Man* and *The Searchers*, among many others, were still ahead.

he let her know he would stand for no more. His green eyes turning hard, he would pull from his mouth the pipe he constantly smoked and knock it against a wall or into an ashtray—a signal for her to behave. Weekends they met at Kate's house and then stole away with elaborate precaution to spend time together on Ford's yacht, the *Araner*. He liked to fish and sail and Kate baited his hook and her own and helped him rig the sails and clean the decks and drop anchor. On Mondays, back on the set, Kate's portrayal of Mary of Scotland began to mellow and form itself more into Ford's concept of the role than her own.

In *Mary of Scotland*, as in all her earlier films, Kate refused to have a stunt woman double for her in dangerous shots. She reveled in undertaking the physically difficult things that no one expected her to be able to do. For a scene in *Sylvia Scarlett*, against Cukor's wishes, she had climbed a rainspout to rooftop height and hung by her hands. Suddenly her fingers started slipping and if it had not been for alert crew members who had caught her she would have been seriously injured. The scenario of *Mary of Scotland* called for Mary, wearing high-heeled pumps and a voluminous gown that weighed fifteen pounds, to run down a flight of stone steps and then, with no pause, vault to the back of a spirited horse, unassisted, and ride away at breakneck speed sidesaddle. Ford insisted Kate let a stunt woman do the scene, which he would shoot from a distance. "Mary of Scotland supposedly did it," Kate balked, "and I'm a damned good horsewoman." Ford refused to back down. In the end, Kate won out and did the hazardous scene, not once but eleven times before Ford, determined to teach her a lesson, was satisfied with the results. As she walked back to her dressing room, the entire crew stood at attention and applauded. No wonder the technicians held her in such great awe. Unfortunately, that kind of derring-do, perhaps because of the courage and grit it displayed, created a negative reaction in her co-actors, who were not athletes and had to use doubles, and in her director, whose authority had been challenged successfully.

With the finish of *Mary of Scotland* in the spring of 1936, Kate returned East to Fenwick for a month and Ford pursued her. They sailed on the Long Island Sound and played highly competitive golf matches at a nearby country club. Neither could stand losing to the other. They went to New York and spent time with Laura and Luddy, much to Ford's displeasure, then they returned to Fenwick. Dr. Hepburn had not been too keen on the young Irish Catholic boy Kate had been enamored of as a young girl. Ford impressed him little better. As far as Dr. Hepburn was concerned, Ford was a philandering married man using Kate poorly. By summer, the romance had diminished.

Work filled Kate's life during the rest of 1936. She had rented a five-acre estate in Laurel Canyon which she shared with a cook-housekeeper, chauffeur, maid, two black-and-white cocker spaniels named Michael and Peter (the monkey having long ago been given to the Los Angeles Zoo), Button, a small French poodle, and Cocoa, a Siamese cat. She never attended any Hollywood parties or premieres. Occasionally she would turn up unexpectedly at George Cukor's on a Sunday afternoon, and Leland Hayward returned to figure prominently in her life.

She followed *Mary of Scotland* with *A Woman Rebels*, based on the novel *Portrait of a Rebel* by Netta Syrett. The story of a woman's struggle against the strict conventions of her time (the 1870s) intrigued Kate for obvious reasons. The rebel in the title, Pamela Thistlewaite, becomes a crusading editor of a women's magazine and has an affair with a young man (Van Heflin*) who leaves her with an illegitimate child. Pamela then refuses the safe refuge of marriage to a man (Herbert Marshall)† who has always loved her.

A Woman Rebels represents an effort on the part of R.K.O. and Kate to re-create the success of *Little Women*. Both films were set in the Victorian period and dealt with the

---

* Van Heflin (1910–1971) made his film debut in *A Woman Rebels*. Later he appeared on the stage with Hepburn in *The Philadelphia Story* in the role played by James Stewart in the film. He and Hepburn were never to work together again. His many films included *Johnny Eager* (1942), for which he won the Best Supporting Actor Academy Award, *Shane* (1953), *Battle Cry* (1955) and *Patterns* (1956); there were notable stage performances as well, among them *A Case of Libel* (1954) and *A View from the Bridge* (1955).

† Herbert Marshall (1890–1966) lost a leg in World War I but successfully disguised the handicap throughout his long career as a Hollywood leading man, perhaps best known for his performances in *The Letter* (1940) and *The Little Foxes* (1941).

revolt of a young woman against convention. But *A Woman Rebels* had none of the vitality or the story detail of *Little Women* and the basic theme of a woman refusing to marry for the sole purpose of legitimizing her child bordered on soap opera. Kate's "well-modulated" performance saved the film from complete mediocrity. Mark Sandrich,* who directed, was entirely out of his element with a film so flagrantly lavender and old lace. Sandrich had directed the first three Astaire and Rogers musicals and went on to do two more. He possessed a lighthearted, light-handed talent for comedy of a sophisticated, contemporary nature. Lacking any depth of understanding of Kate's character, he concentrated with meticulous detail on evoking the period through lighting, camera angles, costumes (Kate had twenty-two changes designed by Walter Plunkett) and set direction. The result was a historically accurate but dull and slowly paced film.

Jane Loring retained her position as film editor on *A Woman Rebels*, but when production began on *Quality Street*† in October, 1936, she was not assigned to do the film, which reunited George Stevens and Kate. Stevens, who had not appreciated Loring's subjective work on *Alice Adams*, insisted she be barred from the set (reminiscent of Jed Harris's refusal to continue rehearsal of *The Lake* until Laura Harding had left the theater). Kate always liked her "gang" close by when she worked. At that time, besides Loring, it included Kate's dresser-secretary, Emily Perkins, and her stand-in, Eve March. Stevens felt this group influenced Kate too deeply. "Kate was confused by them," he said. "Their advice was so diverse, she didn't know what she was doing . . . she had a very good head on her shoulders, but she picked out lightweights to think with, and that was a mistake. She doesn't need a lightweight . . . she needs someone who will question her judgments."

---

* Mark Sandrich (1900–1945) directed *The Gay Divorcee* (1934), *Top Hat* (1935), *Follow the Fleet* (1936), *Shall We Dance* (1937) and *Carefree* (1938), all with Fred Astaire and Ginger Rogers. He also produced and directed *Skylark* (1941) and *Holiday Inn* (1942).

† *Quality Street*, by James M. Barrie, was first presented in London in 1900 and brought to the United States the following year by Charles Frohman. Marion Davies starred in a 1927 silent film based on the play, which had starred Maude Adams.

All the women on the set, Kate included, seemed to be secretly in love with Stevens. Part Cherokee Indian, he possessed striking, dark good looks and could have been called the strong, silent type. He would sometimes pace for hours with his pipe rammed in his mouth, eyes averted, saying nothing while the whole company waited for his next instruction. (Once, during the making of an early Ginger Rogers film, Rogers shouted out, "Eureka!" Everyone turned to look at her. "I know what George is thinking when he paces like that—not a fucking thing!")

Feeling not any better matched to the material of James Barrie's stylized whimsy in *Quality Street* than Mark Sandrich had been to the melodrama of *A Woman Rebels,* Stevens had not wanted to direct this story, about a spinster schoolteacher in 1805 who gets revenge on the man who once spurned her by masquerading as her own nonexistent flirtatious niece. A determined Kate finally got him to agree, but his resentment at his own weakness in doing so remained throughout the making of the film. "I don't think I did her any good," he admitted. "She became precious, and preciousness was always her weakness. . . . *Quality Street* was a precious play, anyway, full of precious people, and that infected her; I myself didn't have sufficient familiarity with the British background to save her." (Why R.K.O. chose to make *Quality Street* after the failure of *The Little Minister,* another one of J. M. Barrie's stylized dramas, is difficult to comprehend.)

During the entire filming of *Quality Street,* Kate was under tremendous stress. Leland Hayward did not come around as often as before and the fact that he was her agent and manager as well made things very difficult. Then, at one of George Cukor's Sunday salons in November—halfway through *Quality Street*—the news came over the radio that Hayward and Margaret Sullavan had just married. Kate managed to get through the afternoon, but the information had visibly shaken her. She sent the newlyweds a congratulatory telegram. For several days, Kate was so distressed by this news that she was sick to her stomach on the set, confessing to co-worker Joan Fontaine how deeply she had been hurt. She kept to herself a lot and looked somehow like "a little lost boy," perched on a stool in either her slacks or a hiked-up costume, leaning forward, arm on knee, puffing away at a cigarette as though she might be sneaking a smoke behind the garage. California suddenly became oppressive, her friendship with Jane Loring had hit a snag, and her expectations of working again with George Stevens had disappointed her. To the surprise of most of her associates, she began to see Howard Hughes on a fairly steady basis. "[I don't know] what she was doing with Howard Hughes," Kate's friend, author and screenwriter Anita Loos,* said. "He had a whole stable of girls, and Kate simply wasn't the type to have anything to do with that kind of thing."

However, that was a challenge in itself to Kate, who seemed to like difficult, individualistic men. Then too, she and Hughes shared several enthusiasms—aviation, golf and films, and Hughes had a monied background like herself.

His vast wealth gave him power that he did not have to seek; his genius gave him "stardom" without personal compromise; he welcomed challenge, breaking new ground and setting new records. Kate had nothing but admiration for such a man, no matter what his other weaknesses. But, perhaps most important, Hughes found Kate's unbound and adventurous spirit irresistible. With her life at sixes and sevens, *Quality Street* a complete failure and her career at low ebb, Kate was susceptible.

"Her Phoebe Throssel needs a neurologist far more than a husband," wrote Frank Nugent at *The New York Times* of her role in *Quality Street.* "Such flutterings and jitterings and twitchings, such hand-wringings and mouth-quiverings, such runnings about and eyebrow-raisings have not been seen on a screen in many a moon." And regarding Herbert Marshall's performance, Graham Greene, at the time film critic for *The Spectator,* wrote, "Mr. Marshall, so intractably British . . . does, I suppose, represent some genuine national characteristics, if not those one wishes to see exported; characteristics which it is necessary to describe in terms of inanimate objects; a kind of tobacco, a kind of tweed, a kind of pipe—or in terms of a dog, something large, sentimental and moulting, something which confirms one's preference for cats" (the

---

* Anita Loos (1893–1981), best known as the author of the 1925 novel *Gentlemen Prefer Blondes.*

latter a reference to Kate's "clawing, scratching, back-arching" performance as Phoebe Throssel).

She went home to West Hartford in time for Christmas with a new admirer and the prospect of doing a play for the Theatre Guild. Most important, she would be near her father, always a steadying influence in her life and never needed more by his headstrong, supremely admiring daughter.

CHAPTER
12

Dr. Hepburn at fifty-seven still looked extremely youthful, his red hair brushed artfully with gray, his strong, angular face dominated as always by his wide-set brown eyes, and his six-foot body kept compact and trim by daily exercise. His agile mind and firm resolve had only sharpened with the years. Whenever Kate spoke to him—and they were in steady contact—she came away mindful of his high intelligence and good common sense. She believed in him completely, trusted his judgment, and constantly quoted his opinions whenever a point was to be made. He showed an enormous interest in everything she did and was a source of infinite strength. More than that, he had never let her down. Kate looked for her father's qualities in every man she met, and found each lacking.

Approaching thirty in 1936, Kate still referred to the men in her life as "beaux." She considered her parents' relationship unique and ideal—one in which a man and a woman could live in the same house and yet respect each other's need for time alone. "In my relationships," Kate admitted, "I know that I have qualities that are offensive to people—especially men. I'm loud and talkative and I get onto subjects that irritate. If I feel these things causing a break, I know something has to give. I never think the man is going to give—or anyone else, for that matter—so I do. I just deliberately change. I just shut up—when every atom in me wants to speak up." Resentments thus accumulated threatened the stability of her close relationships. She rationalized that marriage was not for her anyway. "Well, I'll never marry," she recalled thinking at this time. "I want to be a star, and I don't want to make my husband my victim. And I certainly don't want to make my children my victims."

Nonetheless, she *had* considered marrying Leland Hayward and knew he was a man who liked and wanted children. Howard Hughes was another matter, a man who did not know how, or care, to share anything, particularly the attention of a woman he desired, with demanding, small people.

A long time would pass before Kate would bring Howard Hughes home to meet her parents. "I'm like the girl who never grew up you see?" she told writer Ralph Martin.* "I just never really left home, so to speak. I always went back there [West Hartford and Fenwick] almost every weekend of my life when I wasn't filming. I kept my life there, my roots. . . . And when I went back there I didn't go to *my* atmosphere: I went to *their* atmosphere—of which I was a part. I was going to my father's house . . . that's very unusual, isn't it? Very, very unusual that someone who's sort of made it in the big world could still want to go home to their father's house?"

And home she came for Thanksgiving, 1936, her six-film deal with R.K.O. completed, her popularity slipping, and her feelings for Howard Hughes confused by the too recent betrayal of Leland Hayward. Despite the winter cold, she spent the weekends at Fenwick, swimming every day in Long Island Sound, staying in the water as long as she could bear it, then rushing out, bundling up and, in a short while, dashing back in again. She took long, brisk walks, straight uphill or through the woods, crawling under bushes and climbing over fences in her direct path. Paradise was "getting up at 4:30 or five o'clock in the morning . . . the house absolutely quiet

---

* Ralph Martin (1920-   ), author of *Jennie*, *The Woman He Loved*, and *Cissy*. He interviewed Hepburn at length in 1975.

. . . a big roaring fire. . . and a great big breakfast; bacon, chicken livers, steaks and eggs . . . orange juice and a big pot of coffee . . . then I watched the sun rise. Oh, golly, Paradise!"

Paradise was interrupted by a telegram from the Theatre Guild asking her to accept their offer of $1,000 a week to play Jane Eyre on tour before bringing it into New York. Promptly she demanded $1,500. When the Guild agreed, she pointed out that the extra $500 was payment for the humiliation she had suffered seven years earlier when they had refused a salary increase from $30 to $35 a week during the run of *A Month in the Country*.

The new adaptation of the Charlotte Brontë novel, written by Helen Jerome, had opened in London at the Queens Theatre on October 13, 1936, to mixed reviews. *Jane Eyre* had appealed to actresses as a starring vehicle within only six months of the novel's publication in England in October, 1847.* For Kate, the role was a startling choice. *Jane Eyre* is melodramatic and Victorian to the last inch and Helen Jerome's version retained the speech, the manners and the spiritual essence of the period drama. One would have thought that, after the dazzling failure of her last three costume dramas, Kate would have chosen a more contemporary and lighthearted play in which to return to the stage, especially in view of the unsuccessful, melancholic production of *The Lake*. However, no other play was in the offing; and having learned from her experience with Jed Harris, this time she planned to stay on the road until the play and her performance were polished.

To her delight, Worthington (Tony) Miner, who had been the one responsive person connected with *The Lake*, was to direct. The production was to go into immediate rehearsal in New Haven. This meant she could commute from West Hartford and be home for Christmas as well. Not wanting to drive after a full day's rehearsal, Kate had the company

---

* *Jane Eyre* has had numerous productions in both the United States and England. None of the twentieth-century productions has been successful. An actress named Charlotte Thompson toured the United States intermittently in the first stage adaptation, from 1874 to 1888, with considerable personal success.

manager, Herman Bernstein, hire her a chauffeured car, not easily available in small cities during the depth of the Depression, especially during a Christmas holiday. Bernstein, a resourceful gentleman, discovered that the one available limousine in town was owned by Weller's Funeral Home. The car—a long, sleek, black number—was used in funeral processions. When Harry Weller heard who was to be driven to West Hartford each night, he offered his own services as chauffeur, for Katharine Hepburn was his favorite film star.

Dressed in his best black undertaker's suit, Weller waited outside the theater every evening Kate was in New Haven. A man of old-world charm and sly good humor, he and Kate—who very much enjoyed his Yiddish stories—got on well. One night they had to drive through a terrible ice storm and the trip took twice as long as usual.

"You must be hungry, Mr. Weller," Kate said as they pulled into her father's driveway. "You better come in and have something to eat and drink before you turn around."

Weller explained that he was an Orthodox Jew and that he ate only kosher food. "My wife would kill me if I ate *traif*." He thought a moment. "But then on the other hand, she'd kill me if I didn't go in and see your house." And he followed her to the door.

Jane Eyre opened in New Haven on December 26, 1936. Kate's name appeared at her request below the title and in the same size print as the other actors. The Theatre Guild had settled upon Dennis Hoey,* a reliable English stage and film actor generally featured in supporting roles, to play Mr. Rochester. *Jane Eyre* traveled from New Haven to Boston, and then on to Kansas City, Missouri, Cleveland, Chicago, Pittsburgh, Washington, D.C., and ended its tour in Baltimore on April 3, 1937. Kate's reviews along the way had been mixed, Hoey's notices excellent. But Helen Jerome's retelling of the story of the little governess who goes to Thornfield Hall

---

* Dennis Hoey (1893–1960) made his stage debut in 1918 singing in operettas. He appeared in his first film in 1930. His most famous role was that of Inspector Lestrade in six Sherlock Holmes films during the 1940s. Before *Jane Eyre*, Hoey had finished a season of Shakespeare and starred in an Australian film. *Uncivilized.*

and falls in love with her gruff employer had third-act trouble from the start, and despite constant rewriting on the road and good business, the Theatre Guild was afraid to bring the show into New York. Kate's name had worked miracles at the box office in cities that weren't often able to see a film star onstage. Broadway audiences had their choice of the greatest names in theater.

Boston felt she played "her not too exacting role with much simplicity and straight-forward intelligence." Cleveland found her "thoroughly delightful . . . she essays the variety of moods her role calls for with the authority of a more seasoned stage player. Even when sitting still she seems to command the mood of the scene by the flutter of a hand or slight change of posture." Baltimore claimed she presented "Charlotte Brontë's prim, yet volatile, heroine with an illuminating insight into the very veins of the little British governess," and Washington "applauded her the more for the fine fervor with which she tackled a difficult part," then added, "Her voice remains her least prepossessing quality as an actress. . . . One wonders . . . if her own vivid personality does not obscure the character she plays—wonders if it is not easier to see Katharine Hepburn in Jane Eyre than Jane Eyre in Katharine Hepburn."*

Theresa Helburn, representing the Guild, had stayed with the show whenever possible. "Kate . . . knew how to do the little pieces of the mosaic by which a film is built up, but she had no conception of building a character through three acts. It was wonderful to watch how she did it, groping her way from a stale performance that had a certain brilliance and charm, but no solid characterization, to the full realization of the woman whom she was portraying."

The tour had been a grueling experience for Kate, more because of the loneliness of the road than because of the hard work. Her friendship with Tony Miner helped, but they did not have the kind of intense camaraderie Kate demanded of close friends. And, although she had insisted upon equal billing with other members of the cast, her interest in them

* *Jane Eyre* ended a fourteen-week run in Baltimore on April 3, 1937, after a record road-tour gross of $340,000.

went no further. Howard Hughes's surprise appearance when the show opened in Chicago was therefore much welcomed. Their meeting also made national headlines. Speculation had them about to marry. Once more, as with Leland Hayward, Kate played the Garbo role with the press, taking great joy in sneaking in or out of a theater without being photographed either alone or with Hughes.

With *Jane Eyre* dissolved, having never been brought into New York, Kate returned to her house in Turtle Bay, now buying and paying the full price (thirty-three thousand dollars) for it so that it became hers outright. She spent a blissful summer, mostly at Fenwick, bolstered by the closeness and warmth of her family as well as by the renewed loyalty of Luddy and Laura. Hughes visited her at Fenwick. The relationship was not on solid ground, but his attention was reassuring and his influence at R.K.O. more than helpful.

Leland Hayward now negotiated a new film deal for her at R.K.O. for seventy-five thousand dollars per picture, a feat that would seem impossible considering the failure of her last three films. She refused the project first offered her* and suggested she play the role of Terry Randall in Edna Ferber and George S. Kaufman's *Stage Door*, which had been a huge hit during the 1936 Broadway season with Margaret Sullavan in the same part.† Not until she reached Hollywood in September and read the final screenplay was Kate aware that another part in the film—Jean Maitland, to be played by Ginger Rogers**—had been built up to equal hers in importance. The inclusion of a star as popular as Ginger Rogers indicated that with seventy-five thousand dollars riding on Kate in one film, R.K.O. wanted to hedge their bet. A second shock came when she received a tentative credit sheet that ranked her name in third place after Ginger Rogers (star

---

* *The Mad Miss Manton*, made finally and unsuccessfully in 1937 (released in 1938) with Barbara Stanwyck in the lead.

† After twenty-two weeks of full houses, *Stage Door* had abruptly closed because Margaret Sullavan (Hayward) was to have a baby. Brooke Hayward was born six months later.

** Ginger Rogers (1911–   ) was at the height of popularity at this time with *Roberta* (1935), *Top Hat* (1935), *Follow the Fleet* (1936), *Swingtime* (1936) and *Shall We Dance* (1937) behind her. Rogers also received seventy-five thousand dollars for her work on *Stage Door*.

billing) and Adolphe Menjou. The studio front office had taken note of the fact that Kate had appeared in seventieth place and Ginger Rogers third on the most recent box-office popularity poll.

Howard Hughes and Leland Hayward had been able to negotiate a high-figured contract for her, but nothing more. Kate confronted Pandro Berman, who was producing the film, demanding better billing. Berman replied, semijokingly, "You'd be lucky if you played seventh part in a successful picture." *Stage Door* now took on the aura of a championship battle.

Director Gregory La Cava* had been hired without Kate's approval. La Cava was a legend, and his ability to handle comedy with a delicate but firm and sophisticated touch was well accepted. W. C. Fields gave La Cava credit for having the best mind in Hollywood for comedy, next to Fields's own. Two of his recent films, both screwball social comedies, *She Married Her Boss* (1935) and *My Man Godfrey* (1936), had been tremendous box-office successes. *Stage Door* was more of a comedy-drama, but R.K.O. wanted to be sure that the film never tipped the scale into bathos; and the tearful quality of some of the story could have caused this to happen.

La Cava leaned strongly toward improvisation. He would gather his cast together on the set and say, "The situation for today is thus and so. Talk and act as you naturally would under those circumstances." Kate would spend hours after a day's shooting discussing the next day's scene and arrive early on the set the following morning to discuss it alone with him again. Because Kate did not trust improvisation, she would work on a scene herself before playing it, writing in and memorizing bits. The main text of the famous calla lilies speech, which constituted Terry Randall's big moment on-

---

* Gregory La Cava (1892–1949) came into his own with sound though he made numerous silent films. Ephraim Katz (*The Film Encyclopedia*) says that "La Cava was known for his ability to overcome weak scripts with his vitality and comic instinct and for his knack of drawing superior performances from actors." Andrew Sarris (*The American Cinema*) adds, "La Cava was most effective when he could work between the lines of his scenarios and against the conventions of his plots." He was nominated for an Academy Award for *Stage Door* and did several films before his premature death, *Unfinished Business* with Irene Dunne and Preston Foster (in a take-off of Billy Rose) being the best of these.

stage, Kate lifted from *The Lake* and was a scene she had played previously well over eighty times.

What saved Kate during the trying production was the beginning of a fine, lifelong friendship with the well-known middle-aged stage performer Constance Collier,* who played the role of a drama coach in the film. Collier's experience in Shakespearean productions and her highly acclaimed theater background very much impressed Kate, who turned often to her for advice on interpretation. But, also, the older woman had a warm, generous nature and a lively intelligence.

Midway through the film, Kate's role somehow became more dominant than Ginger Rogers's. Temperaments flared and La Cava used his two stars' rivalry to the film's advantage. When La Cava shot Kate's calla lilies speech, he made sure Ginger Rogers was not on the set. "Ginger is strictly the menthol type," La Cava later explained. "The only way I'd ever been able to get her to cry before was to tell her her house was burning down." Rogers was required by the script to shed tears after Kate's speech. When Kate was finished with the scene, Ginger Rogers was called onto the set. La Cava committed the impossible. He now told her dramatically that her house had burned to the ground. She wept. (A story spread throughout Hollywood that during the filming Kate had deliberately thrown a pail of water on Ginger Rogers's new mink coat with Ginger in it and then screamed, "If it is real mink, Ginger, it won't shrink!")

Terry Randall in the final film version of *Stage Door* is a rich society girl who desperately wants to be an actress. To help her succeed, her father backs a production so that she can play an important role. Kaye, the girl whom she replaces (Andrea Leeds),† commits suicide. During all of this Terry has been living at The Footlights Club, which is home to a less affluent group of would-be actresses. Terry is disliked by one

---

* Constance Collier (1878–1955) was born Laura Hardie in Windsor, Berks, England, and made a grand success as a dramatic actress before she was twenty. She appeared in more than one hundred theater productions. She made her film debut in 1916 in D. W. Griffith's *Intolerance*. Later she was in nineteen films, mainly playing women in the grande dame manner.

† Andrea Leeds (1914–1984) was nominated but did not win the Academy Award for Best Supporting Actress for *Stage Door*. That award in 1937 went to Alice Brady for her role in *In Old Chicago*.

and all, but her most violent antagonist is her acid-tongued roommate, Jean Maitland (Ginger Rogers). The tragedy of Kaye's death-leap from a high window dispels Terry's arrogance and adds great emotion and meaning to the role she has taken from her. With her humble curtain speech, Terry wins the respect of Jean Maitland and the rest of the girls at The Footlights Club.

(In the stage version, Terry Randall suffers all manner of setback but sticks to her guns and becomes a legitimate actress while Jean, her roommate, goes to Hollywood and loses what talent she had.)

The film, though certainly not a probing drama of any great insight, had much more logic and vitality than the play, and La Cava's smooth comedy touches and the abundance of smart repartee gave the picture style and pacing.

The critic for *Life* magazine wrote: "To both of its female stars, *Stage Door* is likely to be a career milestone. Before this picture Katharine Hepburn, following a succession of costume pictures which stifled her talent, was in danger of losing her status as a star. Ginger Rogers on the other hand had become No. 3 box-office attraction as one-half of a dancing team but still faced the problem of what she would do without Fred Astaire in a straight dramatic role. *Stage Door* answers both these problems. It proves that Miss Rogers is a talented comedienne and that Miss Hepburn really is, as her early pictures indicated, potentially, the screen's greatest actress."

La Cava said of Kate, "She is completely the intellectual actress. She has to understand the why of everything before she can feel. Then, when the meaning has soaked in, emotion comes, and superb work."

George Stevens agreed: "Moreover, when the emotion takes hold, she isn't the kind of actress who counts six steps forward, then two to the left. She goes into a scene and lives it, and you have to steer her like an automaton through the mechanical part."

Kate felt certain the bad years were behind her and that she had won over the critics and Hollywood. *Gone With the Wind* had been published the previous year and she had wanted to play Scarlett O'Hara from the time she read the galleys.*

---

* R.K.O. was, in fact, the first studio to receive the galleys of *Gone With the*

Pandro Berman had not been enthusiastic about the idea of another costume picture when the second set of galleys was sent to him, and so, to Kate's great disappointment, R.K.O. had passed on the project, and the option was picked up by David Selznick. Scarlett O'Hara had still not been cast when Kate finished *Stage Door*, and she badgered Selznick for a chance to do it. Selznick refused to commit himself. He did not think Kate had the necessary sex appeal for the role. La Cava had felt quite differently. To him, Kate generated great sex magnetism on screen—a kind of excitement no other actress had. "To win her, to beat down that proud, impervious hauteur, is a challenge only the most virile and dominant male could afford to take up. That's the sort of man who should play opposite her . . . and if he were strong enough to make her melt—oh—that would be worth filming. She's never had a leading man like that. They've always let her be the master."

Against R.K.O.'s advice, Kate now became a leader in a theatrical union jurisdictional fight between actors' unions and stagehands. Newspapers carried headlines like HEPBURN HURLS BOLT AT AFL IN THEATER BATTLE.* Issuing a strong statement that indicated she would participate in a theater actors' strike if the AFL disregarded the claims of the actors' union, the Associated Actors and Artists of America, she threatened to fly to Atlantic City to protest at an AFL convention (which she did not do). The image of the battling activist was not helpful to her popularity, no matter how right her cause might have been.

When Kate began work on a new film—*Bringing Up Baby*, opposite Cary Grant—Laura rejoined her on the West Coast. Howard Hughes, after two years, was still chasing her and, not unlike Scarlett, Kate had succeeded in keeping him interested without any commitment on her part. *Bringing Up*

Wind from Macmillan Publishers. The studio turned the property down without any negotiation or bid on their part. Warner Brothers bid for the book on Bette Davis's behalf, but refused to go over forty thousand dollars. Selznick bought it for fifty thousand dollars.

* AFL: Associated Federation of Labor. This dispute had at its heart the AFL's wish to control the hiring of all theater workers. It was to continue for many years and spread further into the film industry, where a strike did occur.

Baby was a zany madcap farce. The "baby" of the title is an eight-year-old leopard named Nissa, owned in the film by a spoiled heiress who manages to persuade a zoologist (Grant) whom she fancies to take care of it, with the sole intent of winning his affections—the zoologist's that is.

Kate had no qualms about working with Nissa and even agreed to the trainer's* request that she wear a certain perfume that never failed to make the leopard playful. Nonetheless, Kate did put resin on the soles of her shoes to prevent a sudden slip that might alarm Nissa. Nissa's impressed trainer commented, "If Miss Hepburn should ever decide to leave the screen she could make a very good animal trainer. She has control of her nerves and, best of all, no fear of animals."

Both Kate and Cary Grant reacted well to Howard Hawks's "bullet-speed direction."† Hawks was not fully appreciated by the critics in 1938, perhaps because of the eclectic list of credits he had at the time—from the violent *Scarface* (1932) to the slapstick *Twentieth Century* (1934) on to the adventurous *Ceiling Zero* and *The Road to Glory* (1936). *Bringing Up Baby* had a theme that almost all his later films contained: the concept that "a man is measured by his work rather than his ability to communicate with women." Kate respected Hawks's good sense and firm attitudes. The admiration was returned. Hawks said of Kate, "She has an amazing body—like a boxer. It's hard for her to make a wrong turn. She's always in perfect balance. She has that beautiful coordination that allows you to stop and make a turn and never fall off balance. This gives her an amazing sense of timing. I've never seen a girl that had that odd rhythm and control."

As filming neared completion, the Independent Theatre Owners Association published the names of performers who

---

* Mme. Olga Celeste was the trainer. Another animal also appeared with Hepburn in the film: a small wirehaired terrier named Skippy, who had won renown as Asta in *The Thin Man* series and as Mr. Smith in *The Awful Truth*.
† Howard Hawks (1896–1977) later directed *Only Angels Have Wings* (1939), *To Have and Have Not* (1944), *Red River* (1948) and *Gentlemen Prefer Blondes* (1953), among other films. Critic Andrew Sarris lists Hawks as one of Hollywood's fourteen pantheon directors.

were "box office poison." Kate's name led the list, which included Joan Crawford, Greta Garbo and Marlene Dietrich. That all these women portrayed mature, independent, often rebellious, characters and that the most popular "women" on the box-office poll were Shirley Temple, Deanna Durbin and Ginger Rogers provides insight into the taste of cinema audiences in 1937–38. With Europe in ferment and the Depression not yet behind them, American filmgoers looked to movies for easy forgetfulness. *Bringing Up Baby* would one day be an acknowledged classic. But despite its farcical content, its major characters were intellectuals (Grant even wore glasses), and the dialogue was considered too literary.*

R.K.O. took the press's verdict on Kate seriously. The film, by the time of completion of principal photography, had cost nearly one million dollars; but the studio decided to shelve it rather than invest another hundred thousand or more to edit, score and advertise it. Howard Hughes came to the rescue, bought it from R.K.O. and sold it to the Loew's chain.

"For *Bringing Up Baby* [Hepburn] plumps her broad A in the midst of a frantically farcical plot involving actor Cary Grant, a terrier, a leopard, a Brontosaurus skeleton and a crotchety collection of Connecticut quidnuncs, and proves she can be as amusingly skittery a comedienne as the best of them," wrote the *Time* critic. Others labeled her performance "invigorating," "breezy," and equal to "Miss [Carole] Lombard's best." She had now proved to be "a comedienne of the highest order," but she had been late in making such a film. The vogue for screwball comedy was over.

Despite Howard Hughes's bailout, *Bringing Up Baby* lost $365,000 for R.K.O. The studio was in a quandary as to what to do about Kate, to whom they were committed to pay $75,000 for each of two more films. The front office was well aware of Kate's considerable personal fortune. They also had first-hand experience with her tolerance level for any attempt to undermine her position (her fight to gain top billing in *Stage Door* over Ginger Rogers being proof). To follow

---

* The screenplay of *Bringing Up Baby* was written by Dudley Nichols (1895–1960) and Hagar Wilde (1904–1971) from the latter's original story. Nichols had also written the screenplay of *Stagecoach*.

Bringing Up Baby, the studio perfidiously offered her one of the leads in *Mother Carey's Chickens,* a small-budget film scheduled as a programmer to fill out a double bill, a step above a short subject. Kate refused. The studio insisted she would have to appear in it or *buy out her contract.* With her father's approval, she decided (as the studio moguls had hoped she would) to do the latter, at a cost of $220,000, confident that one of the major studios would offer her a good role in a top film for a commensurate salary. Metro-Goldwyn-Mayer, despite the fact that Joan Crawford had also been labeled "box office poison," had re-signed her to a new five-year contract for $1.5 million a year, three pictures a year, and had cast her opposite one of the top box-office favorites—Spencer Tracy—in *Mannequin.* Leland Hayward let it be known that Kate was available and would feel comfortable at a studio where good stories were a prime consideration for their stars. Metro offered her $10,000 for a one-film deal, but George Cukor came to Kate's rescue.

Cukor was set to direct a remake of *Holiday* for Columbia Studios.* Harry Cohn, Columbia's studio head, wanted the film to reunite Irene Dunne and Cary Grant, who had scored a hit the previous year in *The Awful Truth.* Cukor urged Cohn, who was renowned for his pursuit and conquest of beautiful women, to sign Kate for the role. Forty-six years old at the time, his hair thinning and his broad, short body tending to flab, Cohn nonetheless retained a striking appearance that many women found attractive. He had the sharp-cut features, a square, firm jaw, decisive body movements and intensely blue eyes that let a woman know in a most unguarded fashion that he desired her. Chameleon in his approach to women, he could be courtly with a regal actress like Ethel Barrymore and blunt with a woman he either knew or suspected might not be exactly as she seemed. At the end of a private conference with Margaret Sullavan, he had remarked, "Willie Wyler tells me you're great in the hay." Sullavan rose and replied scornfully, "You didn't hear that

---

* *Holiday* had previously been filmed in 1930 by R.K.O. with Ann Harding playing Linda Seton, Robert Ames as Johnny Case, and Mary Astor as Julia Seton. Columbia had paid eighty thousand dollars to R.K.O. in 1936 for a group of old scripts, *The Awful Truth* and *Holiday* among them.

from Willie. He is too much of a gentleman to discuss such things with you." As she reached the door on her way out, she paused a moment to add, "But I am."

He used the same line with Kate, substituting Leland Hayward's name for Wyler's. Kate went on talking at a fast clip as though she hadn't heard him. Cohn repeated himself. Kate still did not pause in her conversation or give any indication that she had heard what he said the second time either. He agreed with Cukor that she should play the role she had once understudied on Broadway and never made another stab at a come-on again. Once the picture was in production, he spared no cost in making *Holiday*.*

Kate worked well with Grant under Cukor's suave, knowing hand, and the additional smart, literate dialogue inserted into the Barry play by screenwriter Donald Ogden Stewart† helped immeasurably. Howard Barnes at the *New York Herald Tribune* called Kate's Linda Seton "a vibrant, moving performance . . . first class screen acting." *Time* was certain her performance as Linda Seton would "refute the argument of New York's Independent Theatre Owners Association . . . that her box office appeal was practically nil." The usually dissenting Frank S. Nugent of *The New York Times* wrote that "Miss Hepburn—the 'New Hepburn' according to the publicity copy—is very mannish in this one, deep-voiced, grammatically precise, and is only a wee bit inclined to hysteria," but added, "*Holiday* comes close to being one . . . and a pleasant one too."

Film audiences of its time unfortunately did not agree. In 1938, when any decent job was still hard to come by, Johnny Case's terribly impractical plan to give up solid, high-salaried employment to see the world while young enough to enjoy it,

---

* Bob Thomas, Harry Cohn's biographer (*King Cohn*, 1967), wrote, "Cohn liked to surround himself with beautiful things and beautiful people. He supervised with meticulous care the glamour trappings of his female stars; he would sometimes order three revisions of a simple hairdo. Many an expensive gown was scrapped because Cohn declared, 'It *looks* cheap.'"

† Donald Ogden Stewart (1894–1980), formerly an actor, had played the role of Johnny Case's friend, Nick Potter, in the stage version of *Holiday* that Hepburn had understudied. (Philip Barry had in fact written the role with his friend Stewart in mind.) He scripted three more Hepburn films: *The Philadelphia Story* (1940), *Keeper of the Flame* (1942) and *Without Love* (1945). He was the author, as well, of several books.

and Linda Seton's supposed courage in breaking away from her gilded existence to join him, did not inspire enthusiasm. Columbia did not offer Kate a second picture.

Cukor, who had just been signed by David Selznick to direct *Gone With the Wind*,* tried to convince him that Kate would be a splendid Scarlett O'Hara. Selznick still disagreed, feeling it would hurt "the quality of the picture having a girl who has the audience's dislike to beat down." Kate confronted Selznick directly and, after an exhausting hour of her insistence, he offered to test her. Kate refused, telling him, "You know what I look like on the screen. You know I can act. And you know this part was practically written for me. I *am* Scarlett O'Hara. So what's the matter?"

"All right, I'll tell you," Selznick said. "I just can't imagine Clark Gable chasing you for ten years."

Kate shouted back, "I may not appeal to you, David, but there are men with different tastes!" When she had calmed down and her good sense returned, she reminded him, "Well, you've gone out on a limb to find an unknown girl—and you can't tell me you're going to be stupid enough not to find one! So, let us say this, if you get within two days of shooting—and the man who's doing the costumes has dressed me many times—Walter Plunkett†—he could do the first dress in forty-eight hours—you send for me . . . you wouldn't have to pay me anything—and I know you well enough to know you *wouldn't* pay me anything." She then cautioned him about making any premature press announcements concerning her possible casting that could be refuted later if an unknown was found, for that would be humiliating.** Selznick promised

---

* George Cukor was replaced on *Gone With the Wind* by Victor Fleming after three weeks of shooting. Differences of opinion between Cukor and Clark Gable, cast as Rhett Butler, have been generally thought to have precipitated the change. A much more likely reason would be Selznick's feelings that Cukor was undermining his control.

† Walter Plunkett (1902–1982) designed Katharine Hepburn's costumes for *Little Women*, *The Little Minister*, *Alice Adams*, *Mary of Scotland* and *Quality Street*.

** Whether Selznick was responsible or not, Hepburn's name did appear in publicity releases, first as having been Margaret Mitchell's choice for Scarlett O'Hara (denied publicly by Miss Mitchell) and then as being one of the "hottest contenders." However, Selznick used Paulette Goddard, not Hepburn, as a backup, for he never considered her right for the role.

and Kate got ready to leave Hollywood. A few days before her departure, the annual Academy Awards dinner (for films made the year before, 1937) was held. *Stage Door* had received four nominations, but neither she nor Ginger Rogers was nominated for Best Actress.*

Luise Rainer† won her second Oscar as Best Actress for her role as O-lan, the Chinese peasant woman in Pearl Buck's saga of Chinese farm life, *The Good Earth*, and Spencer Tracy, who had played the role of Manuel, a Portuguese fisherman in Rudyard Kipling's *Captains Courageous*, was named Best Actor.** Tracy's wife, Louise Treadwell Tracy,‡ accepted the Oscar for her thirty-eight-year-old husband, who was at the Good Samaritan Hospital in Hollywood, recuperating from a hernia operation. After a lengthy and emotional acceptance speech by Rainer, Mrs. Tracy, tall, slim, dark, and dressed and coiffed elegantly, had risen and said simply, "I accept this on behalf of Spencer, Susie [their daughter], Johnny [their son] and myself." Her few words were met with a thunder of applause. The next morning Ed Sullivan wrote in his daily column, "Mrs. Tracy stole the show. She is just the sort of person you expect Spencer Tracy's wife to be. Simple and unaffected."

Just one week before the Awards, another columnist had announced that the Tracys were separating. Rumors circulated that a longtime liaison between Tracy and actress Loretta Young was the cause. So when Mrs. Tracy mentioned her children, herself and Tracy in her acceptance, "everyone

---

* *Stage Door*'s four Academy Award nominations were: Best Picture (won by *The Life of Emile Zola*), Best Supporting Actress, Andrea Leeds (won by Alice Brady in *In Old Chicago*), Best Director (won by Leo McCarey for *The Awful Truth*) and Best Screenplay (won by *The Life of Emile Zola*). Nominees for Best Actress had been Luise Rainer (*The Good Earth*), Greta Garbo (*Camille*), Janet Gaynor (*A Star Is Born*), Barbara Stanwyck (*Stella Dallas*) and Irene Dunne (*The Awful Truth*).

† Luise Rainer (1910–   ). Born in Vienna, she won two successive Academy Awards. Her first was for *The Great Ziegfeld*, in which she portrayed Anna Held, one of Ziegfeld's wives and one of his greatest stars. Her meteoric career was short. She made only six more films after *The Good Earth*, *The Great Waltz* being the best of them.

** When Tracy examined his statue, he found it to be misinscribed "Dick Tracy."

‡ Louise Treadwell Tracy (1896–1983) appeared in minor roles and performed in stock. She married Tracy in 1923, appeared with him in some stage productions, and then retired to have and raise their children.

present got an immediate picture of a family of four challenging the world to break it up." The rumor that circulated among those attending the 1938 Awards was that Tracy's hospitalization was really to help him "dry out." Tracy was an alcoholic, some went as far as to call him a drunk.

Kate had never met Spencer Tracy, but she had seen all his films and claimed, by her own count, to have sat through *Captains Courageous* fifty-two times and cried each time when Tracy "went down, smiling with his ship." That kind of courage moved her. She admired Tracy as an actor, but she also liked his looks: the craggy, granite face, the intelligent eyes, the gruff, deliberate voice that could contain such a surprising degree of tenderness when directed to do so. She had not attended the Awards, and never would attend such an event; she claimed they gave her dyspepsia. If she had known Spencer Tracy then, she might have repeated one of her father's axioms to him: "If you must drink, drink when you're happy. It'll make you happier. If you drink when you're miserable, it'll only make you more so." Or Dr. Hepburn's opinion that "Drinkers are people who're looking for easy solutions to their problems. The short cuts. There aren't any. Problems have to be faced and solved. You don't do anything with them by getting besotted and pretending they don't exist."

Spencer Tracy's problems were not likely to disappear. A Catholic who did not believe in divorce, a husband who was no longer in love with the wife he respected more than any other woman, a father who had had to come to terms with the physical disability of his only son, and an actor caught in a studio system diametrically opposed to his own free spirit— Spencer Tracy felt desperately alone. So did Kate. But when such feelings overwhelmed her, she headed home to her father's house.

CHAPTER
13

Kate, accompanied by Laura, in the spring of 1938, returned to New York by train. Marlene Dietrich, Gertrude Lawrence* and Noël Coward were also onboard, Coward having just spent three weeks in Hollywood where he had been "the belle of The Thing." Much time was spent in Noël's drawing-room accommodation discussing the published list of film stars named the biggest poison at the box office, which had been headed by Kate, Marlene and Garbo. Kate insisted that figures proved her the biggest poison. Marlene argued that since Paramount had simply paid her good money *not* to make another film (Kate, after all, *had* been offered *Mother Carey's Chickens*), she took first place. Marlene and Gertie Lawrence had a serious debate regarding the size and splendor of the gifts given them by admirers. Marlene lost this round for she had never received a yacht and Gertie had.

In New York, Kate spent a few days shopping for presents for her family. She then left for West Hartford alone, the usual pattern being that Laura would stay at her home in New Jersey when Kate was either in West Hartford or at Fenwick.

Kate's arrival, as always, generated much excitement. For several days the family clustered about, listening to all her

---

* Gertrude Lawrence (1898–1952) was returning from the West Coast where she had been on tour with Noël Coward's *Tonight at 8:30*.

tales of Hollywood. But soon it seemed as though she had been home for months. Marion was planning to be married to a Harvard man, Ellsworth Strong Grant, on June 12, in exactly the kind of society wedding Kate had once shunned. Marion had graduated Bennington College in Vermont and had recently returned from Washington, D.C., where she had helped the C.I.O. (Congress of Industrial Organization), a labor union, picket hotels for better wages for hotel employees. Their younger sister, Peggy, still attended Bennington, where the tuition was high, the enrollment small and select and the curricula the last word in progressive education.* Brother Dick wanted to be a playwright and from under his closed door the click of the typewriter could be heard at all hours of the day and night. Bob, following in his father's footsteps, had just completed his internship at Boston Hospital.

Golf at the Hepburns' country club occupied a good portion of Kate's time. She played an awesome thirty-six holes a day and then enjoyed going into the caddy house and chinning with the club's "pro" about her game. She always passed up the club room and its jolly drinkers; though a heavy smoker, she had no tolerance or liking for liquor. She never lunched at the club, coming home between games. The Hepburn luncheon table remained lively, and even Dr. Hepburn joined his family when he could. Kate was intensely concerned with all of his current cases and discussed the medical details without any sign of squeamishness. The half hour or so after lunch was set aside as a time for Kate and Mrs. Hepburn to confer. Kate remained intensely proud of her mother's continuing hard work on behalf of birth control. A family friend commented, "Every time Kate looks at her mother, she recalls the meaning of service to others." Certainly in this aspect of Scarlett O'Hara's character, Kate *was* Scarlett, not surprising when one learns that Margaret Mitchell's own mother was a suffragette who fought valiantly and outspokenly for many of the same causes so revered by Mrs. Hepburn, and that Mrs. O'Hara was molded after the author's mother.

---

* The tuition at Bennington College in 1938 was $1,675 a year, making it one of the ten most expensive colleges in the United States. The enrollment was 276.

Howard Hughes visited Kate during the spring and summer of 1938, both at West Hartford and at Fenwick. After one of his visits, Dick began working diligently on a new play. Four weeks later he gathered the family together in the living room of their Bloomfield Avenue home and read it to them. The play centered on a "handsome and attractive young millionaire who comes to visit the family of a girl who happens to be an actress." Writer-director Garson Kanin,* a new friend of Kate's at that time, read it and thought highly of it. "It seems to me," he said, "a fascinating and entertaining portrait of a kind of American family. In style it is not unlike Noël Coward's classic *Hay Fever*. The character representing Hughes is sympathetically drawn, acting as a catalyst to reveal many things about the members of the family to themselves and to one another. It may have been written before its time."

The Hepburns, however, were shocked and offended that "a member of the family had so blatantly invaded their privacy." Dick was equally shocked by his family's request that he destroy the work. Labeling their attitude an attempt to throttle his own right to freedom of expression, he stood his ground and vowed he would proceed to try to get a theater producer interested in presenting it.† In the end, though the work received some attention, no producer wanted to chance a possible lawsuit from either Hughes or the Hepburns. But this rebellious act on the part of Dick Hepburn was only one dissident note in the usual Hepburn harmony.

Kate went to Fenwick in May to remain throughout the summer, returning to West Hartford as maid of honor for Marion's formal garden wedding, at which she wore a huge, soft-brimmed, white garden hat tied with bright ribbons about her neck and a pastel-blue, short-sleeved, organdy and

---

* Garson Kanin (1912–   ) made his Broadway debut as an actor in 1933. He directed his first play in 1937 and went to Hollywood the following year, working at R.K.O. just at the time of Hepburn's troubles there. They met briefly then but became close friends later. Kanin became a screenwriter in 1946, and his play *Born Yesterday*, made into a film starring Judy Holliday, has become a film classic.

† Kanin wrote, "There were Shubert Alley [Broadway] rumors about the play and a false report that Kate had bought it to keep it from being produced."

lace full-length gown.* She carried a large bouquet of summer flowers and almost stole the show from the bride. Dr. Hepburn seemed surprised that any one of his daughters had caught a man and told Kate, "All you New England girls look at a man like a bull about to charge. You're very forthright and truthful but you do sort of put a man off."

Swimming and walking the beach were Kate's main occupations at Fenwick. Though approaching her thirty-first birthday, she seemed unconcerned about remarrying. "Health is youth," Dr. Hepburn told her, and she believed his axioms and followed through on her regime of exercise as she always had. When not working, she regarded physical exercise as a must to keep her body in shape, just as discussions were necessary to keep her mind alert. Kate still took "endless cold showers," sometimes as many as seven or eight in the course of a day. Aside from her belief that cleanliness was next to godliness, "she use[d] cold baths, as a hair-shirt-sort-of self-discipline, to strengthen the character and drive."

In view of Kate's adamant stand about her brother Dick's manuscript, her enthusiasm for the play Philip Barry brought to her that summer is puzzling, for *The Philadelphia Story* also bore many parallels to her own life. However, it did not contain actual biographical detail. Tracy Lord was not an actress, her father not a doctor, her mother was light-headed where Mrs. Hepburn was the antithesis, and no character even vaguely resembling Howard Hughes appeared. Barry visited her often at Fenwick where they discussed the project at length, and there remains no doubt that he wrote Tracy Lord with Kate in mind.

The possibility of appearing on Broadway in a new Philip Barry play fired Kate's energies. She never looked more radiant. Bronzed, trimmer and leaner than ever, she glowed with a happiness that the Hollywood doom predictors could not understand. Hughes courted her in fine fashion, flying a private plane in and out of Old Saybrook and bringing her costly presents, much to the disapproval of Dr. Hepburn, who thought expensive jewelry and the like an indulgent frivolity. And, indeed, Kate seldom adorned herself with

---

* Hepburn wore almost this identical outfit in the wedding scene of *The Philadelphia Story.*

jewels. Not much for swimming or walking at the kind of pace Kate set, Hughes let her fly his plane or went boating with her. She talked to him about *The Philadelphia Story* and he flew her to Maine for further conferences with Barry.

By the end of August, Barry had completed his work. Kate convinced him she should ask the Theatre Guild to produce it. The Guild liked the play as much as she did but was not in a financial position to be the sole backer. After consulting with Hughes and Dr. Hepburn, Kate proposed a deal for the Guild to put up half the backing and she and Hughes the remaining half. The optimism of all involved is amazing; for the Theatre Guild had had a recent succession of failures, Barry's three preceding plays had flopped, and Kate's last six films, including *Stage Door,* had not been money-makers.

Kate now owned one quarter of the play, securing herself an equal amount of profits should there be any. Next, she bought the screen rights from Barry for an additional twenty-five thousand dollars. Instead of a guaranteed salary, she took 10 percent of the gross profits from the New York run and 12½ percent of profits on the road. With Howard Hughes's backing, Kate had become an entrepreneur.* For the first time in her professional career she could (or thought she could, at least) have some control over a play in which she was to star. Her one proviso was that the play would be postponed for the time it would take to make *Gone With the Wind* should Selznick call her to Hollywood to play Scarlett O'Hara.†

The hurricane that swept the Connecticut seaboard in

---

* *The Philadelphia Story* played 415 performances in New York, grossing $961,310.37, of which Hepburn took her 10 percent ($96,131.03) as salary plus 25 percent of the net in return for her investment of $10,000. It played 254 performances on the road, grossing $753,538.50. Screen rights were sold to Metro for $175,000, plus Hepburn's acting fee of $75,000. Hepburn made over $500,000 from *The Philadelphia Story.*

† On November 21, 1938, David O. Selznick sent a memo to Daniel O'Shea (secretary of Selznick International), ". . . I think we should make it clear to Katharine Hepburn, Jean Arthur, Joan Bennett, and Loretta Young that they are in the small company of final candidates. . . . The final choice must be made out of this list plus [Paulette] Goddard and our new girl [Doris Jordan] plus any last-minute new girl possibility that may come along." (Doris Jordan, renamed Doris Davenport, had a brief film career. She appeared opposite Gary Cooper in 1940 in *The Westerner*.) Hepburn was alerted by the Selznick office of her status.

September was a devastating blow in more ways than one. That Fenwick had been destroyed seemed inconceivable. No Fenwick meant no home! Kate's dash for higher ground and a neighbor's shelter with her mother and the Hepburn maid was too much like Scarlett's escape from burning Atlanta to seem real. Of course, there had been no newly delivered mother or newborn children to protect, but, like Scarlett, Kate had had to crawl over and through brambles and rubble and flooding lands with her two charges. Unlike Tara, nothing was left of Fenwick except the love it had inspired in its occupants.

Fenwick had to be rebuilt, that was certain. Kate spearheaded the project, but all the Hepburns joined in with the planning. Work was scheduled to begin in the spring so that Fenwick could receive them all for the summer. The first week of January, Kate learned through a press release that Vivien Leigh had been signed for *Gone With the Wind*.* *The Philadelphia Story* went directly into rehearsals. Barry began a rewrite of the third act, which Kate and the show's director, Robert B. Sinclair,† did not feel sufficiently resolved the story.

At this stage, great emphasis was placed upon the hostile relationship between Tracy Lord and her father, who was having a fling with a Russian ballerina. Kate never felt comfortable in the scenes where she righteously upbraided Seth Lord for his unseemly behavior, and Barry was reducing these daughter-father confrontations to a minimum. The play, which opened in New Haven before the new third act was finished, was well received by audience and critics. Whether this version would have met with equal or more

---

* Selznick met Vivien Leigh (1913–1967) for the first time on December 10, 1938, when the first scenes of the burning of Atlanta were being filmed. On December 12, 1938, he wrote his wife, Irene, ". . . Not for anybody's ears but your own: It's narrowed down to Paulette, Jean Arthur, Joan Bennett and Vivien Leigh." Hepburn was out as of this date but was not informed.

† Robert B. Sinclair (1905–1970) had previously directed stage versions of *Dodsworth*, *Pride and Prejudice*, *The Postman Always Rings Twice*, *Life Begins*, *Babes in Arms* and *The Women* before *The Philadelphia Story*. His stylish direction of *The Women* convinced Hepburn and the Theatre Guild of his ability to direct Barry's urbane comedy. Sinclair went to Hollywood directly after. Except for *Mr. and Mrs. North*, none of his films was noteworthy. He and Hepburn subsequently worked together on the stage production of *Without Love*.

success in subsequent productions is unanswerable. The third act was still not ready when the play opened in Philadelphia on February 16 to even more enthusiastic reviews. Finally, the new act was included in their Washington, D.C., performances. The play was now light and romantic, filled with laughter and sharp, sophisticated dialogue.

At the end of the short Washington run (which played to consistently full houses), Kate, Phil Barry, Theresa Helburn, Bob Sinclair and Lawrence Langner (of the Guild) sat around the hotel most of the night balancing the pros and cons of whether they should or should not take the show into New York.

"For God's sake," Kate exclaimed, "don't throw away your money. Let's be practical about this. We've got a fortune if we stay out of New York [and tour]."

Theresa Helburn thought that by keeping the show on the road for a long time, "the bloom would be off it" by the time they did bring it in. Barry agreed a risk was involved in going to New York but felt the risk was worth taking. Langner and Sinclair weren't sure which course would be more hazardous. Finally everyone but Kate decided the show should go to New York.

Kate threw up her hands. "Do anything you want," she said in a tone of foreboding. "Throw your money away." (At this stage, Kate had already recouped her ten-thousand-dollar investment.)

From the start, Kate had wanted and obtained Van Heflin as Mike, the young newspaperman who falls in love with Tracy Lord, and Joseph Cotten* as her ex-husband, C. K. Dexter Haven. But Kate liked all her fellow players in *The Philadelphia Story* and, perhaps because the play was so close to her, a family atmosphere developed during rehearsals and remained throughout the tour and the long run. Rumors abounded that she and Heflin were having an affair. They were particularly close during the early part of their associa-

_____

* Joseph Cotten (1905–   ) had been a member of Orson Welles's famous Mercury Theatre. He became an immediate film success after co-starring with Welles in *Citizen Kane* (1941). His most memorable film performances were early in his career. Among them were *The Magnificent Ambersons* and *Journey Into Fear* (1942) and *The Third Man* (1949). In 1973, he and Hepburn were reunited in the film adaptation of *A Delicate Balance*.

tion; but when the run of the play continued into the second year, he returned to Hollywood to make *The Santa Fe Trail*.

As March 28, 1939—opening night—approached, Kate grew increasingly nervous. Because of *The Lake* she regarded New York as "the enemy." The evening before the opening, she checked into the Waldorf-Astoria Hotel accompanied by her dresser-secretary-good friend, Em Perkins, having been seized with a terror of failure "so keen it was a kind of death." No one knew where she was. No calls reached her. The shades were drawn so that day and night had no meaning. Pacing the room endlessly, she kept repeating, "This is Indianapolis, this is Indianapolis," in an effort to convince herself that New York would be no different from the cities she had toured. In the car on the way to the theater, she repeated the chant, eyes sealed closed, over and over again.

The house was packed but silent as the curtain rose on the first New York performance of *The Philadelphia Story*. Kate had no entrance, being onstage at curtain, and she was greeted with polite applause. Her terror returned. She claims she was then certain of failure. She could not have been more mistaken.

"The radiant Miss Hepburn brings a loveliness to our stage such as has not been seen hereabouts in years," wrote John Mason Brown of the *New York Post*, adding, "Her fine chiseled face is a volatile mask. If it is difficult to take one's eyes off of her, it is because she is also blessed with an extraordinary personality. Slim and lovely as she is, Miss Hepburn likewise possesses a voice which in her emotional scenes can be sheer velvet." His colleague, Brooks Atkinson at *The New York Times*, on the same day, March 29, 1939, was even more explicit:

"A strange, tense little lady with austere beauty and metallic voice, she has consistently found it difficult to project a part in the theatre. But now she has surrendered to the central part in Mr. Barry's play and she acts it like a woman who has at last found the joy she has always been seeking in the theatre. For Miss Hepburn skips through the evening in any number of light moods, responding to the scenes quickly, inflecting the lines and developing a part from the beginning to its logical conclusion. There are no ambiguous corners in this character portrayal. Dainty in style, it is free and alive in its darting expression of feeling."

At last Kate had won over New York critics. One, Richard Watts, Jr., of the *New York Herald Tribune,* even found "something particularly pleasant about the triumph she has made in Philip Barry's new comedy. Few actresses have been so relentlessly assailed by critics' wit [a reference to Dorothy Parker], columnists, magazine editors and other professional assailers over so long a period of time and, even if you confess that some of the abuse had a certain justice to it, you must admit she faced it gamely and unflinchingly and fought back with courage and gallantry."

Kate's greatest triumph came at the party on opening night. All the Hepburns were there and for the first time Kate discerned respect and admiration in her parents' attitude toward her. With this performance they had finally taken her career seriously. Their movie-star daughter was a fine stage actress. "I still grin to myself when I think of the party Kate gave [that night]," Helburn recalled. "As long as her family was there she served beer; when they had gone she brought out the champagne."

Kate had always been at her best in roles that were familiar to her, characters in which her own personality could be unleashed to their benefit. The role of Tracy Lord allowed those things to take place. But more, Kate's sexuality—and she had tons of it in *The Philadelphia Story*—that elusive something that made a performer real and vulnerable, shone forth.

Broadway's 1939 spring season had the most glittering stage stars to appear in many a year: Judith Anderson in *Family Portrait,* Katharine Cornell and Laurence Olivier in *No Time for Comedy,* Tallulah Bankhead in *The Little Foxes,* Sophie Tucker in *Leave It to Me,* Raymond Massey in *Abe Lincoln in Illinois,* Fredric March in *The American Way,* Frances Farmer in *Golden Boy,* Bill "Bojangles" Robinson in *The Hot Mikado,* and Ethel Merman and Jimmy Durante in *Stars in Your Eyes,* to name some. Yet, *The Philadelphia Story* played every night to full houses.

The stage success of the Barry play mellowed rather than changed Kate. Howard Hughes—tired of pursuing her—had turned to a succession of other women but was still a close friend and business partner. Her life during the run of the play was much as it would have been had she not been appearing in a smash hit. Laura remained nearby and Luddy was close-at-hand to be called upon whenever she needed friendship. She played tennis for two hours every day at Joe Sawyer's East Side Tennis Courts, studied with Frances Robinson-Duff, and took singing lessons at home with a Dr. Isaac Van Grove, who had been recommended to her by composer Kurt Weill. She slept for an hour in the late afternoon, ate a healthy dinner and arrived at the Shubert Theatre an hour before curtain. Van Heflin accompanied her to various of her activities and could be found at the house on Forty-ninth Street most of the time that they were not at the theater.

Whenever she was not supervising Fenwick's reconstruction, Kate spent the weekends at Laura's estate in New Jersey. "I'd find Kate out picking little flowers that nobody else would have picked," Laura recalled. "She loves nature and she loves streams and she loves rain. She's really very Scotch in her love of mist. I used to find her . . . having breakfast under a tree that I'd never sat under. . . . She's friends with all of it and sees things and makes something of it that nobody else would."

Fenwick was completed in time for the summer and Kate spent every free hour there. Neighbors and friends noted that while "still boyishly awkward," she had "learned to move with grace." The strident voice was "slower and richer," its old stridence returning only with her frequent use of profanity. She gave off a feeling of more assurance. The clothes she wore were still unique but less bizarre. She used no jewelry and no offstage makeup except for lipstick "which emphasized the droop of her mouth and the fact that her upper and lower lips are exactly alike."

Within a few days of opening night, Kate had received an offer from Metro of $175,000 for film rights of *The Philadelphia Story*. Negotiations were set in motion but not concluded for nine months, when an additional $75,000 for her to star in the film was added.

"Louis B. Mayer tried to make a tricky deal with me," Kate remembered, "wanting to put Norma Shearer or somebody else in it, and I said: 'Look, Mr. Mayer, I know you are deliberately trying to charm me, and yet I'm charmed,' and he came to a very fine arrangement, with me getting my own way. . . . After Mr. Mayer and I worked out my contract, I [went] downstairs to his lawyer and said, 'You couldn't very well cheat me, because you're Louis B. Mayer's lawyer. That would be a terribly dishonest thing to do.'"

Since 1938, when she had broken with R.K.O., Hayward remained as her representative, but she had made all her deals herself. She did not expect sainthood from men like Louis B. Mayer or Harry Cohn, but she admired their sense of the romance of the film industry and was struck by Mayer's "scrupulous honesty." She didn't have the same illusion about the business of making films and found it at times "personally humiliating because you are, after all, in the position that the common prostitute is in. You're selling yourself, and if everybody begins to say, 'Oh boy, we've had enough of that' . . . then it becomes a little embarrassing. Then it's up to you to say to them: 'Just a minute, fellows Here's something you haven't seen yet.'"

Kate wanted, and got, choice of director (always Cukor), co-stars, and "reasonable script supervision." Her heart was set on Spencer Tracy playing C. K. Dexter Haven, the Joseph Cotten role, in the film. Metro had released four Tracy films in a period of six months and all of them had been tremendous commercial successes.* Kate had still not met her idol, but she respected him as an actor perhaps more than she did any other film star and she thought that his particular projected personality—the masculine stubbornness, the steady, skillful, quietly humorous character he most often played (and which could only be assumed to be part of the man as well as of the actor)—would make a perfect foil for her Tracy Lord. Apart from that, on screen Spencer Tracy was the kind of man who attracted her most, a man's man like her father, not willing to take any guff, proud and strong—stronger than most women. She even mentioned to Cukor that the name Tracy Lord appealed to her at the time because of her admiration for Spencer Tracy.

---

* The four films starring Tracy and released in 1940 were: *I Take This Woman* (February 2), *Northwest Passage* (February 23) (both made the previous year), *Edison, The Man* (May 10) and *Boom Town* (August 30).

Tracy was free when shooting was to be scheduled for *The Philadelphia Story*, but Metro refused to cast him in deference to his need for time off. Their second-biggest box-office star,* in fact the country's as well, Tracy had never licked his alcohol problem. In 1940, with each succeeding film, more and more days had been lost in production when he had been unable to face the cameras. Cukor suggested Cary Grant and Kate agreed with certain reservations. Grant was all charm, slick and romantic, and possessed a wonderful sense of comedic timing. They were a proven team and she had enjoyed working with him. But Grant lacked an element of rugged individuality, of physical virility that would give more depth and reason to the character of C. K. Dexter Haven, a man who loved his boat and the water almost as much as he loved Tracy Lord, and who could be content devoting his life to his *True Love* (his boat's name) with Tracy onboard with him. Grant looked as if he would be a good deal happier aboard an ocean liner's first-class quarters.

Cary Grant, however, was under contract to both R.K.O. and Columbia and concessions had to be made to borrow him. His salary demand of $137,500 was finally met.† What took longer to agree upon was the matter of billing. Grant insisted upon—and received—star billing above Kate. Both his studios believed in the future success of *The Philadelphia Story* (as did Grant) and wanted to be sure that they would benefit accordingly. The matter of billing was a major clause in all Hollywood contracts, a name above the title and/or above the other stars in a film indicating greater status and allowing the studio to demand larger loan-out fees.** Kate had balked at the billing clause for a long time in the negotiations. After all, in *The Philadelphia Story*, Tracy Lord

---

* Clark Gable was number-one box-office star in 1940, but the following year he and Tracy traded positions.
† Cary Grant's salary above R.K.O. and Columbia's loan-out fees (not known) was donated by him to the British War Relief Fund.
** Studios either charged other studios for loaning out their stars, or exchanged one star for another of equal status. Large sums were often made by the studios for the loan-outs, as in the case of Robert Mitchum. In 1946, when he co-starred with Hepburn and Robert Taylor in *Undercurrent*, he was paid $300 a week by his studio, which then collected $25,000 for six weeks from Metro. This happened mostly when a contract player made it big, especially early in his or her career.

was the central and star character. Finally, Kate, with the attitude of "what-the-hell—let's-get-on-with-it," accepted Grant's terms and took the lesser billing along with James Stewart, who had been signed for the Van Heflin role (Heflin was always to feel bitter about this "betrayal").

Despite Grant's top billing, *The Philadelphia Story*—stage and screen—belonged to Kate. As the *Life* critic wrote of her performance in the film: *"The Philadelphia Story* fits the curious talents of the red-headed Miss Hepburn like a coat of quick-dry enamel. It is said to have been written for her. Its shiny surface reflects perfectly from her gaunt, bony face. Its languid action becomes her lean, rangy body. Its brittle smart-talk suits her metallic voice. And when Katharine Hepburn sets out to play Katharine Hepburn, she is a sight to behold. Nobody is then her equal."

During the making of *The Philadelphia Story,* Kate lived in the old John Barrymore house near the top of Tower Grove with a marvelous view of Beverly Hills and a great deal of privacy. Laura came out and spent some time with her, as did her old beau, Bob McKnight. One evening when Garson Kanin had come for dinner, Kate looked as though she might be in pain and he asked if anything was the matter.

"I got too much sun today—sat out in the garden with no clothes on like a fool," she explained.

"What do you mean 'with no clothes on?'" he asked.

"I mean in the nude. . . . I had to. I was posing. . . . Bob McKnight is here . . . he wanted to do a little figure of me and so there we were—what are you looking so peculiar about?"

"Nothing," Kanin answered, but he was certain she must be stretching the truth. Three weeks later, the naked truth sat on a plinth in the living room.

The Philadelphia Story was filmed in eight weeks and, astonishingly, no retakes were required. The entire experience was an exhilarating one. For once Kate had some control over a film and she felt secure, able to trust her best instincts. Her sense of fun returned, the collegiate humor for which Cukor had always chastised her. She had had a friendly but running battle with Jack Greenwood, the script clerk on the film, whose task it was to correct the performers whenever they missed a line or forgot a prop. One day on her way to the studio, she passed a small dead animal—which turned out to be an opossum—on the side of the road and backed up and got it. She then obtained a small, garlanded box lined with satin, put the corpse in it and presented it to Greenwood—who did not find it as amusing as she thought he would.

Joseph L. Mankiewicz* produced *The Philadelphia Story*. Mankiewicz, whom Richard Burton once called "an Oxford don *manqué*," had great wit and intellect. Possessed of a "superhuman poise," he maintained a well-oiled harmony on the set, and he had been responsible for the major changes in the film adaptation: the fusion of the two roles of C. K. Dexter Haven and of Tracy Lord's brother (which gave more body to Grant's character), and the silent prologue (which showed the end of the Tracy Lord–C. K. Dexter Haven first marriage). Mankiewicz was known for his seductive ways with women, but he preferred women over whom he could exert his "Svengali powers" and Kate was not his type.

Kate returned to New York in September and then took the play back out on the road. Her last performance, appropriately enough, was in Philadelphia, on February 15, 1941. Arrangements had been made with the stagehands not to lower the curtain at the end; and after several minutes of enthusiastic applause with the cast frozen in their final attitudes, Kate walked down front and raised her hand for silence. She thanked the audience humbly and brought out the entire crew. Then she said a few words:

"When I started this play, these people knew I was on the spot. They could have treated me as a climber and a phony. Instead, they treated me as an actress and a friend." Then she turned and pointed to a fire screen and a green vase on the set and asked in her strident voice, "See those? I've had my eye

---

* Joseph Leo Mankiewicz (1909–   ) began as a screenwriter during the late years of silent films. In 1936, he turned to producing and was responsible for many major films at Metro—*Fury* (1936) with Spencer Tracy, *The Gorgeous Hussy* (1936), *The Bride Wore Red* (1937), *A Christmas Carol* (1938), and *The Adventures of Huckleberry Finn* (1939) among them. He later became a director and twice won the Academy Award for Best Director: *A Letter to Three Wives* (1949) (also Best Screenplay), and *All About Eve* (1950) (also Best Screenplay). He made two more films with Hepburn: *Woman of the Year* (1942) and *Suddenly Last Summer* (1959).

on them for two years, and now I'm going to get them." She walked over to pick them up and could not lift them; they were fastened to the floor. She gave them a tug. The audience laughed. She pulled harder. The audience roared, then applauded boisterously. Kate threw a regal wave to the gallery and made her exit.

CHAPTER
14

In Hollywood, the man who holds the title Vice-President in Charge of Production is all powerful, a supreme god to the thousands in his employ. His disapproval can smash the career of any one of them. At Warner Brothers during the thirties and forties under the Vice-President in Charge of Production Harry Warner, the brightest stars were made to punch a time card and the studio police force operated like the F.B.I. Louis B. Mayer was a less totalitarian godhead. Still, he held the reins tightly on the people who made his movies.

Spencer Tracy was one of the chosen—*God's own*—so favored because Mayer was certain he could substantially increase Metro's profit and ensure his personal status and fortune. At this stage of her early association with Metro, Kate was not among the elite. *The Philadelphia Story* had been a financial and critical success. But Kate had proved only that she could be good box office *if* starred in a tailored vehicle and backed up by other box-office favorites. And, though the film had won six Academy Award nominations, her performance among them for Best Actress,* she had lost

---

* *The Philadelphia Story* was nominated for Best Picture (won by *Rebecca*), Best Actor, James Stewart (won by Stewart), Best Actress, Hepburn (won by

183

the award to Ginger Rogers in *Kitty Foyle* (ironically one of the parts offered to her for a low fee before she had created Tracy Lord for the stage and screen). Kate's next film, no matter how commercial the property, would have to co-star an actor with the box-office draw of a Grant or a Stewart.* Metro was in the prime of its golden years in 1941, but the studio had, besides Stewart, only three surefire male stars under contract: Clark Gable, Mickey Rooney and Spencer Tracy. On the other hand, they had an abundance of women stars who could compete with Kate for the same roles: Greta Garbo,† Greer Garson, Irene Dunne, Norma Shearer, Joan Crawford and Margaret Sullavan. Added to this list were Hedy Lamarr, Myrna Loy, Lana Turner, Judy Garland and Esther Williams. Intelligently, Kate reasoned that her best chance would be to bring in her own film property, as she had with *The Philadelphia Story,* and it had to be one that Metro would want as much as she did.

In the spring of 1941, while Kate and Laura were vacationing in Florida, Garson Kanin had conceived an idea for a story with Kate in mind. He titled it *The Thing About Women* and based it blatantly on the character and personality of Dorothy Thompson, considered by some to be the first lady of American journalism. *Time* magazine had printed her photograph on a May, 1939 cover and stated, "She and Eleanor Roosevelt are undoubtedly the most influential women in the U.S." Expelled from Germany in 1934 by Hitler's personal order, she had become an international celebrity and returned to America as a columnist and commentator whose political opinions and warnings on the rise of a Third Reich were widely heard and read. Her marriage to the Nobel Prize–winning novelist Sinclair Lewis was the most

---

Ginger Rogers), Best Supporting Actress, Ruth Hussey (won by Jane Darwell), Best Screenplay, Donald Ogden Stewart (won by him), and Best Director, George Cukor (won by John Ford). Cary Grant was not nominated. Hepburn won the New York Film Critics' Award.

* Except for *The Philadelphia Story,* most films Hepburn made at Metro without Tracy failed commercially, even when she was co-starred with other box-office favorites.

† Greta Garbo had made two recent films, *Ninotchka* (1939) and *Two-Faced Woman* (1941), when she decided to retire. She never appeared in another film. But in 1941, Mayer was trying to renegotiate a new seven-year contract with her.

celebrated literary union of the century. In 1935, Thompson had been chosen the Woman of the Year because (as author Mary Roberts Rinehart said in introducing her on that occasion), "she is the woman journalist at her best. She thinks and works like a man but remains very much a woman; and because she has made a success of her marriage with Sinclair Lewis, and that, I fancy, with that brilliant and talented person would be a career in itself for a woman." (At this stage, Kanin had named the Dorothy Thompson character Tess Harding, after Laura Harding, and the name stuck.)

Two years later, a dinner had been staged in Thompson's honor at the Astor Hotel, at which President Roosevelt's mother, Mrs. Sara Delano Roosevelt, acknowledged in introduction, "No other individual so symbolizes the American qualities of courage, intelligence and recognition of the dignity of man. . . ." Tributes were read from Winston Churchill and presidential candidate Wendell Willkie. Shortly thereafter, an announcement was made that Mr. and Mrs. Sinclair Lewis had separated and filed suit for divorce. Give or take a few biographical details, Thompson's life was the basic story of *Woman of the Year* (which the script was soon to be called). Like Thompson, Kate's Tess Harding was also to be an international-affairs columnist and a fighting liberal once expelled from the Third Reich, on first-name terms with and the adviser to many leading political figures. Tess's husband had become a sportswriter (also of great celebrity) for the same newspaper. Kanin had nothing more jotted down than the idea and a few suggestions for scenes between the principals, but he thought it had great potential for Kate and another friend, Spencer Tracy. Kanin, however, had committed himself to the U.S. Army to write and direct two documentaries* and was very involved in cleaning up his affairs. So he turned to his brother, Michael Kanin,† and

---

* The two documentaries were *Fellow Americans* and *Ring of Steel*, both in 1942. Kanin continued to produce documentaries throughout World War II.
† Michael Kanin (1910–   ) had been a musician until 1939, when he wrote the screenplay for *They Made Her a Spy*. He won an Academy Award with Ring Lardner, Jr., for *Woman of the Year* and collaborated with Lardner and with his wife, Fay Kanin, on *The Cross of Lorraine*, but none of his other films was as successful as *Woman of the Year*.

Ring Lardner, Jr.,* with the suggestion that they develop the story further.

The two young writers had never worked together before; the teaming was Garson's invention, confident that Mike could be counted on to adhere to the characters he had in mind and that Lardner would complement him because of his newspaper experience and his knowledge of both the sports and political worlds.

Within three weeks and entirely on speculation, they produced a treatment of about thirty thousand words in the form of a novella, written in the past tense and first person and narrated by the Tracy character. The script, still called *The Thing About Women,* was sent to Garson in New York, who in turn mailed it to Kate in West Hartford.

"It's magnificent!" she told them. Discussion now turned to how best to sell the property as a package with Kate to Metro. The first thing agreed upon was that the script should not carry either of the authors' names. There were two reasons for their remaining anonymous. One, neither had ever earned more than two or three hundred dollars a week (low pay in Hollywood), and Metro would want to pay them accordingly. And two, Lardner was known as a "trouble maker" because of his part in the Screenwriters Guild's struggle for recognition; and William Fadiman, Metro's chief story editor, had said publicly that he would never be employed by Metro. Kate decided that she would submit the property on her own without benefit of an agent so that the authors' anonymity would not be jeopardized. With Lardner's and Mike Kanin's agreement, she now contacted Mankiewicz and told him he would be receiving a manuscript in which she would like to star opposite Spencer Tracy.

"Swell! Who wrote it?" Mankiewicz asked.

"I can't tell you. It's a secret."

Before he could probe further, she disconnected and drove

---

* Ring Lardner, Jr. (1915–   ), son of the celebrated humorist. Lardner had come to Hollywood as a wunderkind in 1937 and worked without credit on the screenplays of *A Star Is Born* and *Nothing Sacred. Woman of the Year* was his first major credit. He collaborated on numerous screenplays during the forties, *Tomorrow the World* (1944), *Cloak and Dagger* (1946) and *Forever Amber* (1947) among them. In 1970, after many years of being a blacklisted McCarthy victim, he staged a spectacular comeback with *M*A*S*H.*

from West Hartford into New York. When she arrived three hours later, he had already called. Returning the call, she learned that he had received the script, read it and passed it on to Kenneth MacKenna, Kate's mentor in her first stage appearance in Baltimore and now one of Metro's story editors, who, in fact, was reading it at that moment in Mankiewicz's living room. Kate asked to speak to him.

"Who wrote it—[Ben] Hecht and [Charles] MacArthur [two extremely successful authors]? How much do they want for it?" MacKenna asked.

"That's a secret for the present," Kate said.

"Look, Kate; I can't send up a story [to the front office] unless I know the author's name and the price he expects!"

"I'm not going to tell you his name, and as for the price, all I'll tell you is that it's going to be high. I own the story, and I'm not going to sell it anyway, unless Tracy will play it."

Within two days, Metro had read the script and sent it down to Tracy in Florida, where cameras on *The Yearling*, his current assignment, had just begun to roll. Tracy liked it and said he would do it when *The Yearling* was finished. Then the unexpected happened. Production on *The Yearling* suddenly halted. Location problems were cited, but the studio, after viewing the first rushes, was not satisfied that either the director or the young boy who co-starred with Tracy were right. *The Yearling* was to be temporarily shelved.* Tracy arrived back in California at about the same time that Kate was checking into a bungalow at the Beverly Hills Hotel. Kate was finally to meet her idol.

Spencer Tracy's affair with Loretta Young had ended years before. Afterward, Tracy had become the kind of Hollywood character he had always despised, a black-tie regular at Ciro's, filmtown's choicest nightclub, but seldom attending without a beautiful young actress—Olivia de Havilland, Judy Garland—you name them, Tracy had dated them. People talked. Tracy was a married man; and though Louise was Episcopalian, Tracy's dedicated Catholicism stood in the way of a divorce. Whenever he was filming in town, he took a

---

* It was filmed and released in 1946 with Gregory Peck in the Spencer Tracy role.

suite at the Beverly Wilshire Hotel; but he still considered his home the Hill (the ranch in the Valley where Louise and the children lived and on which they raised horses) and returned there from time to time.

Though the marriage had eroded, it had turned into a dependent friendship with strong ties. He and Louise had been married nearly twenty years, through tough times and good times, and she had always been there helping out, bolstering his ego, supporting his talent. Her own career—and though not a great talent, she had been more than competent—had been gracefully put aside not long after their son at ten months had been diagnosed as incurably deaf. And after the specialists had tried to convince her that John (named after Spencer's father, John Tracy, an Irishman "with generations of good old Irish fighters behind him") would never learn to speak and that he should be placed in an institution, Louise had dedicated her life with ferocious intensity to learning how to communicate with the child by teaching him to form sounds, to read, and finally to speak.

Close friends said that when Louise realized her son could not hear she took him that very day to a doctor and that when Spencer was told he went out and got drunk. John, an appealing child with Louise's dark coloring and fine-cut features, soon became almost totally dependent on his mother. "I wanted to help with the boy," Tracy confessed, "but I was no damn good at it. I would come in after Louise had been working with him for hours and start undoing the good she had done. Maybe she had been working with him all day on a word like 'shoe,' showing it to him and saying the word over and over, trying to get him to read her lips. So I would pick up the damn shoe and throw it across the room and scare the poor kid half to death. I had no patience, and it's amazing how much she had—and has."

Tracy felt he had failed Louise all along the way with John and considered her entirely responsible for the fact that his son was now miraculously capable of attending college and living a life of his own. Louise had turned her full and considerable energies into helping to fund and build the John Tracy Clinic. By 1941, Louise's dream had almost become a reality. Convinced that a child's parents were his or her first and natural teachers, Louise had formed a group of parents (mostly mothers) of afflicted children and refurbished a small cottage at the University of Southern California, where she conducted meetings, sharing her successful approach in communicating with an unhearing child before the age of two.*

A man of any conscience or character could not easily walk out on a woman like Louise. How many times had she welcomed him home either drunk or from the arms of another woman—or both—without recrimination? Louise understood his frustration and guilt at not being able to communicate with John as she and their young daughter, Susie, did. Still, Tracy could never forgive himself for not learning John's language better or for his own weakness where alcohol was concerned. Yet, somehow, Louise always found it in her heart to forgive him. Nevertheless, years had passed since they had truly been man and wife, a bold truth that seemed to concern him much more than it did Louise.

Spencer Bonaventure Tracy had been born with the twentieth century in Milwaukee, Wisconsin, to fairly prosperous middle-class parents. A staunch Catholic with an unquenchable thirst for hard liquor, John Tracy was general sales manager of the Sterling Motor Truck Company. Young Spencer admired his father's virile personality, but his mother —Caroline Brown Tracy, whose ancestors could be traced back to settlers in the colonies before the Revolution—drew his greatest love and respect. As a kid, he'd "never passed up many fights" and had an early "itch to travel." At seven, he ran away from home, to be found, happily, eight hours later playing with "ruffians from the wrong side of the track." At sixteen, while attending a Jesuit school—Marquette Academy —he felt called to the priesthood.

"You know how it is in a place like that," he later told a close friend. "The influence is strong, very strong, intoxicating. The priests are all such superior men—heroes. You want to be like them—we all did. Every guy in the school probably thought some—more or less—about trying for the cloth. You lie in the dark and see yourself as Monsignor Tracy, Cardinal

* The John Tracy Clinic is now located at 806 West Adams Boulevard in Los Angeles, California, and is the largest educational center anywhere in the world for parents and their preschool deaf children. By 1983, more than sixty thousand young deaf children and their parents had received services at no cost. Louise Treadwell Tracy was the active president of the clinic until her death in 1983.

Tracy, Bishop Tracy, Archbishop—I'm getting goose-flesh! . . . Everytime I *play* a priest—and I've done my share* . . . everytime I put on the clothes and the collar I feel right, right away. Like they were mine, like I belonged in them, and that feeling of being—what's the word?—an *intermediary*—is always very appealing. Those were always my most comfortable parts. . . ."

After serving a year in World War I (he never had to fight abroad), Tracy struggled through two years at Ripon College in Wisconsin, at the end of which time his life work was set out for him. A well-received performance in a class play† made him decide to become an actor. His English professor agreed with his decision and wrote the director of the American Academy of Dramatic Arts in New York suggesting Tracy appear for a tryout. It sounded like "a silly idea" to John Tracy, but he agreed to pay his son's tuition for the first semester if Spencer could live on the thirty dollars a month he received as an ex-serviceman.

He and another future film actor, Pat O'Brien,** lived in a room in the West Nineties, "two steep, shady flights up" illuminated by "one flickering light bulb," freezing in winter "when the gray wind came up Broadway from the direction of Macy's," suffocating in summer when the sun on the slate roof directly overhead made the heat something "out of Egypt." They subsisted mainly on pretzels and water, but Tracy maintained that there was "something about going hungry that makes you discover the utmost of your resources."

Three days after his father's tuition money ran out, Tracy got a nonspeaking part as a robot in the Theatre Guild's

---

* Tracy was to play a priest in four films: *San Francisco* (1936), *Boys' Town* (1938), *Men of Boys' Town* (1941) and *The Devil at Four O'Clock* (1961).
† Tracy played the lead in *The Truth* by Clyde Fitch.
** Pat O'Brien (1899–1983), born in Milwaukee and a childhood friend of Tracy's. Both attended the Jesuit school and joined the Navy together. O'Brien started his stage career as a song-and-dance man. He preceded Tracy to Hollywood in 1929 and had already made a name for himself by 1931 when he co-starred in *The Front Page*. He made more than one hundred films, but will probably be best remembered as *Knute Rockne—All-American*, in which future President Ronald Reagan was to play "the Gipper." O'Brien and Tracy made one film together, *The People Against O'Hara* (1951).

production of Karel Capek's science-fantasy, *R.U.R.* When it closed five months later he took a job with a new stock company of which Louise was a member. From that point, Tracy was seldom out of work as an actor. He and Louise married in 1923. A year later John was born and the small family traveled in stock together. Tracy made his Broadway debut in a speaking part in George M. Cohan's production of *Yellow* at the National Theatre on September 21, 1926. At the end of the final dress rehearsal, Cohan, speaking in front of the entire company, stood up and said, "Kid, you're the best damn actor I ever saw!" and sat down again. Nonetheless, *Yellow* did not make him a star. After it closed, Tracy returned to stock and, with Louise as his leading lady, appeared in a play a week for nine productions.

His big break came in 1930 when he won the lead role of Killer Mears in the all-male cast of the prison drama *The Last Mile.* Tracy was an overnight sensation. Hollywood called and he answered. Tracy and Humphrey Bogart were to co-star in the film adaptation. Within three years, Tracy had made sixteen films. By 1935 he was a major star. By 1936 he had gained the reputation of being one of the worst drunks in Hollywood, and alcohol wasn't his only vice. Fritz Lang,* the autocratic German director who worked with Tracy in 1935 on *Fury,* revealed that "Spencer Tracy had a contract with Metro—because he drank like a fish—that if he had so much as a glass of beer they could throw him out. My friend Peter Lorre, a former drug addict, explained to me that when people are deprived of a craving, they turn to something else—Lorre to drink, Tracy to whorehouses . . . he'd disappear after lunch [and not] come back until four o'clock. I'd be sitting there with the whole crew wanting to work when he'd arrive and say, 'Fritz, I want to invite the crew to have coffee.'"

Tracy would miss hours—sometimes days—of shooting. But he never appeared drunk on a set. Indeed, his preparation for a scene was awesome. Joe Mankiewicz, who pro-

---

* Fritz Lang (1890–1976). Born in Vienna, Lang became one of the world's outstanding film directors. *Fury* (1936) was his first American film. Earlier, his German films, *Metropolis* (1927) and *M* (1931) among them, had made him an international celebrity.

duced *Fury*, recalled a week Tracy spent at Mankiewicz's home in Malibu during production, a precaution he took to ensure his star's appearance on the set for major scenes. Tracy was called upon to crack nuts in one, and he spent one entire night working on the most natural way to crack nuts. "Christ," Mankiewicz says, "he used up five pounds of nuts and then he pretended on the set it had just occurred to him." Despite his drinking, Tracy remained the ultimate film performer, and Metro's great stars—Gable, Crawford, Harlow, Colbert, Lamarr—all wanted him as a co-star because "his masterful technique of underplaying was an unfailing corrective" to their excesses.

His peers considered Tracy "almost the best" actor in films. Asked why, Humphrey Bogart* replied, "The thing about his acting is there's no bullshit in it. He doesn't go in for those hammy disguises some clowns think is acting. . . . Spencer *does* it that's all. Feels it. Says it. Talks. Listens. He means what he says when he says it, and if you think that's easy, try it."

Clark Gable, upon whom Tracy bestowed the title, "the King,"† added, "The only thing I mind about him is that humble act he does once in a while. Don't you believe it. He knows how good he is. And that's as good as anyone has gotten up to here and now in this business. Any actor or actress who's ever played a scene with Spencer will tell you—there's nothing like it. He mesmerizes you. Those eyes of his—and what goes on behind them. Nobody's better than when they act with him."

Kate had not only seen most of Tracy's films over and over, she had heard stories about his brilliance and professionalism from many of his co-stars, directors and crew members who had also worked with her—Joe Mankiewicz, James Stewart, and Ruth Hussey among them. His wry humor was legend, his intellectualism considered unique among actors in films.

---

* Humphrey Bogart (1899–1957) is perhaps best remembered for his roles in *High Sierra* (1941), *The Maltese Falcon* (1941), *Casablanca* (1943), *Key Largo* (1948), *The African Queen* (1951) and *The Caine Mutiny* (1954).
† Clark Gable (1901–1960) often led the box-office poll and, after his memorable performance as Rhett Butler in *Gone With the Wind*, was probably Hollywood's most internationally famous male star.

She had heard equally as many tales about his hard drinking and his womanizing. But one point was always made. Tracy never appeared on the set drunk or unable to perform at his best. If "indisposed," he simply would not appear at all. The ultimate compliment came from Laurence Olivier, who said, "I've learned more about acting from watching Tracy than in any other way. He has a great truth in everything he does."

Had Tracy not remained in Hollywood, Hollywood party talk concluded, he would have been America's best stage performer, the equal of anyone in England, Olivier included. Kate could not help but have been in awe of the man she was about to meet, even had she not been such a longtime fan.

Tracy, on his part, had not seen any of Kate's films and requested a screening of *The Philadelphia Story*. When the lights came up in the Metro projection room, he commented that the lady was "a damn fine actress." Nonetheless, he remained wary of any woman who chose to wear trousers publicly. But he liked the script and agreed with Mankiewicz that he and Kate were both right for it. Mankiewicz reported back to Kate, "Tracy likes it and will do it."

Kate was tall for a Hollywood star, five feet seven inches, and she had learned years before to use her height to her advantage. She owned several pairs of specially built platform shoes which she wore whenever she felt the need to "put down—literally—the men with whom she came in professional contact." Mayer and another Metro executive, Benjamin Thau, were both under five feet seven. Only nine days after Kate's original call to Mankiewicz, Kate, in her built-up shoes (which increased her height by four inches), her hair piled high and her back rigid, joined Mankiewicz, Benny Thau and Mayer in Mayer's office. She looked, to say the least, imposing, but she claims she was terrified, afraid Mayer would talk her into promising something she had no intention of doing. "He began," Kate recalled, "by saying a lot of nice things to me—still not knowing who wrote the story or how much I'd ask. And I said a lot of nice things to him—the final preliminaries to hitting each other over the head."

Mayer wasted no time. "How much do you want for it?" he asked.

"Two hundred and eleven thousand dollars—a hundred

thousand for the story, and a hundred and eleven thousand for me."

Mayer protested that so far all he had seen was a first-draft script; good, *yes*, right for her and for Tracy, *yes*, but still only a first-draft script.

"Listen, Mr. Mayer," Kate replied. "[I agree] we really shouldn't discuss whether two hundred and eleven thousand dollars is a large or small figure until you've read some of the shooting script. . . . I can deliver you sixty pages on Monday."

Mayer was called out of the office to answer a private call and Kate was left alone for a few moments with Mankiewicz and Thau. She grasped her head in a "Victorian gesture" and exclaimed, "This is absolutely terrible! I don't know what I am doing!"

Looking at her coldly, Thau said, "You're doing all right."

As soon as Mayer returned, Kate stood up and said she had to go. Mankiewicz left with her and once outside the office leaned forward and kissed her on the forehead. "What's that for?" Kate asked.

"I've just kissed the Blarney Stone," he answered.

The two of them headed across the lot to get a cup of tea in the commissary. Ironically, Tracy was leaving just as they entered. There she stood in her trick shoes, towering over his wide-shouldered five-feet-nine-inch frame. Mankiewicz introduced them, and Kate's first words were, "I'm afraid I'm a little tall for you, Mr. Tracy."

They shook hands. Kate recalled that she was still trembling from her meeting with Mayer. Tracy remembered that she had a handshake that didn't make the trousers she wore seem unnatural and that he remained disapproving of her clothes. He stared hard at her for a long moment and then a smile plowed its way across his strong, broad jaw. "Don't worry, Miss Hepburn," he replied. "I'll cut you down to my size."*

Mankiewicz felt a chemistry pass between these two in this first confrontation and was more certain than ever that they

---

* In retelling this story, Tracy always claimed credit for this put-down to Hepburn. Mankiewicz insisted he spoke the now-famous line, but said, "*He'll cut you down to his size.*"

would generate the same sparks on screen. He remained convinced of this even when Tracy turned to him and said, "Not me, boy, I don't want to get mixed up with anything like that."

For the rest of the week, Kate, Ring Lardner and Mike Kanin worked on the script day and night. At seven A.M. on Sunday morning, she surprised George Stevens with an unannounced visit to his house to ask him what he thought of the story and to convince him to direct the film. Stevens said he liked what she had and made a few suggestions. Kate returned to the bungalow at the Garden of Allah, where she, Lardner, Mike and Garson Kanin,* "and two clattering typists" worked all night. Kate masterminded it all. She read, responded, scanned, frowned, suggested cuts and word changes, and read aloud, "always with enthusiasm and optimism." She sent out for food—"gourmet stuff from Chasens." By Monday morning, she had 106 pages rather than the 60 she had promised Mayer. (The secretaries' fingers "were too stiff to hold a cigarette.") Kate delivered the script personally to Metro, went back to her own bungalow at the Beverly Hills Hotel and waited. Twenty-four hours later, Sam Katz, another Metro executive, called. "Kate, I will give you one hundred and seventy-five thousand dollars for the whole business," he offered.

"You don't seem to understand," Kate replied, "I really want two hundred and eleven thousand."

"Why the eleven?"

"Ten thousand for my agent† and one thousand for telephone calls and *things*," she replied, obviously deciding she should not have to stand the cost of her own travel and hotel expenses.

"Well, you know we're going to give it to you."

"Yes, I'm afraid I do know that."

"So now you can tell us. Who wrote it?"

After she told him Katz was silent a moment. "Mike Kanin and Ring Lardner have never made more than $3,000 for a

---

* Garson Kanin had not been involved in the writing of the first draft of *Woman of the Year*, but did contribute some ideas to the shooting script. He received no credit. His trip to Hollywood was to tie up his affairs prior to going into the army.
† Hepburn can only have meant Leland Hayward.

script before and we're paying them $50,000 each! This picture should be called *Agent of the Year!"*

The sale of *Woman of the Year* took place early in May, 1941. For the next six weeks revisions were made. Kate had little to do with this stage except for the rewriting of one scene, which involved a speech to be made to an audience of women. Kate sent it to her mother and Mrs. Hepburn returned it without changes, saying in a note that none was necessary.

The story of how Kate had won out over Metro with *Woman of the Year* was soon a Hollywood favorite. Most people were incredulous that a woman had so successfully bucked a big studio on her own. But they had not realized that Kate had been brought up in a family where she was taught to think for herself, to face life with courage and to fight for her convictions. Tracy was not only impressed, he liked Kate Hepburn all the more for her brassiness. He had also read the shooting script and thought it a hell of a good job despite the fact that the majority of the scenes in it now centered on Kate. When Kate asked him what he thought, he replied, "It's all right. Not much for me to do as it stands—but, Shorty, you better watch yourself in the clinches!"

A
Historic
Affair

CHAPTER
15

From the moment that Kate and Tracy faced each other before the cameras, their sexual awareness of one another transferred itself onto the screen. On the surface, they upheld the theory that opposites attract . . . the hard-drinking Irishman and the Yankee lady from Hartford who was stronger and more outspoken than a woman was supposed to be. Stevens saw immediately that they balanced each other's natures, that Kate's defiant personality, her fiery temper and brash manner, and Tracy's "big-bear, Midwestern simplicity . . . his sense of the ridiculous," his bossiness, made them representative of the American female and the American male's fantasies of themselves. To his credit, he also recognized how much alike they really were—both being private people, intellectuals with large and educated appetites for almost everything from food to sports to politics. Both had wit and humor, loved nothing more than a good fight, stood for no nonsense, could not abide sycophants and flatterers. Both were Democrats, admired President Roosevelt with almost religious awe, had outrageous egos, loved their work, and had respect for anyone who was doing a good job or an important task; and both considered the men who built their sets as important as those who produced their films.

When Kate began work on *Woman of the Year*, she had

been dating George Stevens for five or six months. Nobody close to her thought anything serious would come of it. Despite their conflicts on *Alice Adams,* Kate had great respect for Stevens, both as a director and as a man. They had fun, talked much the same language and had many mutual friends. Still, they did not display any of the intimacies of lovers—the exchanged knowing glances, shared cigarettes, an acceptance of each other's choices ("two whiskeys," "steaks rare," "coffee black") that so often announce lovers. Yet, Kate's insistence that Stevens direct *Woman of the Year* or Metro had no deal created an aura of speculation and gossip in the first days of shooting. Curiously, Stevens bore a strong physical resemblance to Tracy.

The initial scene Kate (Tess Harding) and Tracy (Sam Craig) played together took place on a set duplicating the old Herald Tribune bar in New York. "I accidentally knocked over a glass," Kate explained as she recalled that day. "Spencer handed me a handkerchief, and I took his handkerchief and I thought, 'Oh you old so-and-so, you're going to make me mop it up right in the middle of a scene.' So I started to mop it, and the water started to run down through the table. I decided to throw him by going down under the table, and he just stood there watching me. I mopped and mopped and George Stevens kept the camera running. Spencer just smiled. He wasn't thrown at all."

Stevens added, "From the beginning of the picture, and their relationship, Spence's reaction to her was a total, pleasant, but glacial put-down of her extreme effusiveness. He just didn't get disturbed about doing things immediately; she wanted to do a hundred and one things at once; he was never in a hurry. She 'worried the bone'; he just took it and padded off with it. Slowly."

Kate loved to rehearse, to try something new, and make just one more take. Conversely, Tracy acted instinctively, trusting the moment of creation, firmly convinced that performers went stale by overrehearsing. He could work for hours on a piece of business like cracking nuts or peeling an orange in just the right way. Otherwise, he believed that acting should be a matter of instinct rather than design and his best shots were most often his first takes. Kate had to change her approach (since Tracy was not about to change his) or lose her hold on the film. Tracy had spoken the truth when he had warned her to watch herself in the clinches.

Before the film commenced, Tracy had been a bit flirtatious, as was his habit. But when they began to shoot, something happened. He was not the flirt or the star, he was Sam Craig challenged by Tess Harding, trying to maintain an uneasy kingdom, always working to be the ultimate boss of the situation. As another of his leading ladies, Jean Simmons,* said, "He's a sort of sorcerer. I confess I'd never known anything like it. . . . I wasn't me—I was the part I was playing. I fairly broke out. And it would happen again and again—startling really. One never quite got used to it —to him." Kate, however, did, and within a few weeks.

Everyone on the set realized what was happening. The two stars had fallen quite simply and sincerely in love. Stevens backed away from his relationship with Kate in a true gentlemanly fashion (although no alternative seemed viable). Mayer had told him that Tracy was difficult, that he drank. Stevens warned Kate and reaffirmed the facts—Tracy's seriousness where his religion and the vows of marriage were concerned, and his inability to resist alcohol. Kate ignored the first and brewed pots and pots of strong tea and served them on the set as a substitute for the second.

"She was the rarer beast of the two," Stevens said. "Spence would come over before work to my little office and sit and talk, or I'd go in his dressing room. All of a sudden, there'd be a knocking on the door. The door would open and it was Kate. She'd say, 'What are you two conspiring about?' He would say, 'Kate, I like guidance about things, and this man is our director.' She said, 'And what about my guidance?' Spence said, 'How could I be such a damn fool as to get into a picture with a woman producer and *her* director, how can I be such a dumb bastard as that?' "

Midway through the shooting of the film, a new feminine glow could be noted in Kate. The actress who had been a beauty on screen now became one in private. Trousers were

---

* Jean Simmons (1929-   ), English by birth, appeared opposite Tracy in *The Actress* (1953), based on a personal memoir by Ruth Gordon. She starred in many films, among them *Guys and Dolls* (1955), *Spartacus* (1960), and *Elmer Gantry* (1960).

still her habitual garb, but she had suddenly traded the men's clothes and faded patched overalls that had once startled Hollywood for splendidly tailored ones that complemented her figure. About Tess Harding, the character she portrayed, she told a reporter, "I'm alive, alert, enthusiastic—and also egotistical. I love Spencer, but I won't give up too much of myself to him. . . . I try to dominate him, put things over on him. I almost lose him."

In the early stages of their working together, life seemed capable of imitating fiction. Kate, a talented and financially independent woman, also possessed the courage, audaciousness and business acumen that most men did not. She had fallen in love with a strong, stubborn man with private principles as unbending as her own. And, in the beginning, her love for Tracy was stronger than his for her. She could easily have lost him. The majority of her close friends advised her against entering into an affair. They saw it as a no-win situation at best; they reasoned that, if he had not left Louise for Loretta Young when he was younger and less riddled with guilt, he would never set up housekeeping with another woman now.

The curious fact existed that while other stars' or executives' currently nonprofessional wives were referred to in the Hollywood columns frequently by their own names—Mal (Mrs. Ray) Milland, Mayo (Mrs. Humphrey) Bogart, Irene (Mrs. David) Selznick, Rocky (Mrs. Gary) Cooper, Gladys (Mrs. Edward G.) Robinson—Louise had no other identity than as Mrs. Spencer Tracy. Even the newly created letterhead for the John Tracy Clinic bannered the name MRS. SPENCER TRACY, PRESIDENT, which the Metro publicity department used to their good advantage. Tracy's past affairs and former and current drinking bouts were magically diffused by Mrs. Spencer Tracy's new eminence. To publicly humiliate Louise by living openly with another woman, or even by being seen in the constant company of another woman, would have been a kind of blasphemy. If Kate chose to press forward in her relationship with Tracy, she would have to accept the clandestine conditions involved.

For Kate, the restrictions only enhanced the desirability of the affair. Now she could command the privacy that she had attempted to have with Leland Hayward and Howard

Hughes. This time the press would be in her corner. The good deeds and admirable achievements of Mrs. Spencer Tracy intimidated even the most voracious of gossip columnists (and Kate as well, who told confidants that Louise's work—like Mrs. Hepburn's—was more important than what she did). Then too, Tracy's obvious entrapment in a marriage in name only made the gossip scribes sympathetic to his predicament. By the end of the making of *Woman of the Year,* nothing could have stopped the affair from going forward. Kate was deeply, dedicatedly in love and Tracy saw in her all the answers to his unhappy personal life, a woman who could share his work and who would be willing to accept him on *his* terms. For a short time, he even checked his consuming thirst for alcohol.

During the production of *Woman of the Year,* Kate and Laura lived in the Barrymore house high in the hills north of Sunset Boulevard. To more than one of her guests' surprise, Kate's bed was covered with stuffed animals and dolls, which did not seem to fit with her exterior behavior. (The menagerie on her bed was to travel with her from house to house for several years thereafter.) She could well have owned any car she wanted, but she drove an old Ford convertible borrowed from Howard Hughes. She remained as positive as ever in her likes and dislikes and in her strongly pro-Roosevelt political opinions. But, as the weeks of production elapsed, her conversations with those close to her about her personal life and whether it was a good idea for someone in her position to get married revealed a new ambivalence in these areas.

Woman of the Year was the film that gave birth to the legendary affair of Tracy and Hepburn; in the very first days on the set neither participant thought the eventuality possible. Tracy referred to Kate as either "Shorty" or "that woman" with much exasperation until one day—no one seems able to pinpoint the exact time—when they both came on the set as though a truce had been declared. Kate was now "Kate" or "Kath." Everyone relaxed.

A sneak preview of the film was held in early December just a few days before the Japanese attack on Pearl Harbor. The original ending of the Lardner-Kanin script had Tess Harding take an honest interest in baseball (her husband's passion) and become more enthusiastic than he at a game, which implied not compromise but growth and love. But

Mankiewicz and Stevens were concerned that "the average American housewife, seated next to her husband, staring for two hours at this paragon of beauty, intelligence, wit, accomplishment, and everything else, [could not] help but wonder if her husband [wasn't] comparing her very unfavorably with this goddess he sees on the screen." Stevens, who for all his charm was a dedicated male chauvinist, decided with Mankiewicz that Tess Harding had to have her comeuppance. Stevens recalled a kitchen routine he had done in a silent film in which a wife tried to fix a simple breakfast in order to prove her domesticity to her husband and "completely fucked it up." Lardner and Mike Kanin had already left for New York and so John Lee Mahin* was assigned to write a new ending to specifications. When Lardner and Kanin found out they objected strenuously, but the only concession made to them was that they were permitted to rewrite some of the more objectionable lines.

Kate termed the new breakfast-scene ending "the worst bunch of shit I've ever read," but Mankiewicz left it in after women at the next preview cheered, "not only with admiration," he said, "but relief. Now they could turn to their schmuck husbands and say, 'She may know Batista, but she can't even make a cup of coffee you silly bastard.'" Ring Lardner and Mike Kanin agreed with Kate that Mankiewicz's contribution to the film had vulgarized their script, and they never were happy about it.

Filmgoers loved it. *Woman of the Year* was even more successful than *The Philadelphia Story*.† Critics were unanimous in their opinion that Tracy and Hepburn made a fine team, each complementing the other. The critic at the *New York World-Telegram* summed it up when he wrote: "The title part is played by Miss Hepburn, who has never looked more beautiful. It is played with such humor, resourcefulness and contagious spirit that I think it is even better than her performance in *The Philadelphia Story*, and that was just as fine as anything could be. No less satisfactory is Mr. Tracy.

---

* John Lee Mahin (1902–1984) was a Metro writer who could always be relied upon to do a workmanlike job. He had scripted *Captains Courageous* (1937), *Boom Town* (1940), *Dr. Jekyll and Mr. Hyde* (1941) and *Tortilla Flat* (1942).
† Hepburn was nominated for Best Actress but lost to Greer Garson (*Mrs. Miniver*).

There isn't a false note in his characterization of the sports-writer. And the things he can do with a gesture, with a smile, are nobody's business . . . what an actor!"

Kate may have been Woman of the Year, but Tracy received top billing.* When Garson Kanin chided him about this, Tracy, "his face all innocence asked, 'Why not?'"

"Well, after all," Garson Kanin argued, "she's the lady. You're the man. Ladies first?"

"This is a movie, Chowderhead," Tracy replied, "not a lifeboat."

Kate was not the only woman who had fallen desperately in love with a married man, nor the first star to have done so. Vivien Leigh and Laurence Olivier had been lovers for several years before either of them divorced their mates. Rhea Gable had taken no less time to agree to a divorce so that Carole Lombard could marry her husband. In both these cases the studios involved had been tremendously protective of their stars, making sure the public was kept unaware of the truth. For the preview of *Gone With the Wind*, David Selznick insisted Vivien Leigh and Laurence Olivier fly to Atlanta on different flights and stay in separate hotels. Louis B. Mayer paid Rhea Gable one hundred thousand dollars above her settlement to seek a quiet divorce from her husband on the nonsensational grounds of irreparable differences. Until the day Mayer was dethroned from M.G.M. in 1951, he remained grateful to Kate for her handling of Tracy and her affair with him. He must have also blessed the quirks in her personality that made her such a rare and remarkable woman.

From the onset of their relationship, Tracy knew Kate doted on the concept that theirs was a very private affair. Indeed, the public knew nothing about it and would not for years to come. The Hollywood film community remained quite another matter. Tracy and Hepburn (and *he* received top billing even in their personal lives) were the most discussed couple in filmdom. In the beginning, there was speculation about whether Kate would withdraw at the point

---

* Tracy received top billing on all nine of the films he and Hepburn made together.

where Tracy could not function well without her, or perhaps live openly with him without benefit of marriage.

In some ways, the relationship bore a strong likeness to Kate's marriage to Luddy. The secrecy of it kept people guessing—*were* they or *weren't* they? And the fact of it kept all other beaux away. These were positive aspects of the relationship for Kate, who feared marriage, wanted no children, and felt of superior mind, will and stamina to most of the men in her world. Tracy's outspokenness, his intelligence, his quick wit and deliberate nature—the pure maleness of his personality—attracted Kate. She respected his talent, thought him wise and uniquely fair, a man a woman could trust. His staunch loyalty to Louise overshadowed his chauvinistic attitude toward all women, Kate included. She admired his dedication to the principles of his religion in the same way she did her father's dedication to the principles of his oath to medicine.

Tracy, at forty-one, had serious health problems caused by his drinking. His liver and kidneys had been affected. After his periodic binges, he suffered melancholia; before them, he could often be moody, rude and short-tempered. His sarcastic humor contained an edge of cruelty and Kate received no exemption from it, nor from an early introduction to his drinking bouts. Halfway through *Woman of the Year* he disappeared. None of the Metro staff could find him at any of his usual watering spots. Kate went from one bar to another until she located and brought him home, fed him, sobered him and covered for his absence. For a long while, keeping Tracy on the wagon promised to be her mission in life. To Kate, the combination of flaw and masculinity seemed irresistible. Then too, Tracy had a vulnerability "like an animal or a child that 'got to her.'"

Kanin wrote, "On the conscious level [Tracy and Hepburn] jealously guarded individuality. As they worked together, however, there came to be a trading of the other's world. They helped each other in many ways. Spencer kept his partner-friend down to earth. She can be flighty, whimsical, impractical, wildly over-imaginative, and often unrealistic. Spencer kept his sharp eye on her and used the tender weapon of humor to reveal her to herself; to show her a better way."

In the last four weeks of the making of *Woman of the Year* the relationship became even more intense. No dating was involved. Kate and Tracy were together whenever possible. Kate put aside her own ego; she stopped posing and dropped all the sophomoric artifices of the past. Love had matured her at the same time that it placed her in a bondage that she perversely found energizing. Never had she looked so vital. Whatever the problems of her liaison, Kate was a very happy woman.

Between the time of *Woman of the Year*'s completion in October, 1941, and its release in early 1942, the Japanese had struck at Pearl Harbor and America was at war. Hollywood was thrown into instant chaos. Many films about to be released were thought to be too frivolous. Others starred young actors who would soon be off to war, and films and careers in Hollywood were built on continuity. *Woman of the Year* was never in jeopardy. Tracy's age and health exempted him from the armed forces. If the picture worked, the team of Tracy and Hepburn could continue; and, indeed, it met with instant success.

"Actors Hepburn and Tracy have a fine old time in *Woman of the Year*," wrote James Agee for *Time*. "They take turns playing straight for each other, act in one superbly directed love scene, succeed in turning several batches of cinematic corn into passable moonshine."

Donald Kirkley at *The Baltimore Sun* concurred that "each complements the other. . . . Gone for good are [Miss Hepburn's] mannerisms, the tricks, the superficiality which marred much of her previous work. Her performance in *Woman of the Year* shows even more subtlety and depth."

CHAPTER
16

Humphrey Bogart once said that Kate was an expert on subjects as diverse as St. Thomas Aquinas's *Summa Theologica* and the spreading of manure on diochronda. Hollywood considered her an intellectual, dedicated to her own independence, a "high-class," "hoity-toity" woman who looked down on their society. Still, its residents were drawn to her and wanted to believe that underneath that glacial exterior lived a person not entirely unlike themselves.

Tracy was no dummy himself. Basically a simple man, he loved the sea as Kate did. In Hollywood, they would walk the beaches at Malibu and Trancus together. Each loved to paint, and they painted together—paintings of the sea, of the landscape wherever they were, even rooftops through hotel windows. He possessed all the Irish charm and the storytelling that still goes with it. Kate liked to sit at his feet, knees drawn to her chin, and listen to his blarney. She glowed with pride at his masculine appearance. Once she asked a drinking buddy of Tracy's what size shirt he wore. The man replied, "Size 17."

"Spence has a bull neck too," she smiled. "Size 17 is a man's neck."

Their social circle was limited to Kate's closest friends—

Cukor, Ruth* and Garson Kanin, Laura, and producer-director Chester Erskine†—and, to Kate's constant distress, Tracy's drinking companions, Victor Fleming, and actors Lynne Overman, Pat O'Brien, James Cagney and Clark Gable. In addition to Tracy's marital status and Kate's love of privacy, his alcoholism was another reason for their limited social life. "He could be a mean bastard if he got too drunk," one friend commented. At the beginning of their relationship, this was a too common occurrence.

Tracy once told an Associated Press reporter** who was also a drinking cohort, "Kate and I never go any place where you bastards will see us. It's as simple as that [the public ignorance of his and Kate's affair]."

During the period directly following the completion of *Woman of the Year*, Kate conducted a vigorous campaign to separate Tracy from the men with whom he drank. One of them recalls dragging a drunken Tracy to Kate's door where she called him "every name in the book" for being a bad influence on Tracy, and then, once Tracy was put to bed, she came at the unfortunate man with an umbrella she had taken from the front hallway.

Clark Gable and Tracy had been friends since 1936 when they starred in *San Francisco*. Both actors owed their start in films to their stage portrayals of Killer Mears in *The Last Mile*.‡ As well, both had had at different times serious affairs with Loretta Young. *Test Pilot* and *Boom Town* had consolidated the friendship. Alcoholic consumption during

---

* Ruth Gordon Kanin (1896–1985), born Ruth Jones, known as Ruth Gordon onstage and in film. She portrayed Mary Todd Lincoln in *Abe Lincoln in Illinois* (1940) and won an Oscar for Best Supporting Actress for *Rosemary's Baby* (1968). She also wrote several screenplays alone and with her husband, Garson Kanin; two—*Adam's Rib* (1949) and *Pat and Mike* (1952)—starred Katharine Hepburn, who was to become her close friend. Their lives had crossed years before. Jed Harris was the father of Gordon's only son.

† Chester Erskine (1905–   ) was originally from the theater. He arrived in Hollywood in 1932 and made several routine films. He adapted, directed and produced *The Egg and I* (1947).

** James Bacon, for eighteen years the Associated Press's correspondent in Hollywood.

‡ Clark Gable played the role of Killer Mears in the West Coast production of *The Last Mile* in 1930. The production was partially financed by his then future second wife, Rhea Langham. Gable had had five wives: Josephine Dillon, Rhea Langham, Carole Lombard, Lady Sylvia Ashley and Kay Williams Spreckels.

working hours was a serious infraction of Metro rules. But Tracy and Gable regularly dropped into each other's dressing rooms for "a shot or two." Gable had the ability to hold his liquor without showing it, but Tracy "would usually turn ugly and argumentative," at which point Gable would always manage to persuade Tracy to "put the bottle away" to avoid any trouble. Before 1939, when Gable married Carole Lombard,* he and Tracy would take off on drinking sprees to other cities. One time they started drinking in Los Angeles and ended up in Tucson, Arizona, where they got into an improbable but rather wild game of jacks played for extremely high stakes. When Mayer finally reached them by telephone, a drunken, almost incoherent Tracy came on the line. Mayer angrily asked to speak to Gable. Tracy told him that was impossible.

"Why?" Mayer demanded to know.

"Because he's on his threesies," Tracy slurred, and hung up.

In January, 1942, the plane carrying Carole Lombard back from a War Bond tour crashed into a mountain, killing everyone onboard. Tracy was one of the few friends at Carole Lombard's small private funeral (not attended by Kate). Shortly after the tragedy, Gable joined the air force,† and Tracy fell into a deep depression. The Theatre Guild had offered Kate the lead in the new Philip Barry comedy, *Without Love.* She wanted Tracy to co-star but the Guild refused, being concerned about his drinking problem. Determined not to leave him behind, she persuaded him to accompany her on the tour. Instead of Tracy, the Guild cast Elliott Nugent,** who turned out to drink almost as much.

Witty and unsubstantial, *Without Love* revolved around a confused New England widow and a scientist-investor who have both renounced love but marry for convenience only to find love again with each other. With Elliott Nugent signed to co-star with Kate and Robert Sinclair once again the director,

---

* Carole Lombard (1908–1942), glamorous and top-ranking comedy star of the 1930s.
† Gable rose in rank from lieutenant to major and received the Distinguished Flying Cross and Air Medal for numerous bombing missions over Germany.
** Elliott Nugent (1900–1980), director, actor, playwright, screenwriter. His greatest success was as a director of comedy and light romantic plays.

the play was scheduled to open in New Haven on Thursday evening, February 26, for four performances, then run one week at the Colonial Theatre, Boston, and a week at Ford's Theatre, Washington, D.C., before opening in New York some time during the week of March 23.

Kate and Nugent were ill suited personally and professionally. Though possessing a debonair charm, Nugent lacked sex appeal and a certain macho quality, which were the essence of the role written by Barry. "The play never jelled," Lawrence Langner of the Theatre Guild said. "And as a result of Kate's feeling about Nugent not 'working' with her, she overplayed extremely, trying to make up for his deficiency, his inadequacy, and her whole performance failed to soar . . . we all knew it was a blunder. It was very hard on poor Elliott."

The pressures began to mount. Nugent, to the surprise of almost everyone but Tracy, turned up drunk shortly after the play opened in New Haven. Kate was now working desperately to keep both Tracy and Nugent sober and to conceal from the press Tracy's presence on the tour. They did not stay at the same hotel or eat a meal out together, nor were they seen together coming or going to the theater or the train station. What began as a romantic adventure soon became burdensome. To add to Kate's growing dissatisfaction, audiences received the play lukewarmly. A meeting was held in a Washington hotel room the day before the play was scheduled to go into New York. This time the decision was to remain on the road. Kate suggested Hartford as the next stop, and Theresa Helburn, Lawrence Langner and Philip Barry all thought that a marvelous idea. Once the dates were set (April 28–May 3) and the huge Bushnell Memorial Auditorium (capacity 3,277) booked, Tracy returned to Hollywood to film *Tortilla Flat.**

Never before had Kate appeared professionally in her hometown, but she thought she knew the kind of people who lived there and that they would be respectful of her privacy. After all, the local press had not been the ones to plague her

---

* *Tortilla Flat*, from the novel by John Steinbeck, was filmed in March and April and released in late May, 1942. It starred Tracy, Hedy Lamarr (1914–   ) and John Garfield (1913–1952) and was directed by Victor Fleming (1883–1949).

during Leland Hayward's visit years before. Concerned about Tracy, lonely without him, growing more and more impatient with Elliott Nugent, his drinking and his inadequate performance, Kate became touchy, irritable and unapproachable. She refused to be interviewed by a boy from Hartford High School or photographed with a fifteen-year-old girl who had won local fame as a budding actress. At one point, when some fans stood waiting for her outside the Hepburn house (now listed in the local guidebook alongside past residences of Mark Twain and Harriet Beecher Stowe), she called upon the police to preserve her privacy.

On opening night after all reporters had been warned away, Dr. and Mrs. Hepburn and Marion and Ellsworth Grant filed decorously into sixth-row seats. (Peggy had been married in Elkton, Maryland, to Thomas Perry a few months earlier and did not live in Hartford.) Kate received enthusiastic applause at the curtain and took seven bows before standing center stage to make a short speech. She confessed in a charming manner that she had twice before appeared in public in Hartford—once in a minor professional part* and once as a student reciting "The Wreck of the Hesperus." She told of her excitement on reaching the bend of the railroad track just before it hit Hartford. She spoke warmly of the station porters and some of her old friends. *Life* magazine, uniquely covering an out-of-town opening, called it "a nice speech and [she] sounded as if she really meant it." They added that she performed her role "with superb style and all the heatless brilliance of fluorescent light."

Kate and the Guild directors decided to abandon *Without Love* for the present. An announcement was made that "Its Broadway opening is postponed until fall while Miss Hepburn makes another movie with Spencer Tracy, whom she may also enlist as her new leading man [on Broadway in *Without Love*]." Donald Ogden Stewart had sent Kate an adaptation he had done of an unpublished novel by I.A.R. Wylie; but the melodramatic script, *Keeper of the Flame*, was not one that Metro felt appropriate to follow *Woman of the Year*. Kate

---

* Hepburn was, perhaps, referring to one of her backyard theater productions for which admission was charged. There is no other record of her appearing in any production, however minor, in Hartford in her youth.

managed to convince the studio to make the film with Tracy and her because she was fascinated by the character of Christine: a strong, resolute woman placed in the tragic position of learning the dead husband she thought was a hero had been a traitor to his country. Tracy played the investigative reporter who discovers the truth. The part was the first full-blown, mature woman Kate had played. Previously, her roles had been, as she said, "girls, all sorts of girls, shy, whimsical, sensitive, flamboyant, tempestuous, but never a woman." She apparently considered Tess Harding as one of these varieties of girls, for Kate added, "I looked upon Christine as a new acting experience, the one I had been preparing years to play." But, also, Tracy would be working with her and she could keep an eye on him. As an added inducement, George Cukor had agreed to direct. Kate told Stewart she would certainly consider it.

Being in California would relieve the terrible tension she had been under, for when Kate was away, Tracy, who did not cope well with loneliness, sought out his drinking companions and went on binges. During the filming of *Tortilla Flat,* he had taken a suite in the Beverly Hills Hotel, which he was to retain for many years. Possessions had little meaning to him. Nothing personal marked the rooms as his; no photographs or mementos were displayed. Never an apartment or hotel dweller, upon her arrival, Kate set out to find a house for herself.

Garson Kanin tells a story about searching with Kate for a house to rent. After walking twice through one entire residence, she left Kanin and the rental agent in the downstairs hall while she looked through the upstairs of the house again. After an inordinately long wait, Kanin became concerned. He called upstairs several times; and when he received no reply, he went outside to see if she had left by another exit. When his search proved fruitless, he returned. Kate was descending the stairs.

"Where were you?" he asked.

"Taking a shower," she replied.

"A shower?"

"Of course."

"You couldn't wait till you got home? Or don't you have facilities there?"

"Listen, you ass," she said with little patience. "If I'm thinking of renting a house, I've got to find out what it's like taking a shower in it, don't I?"

The house Kate rented in 1942 was in Malibu Beach, then a small artists' colony a long way from the mainstream of things and considered additionally undesirable at a time when seaside homes had to be blacked out at night and gas was being rationed. If she and Tracy could not live or be seen together, with *Keeper of the Flame* about to be filmed, they could at least work together. Her role in Tracy's life was multifaceted: wife, secretary, companion, chauffeur, nurse. Weekdays she drove him to the studio and remained with him there even when she was not needed on the set. At the end of the day, she took him back to her house, cooked for him, bolstered his ego, encouraged him and, finally, drove him home. Weekends she kept him as occupied as she could. They walked, talked, painted. She brought in her small circle of close friends hoping to ease him away from those people she thought were a bad influence. On occasion, she had to drag him from a bar and nurse his hangover. He often ridiculed her mannerisms, calling her his "bag of bones." Sometimes their bantering looked very cruel to outsiders.

They seemed to enjoy the conflict, the confrontations. Perhaps, as a friend said, the bantering was "a big put on" and they found it amusing for people to think they were having a fight. But to be with them was not depressing. Their wits were sharp, the action fast and both saw the fun in everything. To Tracy, save for his religion, President Roosevelt, Louise and the children, nothing and no one was sacrosanct and all things and people were fodder for satire, wisecracks and jokes.

Neither Tracy nor Hepburn appeared possessive of the other. Kate's dedication and, indeed, servitude were an independent choice. Tracy never demanded either of her. Yet, his acceptance of her slavish devotion and his inability to fight his alcoholism on his own were silent screams of need that he knew Kate, being the woman she was, would have to respond to.

For Kate, Tracy represented "the simple and pure things in life. . . . He was like water, air, earth. He wasn't easily fooled. . . . He was onto the human race—but with humor and understanding. Yet he was enormously complicated and tortured. He looked out from a terribly tangled maze, like a web. Yet from the center of this tangle would come the simple statement, the total clarity of his work."

And Tracy's work, the artistry that gave him the quality of always seeming to *be* the character he portrayed, instilled such great reverence in Kate that it made her downgrade her own accomplishments. For the next eight years Kate's choice of film parts were to be entirely dictated by Tracy's needs, not her own. When referring to these years in the careers of these two, Hollywood writers always call them the Tracy-Hepburn years. In Kate's case, this is perhaps true, but not in Tracy's. Kate made ten films between 1942 and 1950, six of them with Tracy. Of the four she did apart from him, one, *Stage Door Canteen*, was a vignette appearance in an all-star cast and can be discounted. The other three—all Hollywood made—were not wholly successful and had been compromises on her part to allow her to be close to Tracy. Tracy, on the other hand, made fourteen films between 1942 and 1950, and seven of the eight made without Kate were not only great hits but they affirmed his place in the pantheon of film actors, while Kate was only to prove that she was a marvelous foil for his talent.

Kate's drive now was to find scripts for the two of them; but seldom do stories have parts of equal weight, and those that were as right for Kate as for Tracy were few and far between. If a decision was to be made, it appears always to have swung in Tracy's direction. Kate's role was substantially smaller than Tracy's in *Keeper of the Flame*. When *Without Love* was filmed, the part of the husband was completely rewritten to feature Tracy. *The Sea of Grass* and *State of the Union* were both more Tracy's films than Kate's. Only in *Adam's Rib* in 1949 did Kate win back the kind of strong role she had played in *Woman of the Year*.

Like *Citizen Kane*, *Keeper of the Flame* opened in Gothic style with the death of a national hero; a journalist (Tracy) who admires him sets out to write a biography. Kate, as the widow, has to conceal the truth that her husband was an undercover fascist. From that point, although it contains cinematic potential—a fire, a chase, a noble death—the film failed because, as Cukor later commented, "The story was basically fraudulent," and Kate "had to float in wearing a long white gown and carrying a bunch of lilies. That's awfully tricky isn't it? And doesn't she give long, piercing looks at his [her husband's] portrait over the mantel? Well. I think she finally carried a slightly phony part because her humanity asserted itself, and her humor. They always did."

Cukor also later admitted to there being "a wax work quality" about the film but defended the excellent acting of his cast, especially Spencer Tracy—"marvelous as the journalist, a difficult part . . . but you believe him." He also agreed that "as a piece of storytelling, the unfolding of a mystery, the first half of *Keeper of the Flame* is what you'd call a damn good show." However, Kate was offscreen during most of that segment of the film.*

The momentum of Kate's career began to grind down once again. The war had drastically altered the sphere of entertainment. Films had to depend on home revenues. Stars whose movies relied on their foreign markets became a poor risk. Garbo and Dietrich were both in this category. Americans became terribly nationalistic. They wanted American faces and American stories.† At home and abroad, United States servicemen could not get enough of the Hollywood pinup girl. The careers of Betty Grable, Rita Hayworth and Lana Turner soared. Actresses representing the girl back home were in demand. Kate fell into neither of these categories. Her attraction was mostly to the thirty-five- to fifty-year-old, upper-middle-class, well-educated men and women who wanted films that would relieve the grim reality that they were experiencing: young men going off to be killed or maimed, Europe in chaos, the threat of Hitler—of fascism creeping into their own country (echoing the theme of *Keeper of the Flame*), the great debts that war incurs for a nation. Kate's timing was curiously askew. Just when she had made film

---

* Twenty years later, writer and critic Gavin Lambert wrote, "The film is . . . full of chilling contemporary echoes. The attack on hero worship really strikes home. . . . The glimpses of the dead man's effects on youth look frighteningly real—the funeral with all those sullen Boy Scouts in attendance, the secretary mouthing official phrases about a great patriot . . . the suggestions of a right wing in the making . . . and Katharine Hepburn as the great man's widow has definite Jacqueline Kennedy overtones."

† The British reacted in much the same manner. English films were far more popular there during World War II than American films were.

audiences conscious of her great comedic talents and her vulnerability and tremendous charm in *The Philadelphia Story* and *Woman of the Year*—just when she could have had her audiences in the palm of her hand—she became once again the unknown quantity. And although *Keeper of the Flame* was a "romantic glamour girl part," Tracy and Hepburn were not lovers in it. The film was gloomy and depressing, a great disappointment to the folks who had bought movie tickets and waited in line to see Tracy and Hepburn in another effervescent charmer like *Woman of the Year*.

Kate agreed to return to New York for a fourteen-week limited run of *Without Love* in November only after Tracy promised to join her there for most of the time. He remained on the West Coast during the brief pre-Broadway tryout of the play in Detroit, where her apprehensions mounted. Philip Barry had done some major rewriting without improving the central problem of superficiality, Elliott Nugent had not been replaced, and being separated from Tracy made her tense, which may have accounted for the stiffness of her performance. Robert Sinclair had joined the armed forces and Kate's old friend Arthur Hopkins had restaged the production; but he had brought no new insight to the direction.

She felt better when Tracy arrived in New York. He stayed at the Waldorf Towers, just a few blocks from Turtle Bay. Kate relaxed and her performance improved. Nonetheless, *Without Love*, which began the Theatre Guild's twenty-fifth subscription season, opened on November 10, 1942, at the St. James Theatre to unenthusiastic notices. The majority of the critics were in agreement that the writing was mainly responsible for the play's failure. About Kate's performance, Brooks Atkinson of *The New York Times* was more wounding than faultfinding. "Even at her best Miss Hepburn," he wrote, "is not a virtuoso actress. As a wealthy Washington widow with a New England heritage, she has several stunning visual moments to contribute to *Without Love*. But it is hard for her to sustain a scene in a trifling play that is generally uneventful."

The lure of the Hepburn mystique managed to keep the play running for the length of its engagement to fairly full houses. Had Kate's major interest not been elsewhere, the daily grind of playing to lukewarm audiences might have been singularly depressing. But Tracy was generally nearby, even backstage during some performances. And after the curtain she could cook a small private dinner for the two of them. Tracy never went into the kitchen when Kate was around. He felt such an act would be an invasion of her territory. According to Kate, he did brew "a hell of a good cup of coffee," but only in Hollywood in his studio dressing room. At Turtle Bay, Kate kept a pot constantly heated to combat the urge for a drink, and she served Tracy endless cups of coffee before and after a meal.

In addition to her dedication to Tracy, Kate's energies were given over to the war effort. Daily, friends and co-workers were leaving for various army posts at home and abroad. George Cukor had just enlisted. Laurence Olivier and Vivien Leigh, whom Kate had met through Garson Kanin and had even accompanied on their wedding elopement, had returned to England.* James Stewart and Clark Gable were both in the air force. The list was long and included many of the theater and film's greatest talents. A strong flame of patriotism burned in Tracy and he would have given anything to have been able to join in this fight. During the Broadway run of *Without Love*, Kate narrated the documentary *Women in Defense* for the Office of War Information; and Tracy, Garson Kanin's *Ring of Steel*. Kate gave time to hosting servicemen at the Stage Door Canteen and donated her salary from her appearance in the film about the Canteen to its upkeep.

Tracy, who was committed to film *A Guy Named Joe*,† returned to Hollywood in late May, 1943, while Kate went up to West Hartford to visit with the Hepburns. Happy in her "father's house" (as she always called the Hepburns' big brick home on Bloomfield Avenue), she dressed "like an old bum" in frayed white shorts and a baggy cotton sweater and rode

---

* Vivien Leigh and Laurence Olivier were married on August 31, 1940, at one minute past midnight in Santa Barbara, California, by Municipal Judge Fred Harsh in the living room of Mr. and Mrs. Alvin Weingand, friends of Olivier's. The Weingands, Garson Kanin and Hepburn were the only people present.
† *A Guy Named Joe* starred Tracy, Irene Dunne and Van Johnson and was released on December 24, 1943.

her "wonderful English racing bike 90,000,000 miles an hour" through the quiet suburbs of West Hartford. "I get my hands way down on the bars," she explained to an interviewer, "and my bottom way up on the seat and I go like mad. People see my bottom in white shorts and my long legs pedaling madly and from the back I guess it *really* looked like I had absolutely nothing on. It was enough to make them say, 'What the hell is that?' Then they'd see it was me and try to be nice."

She weeded her father's garden and made a friend of her four-year-old nephew, Jackie (Marion's son), and just stayed home whenever she wasn't bicycling or playing tennis or golf. Her spirits were splendidly high until mid-June, when Tracy informed her that a decision had been made to postpone production a few months to accommodate the tight schedule of Tracy's co-star, Van Johnson.* Kate, edgy at being separated from Tracy when he had so much time on his hands, anxiously looked for a film property that, if not suitable for the two of them, would at least bring her actively back to Hollywood.

Theresa Helburn reintroduced the idea to Kate of getting Metro to film *Mourning Becomes Electra*. Her hope was that Garbo, who had been off the screen for only a year, might be convinced to postpone her retirement for a project as worthy as O'Neill's American classic. Kate was even more enthusiastic this time and upon Helburn's arrival in California campaigned to get Mayer to agree to have a screenplay developed. But Louis B. found the project too sexually provoking for Metro-Goldwyn-Mayer. Furious at his reaction, Kate went on record with the press saying, "Really deep consideration of the issue of sex, the problems that may arise because of it, has no chance to be translated onto the screen under the present system of censorship. It makes no sense at all when at the same time in musicals and other lighter entertainment you find sex exploited in an intriguing and vaguely peeking sort of way that is more meretriciously

---

* Van Johnson (1916–   ) was catapulted to stardom when he appeared in 1942 for the first time in a bit in a Metro programmer titled *Too Many Girls*. Because of a physical disability Johnson was draft-exempt, and in the absence of established stars who were in the services he was in great demand. In 1942–43, he co-starred in no less than eight major Metro films. He appeared with Tracy and Hepburn in *State of the Union* (1948) and with Tracy in *Plymouth Adventure* (1952).

alluring than artists' dramatic studies and impressions. It all seems so terribly false and unintelligent and even harmful if you want to believe harm arises from such things."

The press had discovered a new Hepburn, a fully mature, most intelligent, political woman, ready to speak out honestly about issues of great consequence to her. They weren't to know, but with *Keeper of the Flame* she was to have played her last glamour girl role. Tracy's influence was now to be seen. Not that he changed Kate in any way. But as a result of his demand that she be the best of herself, all her true intelligence and social consciousness came to the surface. She saw some of her father's support of her mother's activities in Tracy's encouragement of her opinions, and it bound the two of them even closer.

Furthering her crusade on behalf of *Mourning Becomes Electra*, she told a reporter for the *Los Angeles Times*, "I will fight to have this picture produced and others I believe would benefit the screen—there is need to think of the post war world when we will again be appealing to the European public as well as our own. We simply cannot confine ourselves to typical musicals and light comedies and expect in all ways to satisfy the people in foreign countries. . . . I have great respect for O'Neill and I feel that his plays might prove a good means of carrying a message about our creative achievements to foreign countries. If censorship stands in the way, then perhaps there is some need for modification and change. . . . I'm afraid I agree with George Bernard Shaw who said that censors are like decayed teeth—not good for the purpose for which they were intended and the cause of much painfulness besides." She had always been a rebel in her personal life, and now her verbalized rebellion against false values (according to her gospel) had begun.

None of her emotional or intellectual attempts to get *Mourning Becomes Electra* produced succeeded. Mayer simply and flatly refused to discuss the project further with her. Pandro Berman, who had once sworn he would never do another film with her, now came to Kate with an adaptation of Pearl Buck's *Dragon Seed*. The role of the idealistic yet realistic Chinese girl, Jade, appealed to Kate, perhaps because of the challenge of portraying a woman of another culture, but also because the theme was that of the Chinese peasant's long struggle against Japanese aggression. Mayer had approved such a political film for two reasons: one, it showed America's enemy, Japan, as evil; and two, Metro had made a commercially successful film of another Pearl Buck novel, *The Good Earth.*

Starring in a three-million-dollar production placed an extra responsibility on Kate.* *Gone With the Wind* had cost less to make and was a half hour longer. Filmed largely on location in the San Fernando Valley, where an entire Chinese peasant village had been constructed on a 120-acre tract of land, *Dragon Seed* began under the direction of Jack Conway,† who collapsed halfway through the production and was replaced by Harold S. Bucquet.** The pressures mounted. Location was a thirty-six-mile drive and, because of her heavy makeup, Kate had to be on the set by six A.M. Her renewed friendship with Berman and, more important, with his assistant and her longtime friend, Jane Loring, got her through. Tracy was making a very difficult film, *The Seventh Cross,*‡ which Berman was also producing. Struggling to keep off the booze, he drank steaming cups of coffee all day. At night he suffered terrible insomnia (an affliction that he fought for years), and Kate tried as well as she could to help him ward off the tension this created.

Signe Hasso,¶ Tracy's leading lady in *The Seventh Cross,* noted that on the set "he was intense and withdrawn, and had little time for chit-chat. During a scene he never went in for frivolous ad-libbing as many actors do. We used to tease him about his complete absorption [in his role]. He only smiled,

---

* Hepburn's previous films had never been budgeted at more than one million dollars, a high cost for a film at that time.

† Jack Conway (1887–1952), a film craftsman. Among his many fine films (more than one hundred), *Arsène Lupin* (1932), *A Tale of Two Cities* (1935), *Boom Town* (1940) and *Honky Tonk* (1941) stand out.

** Harold S. Bucquet (1891–1946), previously a director of modest films, was responsible for most of the *Dr. Kildare* pictures. *Dragon Seed* was his first major assignment. He directed Tracy and Hepburn in their next film, *Without Love.*

‡ *The Seventh Cross* was directed by Fred Zinnemann and based on Anna Sagher's novel, which was adapted by Helen Deutsch. Tracy plays a German liberal who escapes from a concentration camp. His six compatriots are killed, and he goes on to fight for freedom.

¶ Signe Hasso (1915–   ), Swedish actress very popular in the 1940s.

pretended to be annoyed, but never bothered to answer back."

Having never previously worked with Tracy, Miss Hasso was not to know that he could ad-lib as well, if not better, than any of his fellow actors, but was reacting to the stress of drying out while performing a heavy and responsible task.

Whatever sharp criticism may have been written about Kate's performance of Jade in *Dragon Seed*—the snide remarks about her "Peck and Peckish pajamas" and her "twangy New England Oriental accent"—she does manage to make Jade "a rather wondrous character" and because of it *Dragon Seed* becomes a compelling film. Not to be dismissed were the two splendid performances of Walter Huston* and Aline MacMahon† as Jade's elderly peasant parents. Mayer had been right. The exotic background, the strength of Pearl Buck's popularity and the view of the Japanese as the enemy made *Dragon Seed* successful at the box office, although far less so than *The Good Earth*, and it was not as well received as many less expensive films.

Clearly, what audiences wanted to see was Tracy and Hepburn reunited in a film that paired them in a romantic comedy like *Woman of the Year*. *Keeper of the Flame* had served only to make the public hungry for the team in a lighter, bantering mood. Kate wanted that as well and she finally convinced Mayer to buy *Without Love* as a vehicle for them. Donald Ogden Stewart adapted the play. Onstage, Kate had been the center spectacle, stunning in her Valentina costumes and floating about as she spoke Barry's witty lines. Her brilliance had covered Nugent's weakness and had been the one saving grace of a shallow play. With Tracy's considerable presence, the story now took on more substance. Kate's

---

* Walter Huston (1884–1950). Famous on stage and screen, Huston starred on Broadway in O'Neill's *Desire Under the Elms* (1924), *Dodsworth* (1934) (a role he later repeated on screen) and *Knickerbocker Holiday* (1938), in which he made famous the song "September Song." He won the Academy Award for Best Supporting Actor (1948) for his role as the old prospector in *The Treasure of the Sierra Madre*. Director John Huston is his son.
† Aline MacMahon (1899–   ) had been one of the stars Hepburn played with at the Berkshire Playhouse in 1931 and had been a guest star in *Stage Door Canteen*. She was nominated by the Academy for Best Supporting Actress in 1944 for her role in *Dragon Seed*, but did not win. She never appeared with Hepburn again.

role was no longer a star turn. The personality she created by subduing her performance to Tracy's was less exciting than the original, but she contributed greatly to solidifying Tracy and Hepburn as a team.

An actor's ego no longer controlled Kate. Making a good film and doing it with Tracy did. Always interested in the filming process, she now wanted to become an expert on all facets of production. She arrived early on the set, stayed late and had her nose everywhere, sniffing her disapproval, scenting fresh ground. The set director, Ed Willis, commented, "People always said to me, 'She's trying to do everything.' And my reply was, 'The thing I'm afraid of and you should be afraid of, is that she *can* do everything.' Producer, director, cameraman! That's what she was! Her idea of everything was always better than you could ever have envisioned."

A caption could have been written for the weeks during which *Without Love* were shot: "Kate, happy at last!" She had her work, she had her man, and she had her way. Tracy was off the booze—her hope was that he had won the battle. In the end, it turned out to be only a one-round victory.

CHAPTER
17

Unlike the majority of top stars, Kate was not surrounded by a claque of sycophants, nor had she ever been. Her longtime friendships with Laura and Luddy were of a different ilk. They remained caring family, and their love for Kate and hers for them was tested and had proved to be strong enough to withstand time and separation. With Tracy's importance in her life, Laura and Luddy's influence faded into the background, but that is not to say that their positions had been completely usurped. For one thing, Kate was a person of fierce loyalty. And for another, each had been the recipient of deep affection from Kate and each had proven dedication to her over and over again. For now, both of them had made adjustments in their own lives that compensated for Kate's dwindling need for their companionship.

In September, 1942, when Kate had been on tour with the Barry play *Without Love*, Luddy had filed suit for divorce against Kate in Hartford under the name of Ogden Ludlow. Luddy claimed desertion and told the court that he doubted the legality of the decree Kate had received in Mexico in 1934. The case appeared on the docket simply as *Ogden Ludlow* v. *Katharine H. Ludlow*. Not until the hearing was almost over did the judge realize the identity of the defendant. Kate was not present, but Dr. Hepburn testified in a successful effort to establish Connecticut as Kate's legal residence.

One week later, on September 26, Luddy married a divorced Boston socialite, Elizabeth Albers, who helped to fill his life. Laura, of course, had her own coterie of friends and her family estate in New Jersey. When Kate was on the West Coast, she often used Kate's house in New York. Laura was always to represent a continuum in Kate's life. No matter what vicissitudes, changes or close deaths Kate might suffer, Laura, who never married, was there, a solid support, a constant friend. Kate knew this, cherished their friendship and returned it in kind.

With the end of the war with Japan on August 14, 1945, Hollywood was back to the flurry of prewar production; among many other returning servicemen, George Cukor came home. Cukor's house remained one of the few places outside her own residence where Kate would go for a social gathering. She claimed restaurants made her faint; people stared at her and she became self-conscious about everything —her table manners, her chewing, her voice. She tried dining out on five or six occasions to please various associates, each time with the same cold-sweat result, and then never attempted to do so again.

Ruth Gordon (Kanin) and Kate got on very well. Both of them had strong New England roots, had been stage performers first, and had known many of the same people earlier in their lives. The Kanins were as splendid a team as Kate and Tracy—both witty, quick and eclectic in their interests—and they seemed to "spark off each other." Dining with them one night, photographer-designer Cecil Beaton* noted that in conversation the Kanins knew how to "dispense with all unnecessary impediments, driving right to the point, sticking to it, and brooking no interruptions." Ruth was writing as well as acting, Garson writing and producing. Like Kate, they were workaholics. Also, although not teetotalers, when working they did not allow themselves a single drink because

---

* Cecil Beaton (1904–1980), knighted in 1972, gained fame as a photographer of the British Royal Family and of noted personalities. He was a great artist in design and won the Academy Award for his work as designer for *Gigi* (1958) and *My Fair Lady* (1964).

they felt it claimed a dividend of energy the next day. With Tracy's drinking problem, they were a boon to have around.

Beaton found them "like a couple of athletes; their training is rigorous. . . . It is typical of [Ruth] and her husband that they both have much work in hand while there is much already ready for production. Garson with a couple of film scripts and a play, Ruth with three plays."*

The Kanins were Kate and Tracy's closest companions. They were now neighbors as well, having bought a house next door to Kate in Turtle Bay. Certainly not sycophantic, the Kanins were enjoying huge success, both individually and together. The friendship (on their part at least) was still curious. They themselves liked to live like royalty, but they accepted a kind of subjects' place where Kate was concerned. Also very much unlike Kate, they led an extremely active social life. Beaton wrote that "their extravagances . . . are such that if both of them have a successful play running for the next six years, they will still be behind with their taxes. . . . They see films . . . in a private viewing room . . . have their own chauffeur . . . take their meals at the most expensive restaurants. Ruth buys whole hog from Mainbocher.† . . . Garson showers her with presents so that she resembles a little Burmese idol studded with bulbous jewelry. They consider money is of no use unless spent."

Late in the spring of 1945, Kate and Tracy went to New York. Kate loved to travel, Tracy loathed it, but he did it to please her and so that he could meet her family. The experience was not exactly what he had expected. "The Hepburns all love to talk," he once said. "Even when they look like they're listening, they're really only sitting there thinking what they're going to say next." Kate was present as he told this story to director Frank Capra: "First time I got invited to the Hepburn home in New England [Fenwick]— home, hell! a palace! On half an island and facing a private fenced-off beach a mile long. Well, you know Madame Do-Gooder, here. She'll donate to the Committee for the

---

* One of the plays Ruth Gordon was working on at this time—*Over Twenty-One* —was successful on stage and screen. At the same time, Kanin had begun work on his play *Born Yesterday* (1946).

† Mainbocher—the designer. The Duchess of Windsor also wore his clothes almost exclusively.

Protection of Fireplugs. She'll parade for the civil rights of the three-toed sloth. And you know what? Her family are all bigger fruitcakes than she is. You know—ultra-liberal New England aristocrats that work their ass off for the poor, poor folk, but never see one. Take [Kate's] father. A big doctor. They won't let charity letters go through New England's mails unless his name's on the letterheads. And her mother helps Margaret Sanger with young girls that got knocked up—"

"Mother helps with birth control—" Kate broke in.

"Okay, mother helps young girls from *getting* knocked up. And all the [five] grown Hepburn kids've got pet social rackets of their *own*. What a clan! Well, at dinner my head's this big. Can you imagine listening to [*seven*] Hepburns all talking at *once* about the Negroes, the slums, the Puerto Ricans, abortions, the homeless, the hungry? So I get up and say, 'If you don't mind I'll step outside and lift the lamp beside the golden door.' So I go out on the porch for some peace and to watch the sunset.

"The beach was empty. Had to be empty with those barbed wire fences on each side. And I see a guy, with a fishing rod, a little guy, crawling through the barbed wire about half a mile away, so far away he was a speck. 'Hey,' I yelled to them inside, 'better put on another plate. Here comes a wretched one yearning to breathe free!'

"Old man Hepburn came out running with fire in his eye. 'Where is he?' I pointed to the fence. Dr. Hepburn took down a megaphone off the porch wall and ran out on the beach yelling 'This is private property! You are trespassing! Get off this beach immediately or I will fill your tail with buckshot! Now git!'

"The poor old fisherman dove through that barbed wire and gits for his life up the beach trailing barbed wire from his legs. Papa Hepburn hangs up the megaphone and says to me, 'Getting so a man can't enjoy any privacy anymore. At least twice a week some nervy interloper tries crawling through that fence!' And he goes right inside and joins the hot family discussion about the rights of the poor."

Tracy had been off alcohol for many months and was looking better and complaining less than usual (he had a natural leaning toward hypochondria). Kate was ecstatically happy. April 1 he received a letter from President Roosevelt asking him to tour army, navy, marine and air-force bases overseas to help keep up the morale of the men still on duty. Kate persuaded him to accept. In Washington, D.C., while he was being briefed, the President extended an invitation for him to call at the White House.

After an hour's visit, Roosevelt told Tracy that he wanted him to deliver a letter in Europe off the record for him. Tracy agreed. On April 12, President Roosevelt died, Tracy's tour was canceled and he never found out whom he was to deliver a message to, a blank that was always to frustrate him.

Neither Kate nor Tracy had scheduled a film for the rest of the year, and they were definitely at odds about what to do. Finally, Garson approached Tracy with the idea of playing the lead in a Robert E. Sherwood play, *The Rugged Path*, that he was to direct. Tracy admired Sherwood's work and liked the role but was not convinced that after a lapse of fifteen years he should return to the stage. Kanin says that "Most of all there hung over him the fear of losing so much as a single round in his continuing battle against alcohol. A few days lost in the production of a film was no great matter. The discipline of the theatre was far more stringent."

Tracy told Sherwood straightforwardly, "I could be good in this thing all right. But then, who knows? I could fall off and maybe not show up."

Sherwood's World War II drama was about an idealistic newspaper editor who gets fired for his articles against the encroachment of fascism and becomes, successively, a cook on an American destroyer, a guerrilla fighter and, finally, a dead hero. Although it had the aura of frequently tried ground, the play contained moments of suspense and a few fine speeches, but either Tracy or Kate should have been able to predict the almost certain failure of the enterprise. The only explanation can be Kate's desire to see Tracy back onstage and his own wish to see if he could still perform in the theater.

Finally, with Kate's encouragement and an agreement from Metro that he could do it, Tracy went into rehearsals in the heat of the New York summer. Kate was always close by, ready to ameliorate a situation or simply make sure his needs were taken care of. The play opened in Providence, Rhode Island, and immediately problems set in. The script needed a lot of rewriting and Tracy fell ill with a flu bug. He managed to make it through every performance with Kate nursing him before and after. He did not want the press to think alcohol had caused a possible absence. By the time the show reached Boston he simply could not go on and four performances were canceled. The press hinted darkly at other reasons and claimed he had simply walked out.*

On the morning of November 10, 1945, the date *The Rugged Path* was to open at the Plymouth Theatre, neither Tracy nor Kate could be located. Kanin, checking things backstage, saw a woman on her knees scrubbing the bathroom of Tracy's dressing room. He went in to ask the cleaning woman if she had seen Tracy. Kate grinned up at him. "Damn place is filthy," she said, amending it to—*"was."* Tracy arrived by curtain and, according to critic George Jean Nathan, "gave a performance that injected at least a superficial belief into the unbelievable materials provided him."

Kanin and Tracy shook hands after the curtain. Garson says, "I tried to convey confidence, but his resentful gray eyes rejected me. Ruth and Kate looked on. We had all tried to behave well but knew that the circumstances had sullied our fine friendship."

Tracy's name kept the show going and Sherwood never stopped rewriting until it finally closed after eighty-one performances. Tracy had begun to drink again.

Not long after their return to Hollywood, Kate and Tracy agreed to make a film for Metro based on Conrad Richter's thoughtful novel *The Sea of Grass*, about the conflict between those who would monopolize the range lands for grazing and those who would portion it out to homesteaders and their ploughs. Kate's role as the principal range holder, Colonel Brewster's citified wife, Lutie, had to be developed. A complicated love story with another man (Melvyn Douglas†)

---

* The Burns Mantle Theatre annual for 1945 also claims, "Tracy quit in Boston, walked out one night, but returned a few days later and went on with the play to New York."

† Melvyn Douglas (1901–1981). One of the most popular leading men in films during the thirties and forties, Douglas was also an acclaimed stage performer. He won a Tony for *The Best Man* and by the sixties became a much honored supporting player. He won the Academy Award for Best Supporting Actor in *Hud*, 1963.

and an illegitimate son was superimposed, throwing the script completely off-balance. A young actor-director, Elia Kazan,* who had made only one previous film, *A Tree Grows in Brooklyn,* was hired to direct. Kazan saw the problems from the start but claims to have been "too dumb to quit." Uncomfortable with Kate, who remained cool to him for unexplained reasons throughout the film, intimidated by Tracy, who thought Kazan's acting methods "a lot of high-flown mumbo-jumbo," and not permitted free rein in production, Kazan never was in real control. To make matters worse, *The Sea of Grass,* which was mainly about the grasslands of New Mexico, was filmed without a blade of grass being photographed because Metro had ten reels of background footage of grazing ground in its library that they insisted Kazan use. All outdoor scenes were therefore shot on a sound stage before a rear projection screen.

No one knew quite what to do with the project when filming was completed. Finally, Mayer decided to shelve it, and for a time it looked as though the film might never get a release. Kate tried unsuccessfully to get M.G.M. to back another project, the Anita Loos play *Happy Birthday,* but Eric Johnson, the head of the Motion Picture Association, which formed the censorship board for films, refused to give his go-ahead on the grounds that *Happy Birthday* was pro-alcohol. No matter how ridiculous this verdict (*Happy Birthday* was a light comedy about a thirty-five-year-old teetotaling spinster who gets inebriated on her birthday and wakes up in the morning with a husband), Metro refused to support Kate's wishes to go forward with the project.

For the first time since he had come to Hollywood, Tracy went almost a year without making a film. He was ill for most of the time with stomach problems. Kate nursed and cared for him, although they still had separate homes (Tracy had moved into a modest guest cottage that George Cukor had on

---

* Elia Kazan (1909–   ) went on to become a celebrated theater and film director. His stage credits include: *All My Sons* (1947), *A Streetcar Named Desire* (1947) and *Death of a Salesman* (1949). His best known films are *Gentleman's Agreement* (1947), *A Streetcar Named Desire* (1951), *Viva Zapata!* (1952), *On the Waterfront* (1954), *East of Eden* (1955), *A Face in the Crowd* (1957), *Splendor in the Grass* (1961) and *America, America* from his own novel (1963).

his grounds and Kate into a hilltop house that had once belonged to silent-screen star John Gilbert). Her plan was to help nurse him back to health before considering a film.

They had both lived in California for more than fifteen years, yet they still behaved like guests who had simply stayed too long at a party. Possessions were scoffed at, and Cukor's guest house (one of three on the estate)—several acres removed from the director's own luxurious West Hollywood residence—was sparsely furnished. If Tracy's landlord-friend expected that Kate would quickly decorate it, he did not reckon with Tracy, who believed that "everything you own, every possession, gets to be a burden. Nothing—that's my idea of heaven. . . . I like to check in and check out." The interior of the small bungalow remained as monastic while Tracy lived there as it had been before he moved in. He visited the Hill every Friday night to see Louise and the kids, but he never thought of it as his home anymore.

To Kate, home was where her family happened to be— Fenwick or Bloomfield Avenue. Her money was still being sent to Dr. Hepburn, her bills paid by a secretary in Hartford and an allowance sent her. (Once, when she wrote her father that she needed extra money for a dress, he replied, "You already have a dress. What do you need a new one for?" And he refused to send her the extra money.) All personal possessions were kept in her bedrooms in both these homes and in her house in Turtle Bay. Whether her stay in California encompassed a week, a month or a year, she could pick up at any time and transport all she had in a few pieces of luggage. That is not to say that she did not have a nesting quality, because she did. However, it took a simpler, more basic form.

What Kate achieved was a kind of expertise on what was essential in her own and Tracy's day-to-day life. Always a font of information on the most diverse of subjects, Kate knew *exactly* "where in the bedroom the bed should be placed" for privacy, view, comfort and convenience; she found the best dentist, the pharmacy that delivered at any hour, the market that gave the most personal attention to its customers, the shortest way to get to places either of them had to go. Flowers were important to her, and her rooms were brightened with strategically placed vases containing simple arrangements of homegrown varieties. Favorite books were stacked beside the bed or on tables. Afternoon tea was a ritual, and some homey confection usually accompanied it. Somehow, within a week of moving into still another furnished house, Kate made it look as though she had lived there for years.

In essence, Kate ran two households, hers and Tracy's; and although she had plenty of staff, everything could not have gone so smoothly if not for her exceptional talent for "no-nonsense" organization. Tracy believed that men and women had decided roles and that neither should cross the line of the other. Anything connected with the kitchen, interior decoration or household purchases was defined by him as woman's work, and he honestly felt he was being "considerate" in staying out of such matters and letting Kate handle them. Yet he much enjoyed Kate's independence, her ability to manage things alone, and the absence in her nature of supposedly feminine fears, such as being "unprotected" by a man in the house or driving late hours alone. Back in 1939, she had interrupted a burglary in her Turtle Bay house and chased the thief out to the street and into the arms of the law. "Fear is no builder of character," was one of her favorite axioms. She chose not to wrestle with her own fears, to avoid the cause rather than to suffer the effect. Obviously, if she never dined in a restaurant, she was saved the terror of people watching her eat.

Her admiration of Tracy never wavered. Her closest friends felt she idolized him. Pride rose forcefully in her when she spoke about him; and when they were together, no one could doubt the extent of her devotion—or, for that matter, Tracy's for her.

Pandro Berman had sent her the script of *Undercurrent*, a suspense melodrama written by Edward Chodorov, and asked her to consider it. Kate really adored Berman, who had absolutely no intellectual pretensions, and their long history, combined with Chodorov's friendship to her during the debacle of *The Lake*, made a refusal difficult. Often gruff and irascible, possessed by a violent temper that exploded most often around actors (for he had no patience with their egos and their whims), Berman had almost always made an exception with Kate. He had also been responsible for some of her favorite films, *Morning Glory, Alice Adams* and *Stage Door*. Kate accepted.

"I'm sure we'll get along," she told Vincente Minnelli, who was signed to direct. To Minnelli "It sounded like both an order and a threat. Never had I met anyone with such self-assurance. She made me nervous." A director of slick musicals, Minnelli was a strange choice. He had done only one previous straight drama, *The Clock*, starring his wife, Judy Garland, and Kate was not struck with the idea of his directing the film any more than she was with Robert Mitchum* co-starring with her and Robert Taylor.†

For the first few weeks of the production, Kate often locked horns with Minnelli. *Undercurrent* required a different acting style from the one she felt comfortable with. Suspense did not demand her usual in-depth probing of the character she was to portray. Her greatest challenge was "getting the right horrified reaction."

Undercurrent is about a young, rather naïve, woman who marries a charming and wealthy industrialist (Robert Taylor). The husband confesses to her that he has a psychopathic brother (Robert Mitchum) who has committed murder and is a constant threat. When the brother finally appears, the wife is taken by surprise. He is an articulate and sensitive man and to her dismay she finds herself falling in love with him. The doubts she had had about her husband can no longer be suppressed. Is *he* the psychopathic killer? When she realizes this is the case, he is about to murder her. A harrowing horse chase follows in which he is trampled to death and she is saved by the brother. The denouement has the wife being pushed in a wheelchair (she is convalescing from the trauma of the experience) to the piano, where the brother is playing the melodic theme from Brahms's Fourth Symphony, which has been used recurrently throughout the film.

Minnelli produced a fine sense of mood, but the genre was

* Robert Mitchum (1917–   ) catapulted to stardom in *The Story of G.I. Joe* (1945) for which he received an Oscar nomination for Best Supporting Actor. His most memorable films include *The Night of the Hunter* (1955), *The Longest Day* (1962), *Two for the Seesaw* (1962) and *Ryan's Daughter* (1970).
† Robert Taylor (1911–1969), one of M.G.M.'s principal players. Best known for his roles in *Camille* (1936), *Waterloo Bridge* (1940) and *Johnny Eager* (1941).

not one he had yet mastered. Kate knew this as well as she knew that her role was better suited to the talents of an Ingrid Bergman. She grew to like Minnelli personally. He and Garland had just had a daughter, Liza, and Kate took an interest in the child's progress. Until this time, she and Garland had never been close. They had often sat next to each other early in the morning under hair dryers in the makeup department, but seldom exchanged more than a few words. Kate now recognized Garland's shaky emotional state and did what she could to be helpful, including making things easier for Minnelli on the set. Mitchum was another matter.

In one of the last shots in the film, a piece of lighting equipment blocked the line of vision for Mitchum while he was playing a scene with Kate.

"Can you see me, Miss Hepburn?" he asked.

"Not for dust," she replied tartly.

Passing by Mitchum's dressing room shortly after the scene was shot, she caught sight of Boyd Coheen, Mitchum's stand-in, drawing. Curious, she stepped inside and glanced at the work and then started to leave.

"You know young man," she said, pausing, "you have obvious talent. You really should do something with it instead of working for some cheap flash actor like Mr. Mitchum."

Fiercely loyal to Mitchum (who was privately one of Hollywood's most caring people), Coheen replied, "Thanks for the advice, Miss Hepburn. Now, may I make a request?"

"Yes, of course," she agreed.

"Should I survive you, would you bequeath me that lovely collection of bones?" And he shut the door in her face. Shocked, Kate turned to find Mitchum facing her. "You can't be all bad with friends like that," she said and strode away.

Undercurrent was not a great film (not even a particularly good one), but it was well made and generally well acted by a good supporting cast.* Kate gave a "crisp and taut performance." Taylor "brooded meanness" throughout and Mitchum was "appealing." But both screenplay and direction dissipated whatever tension the performers achieved. The best that could be said for *Undercurrent* was that the filming

---

* Edmund Gwenn (1875–1959) played Hepburn's father in the film as he had a decade earlier in *Sylvia Scarlett*.

of it kept Kate active as she tended Tracy and it called so little upon her resources, she had the energy to cope well with her personal situation.

In late 1946, while Tracy filmed *Cass Timberlane* with Lana Turner, Kate made *Song of Love,* an overromanticized story based on the marriage of Clara and Robert Schumann. For her role as Clara Wieck Schumann, Kate studied daily with pianist Laura Dubman, a pupil of Arthur Rubinstein (who made the piano recordings for the film), and she mastered "the proper techniques of playing difficult compositions for close-up shooting." But her technical achievement could not compensate for the sloppiness of the script. *Time* found she portrayed Clara "with skill and feeling. . . . She is fascinating to watch at the piano, using the clawlike 19th Century style; her 'reactions' to the men's music, in various dramatic contexts, are the backbone of the picture." Her portrayal of Clara Wieck Schumann called upon her most skilled effort and Kate delivered. By itself, it reveals one of her finest performances. Seen together with Paul Henreid's torpid Schumann and Robert Walker's* ludicrous Brahms ("[he] plays Brahms as though he were a musician whose fate depended on bobby-soxers"), Clara seems to have wandered into some kind of bizarre fantasy.

Unfortunately for Kate, *The Sea of Grass* was now released. Although it fared much better than all concerned thought it would, it did not help to increase her popularity. Despite Kazan's worst fears, the use of rear projection had not destroyed the visual potential of the film. In fact, the process had worked well enough to fool the majority of the critics. One noted with high regard, the "vast, flat New Mexico desert with the 'sea of grass' high on a table-rock mesa, waving now lazily, now stormily, ended like a sea as far as the camera eye can reach."

Appropriately, the next Tracy-Hepburn film was titled *State of the Union*. In 1948, the state of the union was pretty deplorable and Kate, with echoes of her mother's political outspokenness, let her opinions be heard.

---

* Robert Walker (1918–1951) had played Hepburn's son in *The Sea of Grass*.

CHAPTER
18

Throughout his term of office, Kate had been a staunch Roosevelt supporter* and a dedicated Democrat. But unable to rationalize America's use of the atomic bomb or the growing lack of détente between Russia and the United States, she shifted her allegiance from Truman and the Democrats to Henry A. Wallace, former vice-president under Roosevelt, who was campaigning for the presidency on a third-party ticket as a Progressive, a political organization previously active only in the presidential elections of 1912 and 1924.† (Tracy remained loyal to the Democratic party.)

---

* Hepburn had known President and Mrs. Roosevelt personally since the mid-thirties and had been their guest at several large functions. At one famous picnic in 1934, Hepburn was reported to have been surprised by the President as she waded barefoot on the grounds of the Roosevelts' home at Hyde Park.

† Henry Agard Wallace (1888–1965), Vice-President of the United States, 1941–45. His family had founded an influential agricultural periodical, *Wallace's Farmer*, which he edited in the 1920s. His articles on agrarian matters soon made him an authority. In 1933, Roosevelt appointed him secretary of agriculture. In 1944, Wallace was by-passed for the vice-presidency. Truman was nominated and elected on Roosevelt's ticket. Wallace became secretary of commerce, a post he held until his resignation in September, 1945 (attributed to his strong opposition to Truman's cold war tactics with Russia). In 1948, Wallace helped launch a new Progressive party and appeared as its presidential candidate, with Senator Glen A. Taylor as the vice-presidential candidate. He polled slightly more than 1,150,000 votes. Truman defeated Thomas Dewey by the

Endorsed by the Communist party and the American Labor party of New York State, Henry Wallace and his supporters were looked upon as pinkos, arch-liberals, and pro-Communists.

A shattering time lay ahead for Hollywood and the nation. The House Committee for Un-American Activities (HUAC) was revving up its motor; and J. Parnell Thomas, its chairman and chief investigator, had begun an investigation to reveal subversive Communist and un-American influence in motion pictures. What he had in his corner was the ill-gotten confidence that the masses could be stirred into a lynch mob.* What he had not bargained for was the passion, eloquence and influence of his opponents.

When Wallace was barred from hiring the Hollywood Bowl for a political address (frequently used in this manner) in May, 1947, Kate spoke at an anticensorship rally at Los Angeles' Gilmore Auditorium on Wallace's behalf. "At first I was going to wear white," she remembered, "and then I decided they'd think I was the dove of peace so I wore pink. Pink! How could I have been so dumb!"

Many stars, directors and writers joined her on the platform (Judy Garland for one†), each making a short statement, most directed against Mr. Thomas and his committee of "inquisitors." Kate warned, "J. Parnell Thomas is engaged in a personally conducted smear campaign of the motion picture industry. He is aided and abetted in his efforts by a group of super patriots who call themselves the Motion Picture Alliance for the Preservation of American Ideals. For myself, I want no part of their ideals or those of Mr. Thomas. The artist since the beginning of time has always expressed the aspirations and dreams of his people. Silence the artist and you have silenced the most articulate voice the people have."

---

narrow margin of about 500,000 votes. If Wallace had been stronger, the papers that prematurely printed Dewey had won could well have been right.

* J. Parnell Thomas's committee consisted of nine men, among them future President Richard M. Nixon.

† Garland pleaded, "Before every free conscience in America is subpoenaed, please speak up! Say your piece. Write your Congressman a letter! Let the Congress know what you think of its 'Unamerican Committee.' Tell them how much you resent Mr. Thomas's kicking the living daylights out of the Bill of Rights!"

Mayer was decidedly unamused by the venture of his various "children" (as he often called Metro's players) into the political arena, and he made sure they knew of his displeasure. Kate's name was given in the HUAC investigative hearings, attached to an innuendo that was enough for Mayer to decide not to cast her in a film for several months. Kate, directors Leo McCarey and Sam Wood (both immediately labeled informers by the people whose lives they were destroying) testified, had helped raise eighty-seven thousand dollars for a "very special" political party, which, McCarey added, "Certainly wasn't the Boy Scouts." Kate smoldered with fury, especially when she saw the careers and lives of so many of her good friends—Donald Ogden Stewart, Ring Lardner, Jr., perhaps the closest among them—being torn apart.

Kate believed as Thomas Jefferson had written, "It behooves every man who values liberty of conscience for himself, to resist invasions of it in the case of others; or their case may, by change of circumstances, become his own. It behooves him, too, in his own case, to give no example of concession, betraying the common right of independent opinion, by answering questions of faith, which the laws have left between God and himself."

Though never subpoenaed by the Committee, Kate made it very clear that she would give no names or aid or abet Chairman Thomas in any of his scare and smear tactics.

Tracy was fond of saying, "Remember who shot Lincoln," when asked his political opinions. His contempt for J. Parnell Thomas and his committee matched Kate's; but he held strong to the belief that actors, being emotional people, had no place in politics. Portraying a politician was another matter. Tracy had never done so, but when director Frank Capra* offered him the role of presidential contender Grant Mathews in the film adaptation of the Howard Lindsay and

---

* Frank Capra (1897–   ). The majority of Capra's films, including the classics *It Happened One Night* (1934), *Mr. Deeds Goes to Town* (1936), *You Can't Take It With You* (1938), *Mr. Smith Goes to Washington* (1939), *Meet John Doe* (1941) and *It's a Wonderful Life* (1946), dealt with "the triumph of honesty and justice over selfishness and deceit." *State of the Union* was no exception.

Russel Crouse Pulitzer Prize–winning stage success, *State of the Union,* he enthusiastically accepted. Claudette Colbert had been slated to co-star with Tracy. Three days before production was scheduled to begin, she backed out, giving a feeble excuse. In truth, she had just received the final script and could see that Tracy's role was dominant and that she would be supporting him despite her co-star billing.

In desperation, Capra called Tracy for suggestions. "Waal, come to think of it, Kate isn't hamming it up at the moment," he replied.

Not wanting to count on a miracle, Capra asked if he thought she would *really* do it on such short notice.

"I dunno. But the bag of bones has been helping me rehearse. Kinda stops you, Frank, by the way she reads the woman's part. She's a real theater nut, you know. She might do it for the hell of it—"

Tracy handed the telephone to Kate, who accepted without reservations. She appeared on the set ready to work that Monday morning before a contract could be negotiated or a salary fixed (she asked for and got the same fee as had been allocated to Colbert) and played the first scenes wearing her own wardrobe (pajamas and bathrobe, as it happened) while new costumes were hastily being made.*

Capra was to say, "There are women and there are women—and then there is Kate. There are actresses and actresses—then there is Hepburn. A rare professional-amateur, acting is her hobby, her living, her love. She is wedded to her vocation as a nun is to hers, and as competitive in acting as Sonya Henie was in skating. No clock-watching, no humbug, no sham temperament. If Katharine Hepburn made up her mind to become a runner, she'd be the first woman to break the four-minute mile."

A tense atmosphere settled over *State of the Union* whenever Adolphe Menjou was on the set. Kate had not particularly liked the extreme right-wing Menjou when they worked

---

* Metro costume designer Irene Gibbons (1901–1962), known professionally by her first name, had costumed Hepburn for *Without Love, Undercurrent, Dragon Seed* and *Song of Love,* and so had little problem in hastily providing a wardrobe for Hepburn.

together fifteen years earlier on *Morning Glory*. Now, with his testimony before HUAC, she distrusted him. Menjou had cited every liberal he knew in the industry as pro-Communist. About Kate he had said, "Scratch a do-gooder, like Hepburn, and they'll yell, 'Pravda.'" The remark enraged Tracy, who told Capra, "You scratch some members of the Hepburn clan and you're liable to get an ass full of buckshot."

Kate refused to be goaded by Menjou ("wisecracking, witty—a flag-waving super patriot who invested his American dollars in Canadian bonds and had a thing about Communists") and spoke to him only before the cameras. As Menjou played a conniving politician whom Kate despised in the film, her scenes with him—mainly confrontational—bristle. These and Kate's scenes with Angela Lansbury* ("As the adderish lady publisher, she sinks a fine fang," wrote *Time* critic James Agee) are the best in the film. On the whole, *State of the Union* did not work as well as a movie as it had as a play. One of the reasons was that Lindsay and Crouse kept adding and subtracting relevant world happenings to the dialogue in their script so that it always seemed up to date. The film did not have that advantage, and the dialogue was glib rather than biting. Despite this, *State of the Union*, with its glittering cast and Capra's directorial artistry, is a slick film, more charming than controversial. Kate played her role with a nice balance of humor and conviction, and Tracy was sufficiently honorable and persuadably male; but Angela Lansbury walked away with the acting kudos. For Kate and Tracy, the film achieved the goal of marking them forever in the public's eye as a team.

By winter, 1948, life in Hollywood had grown into a stultifying day-by-day existence. Kate had read dozens of scripts and not found one a suitable vehicle for them. Tracy found it too easy to "go off the deep end" when he wasn't working. Also, in Hollywood, Tracy had Louise and the kids to consider. Appearances had to be kept up and, in fact, a publicity picture of "The Tracy Family, Spencer, Susie (16),

---

* Angela Lansbury (1925–   ) was nominated for the Best Supporting Actress Academy Award for her first film, *Gaslight* (1944). Her role as Kaye Thorndyke in *State of the Union* also won her a nomination, as did her performance in *The Manchurian Candidate* (1962). She became a Broadway star with *Mame* and *Sweeney Todd* as her best known theater roles. She never worked with either Tracy or Hepburn again.

John (24)" appeared in newspapers and magazines across the country in connection with some of Louise's fine work for the John Tracy Clinic. Kate and Tracy badly needed a long stretch of undivided time together. Therefore, when George Cukor approached Tracy to accept the role of the obsessed father in *Edward, My Son,** he took it on with enthusiasm. Besides the fact that Kate's old friends Edwin Knopf (producer), Donald Ogden Stewart (writer) and Cukor (director) were involved, the film was to be shot in England and Kate could go with him. (For a brief time the possibility of Kate playing the wife s role, finally portrayed by Deborah Kerr, was discussed, but Kate was not right for the part and she knew it.) All they needed was a place to be together where the press would not find them.

Garson Kanin, back on good terms with them, contacted his old, good friends, the Oliviers; and Vivien Leigh, being a romantic, warm and generous woman, immediately wrote Tracy extending an invitation to stay with them at Notley Abbey during the shooting of *Edward, My Son.* A suite at Claridge's was engaged for Kate, who arrived (with a remarkable lack of press coverage) a short time after Tracy was ensconced at Notley. In the grim winter of 1948, Britain had not yet recovered from the ravages of the war, and traces remained of the hardships caused by the previous winter (the coldest the country had known in decades) when the gas and coal supplies had given out. Notley's stone walls and cavernous fireplaces, where drafts swept down chimneys and into the oversized rooms, was less than comfortable to a Californian like Tracy, who had been accustomed to mild winters and good American central heat. In addition, food was scarce in England. Gas flickered weakly in stoves. Hot water and electricity had to be conserved. And, in addition, neither Tracy nor Kate had been aware of the serious personal problems Notley's owners were having.

The Oliviers were thought to be the golden couple. Olivier,

---

* *Edward, My Son,* based on the play by Robert Morley and Noel Langley, co-starring Tracy and Deborah Kerr, was a dour film, never fully realized. Tracy's performance is seldom convincing. He seemed, and was, uncomfortable in the role of a man who commits arson, goads two people to suicide and drives his wife to drink and death when she tries to stand in his way of making their son a "success."

only the previous year knighted Sir Laurence, Knight Bachelor, at forty the youngest actor to receive the honor, and Vivien, Lady Olivier, more beautiful, more loved than ever, had recently returned from a triumphant tour of Australia; and he had just released his production of *Hamlet,* for which he won the 1948 Academy and British Film awards. Weekends during the summer at Notley were reminiscent of the glittering days at Pickfair when two other screen idols, Mary Pickford and Douglas Fairbanks, had filled their magnificent estate with the most famous people in the world. Vivien at this time was "the happiest when playing hostess, seeing after her guests, supervising the meals, selecting the linens, the silver, the china, and arranging the flowers she would pick herself. The Notley guest book was a theatre *Who's Here.* There were bucolic pleasures during the day, walks by the Thames, picnics on the banks, croquet and tennis, bicycling into the neighborhood villages, breakfast and lunch on the terrace, tea in the small garden room, cocktails in the drawing room, and lavish dinners in the dining room. Then there would be games until the wee hours. Vivien still adored games and checkers and charades and was masterful at all of them."

Vivien, however, was like a piece of exquisite porcelain. She had only recently recovered from one of her worst attacks of tuberculosis followed by severe emotional problems caused by her then undiagnosed manic-depression. The Australian tour had been a great healer; the overwhelming ovations paid to them, the royal receptions and the tributes had given Vivien a great boost. But when Tracy arrived at Notley, she and Larry had been back from the tour only a few weeks and her strength had not yet caught up with her enthusiasm.

Notley, a thirteenth-century house that had been endowed by Henry V, stood gray and forbidding in the chill November cold. The massive, twenty-two-room stone abbey with its mullioned windows, red-tiled roofs and ancient brick chimneys looked quite unwelcoming to Tracy after his forty-eight-mile drive from London in an unheated car. Nor did the sight of the dark and murky winter waters of the river Thames bordering one side of the Abbey ease his apprehension. Once inside he was only slightly reassured. Vivien had done a masterful job and saved no expense in decoration and restoration. Color had been dashed about brilliantly on drapes and settees and beds. Silver gleamed. Crystal chandeliers glimmered. In the main rooms, Notley's forest had supplied great logs to counteract the lack of other heat. Bowls of bright fall leaves filled the rooms. Yet, just as the halls of Notley received little warmth from the great fires burning inside the rooms, so Vivien seemed chilled when Olivier was not present. Vivien was driven, ill, and no amount of gay banter could disguise it. When Kate arrived, the situation became only more troublesome. Tracy could not very well stay with her at Claridge's and did not feel at ease when they were at Notley, although the Oliviers did everything they could to make their stay a happy one.

On her own, Kate went antiquing, visited museums and walked all over London. She spent time with Tracy on the set and enjoyed being reunited again with Cukor. Talk subsequently turned to Kate, Tracy and Cukor working together on another film. Kate recalled the story Garson had said he and Ruth wanted to develop when Tracy had the time. *The Leading Lady*, a recent play by Ruth, had closed; and in one of Kate's phone conversations with Garson, he told her a screenplay would be ready by her return. And, when Kate arrived home in February, 1949 (leaving Tracy on his own), the Kanins' script was, in fact, ready to go before the cameras. It had been retitled *Adam's Rib*.

The story could have been categorized as conventional situation comedy (a pair of lawyers, man and wife, are placed in the position of prosecuting and defending the same client, a woman who has shot but not killed her husband after tracking him through the streets of New York to his love nest). The humor derives from the personal conflict the case creates in the marriage of the lawyers. Since the court arguments and the theme deal with law and order and women's rights, the script also has a satirical quality.

Years later, critic and writer Gavin Lambert was to say, "Hepburn's antics in the courtroom absolutely prefigured the Chicago Seven. She introduces side shows and absurd characters and turns the courtroom into a circus. Then Tracy argues that we've got to respect the law, we may be against it but we've got to respect it and it's exactly like Abbie Hoffman versus Judge Hoffman."

The Kanins might not have been prophetic, but they were writers with a strong social conscience. The reason *Adam's Rib* works even when the comedy becomes too broad and the action difficult to accept is because the basic script could have played as tragedy as well as comedy and the people are human.

Cukor had chosen to shoot most of *Adam's Rib* in New York on location to get more of a documentary feel. This meant that Kate could stay at the Turtle Bay house and Tracy at the Waldorf Towers just a few streets away and they could both walk to the day's location. New York also guaranteed them a maximum amount of privacy. In Hollywood, not only did all the press know the addresses of the stars, so did tour-bus companies. New York had even more tourists but they did not come to gape at stars and their homes.

Tracy and Hepburn in a battle of the sexes was a sure winner, and *Adam's Rib* rescued their sagging box-office ratings and made a sizable profit.* For several months after its completion, Kate hoped a script might come along that would be right for both of them. When none did, Tracy agreed to appear in another Knopf film, *Malaya.†* One of the things that sold him on the project was that his role as a hard-hitting soldier of fortune constituted a return to the tough-guy portrayals of his early career. The effects of alcoholism had begun to age and bloat Tracy. His gray hair was distinguished-looking; and when he smiled that half-smirky smile of his, the old charm leaped back into his face. He looked more than his fifty years; but because he never relied on being a romantic lead, it did not matter.

Kate, at forty-three, had matured into a handsome woman. Her body remained lean, and her voice, perhaps because of her heavy smoking, had lowered attractively so that some of the metallic quality had been mellowed. Working with Tracy

---

* The Kanins' screenplay was nominated for, but did not win, an Oscar. The only sour note in the entire first-class production was a Cole Porter song, "Farewell Amanda," which *Time* magazine suspected the composer "must have written while waiting for a bus."

† *Malaya* (1950) starred Tracy, James Stewart, Valentina Cortesa, Sydney Greenstreet, John Hodiak, Lionel Barrymore and Gilbert Roland and was directed by Richard Thorpe. The film was only mildly successful.

had given her a new confidence in her acting. She had learned much from him. The artificiality that had often crept into her performances was now gone, and her knowledge and use of film technique were truly spectacular. Like Tracy, she could now play any suitable part and make it a star role. Glamour and romantic illusion no longer concerned her. She felt as though she might be able to tackle anything, even Shakespeare.

The relationship between Kate and Tracy had hit a particularly rough patch at this time. Tracy was drinking again. Kate did everything she could to help him fight it, but he became hostile to her interference and highly resentful of any suggestions from her or friends that he seek some sort of professional help. By the time *Malaya* was finished, he and Kate had reached near estrangement. California now presented insuperable problems for her. To add to her unhappiness over her difficulties with Tracy, HUAC was on the march and the film industry was being purged. On June 8, 1949, the committee had listed several hundred film people—actors, writers, directors—as having "followed or appeased some of the Communist party line program over a long period of time." Kate's name had been included in a staggering and often ludicrous list of prominent people, including Pearl Buck (apparently because she had written novels about China), Lena Horne (because she was married to a white man possibly), and Maurice Chevalier (who was considered a reactionary in his own country).

Most of the celebrities named rushed into print with a statement. Sinatra called the list "the product of liars, and liars to me make very un-American leaders . . . and furthermore, if they don't cut it out, I'll show them how much an American can fight back—even if it's against the state—if the American happens to be right—and I'm Right not Left. . . ."

Through a studio spokesman, Kate said that she "refused to dignify [the] un-American accusation with a reply."

Kate had been in correspondence with Lawrence Langner at the Theatre Guild. Langner wanted her to play Rosalind in Shakespeare's *As You Like It*. The idea of attempting Shakespeare for the first time in the role of a young maiden terrified Kate. Besides, there was the problem of dressing once again in boy's clothes as she had done in *Sylvia Scarlett* with terrible results. But Langner would not give up and finally she agreed. Theresa Helburn, in London on holiday at the time, received a cable from her co-director: "Kate definitely wants to do *As You Like It* . . . both feel that there can be some good casting done in England. As this may be the beginning of a very important series of things for us, Kate says 'Don't be cheap— we only live once' and [I] say 'Don't be extravagant either.'"

Helburn did not engage any actors on the trip but she did discuss with Michael Benthall* of the Shakespeare Memorial Theatre the possibility of directing. She wired Kate of her wish to sign Benthall, and Kate replied that she must meet with him before she made up her mind. Helburn had to persuade him to leave England and make the long trip to Hollywood,† where Benthall's sensitivity and urbane wit made an immediate impression upon Kate. A few days later Kate, accompanied by her old friend Constance Collier (who had played the part of the drama coach in *Stage Door*), and Collier's live-in companion, a young English woman named Phyllis Wilbourn, left for New York. Collier, a fine Shakespearean performer on her own, had agreed to coach Kate in the role and in the art of Shakespearean drama.

As You Like It had not had an outstanding record in contemporary theater. Its longest run in America (and it had not done much better in England) had been sixty performances at the Republic Theatre in New York in 1902 with Henrietta Crosman as Rosalind.** Rosalind is the longest woman's part in all Shakespeare and only four male roles are longer. This has always attracted the theater's greatest actresses—Sarah Siddons, Madame Modjeska, Lily Langtry

---

* Michael Benthall (1919–   ) had directed many plays of Shakespeare for the Old Vic Theatre, as well as productions of *Aida* and *Turandot* at Covent Garden. He later directed Hepburn in *The Millionairess* (1952).

† The jet plane was not in operation in 1949 and the flight from England to New York took thirteen hours. Then another seven- to eight-hour flight was necessary to reach California.

** *As You Like It* had had only six previous recorded professional New York productions in the first half of the twentieth century. The others were presented by the Chicago Repertory Company (1930), The Shakespearean Repertory Company (1932), the Surrey Players (1937), Alfred Drake and Helen Craig (1941) and Sir Donald Wolfit and Rosalind Iden (1947).

and Julia Marlowe among them—to the part. But their successes were primarily on tour and in repertory. Rosalind's lure to Kate was another matter. The role was all dreaming and longing and hoping, wonder and magic, and it reminded Kate of when she first came to New York to try her fortune. "I was so happy and so wild with excitement," she recalled of those early days, "that my feet never touched the pavement, I was always five feet above the sidewalk. . . . We all like to see life in terms of fairy tales." *As You Like It* is romance—"pure, idealized, fabulous romance."

Shakespeare required more breadth and range and color of voice than was needed for any of the modern roles Kate had played on the stage. For three hours a day for six months, while the play was being mounted and rehearsed, Kate worked with Constance Collier on the rhythm of Shakespearean dialogue, learning how to speak her lines naturally for their meaning. Rosalind could easily have become a mannish, forward young woman, a replaying of *Sylvia Scarlett*, and she took great pains to avoid this mistake. After long discussions with Michael Benthall, she decided Rosalind should be portrayed in a restrained, ladylike manner.

A nine-week pre-Broadway tour was arranged. Kate was under tremendous pressure in both her private and professional lives. Tracy, having completed *Malaya*, was finding it impossible to cope without Kate and was on the telephone to her morning, noon and night. Finally, she agreed that he could meet her in Cleveland on tour. Their reunion was like the plot of a cloak-and-dagger film. Tracy's arrival was kept so secret that members of the cast never realized he was in town. He promised to put an end to his drinking. Believing him, she consented to his coming to New York when *As You Like It* opened on Broadway. Proud of working on a project she considered worthwhile, Kate invited her mother to accompany her to a few of the cities on tour. Mrs. Hepburn agreed and Kate played to her mother as much as she did to her audiences.

The out-of-town tour was (as were all other Hepburn tours) a great financial success. The notices were good, and the press mentioned with surprise what a fantastic pair of legs Miss Hepburn possessed. The show opened at the Cort Theatre on

A REMARKABLE WOMAN

January 22, 1950. "There is too much Yankee in Miss Hepburn for Shakespeare's glades and lyric fancies," wrote Brooks Atkinson in *The New York Times*. "Gorgeously attired in some stunning finery designed by James Bailey, Miss Hepburn is lovely to look at, and she plays the part with pride and modesty. But in the opinion of one reluctant churlish theatergoer, Rosalind assumes romantic and disarming graces that are not implicit in Miss Hepburn's nature. She is an honest and straightforward actress whom it is easy to admire. But she is not a helpless, bewitched, moon-struck maiden swooning through a magic forest. . . . Miss Hepburn has too sharply defined a personality for such romantic make-believe. Her acting is tight, her voice is a little hard and shallow for Shakespeare's poetry, she has to design the character too meticulously. And is this a New England accent that we hear twanging the strings of Shakespeare's lyre?"

Hard words were about all Kate received from the critics, but she never let them trample her spirit. She continued to work with Constance Collier, and her performance did improve and the lines at the box office continued. Nonetheless, Atkinson was right. Kate was physically wrong to portray a limpid Rosalind. She would have been better to go with the boyish quality rather than against it. Her persona was too fixed in the minds of theatergoers. Kate represented the epitome of the courageous woman, able to do battle with or for the man she loved, and she was as phony when playing it coy as Scarlett O'Hara was when trying to be a shy maiden with Rhett Butler.

Yet Kate seemed not to see herself as a strong woman. Back in the early days Laura had been the dominant one in their friendship. She had lost interest in Howard Hughes and Leland Hayward when they seemed too eager to give in to her. Jed Harris's chauvinistic treatment had drawn her to him. And part of her attraction to Tracy was his obstinate maleness. Yes, he desperately needed her and he was out of control when she was gone. But, she *did* have to play a game with him, be the compliant female, cook, serve, nurse, be in attendance. The stuffed animals and dolls that rested at the head of her bed perhaps were not such a contradiction after all.

248

Tracy had been good when they had met in Cleveland. Back in New York, he started drinking again, and neighbors saw him reeling into Kate's night after night and leaving shortly thereafter in a condition not much improved. He returned to Hollywood to make *Father of the Bride*, and Kate continued with *As You Like It*.

CHAPTER
19

When *As You Like It* closed on Broadway after 180 performances, Kate and the production went back on the road, touring the Midwest. Tracy was on the telephone daily to her and Constance Collier remained nearby. In each new town, Kate would wait in the theater until the scenery was up. Asked why, she replied, "I don't want it to feel lonely." She also admitted she could not stand to "hang around" when the set was being taken down. Between performances, she slept, ate and curled her hair ("any woman who has corn silk instead of hair will understand when I say it takes a long time to curl my hair").

By the time Kate reached Tulsa, Oklahoma, her nerves were on edge. Her driver had been stopped for speeding with her in the car on their way to the city. Kate was summoned and had to appear in court, where the traffic policeman who had issued the ticket informed the judge that they had been traveling at eighty miles an hour.

Pacing the floor of the courtroom much in the manner of the woman lawyer she had recently played in *Adam's Rib*, Kate glared at the policeman. "We would have been glad to slow down if you had just warned us. You don't have enough sense to be an officer." She stepped back and against an electric heater, scorching her mink coat, and then jumped quickly away as she tore off the fur to check the damage.

"It probably did not hurt that one thousand dollar coat too much, Miss Hepburn," the judge commented.

"One thousand?" Kate snapped back as she smoothed the mink. "This coat cost five thousand five hundred dollars."

"Well, the fine will cost you ten dollars," the judge replied, adding, "but you better leave this courtroom now before I change my mind."

Grumbling, Kate paid the fine and left.

She stayed at Irene Selznick's house in California over the holidays, ironing out her personal problems with Tracy. His drinking had not stopped but he seemed able to control it better. They had a warm few weeks together playing chess, talking endlessly, walking around the grounds of Cukor's estate. Tracy still considered it a matter of principle that they not live together, although both of his children were grown, and John had married. Metro was keeping Tracy busy at this time. He had completed *Father of the Bride* and *Father's Little Dividend* while Kate had been appearing in *As You Like It;* and now the studio wanted him to take on the role of the criminal attorney in *The People Against O'Hara,* * which meant he would have to be in California until the following summer.

Kate was desperate for a script that would enable her to return to Hollywood; but good stories, as always, were hard to find. At forty-four and beginning to take on a more mature look, she could not be cast in parts that required either glamour or youth. Very few stories centered on a middle-aged woman, although such roles for men were plentiful. Then, too, Hollywood was in chaos. Television had risen to challenge movies; and to combat the young intruder, films were attempting to be bigger and better than ever. This meant shooting a film on locations real and exotic, giving movie audiences entertainment that they could not get on their television screens. Major studios were in a period of decline. The postwar market had been a great disappointment, and antitrust laws had forced the studios to divest themselves of their theaters. Nor could they pay their stars the fees and percentages being offered to them by the new independent producers.

---

* Based on the novel by Eleazar Lypsky.

Sam Spiegel (then using the pseudonym S. P. Eagle),* a master promoter, was one of this new breed. Spiegel liked a C. S. Forester† novel, *The African Queen,* and knew the only way to get a film financed was to present a complete package to the money people, including lead players and a director who were considered bankable. Kate did not fall into that category—Humphrey Bogart and John Huston** did. But Spiegel needed good bait to hook them, and Kate, whom he admired tremendously, was it. He therefore gave her the book to read, first telling her (a lie) that he had Bogart and Huston. The book was about the curious romance of Rose Sayer, a prim English spinster, and Charlie Allnut, a "gin-swilling ne'er-do-well riverboat pilot," in German East Africa during the early stages of World War I. Kate liked the character of Rose and especially the idea of working with Bogart and Huston. She readily agreed to go ahead for a promised sixty-five thousand dollars in cash, an equal amount in deferred payments and 10 percent of the film's profits. Spiegel now told Bogart that he had Kate and Huston, and informed Huston at the same time that he had Kate and

---

* Sam Spiegel (1903–   ), born in Poland, reverted to his real name in 1954, but he produced *The African Queen* under his pseudonym, S. P. Eagle. He had produced a few well-received low-budget films previously—*Tales of Manhattan* (1942), *The Stranger* (1945), *The Prowler* (1951), but after *The African Queen,* he made three memorable films—*On the Waterfront* (1954), *The Bridge on the River Kwai* (1957) and *Lawrence of Arabia* (1962)—receiving an Oscar for Best Picture for each of them. In 1959, Hepburn appeared in his film adaptation of *Suddenly Last Summer.*

† C. S. Forester (1899–1966). British author famous for his Captain Hornblower sea novels. He was also correspondent for the London *Times* during the Spanish Civil War and the German occupation of Czechoslovakia.

** John Huston (1906–   ), the son of actor Walter Huston. Huston and Bogart had made four films together, *The Maltese Falcon* (1941), *Across the Pacific* (1942), *Key Largo* (1948) and *The Treasure of the Sierra Madre* (1948). After *The African Queen,* Huston made about thirty films, all of them seeming misguided (*Annie* [1983]) or less than met the eye (*Freud* [1962], *The Bible* [1966], *Reflections in a Golden Eye* [1967]). Huston also acted in some of his own films, and in many others—*Chinatown* (1974), *Breakout* (1975) and *The Wind and the Lion* (1975) among them. He wrote numerous screenplays—*Jezebel, The Amazing Dr. Clitterhouse* (1938), *Juarez* (1939), *Dr. Ehrlich's Magic Bullet* (1940), *High Sierra* and *Sergeant York* (1941), and *The Killers* (1946). He co-authored the screenplay of *The African Queen* with James Agee (1909–1955), novelist and film critic for *Life* and *Time.* Agee had never worked on a screenplay before; subsequently, he adapted *The Night of the Hunter* (1955).

Bogart.* In fact, he did not even own the rights to the property. These were controlled by Warner Brothers, who had bought *The African Queen* for Bette Davis from Columbia Studios, which had originally purchased the rights from Forester himself with the idea of casting Elsa Lanchester and Charles Laughton in the leads. Warners wanted fifty thousand dollars, which Spiegel did not have. He unsuccessfully tried to borrow the money, and then, desperate, went to Sound Services, Inc., which supplied sound equipment to the studios, and told *them* he had Hepburn, Bogart and Huston for the film and that not only would he use their equipment on location, he would give them credit in the titles. Sound Services had never loaned money for a film before, but miraculously they agreed.

Kate returned to the road to complete her tour of *As You Like It* just after the first of the year, not knowing if Spiegel would succeed in obtaining the financing for the venture. The idea of going to the Congo to film a picture fascinated her. Finally, Spiegel informed her that the funds had been raised and the film was scheduled to begin shooting in Africa in April.† Kate had only six weeks from the end of the tour until her scheduled departure for London, where she would be fitted for her wardrobe.

She came home to West Hartford the second week in March, physically exhausted but feeling much more at ease about her future. She claimed she would never marry again. She told a reporter a few months later that "it is difficult enough making friends with your own sex—let alone deciding to spend your life with someone of the opposite sex. It is not easy to be interested—and marriage means to be interested— in someone else all the time." If Kate became the second Mrs. Spencer Tracy, she could not see herself being free to

---

* Bogart was promised (and received) $35,000 cash, $125,000 in deferred payments and 25 percent of the film's profits. Huston was promised $87,000 for his services as director (which he received) and a 50 percent interest in Spiegel's company, Horizon Pictures (which he did not receive).
† Spiegel made a deal with Britain's Romulus Films (James and John Wolff) for £4.5 million and with a Chicago corporation for an additional $1 million. *The African Queen's* final production costs were slightly under $15 million, very high for 1951.

accept a film role that would take her thousands of miles away from her husband. Her status quo with Tracy seemed ideal.

Life on Bloomfield Avenue, despite the fact that her brothers and sisters were all married and living away, had not changed. At seventy-five, her father still went to his office on weekdays. Her mother's devotion to birth control and women's rights had not wavered. More guests showed up for Sunday dinner than were invited; and the decibel level of the conversations, with fourteen grandchildren now in the family, sounded as though a brawl were in progress. As always, afternoon tea was served punctually at four o'clock in the dining room.

March 17, St. Patrick's Day and a Saturday, Kate and Dr. Hepburn came in from a brisk walk a few minutes late for tea. They found the table set, the teapot filled with hot, freshly brewed tea, and the house unnaturally quiet. Mrs. Hepburn seemed nowhere close by. They both sat down for a moment and then, exchanging frightened glances, rose without a word and ran upstairs. Mrs. Hepburn had had a recent small heart infarction and they were not wrong in suspecting what they would find. Kit Houghton Hepburn, at seventy-three, was dead, lying gracefully across her bed, where, apparently feeling faint after setting the tea, she had gone to rest for a few moments until her husband and daughter returned home.* The phone calls began, and the family gathered. For a few days they were closer than they had ever been, grasping each other, remembering the good times, the times when they were whole, trying to put off that moment when each one would finally accept the fact that they would never be complete again.

"The thing about life is that you must survive," Kate later said. "Life is going to be difficult and dreadful things will happen. What you do is to move along, get on with it and be tough. Not in the sense of being mean to others, but tough with yourself and making a deadly effort not to be defeated."

---

* The first press release on Mrs. Hepburn's death stated that her body was found by her daughter Katharine. Another release followed that said Dr. Hepburn had discovered the body. His daughter, he claimed, was at her brother's home in nearby Bloomfield. The word "Bloomfield" had confused the reporter (because of Bloomfield Avenue). Ten years later, Hepburn told the story printed above to an English reporter.

She packed her bags, got all the dreadful shots she needed to travel to Africa and, with Constance Collier for support, boarded the small Cunard freighter-passenger ship *Media*, arriving at Liverpool on April 13. The two women were driven in a Rolls-Royce to London, where they slipped in through the baggage entrance at Claridge's to be ensconced most luxuriously in a large suite (which Kate was certain Sam Spiegel could not afford). The following Monday, Kate, wearing cream slacks, a loose-fitting man's-style jacket, and brown suede shoes, stalked into one of the hotel's ballrooms where a welcoming party had been arranged. "I'm tall, skinny (117 pounds) with a lot of freckles, and I can't stop growing. I'm five feet eight inches now, and I've put on an inch in the last year. You could call me an antelope; swift, lean, graceful (I hope) and freckled,"* she announced.

Humphrey Bogart and his wife, Lauren Bacall,† had arrived in London from Paris just about the same time. Bogart, who knew Kate only casually (although he had known Tracy for years), walked over to say, "Katie starts out as a missionary, but after going down river in Africa with me, she ends up as a woman."

To which Kate shot back, "I'd say I start out as a woman and end up as a missionary trying to save Bogart."

For Kate, Africa evoked exotic images of lush greens and wild animals and tribes of people who had never seen a motion picture, and she could not wait to be off on what

* David Levin in the *Daily Express* (April 17, 1951) commented on her entrance at Claridge's, "She has the air of the professional eccentric who plays her off-screen part with unflagging skill." The *Sunday Express* reporter (no by-line) decreed that, "She wore her favourite attention getting costume—slacks and a severely cut jacket, which made her look like a male impersonator." Lauren Bacall was to have the last word. "There was a press conference at Claridge's for which I got myself all done up in a Balenciaga suit and Katharine Hepburn stole the show in her pants."

† Lauren Bacall (1924–   ). She played minor roles in several Broadway plays before turning to modeling. "Discovered" by Mrs. Howard Hawks, wife of the Hollywood producer-director, she became a movie actress, probably most well known for her roles in *To Have and Have Not* (1944), *Key Largo* with Bogart (1948) and *How to Marry a Millionaire* (1953). Following Bogart's death, she married Jason Robards, Jr. In the late 1960s she appeared successfully on Broadway in *Cactus Flower*, and won the Tony Award for her performances in the musicals *Applause* (1970) and *Woman of the Year* (1981).

promised to be a great adventure. The screenplay of *The African Queen* was written by James Agee, although John Collier had done an earlier draft. Shortly after he had finished, Agee suffered a heart attack, which prohibited his going to Africa. Peter Viertel* had been signed to work on the final draft, concentrating most of his effort on the last scenes. C. S. Forester had never been satisfied with the way the novel had ended and had published two denouements, the original American edition appearing without the last two chapters of the English edition.† Viertel met Huston in Entebbe, where he made his headquarters while scouting locations. As soon as the two of them had completed the script and Spiegel had arrived, they arranged for Kate, Bogart and Bacall to meet them in Léopoldville, which was closer to their chosen locations.

Kate and the Bogarts were to change planes in Rome for Léopoldville, the capital of the Belgian Congo. Because the Bogarts were occupied with the transfer of their baggage, they had not noticed until they were face to face with "a battery of press and klieg lights" that Kate was nowhere to be found. A man said she had been the last to disembark and that he was positive she had gone from one plane to another on the field without bothering to come into the airport lounge. An Italian reporter insisted that was not possible because he had gone aboard the plane and had not seen her. Bogart whispered to his wife to "get on board and look in the ladies room." There, indeed, she found Kate, "laughing uproariously at having outwitted the press."

"We sat chatting for a while," Bacall remembered, "then to our horror the newsreel man with the klieg light climbed on board. Kate stayed locked in the loo—Bogie and I were photographed to pacify the man—the doors closed—Katie emerged."

---

* Peter Viertel (1916–), son of the Viennese director Berthold Viertel and the Polish-born actress Salka Viertel, wrote many scripts for Greta Garbo. Peter Viertel's screenplays include *Saboteur* (1942), *The Sun Also Rises* (1957) and *The Old Man and the Sea* (1958). His best-selling novel, *Black Heart—White Hunter*, was based on his experiences while filming *The African Queen*. He was married to actress Deborah Kerr in 1960.

† A new American edition which included the two missing chapters was subsequently published.

That night they stayed in a hotel in Léopoldville. The next morning they continued on by boat. Spiegel and Viertel were waiting for them in Stanleyville amid a welcoming celebration —"natives dancing in costume; painted faces and bodies." The weather was insufferably hot and humid. Kate, comfortable in safari clothes, was wide-eyed with excitement. The next day the film group crossed the Congo River and boarded a train that consisted of two passenger cars, two freight cars, a tin boat on a flat car and the engine. The small caravan moved deeper into the Congo, past primitive grass-hut villages and gawking natives. In Ponthierville, the company transferred to cars and jeeps and proceeded to the small village of Biondo. Then, after an hour ride, they reached a bank of the Ruiki River, where they drove onto a raft that natives poled with four long pirogues to the opposite bank. Another hour's drive was required before they reached the camp that Huston had had constructed for his company.

The director met his stars at the Ruiki campsite and regaled them until one in the morning with stories of the terrain, the native superstitions, the wild animals that they would encounter, the bugs, and tales of his own hunting forays. The next morning Kate got her first realistic view of what her life would be like while shooting *The African Queen.*

Her bungalow was constructed of bamboo and palm leaves, with small screened windows and curtained closets. The floors were dirt, covered with grass mats. A bottle of water sat by a basin. Outside was a toilet, and as a shower a tin barrel filled with cold water hung over a small platform (an invention borrowed from Huston's wartime army experience). When a chain was pulled, a disk was raised in the bucket and the water came through the pierced holes that had been drilled into its bottom.

Without a traveling companion, Kate was forced to make friends with Huston and the Bogarts. She talked compulsively to cover her nervousness. For two solid days after they arrived it rained torrentially. When it stopped, an army of mosquitoes bored their way through the netting around beds, and Kate, who had brought a bag of remedies, was running about applying salves to the ugly, itching red welts that everyone, including herself, suffered. On the first day of shooting it rained again, but this did not deter Huston.

Charlie Allnut's boat, *The African Queen*, was the real thing, having once been a functioning riverboat. Huston was convinced that no stranger flotilla had ever navigated African waterways than *The African Queen* and its river caravan, consisting of four rafts that were pulled by the power generated from the *Queen*.

On the first raft was a replica of the *Queen*. That raft became the stage, with cameras and equipment on it for photographing mock-up shots.* The second raft carried lights and props; the third the generator. The fourth, conceived by Huston to give Kate some comfort while working under such primitive conditions, contained a privy, a full-length mirror and Kate's very own dressing room. Within a few days, Kate's luxury raft was detached and she had to use the jungle for her toilet and a small piece of the broken mirror for her vanity. The fourth raft had simply proved too much for *The African Queen* to tow. Kate and Bacall would stand watch for each other whenever they had to relieve themselves.

"The natives didn't know what we were about," Bacall claims. "When a match was struck and a flame followed, they'd mumble in Swahili."

For the first few days of shooting, Huston let Kate play her scenes (the burial of her missionary brother) as she saw the character. Her performance just wasn't right; and early in the morning of the fourth day, he came to her hut while she was having breakfast on the veranda. "I hope you're not planning to have breakfast with me every day," Kate snapped, "because I rather prefer to eat alone."

"No, no," he replied. "I only want a few minutes of your time."

Kate sensed the seriousness in his attitude. (Recalling the confrontation later, Kate said, "Now you know I've a sort of hollow face and a sort of a [sharp] jaw and my mouth goes down, and when my face is serious, it is very on the down side. If I can smile I've a lot of nice teeth. I can cheer everything up quite a bit. So I smiled big.")

"Well, what is it John?" she asked.

---

* Mock-ups (a re-creation of the real thing on a sound stage) like boats and cars and building façades are used in films to provide better shooting conditions and angles than could be obtained if the actual object was used.

Huston told her, "Your interpretation of Rosie is doing harm to the picture as well as hurting the character." He then sat down and asked, "Did you ever see Mrs. Roosevelt visiting the soldiers in the hospitals in the newsreels?"

Kate replied that she had.

"Well, I think of [Rosie] a little bit as Mrs. Roosevelt." Then he got up, tipped his safari hat and was off.

"Well," Kate recalled, "it was the most brilliant suggestion. Because [Mrs. Roosevelt] was so ugly that she always smiled. So I smiled. Otherwise he said very little to me on the set. But it was an awfully clever piece of direction. . . . Very right."

The company worked seven days a week from six-thirty in the morning until dark, coping with the most awesome physical obstacles. In view of the tremendous courage of both Kate and Bacall, none of the men dared complain. At one point, the raft with the generator got jammed into the thick growth on the banks of the Ruiki and a boiler toppled, nearly scalding Kate and Bogart and burning Guy Hamilton,* Huston's assistant director. A few nights later *The African Queen* sank. When Huston talked to Spiegel by radio (their only communication), the producer laughed. "I thought you said *The African Queen* sank."

"That's right," Huston replied.

"Oy!"

The fifty-five native workers and thirty English crew members managed to raise *The African Queen* from slime, water and tangled weeds, clean it, patch the holes and get it once again to function.

Not long after that, the location was attacked by black wasps from the forest twice in one day; and Kate and Bogart—almost everyone, in fact—were badly stung. Despite all these hardships, Kate loved Africa. She wrote long daily letters to Tracy, which were taken by native runners once a week back to the village of Biondo and then picked up by

---

* Guy Hamilton (1922–) worked as an assistant director on a number of distinguished British productions, including *The Fallen Idol* and *The Third Man* (1949). In 1952, he began to direct on his own. His James Bond films *Goldfinger* (1964), *Diamonds Are Forever* (1971), *Live and Let Die* (1973) and *The Man with the Golden Gun* (1974) are among his best efforts.

launch, carried to Ponthierville and finally sent on their way to Léopoldville, where a post office existed.

Bogart never liked Africa. An urbane, sophisticated man, son of a fashionable New York portrait painter and her successful physician husband, graduate of Andover and heir to a family inheritance, Humphrey DeForest Bogart came from a background similar to Katharine Houghton Hepburn's. They differed in that Kate looked her real-life role and re-created facets of it for the screen, while Bogart in private life resembled the tough, hardened man whom he portrayed professionally. This dual personality was always the first shock people got upon meeting Bogart. The bloodshot eyes, the sallow complexion, the mouth that seemed mocking even in a smile, added to the low timbre and the clip of his speech, contradicted the innate gentility, grace, grasp of language and intellectual pursuits that lay behind them. Bogart was a well-bred gentleman of the first order. Alistair Cooke observed, "Upon meeting Bogart, [I found I was] dealing here with two characters, one fictional, the other private, almost as sharply defined as Chaplin, the man, and Charlie, the tramp. There was the movie Bogart, a character at once repellent and fascinating; and the complex private man . . . a product of upper middle-class respectability."

Bogart might never have become a star had not playwright Robert Sherwood (against all advice) decided to use him as the killer with the sharp tongue in *The Petrified Forest*, the role that won Bogart a Hollywood contract. Thirty-four at the time, he had spent a decade on Broadway as a "dark haired juvenile who loped through French windows wearing tails or a dinner jacket . . . [seeming] to be cast for life as a Riviera fixture." With one role he had made the swing from the "tennis, anyone?" set (a phrase he had supposedly uttered in one of his ignominious early stage roles) to "the cryptic Hemingway tough, the huddled man in the trench coat who singed the bad and the beautiful with the smoke he exhaled from his nostrils."

The role of Charlie Allnut was a natural culmination of all Bogart's film characters. Here was the aging, caustic, disillusioned tough—self-exiled from the real world but still with a spark of that animal courage that made him, unbeknownst to himself, an extraordinary man. Kate's Rose Sayer was the catalyst who would bring out the best in him at the same time that he unlocked the vulnerable woman harbored inside her hard-shelled exterior. The sparks from the tremendous magnetism generated between these two seeming opposites were evident in the early rushes. Spiegel felt certain *The African Queen* would be a successful film. At the Ruiki campsite, cast and crew were only hoping that they would survive to *see* a finished film. Dysentery and malaria spread through the company. Kate suffered an extreme case of the former, and constant nausea as well. Still, she never missed a day's shooting.

She later confessed, "The big joke was on me because I was rather self-righteous and I thought, 'Well, I'm traveling with two drunks [Huston and Bogart], I'd better not drink anything'—so I drank lots and lots of the water. John [Huston] never got sick, Bogie never got sick—and I nearly died of the dysentery because the water was poisoned—shows how sensible they were."

The day *The African Queen* was declared river-worthy once again and shooting recommenced, the company returned to their camp to find it had been invaded by an army of ants. The floors of the bungalows were inches thick with the crawling black creatures; clothing, toiletries, *everything* was covered—and moving. All night long, kerosene fires were kept burning in hastily dug ditches encircling the camp to keep out further armies of these soldier ants. The company swatted and battled the ants in the compound, with Kate in the middle swinging away; "the Jeanne d'Arc of Ruiki" Huston called her.

The shooting at Ruiki required another three days; and Huston and his crew worked night and day to finish on time because they knew that the ants, which had been temporarily routed, would come back. Bacall and Kate were now fast friends, sharing a greater taste for adventure than Bogart did. Kate described Bacall as "soft and sleek . . . sloe-eyed . . . [Bogart] has penned a lioness. . . . No claws for those she loves—babies—mate—and even friends. . . . But if you do not belong; look out. . . . No Zulac from the bazaar has a sharper knife—"*

---

* *Zulac* was a word purely of Hepburn's invention.

The day they left Ruiki the chief arranged a musical farewell for them and the natives performed ceremonial dances. Bacall remembers that she joined in "with my Bdingo* in hand, and with their drums we had an old fashioned jam session." The company was in high spirits. Almost half of the location shooting was done; and they were moving on to a section near Butiaba, certain that the worst was over. After all, what could top an invasion of devastating ants?

The beginning of the film takes place in a settlement in German East Africa, where Rose Sayer and her brother, Reverend Samuel (Robert Morley†), run a mission that is burned to the ground by German soldiers. The church gone, her brother dead, the spinsterish Rose finds sanctuary with the dissolute Charlie Allnut and the idyll of *The African Queen* is begun. A village was constructed by the film crew for the express purpose of burning it down. Huston needed enough natives as villagers to make the scene seem real, and he contracted with a nearby chief to furnish him with people. The first day of shooting came, but no natives appeared. Investigating the cause, Huston discovered that since cannibalism was still a reality in that area,** the villagers were fearful that Huston's offer was a trap.

Butiaba not only had cannibals, it had black mambas. The deadly snakes took a liking to the company's portable privies, which, once in use on the location site, did more for clearing up the rampant dysentery than any of Kate or Bacall's assorted pills. (Bacall had luckily brought antibiotics, which

---

* *Bdingo*, an African string instrument played like a banjo.

† Robert Morley (1908–   ), English actor and playwright, co-author of *Edward, My Son* (1948). At this time best known for his work in *Marie Antoinette* (1938) and as Andrew Undershaft in *Major Barbara* (1941). In the United States he is recognized now as the television spokesman for British Airways. He is the father of English critic and author Sheridan Morley.

** Huston reported later that while the company was building this village a black hunter was contracted to take care of the food. The neighboring village chief whom Huston had befriended informed him that some of his villagers had been disappearing mysteriously. It seems that when the hunter could not find meat or game for the pot "he got the meat the simplest possible way." The man was executed a few days later, before the advance company moved in. Until Hepburn and the Bogarts left Butiaba, Huston held back the telling of this lurid story, confirmed by his associates.

proved lifesaving when one of the English members of the crew suffered an attack of appendicitis.) While the company was at Butiaba, its home was a 125-foot side-wheel paddle steamer, called the *Lugard II*, with a line of small but comfortable cabins on the main deck. After nearly two weeks in Butiaba the company moved on to Murchison Falls, where again they lived on a paddle steamer.

Huston, who considered himself a white hunter, would go out early in the morning before the day's filming began, or sometimes in the late afternoon when work was finished, to bag deer or game for the pot. Kate, who could not conceive of killing an animal, finally could stand it no longer. "You *seem* to be such a sensitive person," she said accusingly. "How can you shoot anything as beautiful as these creatures? Are you a murderer at heart?"

"Katie, there's no explaining it. You'd have to go and see for yourself to understand."

After a considered silence, she snapped, "All right, I will!"

For several mornings, she accompanied Huston, refusing to shoot anything but carrying his light rifle for him. Nothing could convince her that she should take aim, but the beauty of the jungle and the thrill of the hunt got to her. Huston agreed she could come with him and a supposedly professional white hunter to hunt elephant. After about an hour they found a herd and tracked it. "Presently," Huston relates, "we entered some very heavy foliage and were slowly working our way through it when I heard an elephant's stomach rumble. The sound came from only a few feet away. A few minutes later I heard it again—this time on the other side of us —I had accidentally worked us into the middle of a herd of elephants. The thing to do in such a situation is to retrace your steps as quietly as possible, getting clear of the herd. We started to do this, but the elephants picked up our scent, panicked and trumpeting, began to crash through the jungle all around us like big locomotives. One came bearing down on us. . . . Our white hunter broke and high-tailed it. . . .

"I looked around to see how Kate was taking this. She was carrying a little Manlicher rifle—a peashooter capable of putting out an elephant's eye but nothing more. There she was, one heel to the ground, her little rifle up, and her jaw line clean . . . as game as could be. I was carrying the Rigby .470 express rifle, but I don't mind admitting that I didn't feel safe even with that."

Miraculously, the herd stopped as it drew close and then dispersed, perhaps not seeing Kate and Huston, both of whom stood frozen. The hunters headed back to camp, Kate with her long-striding walk in the lead. Suddenly she stopped, having sighted something, and, leaning her rifle against a tree, raised her eight millimeter movie camera to photograph the object. Huston, coming up behind her, was horrified to realize that the object of her photography was a three- to four-hundred-pound wild boar with enormous tusks. Quietly, Huston said, "Stop, Katie," but Kate kept advancing until her camera ran down, and she paused to rewind.

"By this time," Huston continues, "we were so close I was afraid to shoot the boar because, even with a bullet in his heart, one of these animals can maintain a charge. I was sure he was going to attack—and I was actually squeezing the trigger. At this instant his family ran across the open space in the trail behind him. He turned to look at them, looked back at us and suddenly veered away into the brush to join his family."

Bogart never went out on a hunt. He preferred either to "sit in camp, drink in hand, and tell stories," or to read one of the library of books he had brought along. Best of all, he would have liked the film shot in comfort at the studio. Charlie Allnut had not even been a role he had cared for too much before he had come to Africa. He had been lured into the project by the chance to work with Huston again. Then, "all at once he got under the skin of that wretched, sleazy, absurd, brave little man [Charlie Allnut]," and would say to Huston, "John, don't let me lose it. Watch me. Don't let me lose it."

Sickness plagued the company in Murchison Falls, as it had in Ruiki and Butiaba. After a few simple tests, the river waters were pronounced contaminated. Bottled water brought in from Nairobi was found to be equally contaminated. Spiegel, who had arrived at Murchison Falls for the last segment of the shooting, realized now what his production unit had had to suffer.

"The water was infested with tiny worms carrying a disease called bilharzia.* The worms penetrate the skin and stay with the victim for up to thirty years. The disease affects the liver and weakens you, and can eventually kill you. It's said to be the most agonizing way to die. At one time or another, practically everyone fell into the water. We would quickly fish them out, dry them down, spray them with a disinfectant and pray," he admitted.

Spiegel was bitten on the back of his neck by a tarantula spider, but massive doses of Bacall's penicillin saved his life.

Location shooting for *The African Queen* was completed on July 17, 1951, only two days over schedule. Kate's African adventure was behind her. She came back to London to find Tracy waiting for her, but they did not have the time together she would have wanted. For the next six weeks, she and Bogart filmed from early morning to late day at either Shepperton Studios or at Worton Hall, where the scenes of them bathing in the river, the scenes of Allnut removing and replacing the propeller and shaft underwater, then towing *The African Queen* chest-deep in water through the thick reeds and the sludge, the scene following when he finds himself covered with leeches (these last were studio imitations), and all the scenes with Robert Morley were shot. The footage of the pair going through the rapids and being caught in the torrential rains was also filmed on a back lot at Shepperton using special effects.

The African Queen remains one of Kate's most unforgettable films, and one of Bogart's and her best performances. Together they created a kind of cinematic magic, their contrasting personalities cramming the film with one sharp scene after the other. Toward the end of *The African Queen*'s journey, when it looks as if Charlie and Rose may never reach the safety of the lake whose far shore is British territory, no one could doubt the depth of the tender love of this curiously matched pair. And when they begin swimming gleefully in the

---

* Actress Edwina Booth (1909–   ) contracted bilharzia while filming *Trader Horn* in the Congo in 1931. The role she played, that of a white goddess, had made her a star. It was thought that she had died from the disease as she disappeared from the screen that same year. She is, however, alive and living in Hollywood.

direction of that shore after having sunk the German boat with homemade torpedoes, and *The African Queen* with it, it is impossible to doubt that these two will live a splendid, first-rate life together. Kate had proved that she could send sparks flying on screen with a leading man other than Tracy; and she had done it in a blaze of Technicolor, fiery-red hair and ash-gray eyes being revealed for the first time.

The African Queen is a deeply moving, marvelously funny, mature cinema experience, and with its release before Christmas, 1951 (to qualify for the Academy Awards*), Kate had turned a new corner in her career. The Bryn Mawr society-girl image had been replaced forever by one of a more mature woman, a person who had the strength to endure the worst hardships and survive as ably as any man.

Huston remembers all "the many nights I sat with Katie on the top deck of the paddle boat [at Murchison Falls] and watched the eyes of the hippos in the water all around us; every eye seemed to be staring in our direction. And we talked. We talked about anything and everything. But there was never an idea of romance—Spencer Tracy was the only man in Kate's life."

During the same period of time, Joan Fontaine, in England to make first *Ivanhoe* and then *Decameron Nights,* had dinner with Tracy and their mutual friends Mr. and Mrs. William Goetz† while Tracy was waiting for Kate to return from the Congo. Tracy was withdrawn and not too good company. Later he rang Fontaine at her hotel and asked if she would go out to dinner with him the following night. His manner was flirtatious and Fontaine replied that out of respect to Kate she could not consider seeing him alone. Tracy went on to explain that he and Kate were terribly good friends but that they had a completely platonic arrangement.

"That's what they all say!" Fontaine laughed as she refused his invitation even more firmly. She left for Sweden a few

* *The African Queen* won four Academy Award nominations: Best Actor (Bogart), Best Actress (Hepburn), Best Director (Huston) and Best Screenplay (Huston and Agee). Bogart was the only one to win. Hepburn lost to Vivien Leigh as Blanche DuBois in *A Streetcar Named Desire*.

† William Goetz (1903-1969), Hollywood producer. He had produced the film *Jane Eyre* (1944), which starred Fontaine. His wife, Edie, was Louis B. Mayer's daughter and Irene Selznick's sister.

days later, and he called her long-distance to ask if she might not change her mind when she returned to London. "I'm afraid not," she told him. "Not only is there Kate to consider but you *are* a married man."

"I can get a divorce whenever I want to," was his surprising reply. "But my wife and Kate like things just as they are."

CHAPTER
20

Kate returned to New York in the summer of 1951 both
exhilarated and exhausted. Africa and her trials and experiences there had awakened a new consciousness. She now
wanted to travel and see more of the world. A kind of
restlessness and dissatisfaction with the complacency of her
own life set in. She had been made vividly aware of the
extreme struggle other people had merely to survive. She had
also discovered the extent of her own physical strength and
endurance. At the same time, she recognized her Achilles'
heel—changes within the family structure.

Her brother Tom's death thirty years earlier had marked
drastic upheavals in her life at the same time that it had bound
her closer to her family. Mrs. Hepburn's death had had the
same effect. Her need for family and home were even
stronger. During the time she had been in Africa, Dr.
Hepburn had married Madelaine Santa Croce, the nurse who
had worked with him in his office for many years. Bloomfield
Avenue would never be the same. The realization of this
could not have been an easy thing for Kate to face. Nor could
it have helped that Tracy had backtracked considerably in his
battle with alcoholism.

Loaded down with African artifacts—masks, mementos,
jewelry—Kate, joined by the Kanins, took a train to Califor-

nia three weeks after she had arrived back in the States. Once again she stayed at Irene Selznick's house at 1050 Summit Drive.* While Kate had been away, Ruth and Garson had been working on a screenplay, *Pat and Mike*, tailored for Tracy and Kate. Kate was to be Pat, a physical-education teacher with the potential to be a top all-around professional athlete. Tracy was to be cast as Mike, "a smooth, fast-talking sports promoter." The film was to give Kate a chance to display her extraordinary athletic prowess. By the time Kate and the Kanins had reached the West Coast, any problems in the screenplay had been worked out.

On her arrival, she moved into the Selznick estate, redecorating it with her African artifacts. Tracy still had Cukor's guest house. The double housekeeping chores for Kate began right away, as did her rehabilitation of Tracy, who swore this time he would lick the booze habit forever. Kate worked diligently to see he kept his word.

Tracy had become almost reclusive without Kate. Now completely gray, he read a lot, listened to music (preferably Brahms), smoked cigars, cigarettes, pipes, slept fitfully and drank when things got too closed in for him. Kate did what she could to change his habits. The pots of coffee were forever brewing. She insisted he take cold showers and swim every day no matter what the temperature. Heavier than before, he wore his bulk well and had no problems about the fact that at fifty he looked distinctly older. The pounds and years only gave him a more impressive appearance and promised to allow him to play the kinds of roles that interested him most. He glowed having Kate back again as he said, "in one frame at my feet," and he enthusiastically welcomed the idea of doing another film with her.

Work started on *Pat and Mike* in January, 1952, and ended in mid-March. For Kate, the film was a welcome respite. She got her body back into marvelous shape—even Cukor, who directed the film, could not believe her athletic prowess. "She can swing a golf club or tennis racquet as adroitly as she can

---

* Since 1947, Hepburn had been in the habit of staying at Irene Selznick's house in Beverly Hills whenever she was in California. After her divorce from her husband, Irene Selznick had lived in an apartment in New York at the Pierre Hotel.

an epigram," Bosley Crowther commented. In the film Kate also swam, biked, boxed and played basketball. She looked radiant, amazingly youthful and gave a polished, delightful performance. Together Tracy and Hepburn had never displayed more magic. *Pat and Mike* won the Kanins another Academy Award nomination and the film met with both critical and commercial success. Yet, the fact that it appeared in movie houses within a few months of *The African Queen* was jarring. The old Hepburn, though charming and glib, simply could not hold a candle to Rose Sayer, and Kate knew and quickly accepted the end of this era in her life. Something new and wonderful and exciting was ahead: roles that equaled or bettered Rosie's. *Pat and Mike* was her last film on her Metro contract; and determined to move onward, she did not renew it. Instead, she headed back to New York while Tracy remained in Hollywood to fulfill his Metro commitment for another film, a historical potboiler called *The Plymouth Adventure*.

Like Kate, Tracy felt at the end of his tether with Metro. But he did not enjoy travel as Kate did, nor did he hanker for the insecurity that often attaches itself to independent production. Tracy asked her to come back, but Kate refused. Instead, she accepted one of the greatest career challenges in her life—the lead in a George Bernard Shaw play to open in London after a short provincial tour. The play, *The Millionairess*, had been considered by Kate twice before, once as a follow-up onstage to *The Philadelphia Story* and again as a possible film. Both times she had decided against it. *The Millionairess* was written by Shaw in his late seventies. "I am finishing—practically rewriting—my play called *The Millionairess*," he wrote his good friend, Lady Nancy Astor, in 1936. "People will say you are the millionairess. An awful, impossible woman." The following year the play had its world premiere in Vienna. One year later, with Edith Evans* in the

---

* Edith Evans (Dame as of 1946) (1888–1976), one of the greatest actresses of the twentieth century. During her long career (she first attracted attention in 1912 as Cressida in *Troilus and Cressida* at the King's Hall Covent Garden), she appeared in more than five hundred plays and was noted for her Shakespearean performances. Like Kate, she had played Rosalind in *As You Like It*, as well as Katharine in *The Taming of the Shrew*, Cleopatra in *Antony and Cleopatra* and the Nurse in *Romeo and Juliet*. Her film portrayals include Lady Bracknell in

role, it had its British premiere at Malvern, England, where many of Shaw's later works were tried out. Because of the play's poor reception, it had not continued on to a West End production.

If Shaw had had Nancy Astor—an American society woman—in mind as a kind of model when he wrote *The Millionairess*, Kate would have been well cast. And, in fact, the role of Epifania, the dominating, violent lady of the title who is a symbol of the irresistible and corrupting power of money, was better suited to the flamboyant personality of Kate than to the more disciplined nature of Edith Evans. But Kate was well aware of the problems she faced. To appear in a Shavian comedy in London, having never played in England before, was the least of them. The greatest obstacle was the play itself. The Shavian wit is missing, the plot is weak and, except for Epifania, the characters are dull lampoons. The play also contains a preface titled "Preface on Bosses," which, because it is alert and provocative and displayed Shaw's still skilled talent as a pamphleteer, points up the failure of the ensuing script. Even so, Kate, who believed that an inspired performance would transform *The Millionairess* into a riveting theater experience, spoke to Lawrence Langner and Michael Benthall about it. Benthall, in turn, got Hugh "Binkie" Beaumont* of H. M. Tennent, the theatrical production company, to agree to a British production to star Kate. Kate was elated. When Shaw was asked for permission to produce *The Millionairess,* he inquired, "Is she a good athlete?" He was told she was not only a good athlete but as "strong as a horse."

"Then you'll have to watch out," Shaw said, "for she'll have to play a scene where she applies jujitsu to her leading man and she'll kill him if she isn't careful."

Shaw died many months before Beaumont sent Kate two first-class tickets on the *Nieuw Amsterdam.* Although Constance Collier was to accompany her, Beaumont refused to pay Phyllis Wilbourn's fare. Kate traded in these tickets for

---

The Importance of Being Earnest (1953) and the intrepid aunt in *Tom Jones* (1963).

* Hugh "Binkie" Beaumont (1908–1973), managing director of H. M. Tennent, Ltd., from 1939 to his death. Known as the Czar of Shaftsbury Avenue, he was a considerable influence on British theatrical taste for nearly forty years.

three less expensive accommodations on the liner *America*, and the three women sailed on March 15, arriving in Southampton four days later. The small female entourage occupied one of Claridge's best suites for the run of the play. Rehearsals began almost immediately and Kate immersed herself in the role of Epifania. Beaumont might have been tightfisted where Kate's friends were concerned, but he was most generous otherwise and spared no expense on the production. Kate's lavish costumes were designed by Pierre Balmain and her co-stars were Robert Helpmann,* as the Egyptian doctor Epifania loves, and Cyril Ritchard,† as her yes man.

During the day, Kate would rehearse with Michael Benthall and the company. At night, Collier and Wilbourn would put her through her paces, as Laura and Luddy had once done. Within six weeks of arriving in London, Kate opened in *The Millionairess* in the provinces to cheering ovations and full houses. In Brighton, by the end of the pre-London tour, everyone concerned was certain they had a hit and their instincts proved right.

June 26, 1952, was a sweltering day, the hottest of the year, and the New Theatre, St. Martin's Lane, had no air conditioning to offer the 959 theatergoers who occupied every seat in the house. No one in the audience seemed to care and it did not appear to frazzle one hair on Kate's head as she sledgehammered her way through the evening, playing Epifania "with such a furious, rawboned, strident vitality that it sweeps away likes and dislikes and presents the creature as a force of nature."

The London *Times* found her "so vivid in her vicious arrogance that she brings us quite as close as we want to come to feeling the same horrid fascination that Shaw felt in the middle thirties for unprincipled men and women who are born to boss the world by sheer force of personality."

The London critic to *The New York Times*, W. A. Darling-

---

* Robert Helpmann (1909–   ), knighted 1968, was a principal dancer at Sadler's Wells Ballet from 1933 to 1950; but he had always undertaken dramatic roles and made many film appearances as well, most memorably in *The Red Shoes* (1948), *The Tales of Hoffman* (1951) and *Don Quixote* (title role, 1973).
† Cyril Ritchard (1898–1977), brilliant actor and revue performer, well known for his portrayal of Lord Fopping in Boucicault's *The Relapse* and Captain Hook in *Peter Pan* (1954). He made only a few films.

ton, wrote that Kate had "hit London with such a crack that she might have been a thunderbolt generating the sweltering weather." Nothing like it had been seen in years. Other American actresses could claim British triumphs but none had appeared in a play so overwhelmingly reviewed as bad originally and by sheer personal vitality bludgeoned her way to triumph. And a triumph it was, for even those critics who always had a dissenting opinion applauded Kate's virtuoso performance, which they wrote had "enormous range" *(News Chronicle)* and "rhythmic beauty" *(The Times);* they called her "a human hurricane" *(Daily Express)*, and commented that not only was "opposition impossible" *(The Observer)* but "One feels as excited as the man who went over Niagara in a barrel" *(The Sunday Times)*. Yet once again Kate was hit with the question of whether her performance was acting or an "exhibition of personality which is not at all the same thing."

The *Times* critic* summed up his comments by saying, "This millionairess, the born-boss, who simply cannot help dominating people, and equally cannot help spreading devastation in her successful tracks, is not a live character. Shaw could not make a woman of her and Miss Hepburn does not try. What she has seen in this part is that it makes a superb vehicle for violence and it is on her ability to be violent in about twenty-five different ways that her triumph depends. Every now and then she is quiet for a space and the effect is that of a sudden shutting off of power in a boiler-factory. This is magnificent in its way, but it is still not acting."

Kate would suffer this kind of criticism in the future as she had in the past. From Eva Lovelace in *Morning Glory* to Jo in *Little Women, Alice Adams,* Terry Randall in *Stage Door,* Susan Vance in *Bringing Up Baby,* Linda Seton in *Holiday,* Tracy Lord in *The Philadelphia Story,* Tess Harding in *Woman of the Year* to Rose Sayer in *The African Queen,* critics had on the one hand acclaimed her performances and then slapped her down by negating their original praise with versions of—"ah, yes—but Miss Hepburn after all is really not acting but *being* Hepburn." Could all these women Kate had played really have been the multiple sides of one

---

* The *Times* critic (then, by tradition, anonymous) was known to be A. V. Cookman.

woman—herself? Or was it simply that the roles she chose were almost always unique upper-class women, thereby immediately associating herself with what the public knew of her? By now the mannerisms had mostly vanished, but the distinctive voice remained, along with the lithe, athletic body that moved with animal grace. But *The Millionairess* was as far a cry from Kate's own personality as Rose Sayer had been. *The African Queen*, in fact, had just appeared to rave reviews in London and could be seen at the same time as *The Millionairess*.

Within a few days of the opening, Kate began to struggle with an obstinate case of laryngitis. With queues outside the theater from five A.M. almost every morning and houses playing to standing room only, Beaumont was fearful he might have to close, for there could be no question of substitutes or understudies in a play that hung on one bravura performance. Kate was ordered to be totally silent offstage and she complied without complaint, conducting all her affairs (including the purchase of some antique furniture to take home) with the aid of scribbled notes. This continued for three months, but her laryngitic trouble never ceased. Onstage the problem was discernible only to the keen ear— "a shade more edge and strain were present in the tones of the verbal tornado in the later performances than in the earlier, but all the familiar, almost overwhelming force was there"—and as Kate's voice had a slightly cracked quality anyway, the variation was not easily detectable.

A sizable crowd stood outside the stage door of the New Theatre when, two hours after the ninety-sixth and last London performance of *The Millionairess*, Kate emerged in slacks, hair pulled back, wearing no makeup. The crowd pressed in close with scraps of paper for her to sign. She pushed them less than gently away as a burly stage-door keeper came to her rescue and helped her to make her way through the unruly gathering to her waiting car. Fans stood in front of it to prevent the driver from moving forward. As Kate stepped in she called out loudly (no need to conserve her voice now) to the chauffeur (a warning to all those in their path)—"Drive on. We'll sweep up the blood later!" The door slammed, the motor turned and the group quickly dispersed

Katharine Houghton Hepburn, age two, posing on top of her favorite sled with brother Tom. HOMER DICKENS COLLECTION

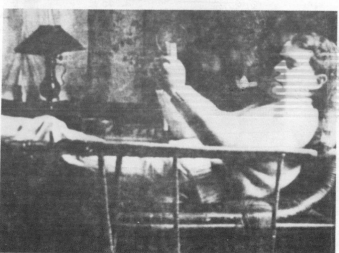

Her father, Dr. Thomas N. Hepburn, called her "Redtop." HOMER DICKENS COLLECTION

Miss Robinson-Duff, Kate's first drama coach, had to tell her she was fired from the cast of *The Big Pond* after only one performance. HOMER DICKENS COLLECTION

On the set of *A Bill of Divorcement* with Billie Burke. Kate played Miss Burke and John Barrymore's daughter in this, her first film, and became a star (1932). HOMER DICKENS COLLECTION

as the car began to roll forward. Then Kate opened the window and waved good-bye.

A few days later, Kate put Constance Collier and Phyllis Wilbourn onboard the *Nieuw Amsterdam,* along with the additional luggage they had all accumulated, and she flew with Irene Selznick to Jamaica, where they were to vacation for a few days with Noël Coward and his good friend Cole Lesley. Irene, now divorced from David O. Selznick,* was a play producer. The two women arrived in an open sports car—unheard of in Jamaica and apparently shipped in by either Kate or Irene. Up until that time, Noël had been firmly warned of the danger of sunstroke and on the insistence of his Jamaican friends had used a closed car. From that point on, he followed Kate's lead and always drove about in an open car on the island, where he had a vacation home. Kate relaxed in the sun, parried loving barbs with Noël and helped Cole play midwife to Serena, the men's much-loved dog of "indeterminate" breed. Serena gave birth to four puppies, Charlotte, Emily, Anne and Bramwell. Emily, "a fat little beige sausage roll," took to Kate at once, gazing up at her adoringly whenever Kate held her.

Kate flew to New York just two weeks before *The Millionairess* was scheduled to open there. The decision had not been easy. Tracy remained on the West Coast and they had not seen very much of each other for the better part of a year. Also, Kate suspected that critical reaction to the play would be no better than in London and that her vitality onstage would not be unique to the American theater. But the Theatre Guild had convinced her she should do *The Millionairess* on Broadway under their auspices. Michael Benthall mounted the play in New York as he had in London and retained the entire original company.

The Millionairess opened at the Shubert Theatre on October 17, 1952, and Kate's suspicions were confirmed. "Miss Hepburn had a lot of physical energy and vocal power," Brooks Atkinson wrote in *The New York Times* review, "and doubtless more endurance than any actress alive. Taking everything at top speed she clears all the hurdles and knocks

---

* David Selznick married actress Jennifer Jones in 1949.

down anything that gets in her way. No doubt this is one way of concealing the infirmities of an untidy and meandering script. Dressed in the most stunning costumes of the season . . . she hammers away on one note from entrance to conclusion . . . she takes every line in about the same key and tempo. What wit there may be lurking in the lines gets short shrift in this treatment. . . . Miss Hepburn can be understood clearly. Perhaps that is the trouble. As a piece of theatre literature *The Millionairess* is not worth all the energy she is squandering on it."

No matter how hard she tried, Kate seemed incapable of conquering Broadway.

When *The Millionairess* closed after a successful ten-week limited engagement, Kate decided the next logical step was to adapt it and star in it for films. This was no easy matter for the rights were controlled by Gabriel Pascal,* who asked for exorbitant terms. Finally, she managed to get Pascal to agree to sell her the rights at an affordable price; and since she could not interest a film company in the production, she put up the money herself. Another few months passed during which she tried to convince several of her old associates— including Cukor and Stevens—to come to work on this project with her. No one supported her idea that it would make a good film. Finally, she approached Preston Sturges,† who was considered to be Hollywood's most brilliant satirist. Sturges, down on his luck, had moved into the house in Turtle Bay and the two of them went to work on an adaptation, emerging two months later with a script Garson Kanin says was "beautifully conceived, hilariously written." The package (meaning Kate as star, the script, and Sturges as director) was then submitted to one major studio after another without success. Kate turned to the independents in both Europe and the States. The answer was no.

At about this time Kate noticed some rough patches on her

---

* Gabriel Pascal (1894–1954) had turned several of Shaw's plays into films, including *Pygmalion* (1938) and *Major Barbara* (1941). Shaw had named him executor of his estate for film rights.
† Preston Sturges (1898–1959) wrote, directed and produced his own films, among them *The Lady Eve* (1941), *Hail the Conquering Hero* (1944) and *Unfaithfully Yours* (1948).

skin and on August 6, 1953, underwent surgery in Hartford Hospital for the removal of several skin cancers thought to have been caused by overexposure to the sun during the filming of *The African Queen*. She went to Fenwick to recuperate and began working again on her plan to film *The Millionairess*. Finally, by January, 1954, Kate thought she had a deal with the Wolff brothers (the same men who had financed *The African Queen*). With Sturges as director and Lester Cowan* (who was to produce), she flew to London and then locked herself into her suite at Claridge's after she realized she had no deal with the Wolffs. She began making frantic calls. In desperation, she offered "to forego reimbursement of her considerable expenditures, work for nothing and pay Sturges" (who had also offered to take a large cut). The answer remained no.

Although everyone agreed that Sturges had written a brilliant script and that the role was tailor-made for Kate, the same problems existed in the film script as in the play.† Even Sturges's gift for satire could not overcome the lack of a story. With great disappointment, Kate gave up and returned to New York. She had made a costly error; and her father, who still controlled her money and doled out her allowance, had allowed her to proceed much against his better judgment. She felt a terrible failure. Things weren't going well with her and Tracy. She celebrated her forty-sixth birthday not knowing what the future held. Then, English director David Lean** sent her a script entitled *Summertime*.‡

---

* Lester Cowan (1904–   ) had made W. C. Fields's classic *My Little Chickadee* (1940) as well as *Ladies in Retirement* (1941), *Tomorrow the World* (1944) and *The Story of G. I. Joe* (1945).

† *The Millionairess* was made in 1960 with Sophia Loren and Peter Sellers. The Sturges script was not used. The film was not successful.

** David Lean (1908–   ), English director. Won Academy Awards for *Bridge on the River Kwai* (1957) and *Lawrence of Arabia* (1962). He also directed *Dr. Zhivago* (1965) and *A Passage to India* (1984).

‡ *Summer Madness* in Great Britain.

CHAPTER 21

In summer a festive atmosphere pervades Venice, that ancient grand survivor of flood, the rise and fall of empires, and centuries of invading tourists. Never mind the aimless, pressing crowds, the stench of the polluted water in the canals and the painful glare caused by the sun blazing like firelight as it hits the water and bounds back and forth between the white buildings of the narrow streets. Venice, sharply outlined against a glowing sky, rose before Kate, Constance Collier and Phyllis Wilbourn as they entered the city by launch and then transferred to one of the flotilla of gondolas that had been hired to taxi the company about. Their final destination —the Bauer Grünwald Hotel—had been chosen because no other hotel in Venice had air conditioning and modern plumbing.

Venetians, it seemed, had seen almost everything but a company of film players. From the time of Kate's arrival, groups gathered to gawk at her. The most persistent comment was "how old and gaunt she was, as compared to Sophia Loren." In fact, Kate did not look well in the summer of 1954. Dysentery still plagued her and some small surgical scars that remained on her face could be seen when she went without makeup. Rumors that *Summertime* was a story about an illicit love affair and that it contained indecent scenes had

As Antiope opposite Colin Keith-Johnston in *The Warrior's Husband*, the role that brought Kate to Hollywood's attention (1932).
HOMER DICKENS COLLECTION

Kate with her dear friend American Express heiress, Laura Harding (1935). They liked to play madcap stunts.
HOMER DICKENS COLLECTION

John Ford, her director on *Mary of Scotland,* nearly left his wife for her (1933). ACADEMY OF MOTION PICTURE ARTS & SCIENCES

Kate's two sisters, Marion (left) and Peggy (right), escort their mother, Kit, from a Washington Senate hearing room where Mrs. Hepburn had defended birth control. HOMER DICKENS COLLECTION

Dressed as a young man in *Sylvia Scarlett* (1936). HOMER DICKENS COLLECTION

Howard Hughes followed Kate to her home in Connecticut after she had been named Box Office Poison in 1938 and became a character in Dick Hepburn's play. ACADEMY OF MOTION PICTURE ARTS & SCIENCES

The Philadelphia Story (1939). (Left to right) John Howard, Cary Grant, Kate and James Stewart.
ACADEMY OF MOTION PICTURE ARTS & SCIENCES

Tracy and Hepburn on the set of *Woman of the Year* (1941). The chemistry they had for each other was obvious to everyone on the film including Kate's then current beau, director George Stevens—the man with the pipe. HOMER DICKENS COLLECTION

A rare picture of Tracy with wife, Louise, aboard the liner *Santa Rosa* en route for South America (1932). They were never to divorce. HOMER DICKENS COLLECTION

Tracy's drinking buddies. (Left to right) Tracy, Pat O'Brien, Frank McHugh, James Cagney and Lynn Overman. HOMER DICKENS COLLECTION

Laura Harding and Tracy. They tolerated each other. (Picture taken at seventieth birthday fete for Ethel Barrymore, 1949.) HOMER DICKENS COLLECTION

On the podium speaking out against the House Un-American Activities Committee's Hollywood witch-hunt (1951). **HOMER DICKENS COLLECTION**

Rehearsing a scene for *The African Queen*. (Left to right) director John Huston, cameraman Jack Cardiff, Humphrey Bogart and Kate (1951). TIME, INC.

During the 1950s Kate traveled extensively. Here with secretary Phyllis Wilbourn (carrying hat box). HOMER DICKENS COLLECTION

Preparing to make up as Eleanor of Aquitaine for *The Lion in Winter*. The role brought Kate her third Oscar (of four). TERENCE SPENCER

On the set of *The Lion in Winter* with (left to right) director Anthony Harvey, co-star Peter O'Toole and producer Martin Poll (1968). PRIVATE COLLECTION MARTIN POLL

Kate sings in *Coco* (1970). HOMER DICKENS COLLECTION

Kate in dining room of her New York townhouse (1970).
CECIL BEATON, CAMERA PRESS, LONDON

With John Wayne on location in Oregon for *Rooster Cogburn* (1975). HOMER DICKENS COLLECTION

Three great legends: director George Cukor, Kate and Sir Laurence Olivier, filming *Love Among the Ruins* for television in England (1975). HOMER DICKENS COLLECTION

preceded Kate's arrival. Of more concern to director David Lean was the Venetians' fear that the filming of it would disrupt the tourism necessary for their economic security. In the first few days there existed a possibility that the *gondolieri* might go out on strike if the company did not move elsewhere. These problems immediately evaporated after a generous contribution by the film company to the fund for restoring the Basilica of San Marco and a guarantee to the cardinal that there would be "no bare arms or short skirts in and around holy places." This last had been prompted by a scene shot of Kate in a sleeveless dress standing outside San Marco, which was then reshot with her in a long-sleeved blouse tucked demurely into a full skirt.

Summertime had been adapted from Arthur Laurents's successful play, *The Time of the Cuckoo.** Jane Hudson, the middle-aged American spinster Kate portrays, comes to Venice to fulfill a lifelong dream. She meets and falls in love with a charming, married antique dealer (Rossano Brazzi).† The affair is brief and one of great delicacy, but when Jane leaves Venice less than two weeks later she carries with her a memory to light up her lonely future. One of the major scenes in the highly romanticized film version is the one where Kate, while attempting to take a photograph of Brazzi's shop, steps back and falls into a canal.

The water in Venice's canals is a polluted mixture of garbage, ordure, mud and putrefaction. Despite Kate's insistence that she not chance further damage to her skin or a rare disease, David Lean was not willing to compromise with realism. Finally, Kate agreed to go ahead when Lean arranged to barricade an area of the canal with plastic sheets lowered from barges and then to flood the enclosed area with disinfectant.

On the long-awaited day, the company all stood by. Kate

---

* Arthur Laurents (1918–   ) had many of his play scripts turned into films, among them *West Side Story* (1961) and *Gypsy* (1962). He also wrote screenplays for *The Snake Pit* (1948), *Anastasia* (1956) and *The Turning Point* (1977), as well as adapting his book *The Way We Were* (1973).

† Rossano Brazzi (1916–   ) had been in Italian films for many years when, in 1954, American producers cast him in *Three Coins in the Fountain* and *The Barefoot Contessa*. In *Summertime*, Brazzi was at the height of his fame as a romantic leading man.

was poised for action when suddenly the water began to foam like a bubble bath, the result of the density of the chemicals.

"If you think I'm going into *that*, you're crazy," Kate stated.

Vincent Korda,* the Hungarian art director, suggested *"vind machines"* and "soon a pair of garbage scows arrived in tow, each carrying a wind machine rather like an old-fashioned airplane propeller and engine with a protective grill around it. A team of technicians anchored them and soon the engines were howling at high speed, producing a gale-force wind and sending the foam down the canal like a tidal wave." Kate, her face and all exposed sections of her body covered in Vaseline as further protection from the water, fell in backward the moment the water cleared. Lean was not happy with the take and Kate, after being pulled out of the water by a gondolier, had her hair dried and replaced her wet dress with an identical dry one before trying again.

"It tastes lousy . . . like a swimming pool in California with all that chlorine," she complained as she stood ready for the next take. Three more takes were to follow before Lean was satisfied.

That night Kate's eyes began to itch and tear. She had infected them with a form of conjunctivitis that would always stay with her, causing the constant teary look that would become so much a part of her performance that no one would suspect the moistness was not induced purposely.

Toward the middle of production, Constance Collier's health grew worse and she and Phyllis Wilbourn returned to New York. Noël Coward visited Kate for five days early in August and Tracy managed a short reunion, fraught with tension. There had been some rumors in the European press of a growing romance between Tracy and Grace Kelly. Tracy had been seen with Hollywood's newest beauty and she had agreed to appear with him in a future project, *Tribute to a*

---

* Vincent Korda (1897–1979), brother of film directors Alexander and Zolton Korda, father of writer and publishing executive Michael Korda. Vincent Korda, a Hungarian who lived most of his adult life in Great Britain, was a talented art director. He often worked on his brothers' films, but *Summertime* was a production of independent producer Ilya Lopart. Michael Korda was visiting his father in Venice when the scene in which Hepburn fell into the canal was shot.

Bad Man, but Tracy claimed the friendship was more business than pleasure. The fact that Kelly had a penchant for married men (Ray Milland, Gary Cooper, Bing Crosby and Clark Gable had all been enamored of her) did not do a great deal to reassure Kate. Uncomfortable in the muggy heat that settled on Venice that summer, upset by the growing discord between Tracy and herself, Kate had not been too gracious to any of the members of the company. After Tracy's departure, she complained, "Nobody asked me to dinner. They went off and left me alone. I felt rather angry about that. I wandered off by myself through Venice feeling very lonely and neglected, and sat down by the canal and looked in the water, and while I was sitting like that a man came over to me and said, 'May I come and talk to you?' Only it wasn't Rossano Brazzi. It was a French plumber.

"I was glad to talk to anyone who looked reasonably all right, so we went off together for a walk through Venice. I suppose they [the film company] all thought I had madly exciting things to do and left me to it. . . . It's my own fault entirely. I have brought it upon myself. I am rather a sharp person. I have a sharp face and a sharp voice. When I speak on the telephone, I snap into it. It puts people off, I suppose.

"Being an actor is such a humiliating experience," she added after much thought. "Because you are selling yourself to the public, your face, your personality, and that is humiliating. As you get older, it becomes more humiliating because you've got less to sell."

The role of Jane Hudson was another performance that added to Kate's reputation of creating her film persona in her own image. Everything superfluous was gone, the elements were refined and complete—"the sad mouth, the head-back laugh, the snap of *chic* in shirtmaker dresses, the dream of enchantment behind wistful eyes, the awakening puritan passion of the girl in love, the 'regular' way with children, the leggy stride, and always the bones"—the magnificent, prominent, impossible bones which a visiting journalist [English], made somewhat exuberant by the deceptively mild local wine, described as "the greatest calcium deposit since the White Cliffs of Dover."

On her way home from Venice, Kate stopped in London to

visit with Ruth Gordon, who was in rehearsal for the role of Dolly Levi in the London production of *The Matchmaker* (later to be the basis of the musical *Hello Dolly!*), and to see her many English friends, including Michael Benthall and Robert Helpmann, who were preparing an Australian tour for the Old Vic. The plan was to present three Shakespearean plays. They now suggested Kate join them and add the roles of Katharine in *The Taming of the Shrew,* Isabella in *Measure for Measure* and Portia in *The Merchant of Venice* to her repertoire. Kate agreed and returned to New York to prepare for the tour, scheduled for May through part of September.

Since Constance Collier was not well enough to coach her, Kate went to Alfred Dixon, who had been recommended by Mary Martin. Dixon had unique methods of coaching, one of which "was to make a mooing noise with lips closed, starting very low on the scale, gradually rising higher and higher and then slowly all the way down again, until at last you had to stop for lack of breath. The result resembled a loud, long air-raid warning emitted by a cow, repeated over and over again." The sounds could be heard up and down the corridors of the Carnegie Hall studios where Dixon coached. Kate was still worried about the throat trouble she had had in *The Millionairess,* and, like Noël Coward, who had also worked with Dixon, she thought the exercise "the best loosener-upper in the world" and a great help in extending her vocal range with ease. Contrary to the advice of Miss Robinson-Duff* and Constance Collier, Dixon's most revolutionary dictum was never to breathe deeply, to inhale just the merest sip of air when needed. Kate's voice cracked less using this method, and she felt much more confident about the difficult repertoire for which she had contracted.

In April, 1955, Constance Collier died, and Kate took her friend's death hard. The years of her close friendship with Collier (1950–1955) had coincided with a certain standoff between Laura and Luddy and herself. More dramatically, the rumors about Grace Kelly, whether true or false, had pointed up Tracy's sudden availability. He had sought out Grace Kelly's companionship in much the same way as he had Joan Fontaine's. And although Kate always gave the impres-

---

* Frances Robinson-Duff had died in 1951.

sion that Tracy was a rock to be depended upon, in reality the situation was reversed. Kate was the strong member of the team, able to cope when trouble hit, working always to improve her talents, her mind and her physical well-being. Tracy, on the other hand, was quite capable of wallowing in self-pity that invariably led to drinking, quarrelsomeness and painful experiences for all those involved in his life and his career. To add to this, his health was failing and he did very little to help himself.

He took Kate's acceptance of the Australian tour as a personal blow, an out-and-out rejection, and he began to drink *seriously* on May 5, the day she left for Australia via Qantas Airlines. Scheduled to begin *Tribute to a Bad Man* on June 1, he could not accompany her. Grace Kelly had backed out of the project and was irrationally replaced by the volatile Greek actress Irene Papas,* who was completely miscast and stood five ten in her bare feet. The script was weak and the director, Robert Wise,† was unknown to Tracy. Location was set in the Rockies near Montrose, Colorado, and Tracy checked in six days late with no explanation to his distraught director. Two days later he disappeared again, causing hysteria on the set. Calls were placed to Kate in Australia. Finally, after a week, he showed up on the location and announced he could not stand the altitude—the plateau on which the set was constructed was approximately eight thousand feet above sea level—and demanded they disassemble the set and rebuild it lower in the mountains.

Metro's vice-president and publicity head, Howard Strickland,** one of the few powerful friends Tracy had left at the studio, arrived on location to attempt to negotiate a peace. He could not convince Tracy to back down and on

---

* Irene Papas (1926–   ) is one of Greece's finest tragediennes. *Tribute to a Bad Man* (1956) was her first American film. Her most vivid performances have been as Antigone (1960), Electra (1962), and opposite Anthony Quinn in *Zorba the Greek* (1964). In 1971, Papas co-starred (as Helen of Troy) with Hepburn in *The Trojan Women*.

† Robert Wise (1914–   ) was known from 1944 to 1954 principally as a director of horror and mystery films. Then he directed *Executive Suite* (1954) and shortly after transferred his skills to sleek commercial musicals like *West Side Story* (1961), *The Sound of Music* (1965) and *Star!* (1968).

** Howard Strickland had been largely responsible for Metro's publicity for *Gone With the Wind*. He remained at the studio through many executive changes.

June 25, Spencer Tracy was fired from a film. A few weeks later his contract with M.G.M. was terminated.*

Even in Australia, Kate heard the stories—Tracy was finished—an alcoholic—sick—and would never be hired again in Hollywood. In Melbourne at the time, working in heavy costume and sweltering one-hundred-degree weather with no air conditioning, Kate had her own problems. The first nine weeks of the tour, with limited runs in Sydney and Brisbane, had been highly successful. But Melbourne audiences had not taken well to her New England cadences superimposed upon Shakespeare. One morning after the company's first production, an ill-chosen *Measure for Measure*, a review on the front page of the major Melbourne paper exclaimed, "I have no idea why Miss Hepburn chose to come to Melbourne, except that it was quite obvious her career must be over as a motion picture star. And Robert Helpmann's is certainly over as a dancer!" Unlike Vivien Leigh, who had toured many of the same Australian theaters with the Old Vic Company in a series of Shakespearean plays seven years earlier, Kate did not enjoy the instant acclaim. Her films had never been successful Down Under and many had not been released there. *Pat and Mike*'s run had been cut short after three days for lack of business. *The African Queen* had done well, but *Summertime* had yet to be shown.

Calls flew back and forth over the Pacific from Tracy, most of them unsettling. Kate immersed herself in the rare beauty of the land and was as fascinated as Vivien Leigh had once been with the Daliesque terrain. "The great shallow blue lakes [near Adelaide] surrounded by glistening white sand, black and white branches of trees sticking up out of the water and birds of every kind and description everywhere." The bird that fascinated her the most was the extraordinary lyrebird, about the size of a guinea hen, with powerful thigh muscles and long-clawed fingers; it sent forth eerie human sounds as it danced in an almost ritualistic pattern, "like an Indian warrior about to go into battle."

* * *

---

* James Cagney replaced Tracy in *Tribute to a Bad Man*. He was shorter by three inches than Tracy; and Papas towered ludicrously over him in the film, which was not successful.

Most of Hollywood thought that Tracy's humiliation at being fired from a film would force him into retirement. Yet the same year he was nominated for an Oscar for his performance in *Bad Day at Black Rock.** Kate was intrenchably in his corner. The two spent many weeks together upon her return from Australia, and a marked change occurred in their relationship. Kate became almost custodial in her care of Tracy. She all but stopped smoking to help him quit the habit because his smoking and drinking seemed to go together. And she determined that she would not leave him for such a long stretch again and that that they would, if at all possible, accompany each other on film locations or any tours she might take. From 1955 on, Tracy was a desperately sick man. Close friends believed he might be dying. Among other things, his heart was weak and his liver seriously damaged. Kate made sure he ate the right foods and took care of himself. She exercised with him and walked with him to help him take off weight. Never, even in the beginning of their friendship, had they been so close, and when Tracy signed with Paramount to star in *The Mountain,*† the story of a plane crash in the Alps, she accompanied him to Chamonix, France, for the location shooting. The high altitude made Tracy's breathing difficult and exerted his heart and lungs. Kate remained in the background as discreetly as possible, but seldom left him alone.

Constance Collier's former companion, Phyllis Wilbourn, was now in Kate's employ as "secretary-companion-assistant-indispensable." She accompanied Kate to France and would travel with her wherever Kate and Tracy went. She quickly became an extension of Kate, although her presence created some thorny moments with Tracy, who, while grateful for her help to him and Kate, found her prim "gentle-gentlewoman" personality a bit hard to take; and "he would often nag or hector or tease her." Tracy was by nature combative, but with

---

* *Bad Day at Black Rock* (1955) was Tracy's last film for Metro. John O'Hara in *Collier's* (July 1955) called the film "one of the finest motion pictures ever made." Compared endlessly to *High Noon* by reviewers, *Black Rock* came out the unanimous winner and Tracy's performance lauded as "one of the best you'll ever see on film." (O'Hara in *Collier's*)

† *The Mountain* (1956) was adapted from an Henri Troyat novel.

Phyllis he sometimes took on a cruel tone that made his resentment at her constant presence most evident.

By the time *The Mountain* was completed, Tracy had achieved a devastating imitation of Phyllis. Kanin says, "He found the precise tone and pitch of her voice, the lovely lilt of her speech, the best of her upper-class British accent, and when the mood struck him, would reply to her questions in her own voice. She would blush and he would continue . . . to twit her, mainly because she reacted so sharply.

"Aeeeeoh! Miss Hepp-bunn," he'd say, becoming Phyllis to the pursing of her lips and the fluttering of her lashes. "Hahow viddy, viddy kind!"

Kate invariably stepped in and tried to ameliorate what Tracy said with some especially warm words or small gesture of appreciation. But Phyllis remained always close-at-hand, ready for any emergency or request for her assistance.

Tracy was equally cutting with Laura, whom he considered too spoiled and too rich. He did like Irene Selznick, whom Kate saw in New York or whenever they both happened to be in California. The two women often went swimming together. "Mind you," Irene Selznick recalls, "nothing as convenient as the pool at George's [Cukor]. Kate would bring masses of towels, a huge lunch, and we'd make a day of it. . . . We'd swim our way across town, from one pool to another, until we reached the surf at Malibu. We gave our patronage to friends and strangers alike, showing up uninvited, unexpected, but we assumed welcome. . . .

"An empty house and a sparkling pool had the effect on us of a formal invitation." Irene had sold her old house in 1953. "[Afterward] . . . on each trip West our first drive about included 1050 Summit Drive to see how it was faring . . . [one time] we were dying to get inside . . . but every door was locked. However, there was one near the pantry that we knew was apt to be left unlocked; it was at the top of the stairs leading from the basement. We knew how to get there through the garage. . . . We felt like Tom Sawyer and Huck Finn.

"For two people so passionate about privacy, this was a hell of a thing to do. We knew better, but somehow felt entitled."

As they were inspecting the bedrooms, they heard a woman's voice, "shrill and frightened from below

"Kate, instantly mobilized, called out, 'We'll be right down. It's all right, I assure you.'"

The woman was startled to see Katharine Hepburn walking down her stairway to meet her and after an uncomfortable few minutes of apologies on Kate and Irene Selznick's part eased up enough to show them the living room as she led them to the front door.

When Tracy returned to Hollywood late in 1955, Kate accepted the role of Lizzie Curry in the film adaptation of N. Richard Nash's successful play *The Rainmaker,* about a tense spinster who cares for her father and two brothers on a southwestern farm plagued by drought. Her co-star was Burt Lancaster,* who played Starbuck, a sensual, good-looking, sweet-talking con man who claims he can bring rain into the area for one hundred dollars but secretly hopes he can turn Lizzie into a woman ready for love before he leaves.

Filming in Hollywood for Paramount, the same studio that had made *The Mountain,* allowed Kate and Tracy to be together (although they still maintained separate domiciles). Apart from this advantage, Kate liked the screenplay, adapted by the playwright himself, and especially loved the comfort of playing a role that, except for one dress, permitted her to wear pants or a cotton shirtdress throughout.

Happily for Kate, Joseph Anthony,† who had directed the play of *The Rainmaker,* was hired by Paramount to direct the film version. Anthony had had a long distinguished career as a stage director but had never directed a film before. He had also had a prestigious if eclectic background as a screenwriter, playwright, actor (theater and films) and premier dancer with Agnes DeMille. Consequently, *The Rainmaker* took on a balletic as well as a balladic quality. Never had Kate moved so

---

* Burt Lancaster (1913–   ). His screen debut in the role of Swede in an adaptation of Hemingway's short story *The Killers* (1946) immediately made him a star. He won an Academy Award for *Elmer Gantry* (1960), was nominated for *Atlantic City* (1982), and won the Venice Festival Award for his performance in *Bird Man of Alcatraz* (1962). In 1961, he appeared with Tracy in *Judgment at Nuremberg.*

† Joseph Anthony (1912–   ) directed such well-received plays as *The Most Happy Fella* (1956), *The Best Man* (1960), *Under the Yum Yum Tree* (1960), *Rhinoceros* (1961), *Mary, Mary* (1961), and the musical version of *The Rainmaker—110 in the Shade* (1963). He made very few films and of them only *The Rainmaker* won even moderate success.

well as under Anthony's graceful direction. Her mannered movements and cracked voice were smoothed into a swell of loneliness that, when it erupts at the climax of the film, has great impact. "Overactive" actresses distressed Anthony. "Don't just *do* something," he once shouted at a leading lady in one of his plays. "*Stand* there!" Kate's performance was the most restrained of her career; and it gave her scenes with Lancaster, as the swaggering pitchman, a startling force. Nonetheless, she never fully captured the sound and manners of a farm woman of limited formal education. Since she had failed so badly years before in *Spitfire* with a country accent, either she or Anthony made the decision that she would simply tone down her own airy vocal intonations. It apparently worked, for Kate won her seventh Oscar nomination for her performance.*

The Rainmaker was finished shortly before Christmas, 1955, and Tracy accompanied Kate to Fenwick for the holidays. The family now accepted the fact that Tracy and Kate would probably never marry. They never felt the same closeness for him as they had (and still felt) for Luddy. Some competitiveness existed between Tracy and Dr. Hepburn. In fact, the two men were too similar in many ways to like each other and both resented the other's power over Kate.

Leland Hayward was currently married to Slim Hawks, former model and ex-wife of film director Howard Hawks. Kate seldom saw Hayward and had been out of touch with him throughout most of the 1940s and early 1950s (although Hayward and Dr. Hepburn kept up a vigorous correspondence regarding Kate's early film earnings, which still came through Hayward's office). However, their paths were once again to cross.

Hayward, now a producer,† had acquired the film rights to Ernest Hemingway's *The Old Man and the Sea*, published

---

* Hepburn at that time had been previously nominated as Best Actress for *Morning Glory* (1933), *Alice Adams* (1935), *The Philadelphia Story* (1940), *Woman of the Year* (1942), *The African Queen* (1951) and *Summertime* (1955), and had won the award for her first nomination. She was nominated again for *The Rainmaker*, but Ingrid Bergman won Best Actress of 1956 for *Anastasia*.
† Leland Hayward produced such theater hits as *South Pacific*, *Oklahoma!*, *Call Me Madam* and *Mister Roberts*, and had assisted in their transfer to film.

that same year. From the start, Hayward was convinced Tracy was the only actor to play the Old Man. Kate, after her experience with *The African Queen*, realized the difficulty of shooting a film in primitive locations, all the more so if the action was to take place in a small boat on rough water. She conveyed her fears to Tracy, whose unstable health promised to make such a precarious venture even more of an ordeal. Hayward had his work cut out for him. He had to persuade Kate and Tracy that the role was one Tracy should play; he had to overcome Hemingway's personal doubts that his masterful short novel (which had helped him win the Nobel Prize in 1954) could make a film; and he had to persuade a film company that a movie about an old man and a boy (Cubans at that) fishing for marlin would be of any interest to moviegoers.

To soften the public and prove the commercial value of *The Old Man and the Sea,* Hayward had proposed that Tracy and a child actor should first read aloud from the book in a series of one-night stands across the country. Hemingway had approved the idea in principle, but Tracy refused to subject himself to the rigors of such a tour. Not to be daunted, Hayward then came up with an alternative scheme. The film would be made as a documentary using "local people on a local ocean with a local boat" and Tracy would then only have to narrate. Tracy found this approach more to his liking and agreed to make the film. By the spring of 1955, with Tracy's name inked to a contract, Hayward managed to gain financing from Warner Brothers, whom he told that Tracy would play the Old Man. Tracy felt that Hayward had used him badly and wanted to back out; but Hayward, still the old charming flimflam man, talked him into visiting Hemingway before he made any final decision.

Kate, at this time, had been preparing for the Australian tour; and Tracy and the Haywards flew to Havana, where they were then driven to the Finca, Mary and Ernest Hemingway's home. Tracy, who was within a few weeks of starting the ill-fated *Tribute to a Bad Man,* was on the wagon so diligently that Hemingway thought he was a teetotaler. Hemingway, "browned to a colour he called 'Indio Tostado,'" was in an especially happy mood as he accompanied Tracy to the nearby small port of Cojímar, originally planned as the location for *The Old Man and the Sea*. Tracy even had the good fortune to see old Anselmo Hernandez (the fisherman whom Hemingway had used as his model for the Old Man) asleep in his shack after having fished all through the previous night. Tracy endeared himself to Hemingway by rising at six-thirty each morning while the Haywards slept until noon.

Back in California, with Kate now in Australia, Tracy slipped back off the wagon. After he had been fired from *Bad Man*, Warner Brothers, who had Peter Viertel working on a screenplay of *The Old Man and the Sea*, grew very nervous.

In January, 1956, Kate flew to London to film *The Iron Petticoat* at Pinewood Studios, with Bob Hope* as her unlikely co-star. Tracy accompanied her (although the press was not aware of this). Born in Eltham, Hope had left England as a child and viewed this—his first return as a star to his native land—as reason enough for accepting a straight man's role opposite a performer of Kate's magnitude. Kate played Captain Vinka Kovelenko of the Russian Air Force, assigned to an American base in Germany.

The Iron Petticoat (originally titled *Not For Money*) was very close to being a remake of the Greta Garbo–Melvyn Douglas 1939 comedy, *Ninotchka*, which succeeded where its imitation would fail. While Garbo was given full rein in the role of the Russian officer who becomes Americanized, Hope arrived with an entourage of gag writers who immediately began rewriting the script to tip the film in his favor. Kate's role began to shrink so that very soon she appeared to be playing straight man to Hope.

Ben Hecht, author of the original story, not only pulled out but asked for his name to be removed from the credits.† Hope's writers now took over completely, and the film began to play like Hope and Crosby on the road to Moscow. Finally,

---

* Bob Hope (1903–   ), certainly one of the great comedians of the twentieth century. He is memorable for his series of *Road* films with Bing Crosby, his radio show and television specials and his constant touring to bring entertainment to overseas troops during both peace and war.
† No screenplay credit is given on *The Iron Petticoat*. The original story is credited to Harry Saltzman, co-producer of this film and of eight James Bond films. *The Iron Petticoat* was released in England in July, 1956, but was not shown in the United States until late December of the same year.

Kate's best scenes (according to Hecht in an open letter published in *The Hollywood Reporter*) were "blow-torched out of the film."

An air of hostility enveloped the set; and to add to Kate's problems, her eyes were giving her trouble, tearing badly, burning and itching, still the result of the polluted bath she had taken in the Grand Canal for *Summertime*. "I used to get by in films on my eyes and my teeth," she told the *Evening Standard* reporter, Thomas Wiseman (who had called her the "Sphinx in slacks"). "For this film I think I might have to manage on my teeth." Tracy was restless; but then the Kanins arrived to help occupy his days, and he soon became the old, sharp Tracy, warm and fun to be with.

Being trapped in a film that promised disaster did not stop Kate from doing her best. Nor did she allow Hope's gagman style to alter her commitment to her role as written. The director, Ralph Thomas,* sorely inexperienced at that time to deal with an ego the size of Hope's, was grateful for Kate's support and cooperation. "She never lost her spirit," he recalled, "but it was very difficult for her to perform with someone whose stock in trade was telling funny stories."

The Iron Petticoat was indeed a disaster, more so in the final analysis for Hope than for Kate, who at least looked the part of a Soviet pilot and played it impressively, whereas Hope, as one critic wrote, resorted "to the cheap tricks that in recent years have made many movie goers give up Hope."

Kate and Tracy flew to Havana shortly after *The Iron Petticoat* was completed. *The Old Man and the Sea* was now scheduled for late April, 1956, with Fred Zinnemann† as director. They were put up in a rambling, fourteen-room villa off the coast of Cuba with a full crew of servants.

Originally the plan had been to use a second unit to shoot all the scenes of the Old Man and the giant marlin at Cojímar, hiring a double for Tracy. This had not worked out because the marlin in the area had not been large enough to satisfy the

---

* Ralph Thomas (1915–   ), British director best known for *Doctor in the House* and its several sequels.
† Fred Zinnemann (1907–   ) was nominated for an Academy Award for Best Director for *High Noon* (1952) and won it for *From Here to Eternity* (1953) and *A Man for All Seasons* (1966).

requirements of the script, which called for a fish weighing one thousand pounds. Also, Zinnemann felt a double could be recognized and would spoil the realism he wanted to achieve. Additionally, Hemingway now had second thoughts about Tracy, who he felt had put on so much weight that he looked "too fat and rich" for the role. Tracy had, indeed, gained about thirty pounds since he had stopped drinking. To Kate's despair, Tracy, in Havana, unhappy about having committed himself to the film, hating what he saw as Zinnemann's plodding, condescending attitude, and fearing the difficulties before him, began to drink again. Rumors of his disruptive behavior in several of Havana's bars, linking Kate with him, traveled back to Hollywood, where Jack Warner was duly alarmed. Hemingway was so upset that he wryly remarked that he "hoped to get through the Spring without killing anyone, himself included."

Zinnemann shot some footage of Tracy and the young boy, Felipe Pazos, at the studio in Havana in preparation for their location work. Hayward and Hemingway did not feel he had caught what they wanted, and Zinnemann was fired and *The Old Man and the Sea* was once again in limbo. This left Tracy and Kate some unexpected free time, and they returned to California having decided to do a film together.

They chose William Marchant's *The Desk Set*, a slight Broadway comedy "about the milder terrors of technological unemployment," which had been successful in 1955. In order to accommodate two stars, the screenwriters* had built up Tracy's role and expanded the story until "it almost burst at the seams." The only thing that made the film tolerable and sometimes amusing for viewers was the occasion of Tracy and Hepburn being together again for the first time in five years. Bosley Crowther wrote in *The New York Times* that "they lope through this trifling charade like a couple of old timers, who enjoy reminiscing with simple routines. Mr. Tracy is masculine and stubborn, Miss Hepburn is feminine and glib. The play is inconsequential."

---

* Henry (1912–   ) and Phoebe (1914–1971) Ephron wrote the screenplay of *The Desk Set*. They always worked as collaborators and had first gained recognition in the theater with *Three's a Family* (1943). They had a reputation for lighthearted comedy but were never as polished or sophisticated as the Kanins.

The film cast Kate as Bunny Watson, head of a major television network's reference library and capable of answering or locating in a matter of minutes any question put to her. Tracy is an engineer who has invented "Emmy," an electronic brain that the network plans to install. Bunny and the girls in her office* fear they are soon to be replaced. Tracy's job as the inventor, Richard Sumner, is to prove to Bunny that Emmy will simply leave her more time for research and him.

One reason Kate had been keen on making the film was that she had been told that it would be shot in New York. However, Twentieth Century-Fox, the studio responsible for *The Desk Set*, refused to spend the additional money that location work required. Production took place in Hollywood. In the end this proved beneficial. The warmth and casual life in California restored Tracy to an even keel so that he could cope with the strenuous work on *The Old Man and the Sea*, which went into production in August with John Sturges† replacing Zinnemann.

After an abortive session back in Cuba, during which tropical storms made shooting impossible, the company with Tracy, Kate by his side, returned to California, where most of *The Old Man and the Sea* was to be shot at the Warner Brothers studios in Burbank. A tank filled with 750,000 gallons of water was built to simulate an ocean and stocked with artificial marlin the size of Hemingway's fisherman's fantasy.**

The year 1957 was not an easy one for Kate and Tracy. It had begun with the news that Humphrey Bogart was terminally ill with cancer. They had their last visit with him on a Saturday night. Bogart, emaciated and in great pain, still managed to smile and joke. After a half hour by his bedside, Kate stood up and leaned over and kissed him. Tracy took his

* The ladies are Dina Merrill (1925–   ), Joan Blondell (1909–1979) and Sue Randall (1935–1984).
† John Sturges (1911–   ) had directed Tracy in *Bad Day at Black Rock* (1954). He hit the peak of his success with *The Magnificent Seven* (1960).
** The final cut of *The Old Man and the Sea* is made up of footage filmed by several location units; background shots include the Cuban coast and Peru's Capo Blanco, Nassau and Colombia. Footage was also purchased from Alfred Cassell, a Houston sportsman, and from a Walt Disney collection. Scenic shots of sky and sea were filmed in June, 1957, in Hawaii, and five weeks were spent at Warners using the tank.

hand. "Goodbye, Spence," Bogart said. Kate was startled. Bogart never said "goodbye," always "good night" or "see you." They left Bacall at the door of his bedroom. Then Tracy turned to Kate and said, "Bogie's going to die." In fact, he lapsed into a coma the next day and was dead twenty-four hours later.

Both Kate and Tracy were conscious of their ages now. Kate was fifty, but looking better than she had since *The African Queen*. Tracy, his hair snow white, his face creased with lines, his body paunchy, appeared much older than fifty-seven. It did not help either of their egos that the reviews of *The Desk Set* referred to them as "getting on." Tracy spoke about retirement, but Kate would not hear of it; and when no films she liked came her way, she contracted to appear in two productions of the American Shakespeare Festival Theatre in Stratford, Connecticut, as Portia in *The Merchant of Venice** (the role she had played on the Australian tour) and Beatrice in *Much Ado About Nothing*. She arrived in Stratford late in June; and although she had been offered a number of charming houses, she chose instead Lawrence Langner's broken-down red fisherman's shack built on stilts out over the Housatonic River, whose rising tides sometimes lapped into the screened-in porch where she slept. The house had once belonged to a woman who sold bait, and "People," she said, pleased, "kept coming to ask if I had any worms. I'd say, 'Sorry not today. Would you like some coffee?'" Phyllis Wilbourn occupied a room with a local family across the road. Kate swam every morning in the chilly waters of the Housatonic and used her afternoon break to speed up and down the river in a red outboard motorboat, sometimes going seventy miles an hour "getting drenched by the water and revelling in it."

Rehearsals for *The Merchant of Venice* went comparatively

---

* Hepburn made the inclusion of *The Merchant of Venice* a condition for her appearance with the American Shakespeare Festival Theatre. The request was awkward, for the horrors of the Holocaust had rigidly excluded the play from the American theater as anti-Semitic. The ASFT placed a questionnaire in their program listing eight possible Shakespearean productions. To everyone's amazement *The Merchant of Venice* was chosen number one above *Hamlet*, *Much Ado About Nothing* and *A Midsummer Night's Dream*. Hepburn's demand was therefore met.

smoothly. Since Portia and Shylock never appear onstage together except for their final confrontation in court, Kate rehearsed separately from Morris Carnovsky, one of the theater's most distinguished performers,* who played Shylock. Carnovsky brought to the role a brilliant poignancy that seemed a new interpretation and certainly was poles apart from Robert Helpmann's baroque, stylized portrayal, which had colored the Australian production. Perhaps because of the separate rehearsals, Kate played her final scene with Carnovsky as though the two characters had wandered in from other productions—Carnovsky being realistic and Kate stylized. Somehow the discrepancy did not detract from Carnovsky's performance, of which critic John Gassner crowed: "If there was a better Shylock than Carnovsky's in the entire stage history of *The Merchant of Venice,* it is not apparent to me from my personal experience or my reading. He has rendered him a completely comprehensible man, capable of wringing a sympathy that Shakespeare, writing in the time he did, could hardly have intended . . . and when Shylock finally leaves the court, he is an unforgettable picture of a human made small by his own malevolence." Carnovsky's dazzling performance served only to discredit Kate's own approach. Walter Kerr at *The New York Times* commented, "Miss Hepburn is a highly giddy adolescent who has been reading far too many novels. . . . I wish I knew what she had in mind for Shakespeare's quick-witted maiden."

Kate took her generally bad notices in stride, having received worse in her life, although she did not feel the reviews were justified. Her interpretation of Portia had not been altered since her appearance with the Old Vic in Australia. Despite the reviews, her contribution to the success of the season was enormous. As always outside New York, many in the audience came just to see Katharine Hepburn, movie star. During one performance, a fan stood up and took a flash photograph. Kate stopped center stage and faced the audience:

"There will be no more of that or we won't go on," she

---

* Morris Carnovsky (1898–   ) had been blacklisted in Hollywood by HUAC since 1951. Besides his fine character portrayals in films, his theater appearances were always well-received.

said, her booming voice met with shocked and silent surprise.
She waited a few moments and then went back into her scene.
When criticized for interrupting the flow of the play, Kate
replied with a laugh, "Well I guess I would have been a great
school principal."

As Beatrice in *Much Ado About Nothing* she had as her
co-star Alfred Drake,* one of the great actors of the musical
stage. During early rehearsals, John Houseman,† artistic
director of the American Shakespeare Festival Theatre, recognized that his company was in danger of being split by the
overwhelming egos of his two major players. Drake's habit,
whenever possible, was to extend his romantic stage association with his current leading lady into real life. "I am sure that
he cherished no serious hope of adding Miss Hepburn to his
conquests," Houseman said, "but he did entertain visions
of a gallant, glamorous stage relationship with his fellow
star."

Kate, however, found Drake a boor; and a terrific contest
of wills—and spite—followed. She mocked and provoked him
backstage whenever she could. Finally, her stinging assaults
(labeled by Drake "unfeminine and unprofessional") made
their way onstage. Drake's Benedick, the pompous wooer,
was too close to reality for Kate to ignore. In one rehearsal
her reading of her lines became so outrageously pointed that
Drake was thrown off-balance and had to stop. Kate laughed

---

* Alfred Drake (1914–   ) has been mainly a theater performer. He starred as
Curly in *Oklahoma!* in 1943. In 1946, he played Macheath in *Beggar's Holiday*,
and starred in *Kiss Me, Kate* (1948) and *Kismet* (1953). He also played Othello at
the American Shakespeare Festival Theatre in Stratford in the summer of 1957.
† John Houseman (1902–   ), born in Romania, became the perfect image of
an upper-class American. A man for all seasons, he has had success in films and
theater as an actor, producer and director. As well as being artistic director of
ASFT, he was a member of Orson Welles's Mercury Theatre. In 1973 he won the
Academy Award for Best Supporting Actor in *The Paper Chase*, a role he
re-created on television. As a writer he was co-author of the story of *Citizen Kane*
(1941) and the screenplay of *Jane Eyre* (1944) and has written three autobiographical volumes: *Run-Through* (1973), *Front and Center* (1979) and *Final
Dress* (1983), which are among the most intelligent and revealing books of
theater memoirs. Houseman had known Hepburn for years. He had been in the
audience when she appeared at the Berkshire Playhouse, and "watched a very
young, inexperienced girl with a wide mouth, wonderful bones and an impossible voice take over the stage." They had met many times, and Houseman had
worked with Hepburn in radio on the Mercury Theatre of the Air when she played
opposite Joseph Cotten in *A Farewell to Arms*.

uproariously at him before the entire company, which remained solemn and silent. Drake stormed off.

After this episode, Houseman hurried first to Kate's dressing room, where he found her "weary but exhilarated—like an athlete after a sports contest in which she felt herself the winner." When he went to Drake's room, Kate's co-star handed Houseman his resignation from the cast. "I reminded him that he had a contract, he declared that he refused to work with the bitch." Houseman finally managed to convince Kate to temper her conduct, and he brought a kind of peace between them that would allow a professional relationship to exist.

Houseman claims that Kate had learned—"at the knee of Constance Collier who had been her coach for many years—that stardom is achieved . . . above all, through the bravura that an audience comes to expect from its favorite performers. In every star role there are one or more opportunities for such peaks. . . . In *Merchant* [inserting her own interpretation of a scene that called for her to enter quietly] . . . a Chinese bungalow rolls silently forward in the dimlit stage. It had barely come to a stop when the door bursts open and [Kate] appears in the brilliantly lit portal. . . . Ravishing to look at in her undernourished way, she swoops around the stage, and, at last, falls into a pool of satin on the floor—to rapturous applause. In *Much Ado* [she] selected [a scene] in which the frivolous Beatrice turns suddenly serious and demands of her lover that he kill . . . her cousin's betrayer. Kate played it as grand tragedy—raging, kicking hassocks around, and howling like a banshee. It was hysterical, insincere, embarrassing and utterly unbelievable, but it shook up the audience and confirmed her star status."

Brooks Atkinson in *The New York Times* found *Much Ado* "not only shrewd but fresh and joyous and admirably suited to the personality of our leading lady." Obviously Kate's star turn had done her no harm, nor had her contest with Drake, for Atkinson added, "Miss Hepburn is an extraordinary star, an actress who commands an audience with glamor and personal magnetism. She is beautiful, debonair, piquant, with a modern personality. Her lovely-looking and humorous-minded Beatrice is one of her best characterizations, and the

Benedick who has been snared into loving this sharp-tongued hoyden is one of Mr. Drake's finest jobs."

Kate's animosity toward Drake is easy to understand. Since her confrontation with John Barrymore during the filming of *A Bill of Divorcement*, she had not had to deal with the personal humiliation of fending off a co-star's advances. For years the degree of her stardom and the caliber of her leading men (and producers and directors) had protected her from such belittling experiences. By the time she appeared with Drake, she had assumed her age, her reputation and the knowledge of her love for Tracy would inhibit such a display.

From the beginning of the Stratford engagement, she spoke openly about Tracy "always with a mingling of loyalty, tenderness and admiration." Several times that summer "she joyfully announced his imminent arrival, then reported that he had been detained or prevented," Houseman recalls. (Tracy was in Hollywood reshooting scenes for *The Old Man and the Sea*.) "Finally, during *Much Ado*, the great day came when Kate, with a young girl's enthusiasm, proclaimed that this time Spencer was really coming. His plane ticket was bought and all arrangements were made. On the evening of his arrival—carefully chosen as an *Othello* day (Kate did not appear in this play), she drove off alone, in a state of high excitement, that she made no attempt to conceal, to Idlewild [Kennedy Airport] to meet him. Soon after she had left there was a phone call from California. Somehow, on the way to Burbank, Spencer had got lost and missed his plane. He never did appear."

Kate went on winter tour in *Much Ado About Nothing* with the American Festival Theatre. Bernard Gersten, who was executive stage manager of the company, drove with her from city to city, with Phyllis and the chauffeur seated in the backseat while Kate did most of the driving. She kept elaborate logs on their mileage; and if they came to a pretty wood, she would park and insist everyone get out with her and hike.

Gersten recalls that they "traveled with trunkloads of food for picnics and with other necessities, including plants she'd been given and couldn't bear to leave behind. Once, someone had apparently neglected to wrap a beautiful, delicate plant against the weather and when [we] opened the trunk [we] discovered it had given up the struggle against the cold. Miss Hepburn cried."

Kate returned to Hollywood at the end of the season. Irene Selznick was in California, occupying the guest suite at George Cukor's. This time the two women were not in the mood for sophomoric pursuits. Irene's father, Louis B. Mayer, was dying of leukemia and she had come West to do whatever she could for him. Mayer was not permitted visitors; but Kate, at his request, went to see him at the hospital. Mayer was quite moved by the visit and told his daughter he was glad "they were such good friends."

Mayer died in the spring of 1957. Tracy was ill and depressed, still talking about retirement. Kate persuaded him to accept the role of Frank Skeffington, a Boston-Irish politician (a dead ringer for Boston's Mayor James M. Curley*), in the screen adaptation of Edwin O'Connor's best-selling novel *The Last Hurrah*. The film reunited both Tracy and Kate (as a bystander only) with John Ford. Ford had directed Tracy's first film, *Up the River,* in 1930, and Kate had not seen him since the end of their affair in 1936. The trials of *The Old Man and the Sea* had depleted Tracy's energy, and she happily joined him at Columbia Studios (where she had filmed *Holiday*) to make sure he took care of himself.

The atmosphere on the set was high-spirited. Besides Ford, most of Tracy's Irish friends, his former Wednesday night drinking circle, were in the cast—Pat O'Brien, James Gleason, Frank McHugh, Ed Brophy and Wallace Ford. A good deal older now, none of the men, including Ford, was the hard drinker of the past. Yet Kate's vigilance could well have been prompted by a fear that any one of them might have encouraged the others to fall off the wagon.

Production began early in 1958. As it progressed, Kate saw the life and artistry return to Tracy. He told an interviewer, "I've joked about retiring but this could be the picture. I'm superstitious—you know that's part of being Irish—and I'm back with John Ford again. . . . I feel this is the proper place for me to end. Even the title is prophetic."

---

* Curley later sued Columbia Studios unsuccessfully on the grounds of invasion of privacy.

A REMARKABLE WOMAN

Kate had been right about *The Last Hurrah*. Released in the fall of 1958 only two weeks after *The Old Man and the Sea*, it counteracted the harsh reviews of the latter.* The film was an unqualified success; and Tracy, far from retiring, was suddenly catapulted into becoming "the grand old man of films."

---

* Reviewers criticized Tracy for not even attempting the Old Man's Cuban accent. In fact, Tracy was extremely good with accents and had used a Portuguese one for *Captains Courageous* to good effect.

CHAPTER
22

When Kate agreed to play Violet Venable in the film version of *Suddenly Last Summer*, Tennessee Williams's New Orleans Gothic horror story of homosexual martyrdom, she thought the film would be made in Hollywood. After *The Last Hurrah*, Tracy suffered severe breathing problems that turned out to be emphysema, and she did not want to be separated from him. Sam Spiegel's decision, however, was to produce *Suddenly Last Summer* in England, where production costs were considerably less than in the United States, even if an entire American cast had to be sent over to make a film.

By the end of the fifties, the major Hollywood studios were in decline, their great resources depleted. Foreign capital was almost a requisite for getting a film produced, and stories that could not be filmed abroad or in Mexico were genteelly postponed. Spiegel, as good a "table-stakes player" as ever, refused to let the Southern background of *Suddenly* hinder his going ahead.

Kate had not only been conned into making a film on location, but the story, which she had been assured would not be as sensational as the play, had turned out to be even more lurid. For a time she considered backing out, but in the end she honored her contractual commitment. She left for London with Phyllis in June, 1959. Tracy was unable to fly until his condition improved. Instead of staying in a hotel, Kate moved into a country cottage not far from Shepperton Studios, where the film was to be shot. This gave her a garden to oversee in her off time and allowed her to bicycle to the nearby village whenever she could.

The role of Violet Venable was one Kate loathed from the start. Why she accepted the part in view of her disgust of the shocking sentiments she had to express in it can only be answered by her respect for Tennessee Williams as a great writer and poet and her mutual regard for the high caliber director, cast and technicians whom Spiegel had assembled.

Suddenly Last Summer had premiered as *Garden District* in January, 1958, as one-half of the double bill with *Something Unspoken* and had immediately become "the most talked about off-Broadway production of the 1957–58 season." The play dealt with such film taboos as "an oedipal relationship, homosexuality, psychosurgery, and cannibalism." Suddenly, during a summer in North Africa, Sebastian Venable, an American poet and son of the very rich and possessive Violet Venable of New Orleans, dies, supposedly of a heart attack, but the death certificate mentions that the body "was somewhat damaged." Catherine Holly (Elizabeth Taylor), Mrs. Venable's niece and Sebastian's cousin, who had been in North Africa with him, returns in a terrible mental state, incoherently speaking of vile acts and insinuating Sebastian's body had been ravaged. Mrs. Venable, desperate to protect her son's name, attempts to bribe Dr. Cukrowicz (Montgomery Clift), a psychosurgeon, into performing a lobotomy on her niece to render her mentally incompetent. The doctor, in love with Catherine, instead administers a truth serum to her, helping her to overcome her amnesia and reveal in detail the psychotic manner in which Sebastian had used first his mother (until her beauty faded), and then Catherine, to lure young men for his homosexual needs. Finally, she breaks down and explains how his body had been dismembered and partially devoured by a group of "starving Spanish urchins, some of whom Sebastian had courted."*

---

* *Suddenly Last Summer* contained many autobiographical elements of Tennessee Williams's life. In his *Memoirs* (Doubleday, 1975), Williams describes the

Once again Kate was to work with Joe Mankiewicz as her director. Their relationship had not been stormy during the making of either *The Philadelphia Story* or *Woman of the Year*. An engraved silver box and inscribed dictionaries presented to him by Kate on the completion of those films attest to amicable terms between them. But Mankiewicz had committed what Kate considered an unforgivable betrayal. In 1950, on its post-Broadway tour, the production of *As You Like It*, starring Kate, came to the old Biltmore Theatre in Los Angeles. Kate left a pair of tickets at the box office for Mankiewicz and asked that he come backstage after the performance. Mankiewicz had just bought a magazine story from *Cosmopolitan* called *The Wisdom of Eve* and was struggling with the screenplay, but he interrupted his work to attend. After the play, he went backstage and was kept waiting at length with Kate's other visitors until she had had sufficient time "to disguise her beauty" by smearing her face with cold cream before receiving her guests. She then talked nonstop as people wafted in and out of her dressing room while an uncomfortable Tracy poured himself a drink—an act which did not go unnoticed by Kate. Mankiewicz wrote the scene almost identically as it had occurred into his script, now titled *All About Eve*, with Margo Channing (played by Bette Davis in the film) doing a fair imitation of Kate. Kate found this an invasion of her privacy, and she had made a point of avoiding Mankiewicz from the time of *All About Eve*'s release until *Suddenly*. When Spiegel had first come to Kate with the property, he had said that George Cukor was his choice for director. Cukor, however, was contracted to do *Let's Make Love* with Marilyn Monroe, and Kate had been caught in one of Spiegel's old-time flimflams.*

---

violence he had encountered in "his own homosexual pursuits" as well as the lobotomy on his sister that his mother, "whose sensibilities were offended by her disturbed daughter's obscene speech," had authorized. Williams had written the first draft of the screenplay, and Gore Vidal the final draft, which was extremely true to the original dialogue in the play.

* Tennessee Williams wrote in his *Memoirs* that he had made his own deal for *Suddenly Last Summer* with Spiegel. "Sam asked what I wanted for the movie rights. . . . I said, 'How about $50,000 plus 20% of the profits?' Sam said, 'It's a deal,' and it was."

She and Mankiewicz were locked in battle from the first day on the set. Kate believed the only way to play such an unsympathetic character was as insane, but Mankiewicz would not hear of it. "Kate wanted very much to direct herself," Mankiewicz explained. "This is a battle I don't think a director can ever afford to lose. . . . I insisted on the performance being played my way."

Kate's first scene was Violet Venable's entrance as she descends in a "gilded, ornately carved elevator cage nestled between two white metal palm poles," to meet the young doctor she intends to bribe. Kate's idea was for her to kick the gate open "with a great flourish" to introduce a kind of irrationality and madness in the character. Mankiewicz did not agree and wanted her to confine her behavior to "haughty eccentricity." At an impasse, Mankiewicz consented to shoot the scene both Kate's way and his before deciding which one to retain, but he never intended to use her version.

The dialogue (which Williams felt contained some of his best writing) so repelled Kate that at times she was certain she could not speak it. Before shooting one difficult scene, she took Mankiewicz aside to tell him, "If you only knew what it means to me when I have to say those things!"

Mankiewicz was not sympathetic. "That's the play and that's what we have to do," he told her, confiding to others that since she had played Shakespeare she thought of herself as the grande dame of the theater. But despite the confrontation with Kate, Montgomery Clift was Mankiewicz's greatest trial.*

Mankiewicz had had a hard enough time in the past dealing with heavy drinkers like Gable and Tracy, but they at least had "worked diligently with the star system, they were big money-makers for their studios, superstars who kept their grief off the set." Tracy had caused film delays and pushed up budget costs, but he had never come onto a set drunk or unprepared for the scene to be shot. Clift was "a crazy drunk,

---

* Montgomery Clift (1920–1966) received an Academy Award nomination for his first film role in *The Search* (1948). All of his subsequent roles contained "a rare psychological dimension," but he did not make many films. Hepburn was to see him again when Tracy made *Judgment at Nuremberg* (1961) with him. He appeared in *Freud* in 1962, and died of a heart attack at the age of forty-five.

a pillhead, confused, quarrelsome . . . no longer a hot property—simply a bad risk," and Mankiewicz was saddled with him to appease his star—Elizabeth Taylor.* (For the first time since her film career began, Kate was supporting another woman star.) Taylor's life was in tremendous chaos. Her third husband, Mike Todd, had been killed in an air crash the previous year; and her current marriage to Eddie Fisher, the singer, had brought headlines, calling her a home-wrecker. (Fisher had been married to actress Debbie Reynolds.) Fisher was with her on the set (which was closed to reporters) and they seemed very much in love, although there were rumors that Taylor was having an affair with political columnist Max Lerner. To complicate matters, Mankiewicz was—if not in love with Taylor—at least badly smitten, feelings that added to his stress.† Taylor's language was obscene both in the script and on the set, and Mankiewicz had to have Fisher talk to her about her constant use of profanity, which terribly offended the British crew. If, because of Taylor, Clift had been cast as the doctor, it was also because of Taylor that he had not been replaced when good sense warned Mankiewicz to do so.

Clift, a homosexual, had been a close friend of Taylor's since 1951 when they had made *A Place in the Sun* together, a friendship that had been consolidated in 1957 when they co-starred in *Raintree County*. During the filming of that movie, Clift almost lost his life in an automobile accident and had to have extensive plastic surgery on his face, one side of which still had little movement. The accident was responsible for giving his speech a curious slur. That he could act at all was a miracle. But, in fact, these impediments, plus a scar from the surgery, gave his screen presence "added strength

---

* Elizabeth Taylor (1932–   ) had just completed *Cat On a Hot Tin Roof* (also by Tennessee Williams) and was one of Hollywood's highest paid actresses. Her appearance in both these films brought her Academy Award nominations, but she won for *Butterfield 8* (1960) and *Who's Afraid of Virginia Woolf?* (1966). Taylor was married seven times: (one) Nicky Hilton; (two) Michael Wilding; (three) Mike Todd; (four) Eddie Fisher; (five and six) Richard Burton; (seven) Senator John Warner.
† On the ill-fated *Cleopatra* (1963), Mankiewicz came in to replace Rouben Mamoulian, and he and Taylor were thrown together again. Taylor was still married to Fisher, but the marriage was in trouble. In the end, Taylor left Fisher, not for Mankiewicz, but for Richard Burton, one of her co-stars in the film.

and pathos." Difficult before his injuries, Clift had now turned to drugs and liquor to ease the pain. Taylor apparently felt that he needed the role as Dr. Cukrowicz to maintain his visibility. After Spiegel saw the first rushes, he told Taylor he would have "to get rid of him." Taylor snapped, "Over my dead body." Clift remained.

Kate now became involved with Clift's problems. In pain a lot, "he washed down his codeine pills with brandy" and could not remember his lines. "He used to have the most peculiar expression on his face," Kate recalled. "Whenever we'd shoot a scene big beads of sweat would pop out on his forehead." She convinced him to spend a weekend with her at her country cottage and tried to talk some sense into him there, but "none of my arguments," she said, "did any good. I thought he was weak. Simpatico but weak."

Despite her protective attitude toward Clift, this one weekend was all the private time Kate gave him. She had little patience with people who did not at least try to help themselves, particularly those who did not appreciate her advice. (Tracy, after all, had gone off the wagon whenever she pressed hard enough.) Taylor and Mankiewicz worked desperately to keep Clift going. "I had all sorts of scenes with Monty," Mankiewicz says, "scenes with me comforting him and his relying on me." He had slept over several times at Mankiewicz's hotel suite at the Dorchester (Taylor and Fisher also had a suite there), Mankiewicz having taken him home to sober him up the same way he had a drunken Tracy so many years before. But Clift "was in a bad shape" and passed out not only at the Dorchester but more publicly "in limousines conveying him and members of the company to several social functions."

Kate's animosity toward Mankiewicz grew as filming progressed. Not only did she disagree with him over her interpretation of her character, she caught on early that by the use of camera technique Violet Venable was being twisted into an utterly repugnant character. Her fury was finally pushed to the limit when he and his cameraman, Jack Hildyard (who had photographed Kate in Summertime), devised a way to transform Mrs. Venable into an aged harridan without (they thought) Kate knowing what they were doing.

Mankiewicz explains: "When [Mrs. Venable] spoke of her son we had her look as young and beautiful as was possible, which with Kate was then very possible [with the aid of diffusion lenses].* At the end I remember we shot her hands [first opening and later closing her son's empty composition book from his fatal summer] after Catherine had told the truth. I wanted them to look like an old woman's hands. Kate didn't like that close-up nor the last one of her before she went to the elevator.† I wanted her suddenly to look old. In other words, the destruction of the legend about Sebastian, her son, destroyed her illusion of youth. I think Kate sensed what Jack and I were up to [that is, removing the diffusion lenses and making her lighting harsh] and she didn't like what I was doing."

Mankiewicz's biographer, Kenneth L. Geist, supposes that "Hepburn wanted to preserve the illusion of her screen beauty, and the comparison of her seamed and freckled hands and face juxtaposed with close-ups of the gorgeous Taylor is especially unflattering." No doubt what he wrote is true, but Kate had never minded sacrificing appearance for performance and had hardly looked glamorous in *The African Queen*, where diffusion lenses were never used. She had an ego, of course, and vanity as well. No one could manage a career in theater and films without both; they more or less came with the territory. To be brazenly deceived was another matter, one of pride. Mankiewicz (and Hildyard too) had been guilty of duplicity, and never was she to forgive either man.

When Mankiewicz had called the final "cut" on the film, Kate strode across the sound stage to him. "Are you absolutely sure you won't need my services anymore?" she asked.

"Yes, I am sure."

"Absolutely?"

"Absolutely."

* Diffusion lenses are often used in films to give a *glow* to a scene as well as to make a star look younger. However, they are put to good use in the latter way. Hepburn's photographers had been using diffusion lenses with greater frequency since *Summertime*.

† The nonfiltered close-ups of Hepburn consist of three full-scale reaction shots and two shots of her hands.

Then, in front of the shocked company, she leaned forward and spat straight into his eye, turned on her heel and marched directly into Sam Spiegel's office, where she asked him the same question, to which Spiegel also replied, "Yes. I am sure."

"Absolutely?"

"Absolutely."

And she spat in his eye as well.*

"To the best of my knowledge she never saw the film," Mankiewicz said. "People tell me that she refused to see it." Kate's close friends say she won't even discuss *Suddenly*, her performance in it or Joe Mankiewicz. The subject is simply closed. But when questioned about the above incident, she commented, "When I disapprove of something, it's the only thing I can think of to do. It's a rather rude gesture, but at least it's clear what you mean."

To Columbia's pleasant surprise, *Suddenly* was more than the *succès d'estime* they had anticipated; it was also a resounding commercial success. And it had a strong impact on the future of films, opening the way for movies with more explicit sexual content and erasing most of the taboos that had been applied to films since their inception. Both Kate and Elizabeth Taylor were nominated for Best Actress† and were unanimously reviewed as having given outstanding performances. (Clift did not fare that well. One reviewer said: "[He] has little to do except to look pained and puzzled, as well he might.")

If Kate did not see the film, Tennessee Williams at least did and came away enchanted with her performance. "Kate is a playwright's dream—a dream actress," he told *The New York Times* shortly after the film's release. "She makes dialogue sound better than it is by a matchless beauty and clarity of diction and by a fineness of intelligence and sensibility that illuminates every shade of a meaning in every line she speaks. She invests every scene—each bit—with the intuition of an

---

* Years later, Hepburn told television interviewer Dick Cavett that her act had not been prompted by her compassion for Montgomery Clift—"I didn't spit for Monty Clift! I spit for the way they treated me!" she snapped.
† Won by Simone Signoret for her role in *Room at the Top*, possibly because Hepburn and Taylor had split the *Suddenly* vote.

artist born into her art. Of the women stars that belong to a generation preceding that of the method [acting], Katharine Hepburn impresses me as having least needed that school of performance in depth. Like Laurette Taylor before her, she seems to do by instinct what years of method training [have done] for her juniors. She is limited only by her ladylike voice and manner. Miss Hepburn could never play a tramp or a tenement housewife. No matter. There will always be parts for ladies and we need Kate Hepburn to play them.

"I don't think [she] was happy with the part of the poet's mother in the screen version of *Suddenly Last Summer*— brilliantly constructed as the screen version by Gore Vidal is—it still made unfortunate concessions to the realism that Hollywood is often too afraid to discard—and so a short morality play in lyrical style was turned into a sensationally successful film that the public thinks was a literal study of such things as cannibalism, madness and sexual deviation. But I am certain Kate knew that what the drama was truly concerned with was all human confusion and its consequence."

Be this last the case or not, Kate was glad to return to Tracy and the States when *Suddenly* was finally finished. For nearly twenty years, Kate and Tracy had maintained their relationship protected from public gossip or censure. Around 1960 stories began appearing in the press coupling their names, but always in a dignified manner, Tracy usually being referred to as "Miss Hepburn's longtime friend." A mystique enveloped them. Everyone knew what a longtime friend implied. Still, seeing it in print did not convince filmgoers that Tracy and Hepburn had actually been engaged in an affair for all those years. Neither had ever played a steamy sex scene on screen or relied upon sex appeal to sell films. Their sex scenes were playful not passionate—bantering, nudging, any touching seeming to be unconscious—the kind of words and gestures usually associated with youth. Kate's aloof manner, her prim appearance, the androgynous way in which she dressed, all were a factor, as was Tracy's father image, his growing reputation as the grand old man of films. People simply preferred to believe that Tracy and Hepburn were really and truly longtime friends, devoted, faithful to each other, and yet faithful to the tenets of Tracy's religion and marriage vows. And perhaps that is the truth. No one but them will ever know.

More important is the fact that Tracy was almost as steadying an influence on Kate as she was on him, and that she liked herself a good deal better for his involvement in her life. One friend remembers Kate as saying that Tracy was probably "the only man . . . man enough to counteract her individualistic femininity." Another friend quoted her as saying, "To most men I'm a nuisance because I'm so busy I get to be a pest, but Spencer is so masculine that once in a while he rather smashes me down, and there's something nice about me when I'm smashed down."

One of Tracy's buddies said in 1960, "What would have happened to Spence if Kate hadn't is a dark thought. He was thrashing about, unhappy, and she put his talent in focus so he could understand it. He's a queer bird with his own way of doing things, and it took a brilliant girl just to begin to see inside him." Kate added that "Spencer sees the ludicrous side to everything. That's why the Irish have the miseries. They see themselves as clowns falling through life."

Misery was an emotion that, when alone, Tracy nurtured. He had had his share of it, his youthful struggle to be an actor, John's deafness. But these had been overcome many years before. Two of his former lady friends claim he had problems of impotency, not surprising in a man who drank as much as he did. According to Larry Swindell, his biographer, he had a deep dislike of homosexuals and any form of perversion.* Yet, in a *McCall's* article,† Garson Kanin claimed that Kate refused to acknowledge the existence of homosexuality at all, and that in a Paris hotel suite in 1961, he and Tracy described homosexual acts in laborious detail to Kate, "who maintained her firm disbelief in the existence of such ridiculous practices." (Curiously, the magazine article is represented as an excerpt from Kanin's subsequent memoir, *Tracy and Hepburn* [Viking Press, 1971], but it does not appear in the text of the book.) How Tracy could describe

---

* Swindell says he "refrained from including these facts in his book, *Spencer Tracy, A Biography*, out of respect to Louise Tracy, who was alive at the time of publication."
† "The Private Kate," February, 1970, pp. 109–110.

acts so supposedly offensive to him is as difficult to comprehend as Kate's presumed refusal to believe homosexuality existed in the face of her many friendships (Noël Coward, to name just one) with self-proclaimed practicing homosexuals and the open manner in which all sexual matters were discussed in the Hepburn home during her youth.

In terms of people, Kate liked only the proven, the familiar, those friends who recognized her as a presence. Not sycophants either, but equals, or at least *almost* equals, otherwise their friendship meant nothing at all. She still loved intellectual debates, which never interested Tracy, but he liked to listen to her while she did all the talking. He would sit back reflectively and wait. Then, when the right opportunity presented itself, he would squash her with one rapier-sharp comment that usually had no connection with the topic under discussion. Kate perversely enjoyed this parry between them. Tracy's harsh wit stimulated her. She also appeared to enjoy mothering him and doctoring him and ministering to him.

In the summer of 1960, with Tracy in better health, Kate returned to Stratford as Viola in *Twelfth Night* and as Cleopatra to Robert Ryan's* Marc Antony in *Antony and Cleopatra*. John Houseman had left to accept a position with CBS on the West Coast, and Jack Landau had taken over as artistic director. Ryan had appeared with Tracy in *Bad Day at Black Rock* and Kate very much respected his talent. He often was cast in the role of a hard, unbending hero or a psychopathic or vicious heavy, but in real life he possessed a quiet, strong personality and was committed to many liberal causes. Kate enjoyed long discussions with him and performed at her peak as Cleopatra, receiving her best stage reviews to date with the exception of *The Philadelphia Story*. She brought to the role a sensual quality that was quite surprising; and in the early scenes, costumed most provocatively, she became "a half-naked woman with a genuine

---

* Robert Ryan (1908–1973) was one of Hollywood's most versatile and reliable performers. He made about eighty films, giving fine performances in diverse roles—the anti-Semitic murderer in *Crossfire* (1947), the washed-up boxer in *The Set-Up* (1949) and, repeating his stage role, the cynical lover in *Clash by Night* (1952). He returned to the New York stage in *The Front Page* in 1968, and was one of the founders of the UCLA Theatre Group, as well as of a nonsectarian children's school.

capacity for enjoying the wanton, sporting pleasures of the bed."

Her Viola was not so well received. Once again she and Morris Carnovsky (as Feste) seemed to be performing in two different plays. But the accolades for her glowing beauty were especially soothing after her experience with Joe Mankiewicz. Walter Kerr, then on the *New York Herald Tribune,* noted, "Miss Hepburn has always been one of the most fetching creatures to have been bestowed upon our time, and fetching isn't the half of it as the lady takes a stubborn, or a petulant, or a slightly fearful stance in her white ducks, brass buttoned jacket and sleek black boater."

Kate again stayed in Lawrence Langner's old red cottage, swam early every morning as she had done during the 1957 season, and seemed to the members of the company to possess "boundless energy." She truly loved playing the Shakespearean roles in repertory. The fact that her salary was $350 a week only added to her pleasure, because it signified her sincerity. She held on to the notion that Britain's theater flourished in a way the American theater did not because England's best performers kept repertory going.

Asked by *Newsweek* reporter Calvin Tomkins if she had any ideas on the possibilities of an American—as distinct from a British—style of playing Shakespeare, she mused, "You'd have to take our greatest actor—who is he? Spencer Tracy, I'd imagine—and contrast him with their greatest— Larry [Olivier] or [John] Gielgud. There's something about the great American actor that's like a clipper ship in action, a sort of heart's directness. Spencer has it. He could do Shylock or Lear, or Macbeth—we could do Macbeth together."

When asked about American playwrights, she said, "Tennessee Williams, now—he uses words brilliantly. But whose time is he writing about? Not mine, certainly. Williams gives us the middle-aged woman's answer to sex—she can go ahead and sleep with her son [*Suddenly Last Summer*]. Or look at Lillian Hellman's new play [*Toys in the Attic*]. All the characters are such jackasses. . . . Shakespeare took into consideration the violence, the waywardness of man, but he also gave him the sun and moon and stars, and his own dreams."

Tennessee Williams had asked her to star in the first production of his newest play, *The Night of the Iguana*, which he claimed he wrote with her in mind (although it is not clear which of the two main women characters she would have played).* Saying no to such a flattering request was not easy, especially since she would not have known that Williams used that ploy quite often in getting a well-known actress for one of his dramas. But Kate liked the subject matter of *Iguana* no better than that of *Suddenly*. Nor did she want to commit herself to what might possibly be a long New York run. Tracy was about to film *Inherit the Wind* for Stanley Kramer,† and she wanted to be available to travel with him.

Kate greatly respected Kramer. Most of the time she sat in a corner of the set wearing a man's shirt with the sleeves rolled up and khaki pants, her lap filled with knitting—a sweater for either Tracy or herself—glancing over the rims of her glasses at the scene being readied or shot. When she had an opinion she spoke out. Tracy had quit drinking and smoking, but his red hair was now pure white and his appearance portly. Kate said that "he was much too impatient for the time and place in which he found himself. His impatience generally displayed itself with agents and lawyers and publicity men and reporters and photographers and directors and the whole damned system." Yet, though irritable and ill, "he stood under the hot lights and perspired through the extra takes and the technical nuisances." When the cameraman, Ernest Laszlo, asked for another take, Tracy would stare back with disgust, but everyone knew he would repeat the scene.

Inherit the Wind required little makeup, which greatly pleased Tracy. It meant that he and Kate had an extra hour before driving to the studio, where he could "breeze in ready

---

* Bette Davis played the part of Maxine (replaced later by Shelley Winters) and Margaret Leighton the other woman's role in the Broadway production. The film starred Ava Gardner and Deborah Kerr.

† Stanley Kramer (1913–   ) began as a film producer and successfully made many prestigious low-budget films: *Champion* (1949), *Home of the Brave* (1949), *Death of a Salesman* (1951), *High Noon* (1952). He directed his first film, *Not As a Stranger*, in 1955. With *The Defiant Ones* (1958) his reputation for "bucking the Hollywood system" as an independent producer-director was made.

for work with no nonsense." Kramer says that "if a makeup man tried to powder-puff his forehead, Tracy would push him away and give him a look as though he were somebody he had just thrown up."

As always, Tracy was prepared for whatever scene was to be shot, had a prodigious memory and could not tolerate less professionalism in his co-stars. Fredric March,* whose wife, Florence Eldridge, was also in the film, found memorization more difficult. March (who had appeared with Kate years before in *Mary of Scotland*) mentioned to her that Tracy was a wizard at retaining long speeches. "It's his concentration— his theatrical background you know," she said.

March, who, unlike Tracy, throughout his career had spent long periods of time on the stage, bowed to Kate and in a sarcastic voice replied, "Thank you, Mrs. Shakespeare."

As the film progressed, the two men became highly competitive. March had a straw fan he used as a prop in many of his scenes; and when Tracy launched into an oration (for his role as the lawyer Clarence Darrow), March would fan himself vigorously. Kramer said, "Tracy had no props, but he got even. He sat behind March and picked his nose during a three-and-one-half minute summation [of March's as the prosecuting attorney, Matthew Horrison Brady]."

Tracy's films always started with a closed set, and *Inherit the Wind* was no exception. Kramer says, "Tracy didn't want a bunch of idiots clambering all over the place. One week later it was like Las Vegas. Everybody was there to see him; bookies, ball players, fighters and press, along with a million actors just there to watch." No one was in greater awe of him than Kramer himself. Another co-star in the film, Gene Kelly,† admitted to Kramer, "I finally stepped out of my class. I just can't keep up with [Tracy]." Kramer confesses, "I was afraid to say, 'Spencer you're a great actor.' He'd only

---

* Fredric March (1897–1975) married Florence Eldridge in 1927. From that time on they appeared in plays together, but only occasionally did she make a film with him. March had been a leading man for more than thirty years.

† Gene Kelly (1912–   ), one of the most innovative dancers and choreographers in film, also has given splendid acting performances in such films as *The Pirate* (1948), *On the Town* (1949), *An American in Paris* (1951) and *Singin' in the Rain* (1952). He began directing in 1952, *The Tunnel of Love* (1958) and *Hello, Dolly!* (1969) being among his best efforts.

say, 'Now what the hell kind of thing is that to come out with?' He wanted to know it; he *needed* to know it. But, he didn't want you to *say* it, just *think* it." Kramer, who by this time had worked with some of the most respected actors in Hollywood—Brando, Cooper and Bogart included—says that Tracy "thought and listened better than anyone in the history of motion pictures. A silent close-up of Spencer Tracy said it all."

The ambience of every Tracy set was that of adulation for *him* above and apart from any other performer. Whatever his image might be to the movie-going public, to his peers Tracy was the consummate film performer. He seemed instinctively to add to the depth of every scene with a look or a nuance that they had not imagined. If Zinnemann and Sturges on *The Old Man and the Sea* had not left him to his own devices, his performance might have been a far different one. But few directors had the temerity to lock horns with Tracy over an interpretation, because he so seldom was proven wrong.

To understand Kate's own veneration of his talent, one has to grasp the impact his acting had upon her. Though she might have made comments to Kramer, they never were about Tracy or his performance. She believed him to be a great artist, deserving of homage, respect and—service. And when he signed next to make *The Devil at Four O'Clock*, which was to be filmed mainly in Hawaii, she put aside all other considerations and went with him. Tracy's co-star was Frank Sinatra.* "Nobody at Metro ever had the financial power Frank Sinatra has today," Tracy commented, adding that his own days as "a box-office favorite were over" as he shrugged and looked quizzical from under his brows, as if hoping for a contradiction.

Sinatra called Tracy "the Gray Fox" and had agreed to Tracy's receiving first billing, emphasizing that he would give the top spot only to Tracy, "the greatest actor in Hollywood." Tracy had a strong personal affection for Sinatra, but he did

---

* Frank Sinatra (1915–   ) turned to acting in 1952 when his vocal cords had suddenly hemorrhaged. For his first nonsinging performance, as Maggio in *From Here to Eternity* (1953), he won the Academy Award for Best Supporting Actor, and was nominated for Best Actor in *The Man with the Golden Arm* (1954). His voice then returned and he became a superstar. He was at the height of his popularity at this time.

not think he approached his work with enough respect. "Tracy was on the set early," his director, Mervyn LeRoy,* said. "Sinatra arrived when he chose, and seldom before lunch. Sinatra was a spontaneous worker. Tracy was tightly disciplined."

Tracy complained that he had to play his over-the-shoulder close-ups with a coat hanger because Sinatra wasn't there. Nonetheless, "he would twinkle and say Sinatra had called him and told him he wanted him for his next picture."

His directors soon found that "still photographers drove him crazy." Kramer had observed that, when a still was to be shot, Tracy "pretended that he didn't care by looking down at the ground or turning half away from the camera. Then he'd argue that that was the way people stood or looked naturally. He posed for a hundred thousand stills in his time and claimed none of them ever appeared 'except in the B'nai B'rith *Messenger.*'"

When looking at some stills with Tracy and Mervyn LeRoy on the set of *The Devil at Four O'Clock*, Kate exclaimed, "Spence, these are wonderful character studies!" Tracy snapped back, "Kate, those aren't character studies, they're just pictures of an old man . . . the truth is I'm old, so old that everyone has changed. . . . Not just the movie business but the whole country." At sixty-one, he did look like an old man, although his abstaining from liquor and cigarettes had improved his physical condition, as had the quiet life-style he and Kate lived.

Now together most of the time, they still maintained two hotel suites when traveling. Unless on the road, they never went out. Their intimate friends came to them a few people at a time because Tracy did not like large groups: Chester Erskine, the Kanins, and Cukor and Kramer in California; Laura, the Hepburns, and again the Kanins (who had two homes) on the East Coast. Tracy held court and exchanged gossip, news and conversation. Kramer claims that "no matter what play or performance or book might be discussed,

---

* Mervyn LeRoy (1900–   ) had directed Tracy in *Thirty Seconds over Tokyo* and had known him for years at Metro. LeRoy had directed such powerful social dramas as *Little Caesar* (1931), *I Am a Fugitive from a Chain Gang* (1932) and *They Won't Forget* (1937) earlier at Warner Brothers. At Metro he made many films as both producer and director.

nothing could match his insatiable desire for plain gossip. What went on at the Daisy Club [a Hollywood night spot] was really a fascination. He announced and savored as a choice tidbit each new pairing off of the jet set. I never understood his sources—most of the time I thought he made it all up—but usually he was right."

Kate continued her domestic position in their relationship, doing the cooking, the cleaning, the carting. Once when some of their close friends were guests, she rose, "casually picked up a big log and threw it on the fire. Tracy calmly watched and then said [harshly], 'Don't ever do that again in front of company.'" Kate giggled nervously and sat down, her face flushed, but more loving than ever in her attention to him, accepting being "smashed down" by him without a whimper because she had crossed the line into his territory.

Her position in his Court was as Consort. She made sure problems other than his work did not filter through to him. He remained in close contact with Louise and still saw her frequently. Kate respected this. John's wife had divorced him, a fact that deeply troubled Tracy. Susie's accomplishments as a fine photographer and a good musician gave her father great pride. From 1959 to 1962, except for the summer season at Stratford in 1960, Kate devoted herself to Tracy's care. In 1961, when Kramer begged him to take the role of the American judge in *Judgment at Nuremberg,* which was to be filmed in Germany, she once again set off to be with him, but only after a shaky start.

As they approached the check-in gate at Idlewild Airport, Tracy suddenly had second thoughts. Breathing was always difficult for him on planes and he had not felt well for a few weeks. He had doubts that he could stand the trials of location shooting. Some of the film company's executives, who had accompanied Kate and Tracy to the airport, were frantic—shooting was scheduled to begin in five days. Kate took Tracy aside and talked to him for about five minutes. Then she planted a kiss on his cheek and he walked back with her to board the plane. They flew together; but when the car that had picked them up from the airport near Nuremberg was within two blocks of their hotel, Kate ordered the driver to stop, got out and walked the rest of the way alone, entering the hotel where they both had suites through the service door.

The press knew Kate had accompanied Tracy, but she managed to be elusive enough to avoid photographers.

Montgomery Clift, *very* ill now, was also in *Nuremberg*. Clift had even more difficulty in remembering his lines than he had had in *Suddenly*. According to Kramer, "he was literally going to pieces. Tracy just grabbed his shoulders and told him he was the greatest young actor of his time and to look deep into his [Tracy's] eyes and play to him and the hell with the lines." It pulled Clift through for he did exactly that—speaking in character but often in his own words.

The theme of *Nuremberg* was summed up in a statement made by Tracy at the close of the film: "This, then, is what we stand for: truth, justice, and the value of a single human being." Because Tracy believed in *Nuremberg* and felt it outweighed in importance any of the other films he had made in his long career, his earnestness had a tremendous impact on both the making of the film—for his fellow actors caught his fervor*—and the final product.

The critic for the Hollywood *Daily Variety* wrote: "As the presiding judge, Tracy delivers a performance of considerable intelligence and intuition, a towering but gentle figure, compassionate but realistic, warm but objective, a man of insight and eloquence, but also a plain man who finds himself caught between politics and justice. He's calm, unflappable, but the wheels of his jurist's mind are always sensed working behind that wise, sometimes tired brow, and you never feel that there is any shred of inordinate pride in the man. It's Tracy's point of view through which we see and feel the events of the trial and outside the courtroom. . . . Tracy seems to be Kramer's *alter ego*—he actualizes on screen Kramer's own bewilderment, his horror, his passion about the primacy of conscience. . . . 'I want to understand,' Tracy says with humility and a kind of epic bereavement for all the unnamed and unknowable dead who were the victims of Hitler's madness. 'I really do want to understand. I have to. I *must*.'"

At the end of the film, Tracy had a speech that ran thirteen minutes and forty-two seconds, a record for movies at that

---

* Co-starring with Tracy were Clift, Burt Lancaster, Judy Garland, Marlene Dietrich, and Maximilian Schell, who won the Academy Award for Best Actor for his performance.

time. Most actors would have split it and done it in two or three takes that would then have been spliced together. Tracy insisted on shooting it in one; two cameras were used so that different angles could be filmed.

Some months after Kate and Tracy returned to the States, Ely Landau, who had produced Eugene O'Neill's *The Iceman Cometh* with Jason Robards, Jr.,* for television, and now had the rights to produce the playwright's great autobiographical work *Long Day's Journey into Night* as a low-budget film, approached Kate with the idea of her playing Mary Tyrone. She read the script, brilliantly written by O'Neill himself,† and knew that she wanted to do it and that she could do it well. But she did not think that she should leave Tracy for the time such a project would take. Landau thought he had the solution. Tracy would be ideal for the role of her husband, James Tyrone. Kate asked Landau to come for breakfast at Tracy's the next morning, and she would have him read the script that night.

Landau quickly accepted the invitation. "It was extraordinary to watch her with Spence," he said. "She was a totally different person. She turned really submissive—it's the only word I can use—and hardly opened her mouth, other than introducing us. She smiled, laughed at everything he said—which, by the way, was quite justified; he was the most charming man I've ever met—and finally when we got down to business I explained to him, 'I don't have to tell you what it would mean to have you.' He replied, 'Look, Kate's the lunatic. She's the one who goes off and appears at Stratford in Shakespeare—*Much Ado* and all that stuff. I don't believe in that nonsense—I'm a movie actor. She's always doing these things for no money! Here you are with twenty-five thousand

---

* Jason Robards, Jr. (1922–   ), son of the famous American stage and film actor, Jason Robards, Sr., did not come into his own until the production of *The Iceman Cometh* (1953). He has appeared in a rather mixed bag of films but has given some brilliant performances. He won Best Supporting Actor for *All the President's Men* (1976) and *Julia* (1977). He later married and divorced Lauren Bacall.

† O'Neill began work on *Long Day's Journey into Night* in the early summer of 1939 at the age of fifty and completed it the following year. He died in 1953, noting in his will that the play was not to be presented until twenty-five years after his death. His widow, Carlotta, decided to ignore the will and gave her approval for the 1956 Broadway production.

each for *Long Day's Journey*—crazy! I read it last night and it's the best play I ever read. I promise you this: If you offered me this part for five hundred thousand and somebody else offered me another part for five hundred thousand, I'd take this!' and Kate exclaimed, 'There he goes! No! It's not going to work!'" Indeed, she tried to change Tracy's mind but could not. Tracy, after the hard assignment on *Nuremberg*, simply did not feel well enough to tackle such a tough role knowing as he did that the film would be made for under four hundred thousand dollars and would require many sacrifices on the part of the cast and crew.

In the end, Kate, with Tracy's urgings, decided to accept the role. Abe Lastfogel, who had been Tracy's agent for years, now represented Kate; and a deal was made with Sir Ralph Richardson* to play James Tyrone, with Robards playing their son Jamie, the character molded after O'Neill.

Tracy was not wrong in expecting the shooting schedule and working conditions of the film to be trying. In the fall of 1961, the cast and Sidney Lumet†, the director, at greatly reduced salaries, rehearsed for three weeks in New York, enabling them to shoot the film in thirty-seven days. First, all the exterior scenes were shot on location at an old Victorian cottage on City Island in the Bronx. Then the company moved to Production Center Studio in lower Manhattan for the interior scenes. Lumet approached his task in the manner of filmed theater, and the critics would complain about this. But, whatever it might be called, *Long Day's Journey into Night* is a riveting film. The experience was an exhilarating and exhausting one for Kate.

The role of Mary Tyrone was both physically and mentally demanding. Kate allowed herself to be photographed with no

---

* Ralph Richardson (1902–1984), more noted for his stage work, formerly a leading member of the Old Vic and one of their most prestigious players. He gave memorable performances, however, as Karenin in *Anna Karenina* (1948), as Buckingham in Olivier's *Richard III* (1955), in *Our Man in Havana* with Alec Guinness (1959), and in *The Fallen Idol* the same year he was knighted (1947). His portrayal of Dr. Sloper in *The Heiress* (1949) brought him a nomination as Best Actor.

† Sidney Lumet (1924–   ) had directed *Stage Struck*, the 1958 remake of *Morning Glory*, the least successful of this sensitive, intelligent director's films, which include *Twelve Angry Men* (1957), *The Fugitive Kind* (1960), *The Pawnbroker* (1965) and *Network* (1976).

filters and no artful lighting. Her part required her to grovel on the floor, her hair disheveled, telltale traces of age exposed and naked of makeup. Though she lost the Academy Award that year* to Anne Bancroft for *The Miracle Worker,* the role of Mary Tyrone was her greatest professional achievement. There seemed to be not one dissenting critic. Most thought she had either capped her "distinguished career" or "surpassed even herself."

Arthur Knight of *The Saturday Review* wrote: "Her transformations are extraordinary as, in recollection, she suffuses her tense and aging face with a coquettish youthfulness or, in the larger pattern of the play, changes from a nervous, ailing but loving mother into a half-demented harridan. Her final scene, which contains some of O'Neill's most beautiful writing, is in every way masterful. . . ."

As Pauline Kael commented: "From being perhaps America's most beautiful comedienne of the thirties and forties," Kate had "become our greatest tragedienne." Viewing the film nearly twenty-five years later one is startled, no, perhaps *assaulted,* by this realization. The performance is brilliant, shattering. Kate simply *becomes* Mary Tyrone—"that terrible smile, those suffering eyes—" Kael called her "the Divine Hepburn." Her career had reached an apogee that could not have been foreseen even in the time of *The Philadelphia Story* or *The African Queen.* Kate's destiny as the reigning queen of films had been fulfilled. One producer dusted off a screenplay about Sarah Bernhardt, another wanted to remake Garbo's great classic, *Queen Christina,* with Kate in the title role.

But Kate's private life had taken a tragic turn. During the filming of *Long Day's Journey into Night,* Tracy (on the West Coast) had suffered a serious attack of emphysema and her father had taken very ill in West Hartford. She hardly knew in which direction to go first. Some weekends she drove to West Hartford late Friday, spent Saturday there before flying to California Saturday night to be with Tracy for a few hours on Sunday, and then returned to New York that same night to be ready to film the following morning. When her work was completed on the O'Neill film, she commuted weekly for

---

* Hepburn did win the 1962 Cannes Film Festival Best Actress Award for *Long Day's Journey into Night.*

several months between California and Connecticut. On November 20, with all his children at his bedside, Dr. Hepburn died.

They say that one doesn't really mature until both of one's parents are dead. In many ways and for many people that thesis is valid. But often life—and death—are not quite so straightforward. Kate's relationship with each of her parents had been unique. They were, of course, extraordinary people, but Kate's attachment at age fifty-five to family and home, considering her worldly experiences, her independent life, and her rebellious nature, was a key to the essence of her personality. Her mother's death had been more difficult for her to cope with than her father's. Dr. Hepburn's remarriage within months of his bereavement could have been seen by Kate, as both a woman and a daughter, as a kind of betrayal of Mrs. Hepburn. The great reverence she had felt for him, the joy of comradeship, had transferred itself to Tracy. One cannot say Tracy had become a father image to her; but Kate was very much the submissive young thing with him. The verbal cuffings, the smashing downs, were merely to show her who was boss and, at the same time, were regarded as a display of his true love for her. To discipline meant to care; and if Kate was strong-tongued or dictatorial with her close friends, her words were meant to show them how much she cared.

Although Dr. Hepburn was dead, his former secretary, Gloria Roberts, now on Kate's payroll, continued to send her a weekly allowance from Hartford to wherever she might be, and Fenwick was still there to harbor the Hepburn clan.

To Leland Hayward she wrote, "Dad had a stink of a time for nine months. He said 'thank God it was me and not your mother.' He heaved a sigh and was gone with a little sigh. . . . How lucky I have been to have been handed such a remarkable pair in the great shuffle."

Kate remained on the East Coast for a week after her father's funeral, sharing Thanksgiving with what was left of her family before flying to California and Tracy, determined that she would never leave him again and that she would fight for him to remain alive and productive with all her strength and good sense. Unlike Mary Tyrone, she did not have to grope back to the past for "dimly remembered moments of happiness." She still loved being with Tracy, a great artist (she conveyed to close friends that her Mary Tyrone would not have seemed so "towering" if Tracy had played James Tyrone, for his performance would have "pierced the sky") and her best friend in the world. Nothing would have been too much of a sacrifice to make for him. It turned out to be five years of her life, years that had promised, with *Long Day's Journey into Night,* to be the most rewarding of her long career. She traded them gladly for her chance to prolong Tracy's life and to be with him until the end.

CHAPTER

23

Kate still kept up appearances. She rented a hillside house close to Tracy. Their liaison was a known fact. In January, 1962, *Look* magazine published a story that revealed that Tracy had been an alcoholic, that he had "a mean streak," that he had not been living with Louise for years and that he and Kate were "something more than frequent co-stars." Even so, Tracy still held it as a matter of principle that they not live together in an unmarried state. He continued to see Louise at least once a week at the Hill, visiting with her for several hours. Her attitude toward him was one of loving regard, and he had supported her exceptionally well through the years. Not only had her life-style never had to change, he saw to it that she had the resources to continue her "good work" (a term he frequently used). In 1956, she had won the Save the Children Foundation Award. The New York *Journal American* (referring to her throughout the article as Mrs. Spencer Tracy) had called her "one of the great women of the American progress, in the humanitarian tradition of Clara Barton and Jane Addams" (two women who were dignified by the use of their first names). Four universities had bestowed honorary degrees upon her.

A kind of deification clung to Louise. Those close to her are ready to vow that there had been no man in her life except Tracy and that she accepted Kate's presence in his life with "continuing good grace." Until 1962, on occasion, she and Tracy were still photographed together for the purposes of publicizing the John Tracy Clinic, and his name remained on the letterhead, although he had nothing more to do with the organization than to encourage and finance Louise in her work—in which her absorption was total. The only social affairs she attended were those connected with raising funds for the clinic or in celebration of an award she might have been given.

Tracy had been deified in another way. Fellow actor David Niven called him "the Pope" and the name stuck. More and more, his whims had become law. On the set, no one dared eat or play cards while a scene was being shot. His co-stars and his directors treated him with a mixture of respect and obeisance generally given to aging geniuses—Picasso, Chaplin, Rubinstein. At sixty-two, he had taken on, but only within the world of film, the veneration these men received at eighty. As a so-called movie star, his popularity had waned. Gable at the age of sixty had retained his sex appeal sufficiently to star romantically opposite Marilyn Monroe.*

From Christmas, 1962, Kate sincerely believed Tracy could not function without her. On days when they weren't to be together—visiting days to Louise or when she had errands to run—she would cook and pack his lunch and dinner in a basket and leave it on his front doorstep. She made sure the refrigerator had plenty of milk (he drank it with ice cubes like a cocktail) and just enough beer for the one a day the doctors permitted him (he claimed he could not survive without it). She insisted he exercise. Since he no longer was able to take the icy swims she had once prescribed for him, she accompanied him on "long, slow-paced walks in the hills." On warm, windy days they flew kites together. Other times they painted or read to each other.

Abe Lastfogel knew enough not to submit any scripts to her. Kate was determined to dedicate 100 percent of her time to Tracy. But in the spring of 1963, with Tracy miraculously improved from eighteen months of Kate's close supervision, both Lastfogel and Stanley Kramer convinced her that Tracy's

---

* Gable had died in 1960 only a few months after the completion of the film *The Misfits* (1961) in which he co-starred with Monroe.

spirit needed some energizing and that she should persuade him to take a role in Kramer's next film, *It's a Mad, Mad, Mad, Mad World*. The film was to be shot on location in the desert not far from Los Angeles, and the doctors assured Kate that the dry climate was good for Tracy's emphysema. Although Tracy received top billing over such stellar performers as Milton Berle, Sid Caesar, Ethel Merman, Jimmy Durante, and Mickey Rooney, to name only some of the great comedians Kramer gathered together, he did not appear in more than 20 percent of the footage. This meant his presence would be needed for only a number of weeks—not months. As an added inducement, Kramer agreed that Tracy's working day would never exceed six hours.

At its roots, Kramer's comedy was really about greed, and Tracy plays his role of a police captain out to recover a stolen fortune in a cynical manner that gives the film whatever validity it has. Bosley Crowther at *The New York Times* wrote: "Mr. Tracy seems the guardian of a sane morality in this wild and extravagant exposition of clumsiness and cupidity. While the mad seekers are tearing toward the money in their various ways—in automobiles that race each other in breathtaking sweeps of hair-pin turns in the wide open California desert, in airplanes that wobble overhead—Mr. Tracy sits there in wise complacence, the rigidity of the law. And then, by a ruse I dare not tell you, he shows how treacherous his morality is."

When the film was finished, Tracy once again announced his decision to retire. No one but Kate and Kramer believed him. Kramer recalled that "During the filming of *Mad World* . . . Spencer Tracy was in poorer health than I could remember; he had bad color and no stamina whatever. But then, even though this lack of energy showed, I think he had his best time ever during the making of a film. The comedians worshipped him. Never before or since has a king had the court full of jesters who strove only to entertain him so that his majesty might say 'that was funny,' or just laugh or smile."

Kate's concern for Tracy kept her from fully enjoying the antics of the comedians on the set. The film and the heat of the desert had taken their toll on Tracy's ebbing strength. He returned home hardly able to walk. During the early summer of 1963, he seldom left the cottage, except to sit on the terrace or move a short distance to a cool spot under some giant elms. By the beginning of July, he had recuperated enough to drive the car. He visited Louise, and he and Kate took rides down to the beach. On July 21, with a picnic-basket lunch in the back of his Thunderbird, he and Kate headed for Malibu for a picnic. As they neared their destination, Tracy suddenly began to gasp for breath. Kate brought the car to a jolting halt at the gas station they were just passing, jumped out and called the local (Zuma Beach) fire department and then— fearing this might be a final attack—Louise, to alert her to stay by the telephone. When she returned to the car moments later, Tracy had slumped into unconsciousness. Kate loosened his collar and began mouth-to-mouth resuscitation. The rescue car from the fire department arrived in less than five minutes, an ambulance shortly after. The interns were certain Tracy had suffered a heart attack. On the way to the hospital he regained consciousness and smiled weakly at Kate, who had left the car to go with him. On their arrival at the hospital, the heart attack was diagnosed as pulmonary edema. Kate called Louise, who came directly over. For two weeks the women set a schedule so that each would have time alone by Tracy's bedside. At the end of that time, his health had improved enough for him to go home with a nurse to care for him under Kate's supervision.

They now saw even their closest friends infrequently. Tracy's house looked like a nursing home. An oxygen machine sat in the corridor outside his small bedroom, which had taken on a monastic, cell-like appearance; all unnecessary clutter had been removed in case any equipment had to be wheeled in for an emergency.

Further complications arose in September, 1965, when Tracy was diagnosed as having prostate problems. A prostatectomy was performed in the hospital, and for the next six weeks he struggled to hold on to life as his lungs and heart suffered from the trauma. Again, Kate and Louise arranged their visits so they would not conflict, all reports on Tracy's health being issued by his wife.

By now Hollywood knew that Spencer Tracy was dying.

People spoke about him in a hushed way and of Kate's devotion with much admiration. Cukor came down from "the big house," the Erskines dropped by, Abe Lastfogel and the Kanins visited when they were in town, Phyllis still handled all secretarial chores, Kramer kept bringing scripts. Tracy never abandoned his love of gossip and "as soon as a visitor came through the door, he started digging for the latest dirt, his face crinkling with mischief as he caught up on who was doing what with whom."

Kramer gave Kate the script of *Ship of Fools* (based on Katherine Anne Porter's novel) in the hope that she might play the role of Mary Treadwell, the aging but beautiful grande dame who strikes back at a drunken lothario with the stiletto heel of her evening pump. Kate refused and Kramer cast Vivien Leigh. Tracy and Hepburn visited the set on several occasions; and Vivien, divorced from Olivier now and not well herself, came by the cottage to visit with them and her old friend Cukor.

By the fall of 1966, Kramer, a frequent guest, could see the miraculous improvement Tracy had made. He felt Tracy needed to work again and told Kate about a script, *Guess Who's Coming to Dinner,* that Tania and Bill Rose* (writers of *Mad World*) were working on. The story was a social comedy about a liberal couple whose daughter brings home a black fiancé. Kramer had signed Sidney Poitier† as the fiancé and asked Kate and Tracy to consider playing the girls' parents. The suggestion took a great deal of courage on Kramer's part. He knew he could not get insurance on Tracy and that if he died halfway through the film, that would be it. Kate and Tracy knew this too, and perhaps this extraordinary act of faith on Kramer's part was the deciding factor in Tracy's agreement to make the film with Kate, even before

---

* William Rose (1918–   ), though an American, won his first international success as the author of the British film *Genevieve* (1953). His credits include *It's a Mad, Mad, Mad, Mad World* (1963) and *The Russians Are Coming, the Russians Are Coming* (1966).

† Sidney Poitier (1924–   ) had starred in two previous Kramer films—*The Defiant Ones* (1958) and *Pressure Point* (1962). His success in films paved the way for other black performers in commercial cinema. He won the Academy Award for Best Actor for *Lilies of the Field* (1963) and gave outstanding performances in *In the Heat of the Night* and *To Sir with Love* the same year (1967) as *Guess Who's Coming to Dinner* was made and released.

either of them had read the script. Incredibly, as soon as the decision was made, Tracy began to show signs of dramatic improvement. The old vigor came back into his attitude, his step became steady and the feisty humor returned.

Kramer made a deal with Columbia Pictures only after Kate and Tracy agreed to place their salaries of about $250,000 each—as did Kramer his salary of $500,000—in escrow to guarantee the studio against loss in the event of Tracy's inability to complete the film.* Kate and Tracy accepted such stiff terms only after Kramer swore to them that he would not make the film without them. A ten-week shooting schedule was set to begin in February, 1967. The San Francisco home of Tracy and Kate's characters in the film, Matt and Christina Drayton, was built on the Columbia back lot as Kramer assembled the rest of his cast. News was made when Kate's niece, Marion's daughter, Katharine Houghton (Grant), was signed by Kramer to play Kate's daughter. Kathy had not had any previous film experience, but she had played a small role in the Garson Kanin–Ruth Gordon Broadway comedy of the previous season, *A Very Rich Woman.*

On February 19, the eve of the scheduled start of production, Tracy suffered a severe attack of emphysema. Kate called the local fire-department rescue squad. Production was postponed for a few days while Tracy regained his strength, and it only went forward after Kramer agreed that Tracy's scenes would all be shot between nine and twelve in the morning, when his energy was at its peak. The entire schedule was arranged around him. Most of his dialogue scenes were shot so that when the camera came in for a close-up on the other person, a stand-in was substituted for Tracy. And luckily the script did not call for many scenes in which he had to be part of a group.

The first morning of shooting, Kate, "all dowdied up in her trouser-suit," appeared on the set before Kramer, Tracy or any other member of the cast, even though the schedule did not call for her services that day. As she checked the interior

---

* Provision was made for a percentage of profits to each of the three if the film was released and made back its negative cost.

set, she announced to the crew, "In case my niece drops dead from the excitement, I'm here and I know all her lines, too." When Kramer appeared, she turned to him to complain about the fake fireplace in the living-room set. He assured her that once lit the fireplace would not look fake, but not until she first demanded it be torn out and replaced by the real thing. She then went on to discuss with the lighting man the placing of a key light, insisted the wardrobe woman select other accessories for Kathy to wear with her first costume in the film, and engaged a hairdresser in a discussion about shampooing ("I'm the best hair washer in the world," she proclaimed). By now the first shot had been set up—a short confrontation between Tracy and Sidney Poitier. Kate crouched and squinted through the camera viewfinder and reported to Kramer that the angle of the shot did not look quite right to her.

Kramer grumbled that she had repressed directorial ambitions. "I'll give you the whole thing," he said, turning away as if to leave.

"Now, now, Stanley," she cooed, "let's not lose our equilibrium. I'm only trying to keep the set alive so everyone won't go to sleep."

Tracy entered and hostilities immediately ended. Kramer reflects that "[Kate] and I had a strange relationship, because I loved Tracy, and I think he loved me, and in a way, I felt for a while Kate and I were rivals. We had some tensions on the picture. I was irritated by her fear over her so-called 'ugly neck'*—she wore scarves and high collars, and 'played low.' . . . Many times she would come into a room and kneel, or sit down at once, so people wouldn't be aware of her neck. During rehearsal, Tracy would be sitting there; suddenly she'd come in and she'd kneel. He'd say, 'What the hell are you doin', kneeling?' and she'd say, very grandly, 'Spencer, I just thought it would be appropriate,' and he'd mock her high-falutin' accent, saying '*Spensuh!* Christ you talk like you've got a feather up your ass all the time! Get out of there,

* Wrinkles had formed in the five years since Hepburn had been off the screen, giving her what she called a turkey neck. This part of her anatomy remained covered in all her subsequent films. Even on television interviews, she wore her shirt collar turned up and a scarf around her neck.

will yah?' and she'd start to say, 'I just thought that—' and he'd snap out, 'Just do what the director guy tells you, will yah?' and she'd reply, humbly, 'All right.' She'd take anything from him. She'd take nothing from anybody else."

Thinking for a moment, he added, "Spencer Tracy is the greatest actor I ever worked with. He had no physical energy for the shooting of this film. . . . Columbia doesn't know to this day that we shot only half-days. They didn't believe the film would be a commercial success, anyway, and if they'd known our schedule would have been doubly furious."

In describing Kate's attitude on the set, Kramer comments, "She had to run free, with and around a director. She was always creative, one of the two or three most creative artists I've ever worked with. I've never known anyone who matched her in terms of independence *vis-à-vis* a director. She *thinks* like a director. She's a set-decorator also . . . a driving worker. Work, work, work. She can work until everybody drops." Tracy, Kramer claims, was a *reactor*, Kate a protagonist. "With Spencer, you could give another actor all the pages, he'd listen—and he'd steal the scene, nobody would look at the man who read the lines."

At five A.M. on shooting days, Kate would drive through the heavy early morning California fog to Tracy's house to rehearse with him until the time they had to leave for the studio. Kramer nostalgically recalls that when "he had finished a scene that was satisfactory from his viewpoint," Tracy would yell to Sam Leavitt, the cameraman, "'Did you get that, Sam?' and wait apprehensively until Sam waved him a sign of approval."

Although there was a difference of thirty-eight years in their ages, Kate and her niece Kathy shared a strong family resemblance. The similarities were more than physical. Kathy quickly picked up Kate's work ethic. Late afternoons they would return from a day's shooting (Kate remaining to film her scenes after Tracy had finished) to "Aunt Kat's" house for "force-feed sessions." "I had the part down cold," Kathy says. "So what she got me to do was go at it intellectually to begin with and then forget what I knew about the character and just fade into her. Whenever I tended to lapse into thoughtfulness, she'd say, 'I can hear the wheels turning.'"

Kathy also had much of her aunt's distaste for the press. Kramer, who was not happy with her casting, found the young woman uncooperative: "the publicity guys would want to take stills of her, and she'd say, 'I don't want to do that kind of publicity.' We had a *Vogue* layout all ready to go . . . and she nixed it. My publicity man, George Glass, had aggravation all the time." Kate, to the contrary, was cooperative with the press for one of the few times in her life.

Jack Hamilton, senior editor for *Look,* who had been given the okay to come on the set for an interview with her, found to his surprise that "She had declared herself an ally something like China coming over to our side." Nonetheless, when Hamilton arrived for their meeting, the sight of her wearing what she called her "Civil War veteran's rags" and red socks, scruffy shoes and no makeup unsettled him. He recalls, "She was fiercely protective of Spencer Tracy who was sitting there . . . looking like a marvelous, quiet king lion. Here was Katharine Hepburn of legend, who always considered the press 'her natural enemy,' and was as untouchable and removed as Garbo." Why was she cooperating? "We figured out later she must be feeling mellow about their [Tracy and herself] working together again, and the movie bow of her young niece."

"Listen, I'll be the easy one to get," she confided to Hamilton. "I gab a lot. It's Spencer we'll have to work on. He gets melancholia if he thinks too much about the past. He's an uncommunicative kind of fellow anyway. Doesn't like discussions. Not interested in the give and take of philosophical opinions."

Once Kate started talking, she could hardly be stopped. "People say the story's a shocker [*Guess Who's Coming to Dinner*]. Even anybody with a pint-sized brain knows the day is soon coming when interracial marriages won't be funny, or surprising or anything else. It will be just: 'There it is.' It's a defenseless position, to judge people by their color. Sidney Poitier is black, but he and Kathy don't look odd together at all. I'm spotted [a reference to her freckles], he's black, she's white, so . . . ? . . . . We're living in very odd times, you know. We insist on knowing everything about everything. What the dickens, are you going to accept only what you know? What about the mystery of life? . . . religion? . . . sex? Sex! Are you going to have some sort of draughtsman tell you what the delights of sex are, or are you going to allow your own imagination a little more free range? . . . Is it the man's walk, or the spring in his walk, the lift in his walk, that intrigues you? We are becoming so literal minded. . . . I think disillusioned authors are destroying the sex act.

"You think I'm dated? I think life is rather a romantic episode. It's romantic as the blue sky and the bright clouds and Kathy suddenly getting an opportunity.* This is romantic, life is romantic. And I think young girls are the same as when I was a young girl. I think a few of them hop into bed more often than they used to. . . . My mother encouraged me to live in the image of George Bernard Shaw and lead a colorful life. Now, everybody is drafted and they are stood up naked and stamped and sent on, and it doesn't encourage individuality."

When Kate talked like this, Tracy would smirk at her and then start to rise—a cue to her to bring him into the conversation, to persuade him to tell some story she knew he told well. Her behavior with the press was perhaps attributable to the knowledge, learned from Tracy's doctors, that this film was to be his last, and she wanted to do everything possible to help make it a tremendous success. During the filming, everyone involved thought the subject matter would put the public off *unless* it was both intrigued by and used to the theme by the time of its release. Therefore, her seduction of the press.

Four days before the last shot was filmed, Tracy put his arm around Kramer and said, "You know, I read the script again last night, and if I were to die on the way home tonight you can still release the picture with what you've got." After Kate had finished a scene during one of the last shooting days, she rushed to her dressing room and, as was her habit, immediately changed back into a pair of trousers and a comfortable shirt. Tracy was being set up for a close shot when she returned and she slipped behind him and into a director's

---

* Although Houghton received generally good reviews and photographed well, she has yet to fulfill her promise.

chair out of camera range preparing to feed him lines. His back to her, she propped her feet up on a set piece and gave him his cue. Tracy, without turning, asked, "Do you intend to sit there with your feet up like that?" an edge to his voice.

Kate, not having realized he had seen her, was taken by surprise and was unable to answer.

He then told her slowly, the way a father might reprimand a child, "We can begin when you put your goddamn feet down and sit like a lady!"

Kate dropped her feet and with a little smile adopted a ladylike posture. She fed him the line again, and Tracy nodded to Kramer that he was prepared to begin. The line he spoke comes after a scene where Drayton has listened carefully to all his daughter and her black fiancé have to say in defense of the rightness of their marriage. After they have finished speaking, Drayton turns to his wife, who is seen for a moment from his point of view. Then the camera comes in close to Tracy. "If what they feel for each other is even half what *we* felt"—he tells her, his voice cracking—"then that is everything." Kate was so moved that she had to bite back her tears.*

Production ended on May 26 and an on-the-set party was given to celebrate the windup. Tracy's strength had all but given way and he could not attend. But he called Garson Kanin in New York and jubilantly and incredulously cried, "Did you hear me, Jasper? I finished the picture!" While Tracy rested, Kate mixed with all the members of the company, sharing memories of the film's funny and sticky moments. During dinner Kramer stood up and proposed a toast: "To Spencer Tracy, the greatest of all motion picture personalities." At this point, Kate "rose from her chair and the long-legged figure in the white slack suit" strode to the microphone and spoke with much emotion to the crew:

"You are the people who make an actor able to act, and I don't know how many of you realize that. But I want you to know that I shall be everlastingly grateful to you all. And I

---

* In the final cut, as Tracy says these words, the camera reveals his profile on the left foreground of the screen and Hepburn, her eyes brimming with tears, on the right background, looking at Tracy. Actually, the shot was two separate shots spliced together in the final cut.

know that your help . . . made a hell of a lot of difference
. . . to Spence."

Guess Who's Coming to Dinner was released the following
November, and the film was to be one of Kate's greatest
box-office successes as well as a personal triumph. The critics,
however, "virtually unanimously" found it "loathsome." As
one maintained: "the race issue is prettified and pre-
guaranteed a happy solution here because of the extraordinary character of this black man, and the built-in liberal
stance of the parents, especially since Poitier represents the
quintessentially respectable and unthreatening black, and
Tracy and Hepburn represent the settled, establishmentarian
liberals who can win over any case and make the nastiest
world safe for love and ideals."

Poitier had quite different feelings about the character he
portrayed: "People said I was cast as the stereotype of the
intellectual black man with no flaws. . . . There was a great
hue and cry. . . . They said I should have played a garage
mechanic, or someone like that, brought home to this wealthy
San Francisco family by the daughter and presented as a
candidate for marriage.

"Well, this objection has absolutely no historical sense. In
1967, it was utterly impossible to do an in-depth interracial
love story, to treat the issue in dead earnestness, head on. No
producer, no director could get the money, nor would theaters in America back it. But Kramer made people look at
the issue for the first time. . . . He treated the theme with
humor . . . delicately . . . humanly . . . lovingly. . . . *Guess
Who's Coming to Dinner* is a totally revolutionary movie, and
this is what so many critics failed to see. For the very first
time, the characters in a story about racism are people with
minds of their own, who after deliberations in a civilized
manner, and after their own private reflections, come to a
conclusion—the only sensible conclusion that people could
come to in a situation like this!"*

No matter what barbed criticism was thrust at the content
of the film, all the critics shouted *Bravo! BRAVA!* for Tracy
and Hepburn. "Mr. Tracy," began Brendan Gill at *The New*

---

* The film ends with the interracial couple receiving final blessings to marry
from both sets of parents.

Yorker, "gives a faultless performance [and has] turned his role into a stunning compendium of the actor's art . . . as if he were saying . . . to generations of actors not yet born, 'Here is how to seem to listen. Here is how to dominate a scene by walking away from it.'" Penelope Mortimer of the London *Observer* felt that "while either [Tracy or Hepburn] or both are on screen the most savage criticism [of the story] is replaced by gratitude. To me, at any rate, Tracy's craggy face and burly build, the exploding humour, extraordinary gentleness and toughness of old leather, have always represented the ideal man. . . . Miss Hepburn is, of course, unchanged and unchangeable. Anyone who feels as I do about this pair will go and see *Guess Who's Coming to Dinner* regardless of its fallacies and its hokum."

Tracy was never to know the controversy that surrounded the film upon its release, nor the glowing reviews received by both him and Kate, nor the incredible success of his eighty-fourth movie. At around six A.M. on Saturday morning, June 10, just fifteen days after the completion of principal photography, Tracy was stricken with a fatal heart seizure as he drank a glass of milk in the kitchen of his small house. Kate arrived unsuspecting a short time later to find him hunched over the kitchen table. She called the doctor, Cukor, and Tracy's brother, Carrol Tracy, who, in turn, notified Louise. Tracy was moved to the bed in his monk's cell of a bedroom, which contained only an oak chest, one chair and an old bed. (Cukor had said that the room "had the aura of a place where a man might do penance.") Kate was left alone with the body. About ten minutes later she emerged from his room, eyes moist but tears in control, and walked out of the cottage on Cukor's arm. A few moments later, Louise arrived with John and Susie.

Kate did not attend the requiem low mass said for Tracy at the Immaculate Heart of Mary Roman Catholic Church in Hollywood. Six hundred people were present at his burial at Forest Lawn Cemetery. All of Hollywood seemed to have turned out to pay their respects to one of their great ones and to his widow, daughter and son. Louise, cloaked and veiled, a brave and sad looking figure, held on to the arm of Metro's Howard Strickland. Kate had remained at her home, secluded, refusing to talk to any reporters. Phyllis was with her, and Laura flew out to help her through the first difficult days. Forty-eight hours after the funeral, Kate paid her respects to Louise. Then, with Phyllis and Laura, she flew back to the East Coast and Fenwick, where the sea and her beloved home waited and would, she hoped, help her to heal her wounds.

A
Life
on
Her
Own

CHAPTER
24

Summers at Fenwick were a festival of life. The rooms Kate had so lovingly helped to design were once again filled with the sound of Hepburn voices, many of them very young, for Kate's sisters and brothers were now grandparents. Early every morning "Aunt Kat" could be seen walking along the shoreline before swimming out to meet the incoming tide. She never seemed too tired for sports or games—three-legged races, blindman's buff. Watching her dynamic energy, one could hardly believe the woman was approaching her sixtieth year. Yet, for all this activity and for the first time, Fenwick could not console her. The children were not hers and she had no husband to send back to the city on Sunday nights, no patient to care for, no parent to answer to. Katharine Houghton Hepburn was a woman on her own—alone, and even Fenwick could not ease her sense of loss or overcome her fear of a solitary future.

After two weeks, with Phyllis as a companion, Kate left Fenwick and took a small cottage at Martha's Vineyard. Her habits did not change. She still walked the shoreline with the rising of the sun and swam out to meet the incoming tide. Within a matter of a few weeks, she was ready once again to tackle life as she did the waves, by refusing to let it overpower her. She did not know yet what position toward Tracy she would take—grieving friend, companion, widow? All three?

Or only the first two? Louise remained—and would always remain—Mrs. Spencer Tracy.* Kate could not know at the time that within a matter of months the press and the public would cast her in the role of widow *manqué*. The secret that had been kept so assiduously for so many years, and even when leaked had not been really accepted, now became common knowledge.

The public reacted in a manner that might have surprised Tracy. Yes, of course, a *Mrs.* Spencer Tracy existed, but she and her husband had not lived together for nearly thirty years. And—hadn't it been admirable, noble really, of the two stars to so respect the covenants of Tracy's Catholic faith? In fact, only two days after the funeral, Charles Champlin of the *Los Angeles Times* called their liaison "a remarkable legacy of an association as beautiful and dignified as any this town has ever known." Louise might have worn the public mourning, but Kate was looked upon as Tracy's true widow. Kate would soon discover this for herself and use a kind of professional widowhood for her personal protection ever after. But in August 1967, what was uppermost on her mind was finding work that would excite and involve her.

Toward the end of her stay at Martha's Vineyard, Kate was sent *The Lion in Winter*, a script based on James Goldman's twelfth-century drama about Henry II and Eleanor of Aquitaine, which had been produced on Broadway in 1965. Kate read it and then gave it to Phyllis to read. Both women believed the role of the aging and anguished Eleanor, who never loses her astonishing queenliness, ideal for Kate, and she quickly accepted the offer. Martin Poll, the film's producer, had no trouble in signing Peter O'Toole† to play Henry II, Eleanor's more youthful husband. But Poll could

---

* Louise Tracy never remarried and was, indeed, known publicly as Mrs. Spencer Tracy until her death in 1983. Tracy named her his beneficiary and executrix in his will and she received somewhere around five hundred thousand dollars and full title of the Hill.

† Peter O'Toole (1933–   ) is Irish by birth but grew up in Leeds. He began his acting career with the Old Vic and became a top film star in 1962 with *Lawrence of Arabia*. *Becket* (1964) and *Lord Jim* (1965) consolidated his position. When Hepburn eventually co-starred with him in *The Lion in Winter*, O'Toole was one of the leading international box-office attractions and, like Tracy, had star billing over her.

not immediately arrange financing and distribution. Goldman's script, adapted from his play, was considered too intellectual and special to be a commercial venture. In September, 1967, it looked as if *The Lion in Winter* would never be made.

Ely Landau offered Kate a role in the adaptation of Jean Giraudoux's play *The Madwoman of Chaillot*—that of Aurelia, the eccentric countess intent on saving Paris from a group of men who planned to turn it into a giant oil field. She read it and told him, aghast, "Oh *no*. What's all this about? I'm a simple, nice person. I like to make Christmas wreaths, sweep floors. I don't *understand* all this complicated stuff. I'm rather like my sister [Peggy] who's a farmer and says that the most difficult thing she likes to attempt is carrying two pails of milk over a fence!"

Landau kept pressing. Although Kate was not convinced that she could be totally effective as Aurelia, *Madwoman* was to be produced by Landau, with whom she had worked so well in *Long Day's Journey into Night;* and another old friend, John Huston, was scheduled to direct. She claims she finally accepted the role "in order to better understand what [the play] was all about." No sooner had Kate agreed to appear in *Madwoman* than Martin Poll announced that he had obtained the financing for *The Lion in Winter* and hoped to begin production within a matter of weeks. Landau consented to postpone *Madwoman* until Kate's first commitment was honored. Both films were to be made in Europe (*Lion* in Wales, England and France; *Madwoman* in France), and Kate and Phyllis would be away from the States for nearly a year.

The idea of being abroad for so long suited Kate's mood, as did the chance to submerge herself in work. She was determined to make a new life for herself. She had always been thoroughly capable of holding her own in a man's world. Few if any other women stars had experienced the success that she had making her own deals, calling her own shots. For more than thirty-five years, she had been a queen of international renown, and she held herself with an enduring grace that lent as much luminosity to her appearance at sixty as it had at twenty-five. Bette Davis and Joan Crawford, those two colorful ladies whose reigns had coincided with Kate's, were now working in horror films,* while she still commanded the best leading men and the most prestigious scripts. There seemed suddenly to be a plethora of exceptional stories with a strong middle-aged woman as the pivotal character, and Kate was offered the very best of these.

Before she and Phyllis left for Europe to begin her two-picture schedule, Kate's old friend Irene Selznick discussed with her the possibility of playing the role of the ageless Parisian couturière Coco Chanel in a musical written by Alan Jay Lerner and planned for a year hence. Kate laughed loudly at this suggestion; the only public singing she had ever done was one chorus of "Onward Christian Soldiers" in *The African Queen*. Mrs. Selznick begged her not to say no without trying, and so Kate spent ten days in New York working with Roger Edens, Metro's former music coach.†

"When she came to my house that first Sunday morning I got out about fifty songs," Edens recalled. "But she just moaned about her repertoire. 'I might just sing *Onward Christian Soldiers*,' she said seriously. So we started from scratch to learn a few songs. At six o'clock I knew she was the third woman in my life [the other two, Judy Garland and Ethel Merman, were also Eden's *students*]."

The audition was held in the elegant living room of Irene Selznick at the Pierre Hotel. Kate, her hair still up à la concierge and dressed in gabardine trousers, sandals and several layers of sweaters that allowed little more than her chin to protrude over the edge of a thick wool turtleneck, stood by a grand piano sipping tea. Halfway across the room sitting in a semicircle and waiting nervously (after all, what could one say to Katharine Hepburn if she was absolutely

---

* In 1962, Davis had made the horror classic *What Ever Happened to Baby Jane?* with Joan Crawford. Davis went on to do a string of such films—*Hush, Hush Sweet Charlotte* and *The Nanny* (1965), *The Anniversary* (1971), *Madame Sin* (1972), *Burnt Offerings* (1976) and *Return from Witch Mountain* (1978). Crawford went the same route with *Strait Jacket* (1964), *I Saw What You Did* (1965), *Berserk* (1967) and *Trog* (1970).

† Roger Edens (1905–1970) was known at Metro as musical supervisor for nearly twenty-five years. He was also a fine arranger and composer and won Academy Awards for his scoring of *Easter Parade* (1948), *On the Town* (1949) and *Annie Get Your Gun* (1950), a three-year sequential record.

God-awful?) were Freddie Brisson,* the producer, Mr. and Mrs. Alan Jay Lerner, Patricia (Kennedy) Lawford, Phyllis and Irene Selznick. Edens sat poised, ready to accompany Kate on the piano. Kate put the teacup down on a nearby table and nodded to him to begin. After a few bars of Cole Porter's campy "Mrs. Lowsborough—Goodby," everyone relaxed.

Her style was what Lerner called "talk-singing," and he later commented that "She's remarkably musical and unlike most actors who forget to act when they sing, she was always acting." Edens led her from Porter to Lerner and Loewe ("Camelot") and back to Porter again ("Miss Otis Regrets").

When she and Phyllis arrived back home in Turtle Bay, she called Stanley Kramer on the Coast. "I sang for them," she announced. "They seemed to like me. They must be desperate."

So now Kate had three projects to look forward to: the two films and the musical based on Chanel. She was guaranteed of work for somewhere between one and two years. She had got on with her own life very well indeed.

With Phyllis, she flew to Paris late in October for a one-week holiday and then continued on to London where, within a few days, Kate, O'Toole, the director, Anthony Harvey,† and the rest of the cast of *The Lion in Winter* gathered on the bare stage of the Haymarket Theatre to rehearse. Harvey, who had made only one previous film, the small-budgeted *Dutchman,* commented that "working with [Miss Hepburn] is like going to Paris at the age of seventeen and finding everything is the way you thought it would be."

Kate had a great fondness for the character of Eleanor. "She must have been tough as nails to have lived to be 82 years old and full of beans," she told a reporter. "Both she and Henry II were big-time operators who played for whole

---

* Rosalind Russell (1912–1976), Mrs. Frederick Brisson, had originally been slotted for the role of Coco, but she was suffering from acute arthritis and so another Coco had to be found.

† Anthony Harvey (1931–   ) began his film career in England in 1949 as an editor and turned director in 1966 with *Dutchman.* That film and *The Lion in Winter* are his two best screen works. He has made several films since then, none of them as successful.

countries. I like big-time operators." The gentleman of the press, to his surprise, was welcomed quite magnanimously by the formerly press-shy Hepburn. He watched with fascination as Kate stalked "about the stage as Eleanor, laughing, shouting and once startling the rest of the cast by crying real tears."

"If we'd had a camera," Harvey later commented, "and everyone had been in costume, we could have filmed it and released it."

At a break in one rehearsal, Phyllis gave Kate a newspaper with a photograph of her on the front page hurrying from a car in trousers and a scruffy raincoat.

"Look at this!" Kate exclaimed, slapping the newspaper so that it made a cracking, call-to-attention sound. "He *did* get a picture of me after all. Don't I look awful? We thought we'd escaped the son-of-a-bitch. He chased us all over the West End. He could have saved us the gas." Another day she bragged, "We lost [a photographer] in Camden Town. Now I'm one up on them. I love winning. I like to prove I'm the best guy. These London boys are amateurs."

In the film, O'Toole might have played the King and Lion, but no one in rehearsals doubted who really wore the crown. "Peter, stop towering over me," Kate would order. "Come and sit down and try to look respectable." And he instantly would oblige, to the amazement of the cast who knew his reputation as a tyrant on the set. O'Toole was quick to admit that Kate's presence reduced him "to a shadow of my former gay-dog self. . . . She is terrifying. It is sheer masochism working with her. She has been sent by some dark fate to nag and torment me."

Kate scowled as she replied, "Don't be so silly." Then she smiled patiently. "We are going to get on very well. You are Irish and make me laugh. In any case I am on to you and you to me."

She relished sparring with O'Toole, who was twenty-four years her junior, and soon it became a kind of bantering, affectionate warfare. After three weeks of rehearsals, Kate and Phyllis left for Ireland, where part of the film was to be shot in a replica of a twelfth-century castle in County Wicklow.

To the company's amazement, she swam twice a day in the winter sea, early in the morning and during her lunch break. To O'Toole's question, "Why on earth would you do a thing like that?" she replied, "It's the shock—so horrible that it makes you feel great afterwards." Whatever free time she had she spent roaming the Wicklow hills and collecting broken glass from Georgian ruins, which she had decided she would ship home to make into a chandelier.

From Ireland the company moved to Wales and then France. *The Lion in Winter* was the second time Peter O'Toole had played Henry II in a film. In *Becket* he had portrayed him as a limp, ineffectual king. In *Lion*, he imbued Henry II with a bold dynamism. History indicates that the former interpretation was probably closer to the truth; but there seems no doubt of Eleanor's tremendous independence and strength of character, and the reviewers were to be much in accord that as Eleanor Kate was "Triumphant in her creation of a complete and womanly queen . . . an aging beauty who can look her image in the eye, a sophisticate whose shrewdness is matched only by her humor." One could say that these words also applied to Kate.

Working with the volatile O'Toole had generated exactly the right sparks to pull Kate out of the depression that followed Tracy's death. She was sorry when shooting on *The Lion in Winter* ended and was pleased that she had no time between the end of that film and the start of production at Studios de la Victorine in Nice on *Madwoman of Chaillot*. She moved into a gracious old house on St. Jean-Cap-Ferrat overlooking the Mediterranean, which in March is gray and cold, although no more so in that month than the waters that bordered Fenwick. She swam daily and bicycled. Most of St. Jean-Cap-Ferrat's aristocratic houses were shuttered while their occupants either followed the sun or traveled the ski circuit. The small village on the Cap was active with shops and sidewalk cafés catering at this time of year to the less affluent year-round residents. The town of Beaulieu-sur-Mer, with its early Wednesday morning open market, was only a mile's walk. The Port of Petite Afrique, where a café had been named *The African Queen*, was just a fifteen-minute bike ride away. In March, few people in this area spoke

English, so that even when they did recognize her, they were hesitant to speak, supposing she would not be able to understand them.

Tracy had left her very few material mementos, but she had a tattered old red sweater of his which she often wore over a motley selection of other sweaters as she pedaled about in her slacks and beat-up tennis shoes. She had begun to smoke again, but never until late afternoon. Then she puffed "her way through packs like a Foreign Legion trooper." She went to sleep at eight-thirty, whether or not she had a call to work the next day. Dame Edith Evans, who was playing with her in *Madwoman*, told her she was sleeping her life away. "It's true," she replied. "I don't go out much. But when I do, I decide I don't miss much." Phyllis was not athletic, and so Kate usually swam and biked alone. Her vitality seemed to have grown with the years rather than diminished.

On work mornings, she'd stuff her bicycle into the trunk of the car and, dressed in trousers, shirt and sweaters, and an old forage cap that had also belonged to Tracy, she would seat herself beside her chauffeur and let all other passengers ride in the backseat for the half-hour journey to the studio, keeping up a stream of conversation that she flung over her shoulder in her tremendous voice "like machine gun fire deliberately aimed."

"Deaf people love me to talk to them," she once commented. "No one who's hard of hearing has any trouble making me out."

Her appetite had not diminished. She never left her villa without stowing away one of her lumberjack breakfasts. She munched chocolate all day and had a steak and fresh fruit for lunch. Four o'clock tea was observed and was not complete without a plate of sweets. What she called a light supper was pretty solid fare to most people, and it was usually topped at bedtime with a glass of milk and a sweet. But with her Amazonian energy she never put on a pound.

At the Studios de la Victorine, she would climb the cherry trees behind the executive offices for the fruit and often upon coming down would tell the gaping workmen, "Hide the ladder so no one'll get the big ones."

Ely Landau had gathered together a most extraordinary

cast for *Madwoman*. Besides Dame Edith, there were Danny Kaye, Yul Brynner, Charles Boyer, Giulietta Masina, Margaret Leighton, Donald Pleasence, Richard Chamberlain, Nanette Newman, John Gavin and Oscar Homolka. To Kate's great disappointment, John Huston had walked off the film just before production began. Landau had wanted the nineteenth-century story updated and Huston had not believed a contemporary background would work in a fantasy. Bryan Forbes* had been signed only eighteen days before shooting started, during which time he had rewritten the script to Landau's recommendations. Kate liked Forbes but kept her distance from him throughout most of the film. Despite the stellar quality of her fellow players, she remained both "the Star and Autocrat." For the first few weeks, she would not talk to journalists nor pose for photographers. When Yul Brynner (who had given her the bicycle she rode) took out his camera to shoot a candid picture of her, she ordered him off the set as if he were a schoolboy being sent by a school mistress to the principal's office. Then, early in April, she seemed to do a complete turnabout.

Previously, she had uncategorically refused to appear in any form of television, believing the medium was unsympathetic and unflattering to film performers. But she had been asked to film a short segment in Nice for the upcoming Academy Awards presentations and she agreed. *Guess Who's Coming to Dinner* had been nominated in ten categories, her performance and Tracy's among them. Perhaps she accepted because of her conviction that Tracy would win Best Actor. Whatever her reason, she was seen introducing a section of a film montage covering many of the winning performances in the forty years of Oscar history, including a scene of Tracy as the Portuguese fisherman in *Captains Courageous*. The audience at the Awards, held in the Santa Monica Auditorium, was well aware of the poignancy of this moment, especially

---

* Bryan Forbes (1926–   ) is as well known for his screenwriting as for his direction. He directed his first complete film, the critically acclaimed *Whistle Down the Wind*, in 1961. *The L-Shaped Room* (also screenplay) (1962), *King Rat* (also screenplay) (1966), *The Whisperers* (also screenplay) (1967) were among those that followed. He married Nanette Newman, who has appeared in many of his films.

since Louise, accompanied by John and Susie, was present, ready to accept the award for Tracy as she had done years before.

To Kate's disappointment, she, not Tracy, won an award. Rod Steiger had taken Best Actor for *In the Heat of the Night*. When informed, Kate said, "Well, I suspect my award was really given to the two of us."*

A few days after the Awards, she told British journalist Alexander Walker, "I had twenty-five years of perfect companionship with this man among men. He had been a rock, a protector. . . . There are very few great actors. Spencer was one. I'm not in his class. Inside him was a light that did a disservice to some poor movies he made—it made them that much shoddier. . . . Our films assumed that if the relationship between us was valid enough, the spontaneity would be there. . . . If people ask why our partnership was so successful, that's why—it was based on a natural and truthful completion of needs."

She cabled the Academy her thanks with these words: "I'm enormously touched. It is gratifying to find someone else voted for me apart from myself." And to Roderick Mann of the *Sunday Express*, she confided that she hadn't wept when either her parents or Tracy had died. "I don't have pictures of them about, nothing like that. I don't believe in guilt or regrets. The only thing is to hope you did your best for people and made them happy sometimes."

The day she won the award she put on Tracy's worn red sweater and cycled off the set of *Madwoman* to where a small

* George Cukor received the award for Hepburn. *In the Heat of the Night* won Best Picture for 1967 over *Guess Who's Coming to Dinner*, *Bonnie and Clyde*, *Doctor Doolittle* and *The Graduate*. William Rose won for Best Story and Screenplay (written directly for the screen), the only other Oscar awarded to *Guess Who's Coming to Dinner*. After Hepburn was notified that she had won the Oscar for *Guess Who's Coming to Dinner*, she cabled Screen Actors' Guild president Gregory Peck: "It was delightful a total surprise I am enormously touched because I feel I have received a great affectionate hug from my fellow workers and for a variety of reasons not the least of which being Spencer Stanley Kathy and Bill Rose. Rose wrote about a normal middle aged unspectacular unglamorous creature with a good brain and a warm heart who's doing the best she can to do the decent thing in a difficult situation. In other words she was a good wife. Our most unsung and important heroine. I'm glad she's coming back in style. I modeled her after my mother. Thanks again. They don't usually give these things to the old girls you know."

band of newsmen and photographers had assembled. She submitted graciously to their cameras and questions. "Much of what I know about acting I learned from Spencer Tracy," she said, her eyes glimmering. She called him a "sturdy oak buffeted by the wind—a throw-back to an age of rugged heroism . . . that vanishing American, the self-made man. He was what we imagined our grandfathers to be." These words opened the way to queries about their longtime relationship and she replied, not with intimate memories but with the eulogies she would utter frequently for the rest of her life. Louise had had the respect, the *title*, until Tracy's death. Now the turn was Kate's.

CHAPTER
25

❧

By the time Kate finished *Madwoman*, Alan Jay Lerner and *Coco*'s composer, André Previn,* had not worked out their problems with the book. *Coco* would be postponed at least another season. Kate had no immediate plans and decided to stay for a while in the south of France with Phyllis. William Rose, who had written *Guess Who's Coming to Dinner*, visited her for a week, bringing with him an original first-draft screenplay which he promised would enable Kate "to end her sixteen year film career in a blaze of glory." Kate had, of course, been a star for many more than sixteen years and had no intention of ending her career, *period*, and she did not like Rose's projected story. To Kate's further consternation, the American and English press carried a story that she and Rose planned to wed. Rose, who was in the midst of divorcing Tania, his English wife and co-author of many of his screenplays, returned to London where he "confided" to the *Sunday Express*, "I'm rich, fat, burned out, and I'm looking

---

* André Previn (1929–   ) was born in Berlin and came to the United States at age ten. In his late teens, he became a top arranger for Metro. In 1954, he composed the background score for Tracy's film *Bad Day at Black Rock*. He won four Academy Awards, three for scoring of a musical film—*Gigi* (1958), *Porgy and Bess* (1959) and *Irma La Douce* (1963), and one for *My Fair Lady* (1964), for musical supervising and conducting. After *Coco* he became more involved with conducting and is currently conductor of the Los Angeles Philharmonic.

for someone to come with me in my claret-coloured Maserati to Italy next month. I've rented a villa in Portofino and I want to be there for my 51st birthday at the end of August." Portofino was entirely too close to Cap Ferrat for Kate's comfort, and she and Phyllis left France to spend the rest of the summer at Fenwick.

While *Coco* was still going through rewrites, Irene Selznick, who had been successful as a Broadway producer with *A Streetcar Named Desire* and *The Chalk Garden*, thought she would like to try her hand at film producing; and she approached Kate with an offer for her to direct. Mrs. Selznick owned the rights on two related novels—*Martha, Eric, and George* and *Martha in Paris*—by British author Margery Sharp. Their plots centered around the unusual career of a gifted English girl who goes to Paris to become a painter, a role Kate might well have played herself thirty years earlier. Kate had always been interested in directing and had discussed the possibility with Louis B. Mayer not long after *Woman of the Year*, but nothing had come of it. In 1958, John Ford had encouraged her to follow up on the idea, but then Tracy had become too ill for her to tackle such a big task. Her great enthusiasm for striking out on this new career ended in the spring of 1969, by which time several attempts to adapt the lengthy books into a tidy screenplay had failed.

The Oscars for 1968 were awarded on April 14, 1969, on the stage of the glittering Dorothy Chandler Pavilion in the new Los Angeles Music Center. Ingrid Bergman, looking radiantly beautiful, opened the envelope containing (supposedly) *the* winner for Best Actress for 1968. For a moment, a look of astonishment came over her beautiful face. In a stunned voice, she cried out, "It's a tie!" and then read off the names, "Katharine Hepburn for *The Lion in Winter*," and then had to wait a moment until the applause quieted down before she added, "and Barbra Streisand for *Funny Girl*." Streisand, wearing a shocking, see-through, jeweled black-chiffon pajama outfit with starched white puritan cuffs and collar, ran up to collect her award while Anthony Harvey followed her to the microphone to accept on Kate's behalf. Streisand held up her golden Oscar and in strident Brooklynese said, "Hello gorgeous!" Then she graciously declared, "I am honored to be in such magnificent company as Katharine

Hepburn." The two women were the first co-winners since Fredric March and Wallace Beery had shared the award in 1932.*

Kate's Oscar made her the first three-time winner for Best Actress. Furthermore, with the *Lion* nomination, Kate's eleventh, she became the most nominated screen performer in the forty-one years of the Academy Awards. Kate had remained adamant about not owning a television or other "household noise makers," but she did watch the televised program in New York with Laura and Phyllis at Irene Selznick's apartment and laughed heartily when Ruth Gordon, looking much younger than her seventy-two years, snapped into the microphone, "I don't know why it took so long," when presented with her first Oscar for Supporting Actress in *Rosemary's Baby*.

During the filming of *The Madwoman of Chaillot*, Kate had said, "I think *The Madwoman of Chaillot* has more relevance today than it did twenty years ago. The world has gone cuckoo. We're still dominated by greed, and that's what Giraudoux was talking about. *The Madwoman* represents the possibilities of man, she represents hope." But the final film of *Madwoman*, which failed either to make this point or to be an arresting movie, was a disappointing follow-up to Kate's sequential tribute at the Awards. Huston had been right—the contemporizing of the story bound it to the earth when it should have taken off in enchanted, whimsical fantasy. Kate's interpretation of the Madwoman presented her as far too sensible a woman to be living in the past and only added to the discomforting reality of a story meant to be whimsy. In fact, despite the stellar supporting cast, only Danny Kaye as the ragpicker seemed to belong in Giraudoux's *The Madwoman of Chaillot*.†

Kate spent no time feeling sorry for herself. On Alan Jay Lerner's insistence, she flew to Paris to meet Coco Chanel. "I

---

* Wallace Beery won his 1932 Oscar for *The Champ*, Fredric March for *Dr. Jekyll and Mr. Hyde*.
† Tennessee Williams commented, "Has anyone ever understood the irresistible gallantry and charm of old ladies, in and out of the theater, so well as Giraudoux in *The Madwoman of Chaillot*? Kate Hepburn was just not quite old or mad enough to suggest the charisma of their lunacy."

was scared to death to meet her," she says. "I had worn the same clothes for forty years, *literally,* even the shoes. I thought, 'If I don't like her, it will be an *agony.*' Finally, Alan Lerner said, 'Don't be silly, you'll like her.'

"So we went to her apartment over her salon in Paris.* I brought her a little African brass medallion [from among her mementos of *The African Queen*]. I didn't give it to her. I left it on a table with a note. It was hard to talk to her. She spoke only French and my French is very faltering. We had a delicious lunch and she—after a carefully delayed great entrance—was *enchanting*. Alan and I went to see her fashion show afterward, sitting on the stairs. Then she went back to her apartment and found the medallion. She was like a little girl, she was so tremendously pleased by discovering the gift. I liked her at once, she was amusing, tough in a good sense, and *fun*. She got to me. The essence of her style was *simplicity*. Exactly what I appreciate most."

Chanel, on the other hand, commented privately to Lerner, "She's too old for the role. Why, she must be close to sixty!" (Chanel was in her mid-eighties at this time.) When Chanel had first optioned her life story to Brisson, she had been told that in the book Lerner would encompass only her youthful years—the 1920s and 1930s. During the many rewrites, Lerner had dropped that idea in favor of presenting Coco in 1959 in her seventies after she had been in lengthy retirement. Coco was enormously displeased when she discovered what Lerner had done, especially since she had trusted him implicitly. A story about a young Coco, in far-removed time, was romantic history. But Kate was to play a seventy-year-old Coco—*impersonating* Coco as she still saw herself—a vital, older woman. (Coco had once declined a marriage proposal from the Duke of Wellington by saying there had been several Duchesses of Wellington, but only *one* Coco Chanel.) After years of sermonizing on the right of privacy to which celebrities were entitled, Kate apparently closed her eyes to the fact that, when she played Coco Chanel on the stage, she would not only be invading the fashion

---

* Chanel also had an apartment at the Ritz Hotel across the street from the salon that she had maintained for years.

designer's privacy but creating a portrait of the woman that might be both erroneous and unacceptable to the woman she portrayed.

As soon as Kate returned to New York, she began work with two music coaches, Susan Seton and Alfred Dixon's former assistant, Lynn Masters. To Kate's shock and grief, Roger Edens, who had given her the confidence she had needed to accept the challenge of a singing role, had died suddenly just before the show was scheduled for rehearsal. Under Edens's brilliant guidance, she had learned to interpret a lyric as she would dramatic lines in a script. He had also helped her with her phrasing, and Previn had tailored Coco's songs so that they did not exceed Kate's limited range.* Masters taught her how to project and yet save her voice for eight performances a week, while Seton concentrated on the actual songs that she must perform.

Coco was budgeted at close to nine hundred thousand dollars, which made it at that time the most expensive show in Broadway history.† The decision was to rehearse for six weeks and preview the show in New York for five more weeks before the scheduled December 18 opening. The first rehearsal at the Mark Hellinger Theatre was called on September 29. Kate swept onstage, where the company had been gathered. She was dressed in clumsy looking sandals, baggy beige gabardine trousers, a white cotton T-shirt and a black, long-sleeved, high-necked outer sweater. Lerner commented that she got most of her energy "from simplifying her life. She has 20 pairs of beige slacks, white shirts and black sweaters. When she gets up in the morning, she knows what she's going to wear. She never considers what she's going to have for

---

* Because of Previn's commitment with the London Symphony Orchestra, he and Lerner were separated by the Atlantic Ocean during much of their collaboration. Previn claims that some of their conferences were conducted over the noise in airport lounges. Lerner had recently ended his long collaboration with Frederick Loewe (with whom he had written *Paint Your Wagon*, *My Fair Lady* and *Camelot*, among other shows) and was floundering for another partner. Previn and Lerner, as men and as artists, did not seem to be simpatico, and the resulting music and lyrics are at odds with each other. Lerner wrote glib, sophisticated but straightforward lyrics which Previn mismatched with nonmelodic music that took awkward twists and turns in an attempt to be modern.
† *Coco* was wholly capitalized by Paramount Pictures, which also put up $2.75 million for film rights.

dinner, because her cook knows she eats simply (a steak, potato and salad). All the decisions that exhaust the normal person, she has eliminated."

From the beginning, Kate was the first to arrive for rehearsals and the last to leave. She knew not only her own lines but the entire script. *Coco* was to run two and a half hours and Kate's role called for her to be onstage for all but twelve minutes. Very few scenes could be rehearsed without her. But she never complained of the demands of the script, the complicated machinery of the main set, or the constant revisions she was forced to memorize every night. "She's Man Mountain Dean," Jerry Adler, the production stage manager, told a *Time* reporter. "She leaves the younger folks for dead at the end of the day. When she's not in a scene, she perches on a staircase munching things—packets of meat and cheese and fruit she has brought from home—listening and watching the onstage action over and over."

Cecil Beaton had designed two basic sets, Chanel's salon and the apartment over the salon. These were constructed on a giant turntable that rose, split, revolved and descended in whole or in part, depending upon the needs of the script. This "mechanical marvel" was more of a monster to the players, who found themselves having to improvise rather athletically when it malfunctioned. The first night of previews, Kate was faced with playing a scene with another performer across a four-foot chasm when the two sections did not reunite as planned. The stage manager was about to lower the curtain when to his amazement Kate leaped across the aperture, even though, had she made a misstep, she could have dropped about twenty-eight feet onto a concrete floor. Kate and Beaton were no more than polite to each other. Each respected the other's reputation but Kate had felt both the set and the costumes were too complicated to work with and that they owed more to Edwardian England* than to Chanel's Paris salon.

Coco's finale featured a fashion show of Chanel designs from 1918 to 1959. The set was transformed into mirrors, platforms and rings, each going in different directions, every-

---

* Beaton had designed the sets and costumes for the film version of *My Fair Lady* and the costumes for the stage version.

thing flashing and turning at once. This production number clearly pointed up where Lerner, Previn, Beaton and director Michael Benthall went wrong. The essence of Chanel was simplicity, and the production of *Coco* was a great dinosaur of a musical that managed to overwhelm the uninspired music, lyrics, and story, but still could not KO Kate.

Kate played a seventy-year-old Chanel who, after fifteen years in retirement, decides to make a comeback by reopening her salon. She succeeds, but her collection is a flop with the Paris fashion world. After she believes she has been bankrupted, four department store buyers from across the Atlantic* save her. Through a series of flashbacks using filmed sequences shown on mirrored screens, Coco's past love affairs are recalled, but never is her current life shown to be in personal jeopardy. She develops a motherly feeling for one of her young mannequins and becomes more meddlesome than an active participant in a flimsy triangle involving herself, the mannequin and the girl's lover. A venomous designer who "has gone way past homosexuality" gives Coco a setback or two, but he never threatens her ability to survive imperiously as Coco Chanel.

"I've felt all along that Coco and I were alike," Kate said at the time, "that we're two females who have never been intimidated by the world, who never shifted our stripes to conform to public opinion. She is practical, vulnerable and a fighter. She's not afraid to put herself on the chopping block. She's taken some real body blows. And her capacity for survival is what fascinates me. You know, I'd play this part for free. Because that's me, Coco, on the chopping block now." But none of these qualities was in Lerner's script. For *Coco*'s audiences, the heroine existed purely as a reflection, an extension, of the personality and life of Katharine Hepburn.

Kate had not submitted to Coco any more than she had to Tracy Lord. Both were indivisibly Kate. "Now that I've become like the Statue of Liberty or something—now that I've come to an age where they think I might disappear—they're fond of me," she said of her audiences, who packed

---

* The New York stores represented were: Saks, Best, Ohrbach's and Bloomingdale's.

the house for every performance. Unable to dance, she kicked and pranced outrageously. Confined to a small singing range, she nonetheless expanded it by using the pattern of her voice to imply singing. Locked into a book that had little charm, she managed to dissolve her audiences into gales of laughter on the strength of her delivery of a constant stream of sharp, often catty, one-liners. Striding across to mid-stage and pausing, she could spew the word "shit!" in a rasping Hepburnian contralto that implied she had just invented the expletive. This last device, which had been her own idea, opened the second act, and Coco Chanel was appalled when she heard of this "vulgarity." The rich and middle class looked to her and to her designs for true elegance, a legend that Kate seriously threatened by suggesting Coco Chanel could be publicly profane.

Kate might have been adored by her audiences, but the company was not entirely enamored of her. For one thing, she set a terrible pace for everyone to follow; and for another, during rehearsals, she insisted the theater be kept at a cool 60 degrees with the stage door open to the winter winds. By the time of the previews, almost everyone in the cast had colds. After listening to their complaints, Kate arrived one morning with a huge box of sweaters. Dumping them in her dressing room, she informed the cast that anyone who was chilly could have a sweater but that, since she liked the cold, the door would remain open and the thermostat down.

December 18, opening night, was like "a disastrous party. Everyone who was anyone was there," *Time* reported, "primed for some kind of theatrical night of nights. Dramatically, the champagne was flat, the hors d'oeuvres tasted of sawdust and the small talk on- and offstage sagged into yawns."

Clive Barnes, of *The New York Times*, wrote that "[Miss Hepburn's] . . . presence is a blessing. She growls out the most ordinary lines as if they were pearls of great price, gems of wit, nuggets of wisdom. She grins and she is enchanting. She prowls gloweringly down to the footlights, mutters a word for ordure in an idiomatically terse fashion, and remains devastatingly charming.

"This is not acting in any of the accustomed fashions of

acting. Her singing voice is unique—a neat mixture of faith, love and laryngitis, unforgettable, unbelievable and delightful. Dear Miss Hepburn—perhaps they should have made a musical of your life rather than a dress designer. They say some beauty is ageless—yours is timeless."

Most of Kate's good friends attended the after-the-opening party—Luddy, Laura, Ruth and Garson, Lauren Bacall, Sue Seton, Irene Selznick. Alan Lerner's wife, Helen, wore a marvelous Chanel gown, but Kate appeared in beige pants and black sweater. The one person who had not attended the opening—although Lerner had believed until the last minute that she would—was Coco Chanel, who never did see the musical based on her life. If she had, one cannot help but wonder what she would have thought or if any part of it would have been familiar to her. The story had become pure fiction and Kate's performance a parody of her own personality rather than Coco Chanel's. Indeed, Kate had been honest when she had said, "That's me, Coco."

Despite reviews that were uniformly harsh to the production, Kate, by sheer force of her personality, not only kept *Coco* running for more than seven months but she filled the theater every performance. Those reviewers who had pointed out what had gone wrong with the show were now asking themselves, "Can Hepburn single-handedly be keeping this outdated musical showboat afloat?" The answer became clear after August 1, 1970, the night Kate waved farewell to her last audience, who stood and cheered until she raised her hands for silence.

Tears welled in Kate's eyes and a kind of breathless emotion charged her voice as she spoke. "It's obviously an enormously confusing experience to stop in the middle of something that means as much to me as this play did—has—does—and the things that it has represented to me in what people can do for each other. Alan Lerner had the confidence to trust me to do it. I had two good friends—Roger Edens—who's dead, and Sue Seton—who teaches me every day—who had the force to convince me that I would be able to do this. Then I started rehearsals and I was very, very frightened—and all these people whom you see in back of me *really* gave me the faith to go on. Then there was the terror of the opening night, and for some wonderful reason for me, you people gave me a feeling that you believed that I could do it. I've lived a very, very fortunate life because I had a father and mother who believed in me. I had brothers and sisters who believed in me—and a few friends who have believed in me—and I cannot begin to thank you enough—and I hope that *you* learn the lesson that I have learned. That is—I love you and . . . you love me."

A few days after *Coco* had opened, Walter Kerr had written in *The New York Times:* "The show has become a showcase, a form of endearment, a gesture of assent, an open palm of respect. Miss Hepburn will never be old enough or tired enough to undergo one of those official evenings of tribute at which everyone gathers to summarize and reminisce. And so it's been arranged right now, with her doing all the work. If *Coco* is anything, it is Miss Hepburn's gala Benefit Performance for our benefit." Kate's "I-love-you-and-you-love-me" speech was a fitting ending to such a benefit.

Kate's audience had not reseated themselves for her farewell words. As she finished, bowed slightly and then with a grand sweep of her hand paid tribute again to the cast, her fans moved forward toward the rim of the stage. Kate smiled a last smile and hurried off.

What happened at the Mark Hellinger Theatre that night exposed the same kind of audience-performer interaction that had existed at Judy Garland concerts. That Kate should become a cult figure was ironic, for she had been expounding on her disregard of public adulation for nearly four decades. "Just do your job and get on with it" had been both her and Tracy's motto. But by the end of *Coco* she had recognized the truth, that all along she had needed the love of her audiences, and had tested them—as she had Tracy and her father—by being as difficult as she could. Several times during the run of the play, when a flash camera went off in the theater, she halted the performance by moving to the footlights to address the culprits like a high-school principal who had just found a student smoking marijuana. At least once she refused to continue until two people in the audience stopped talking. Another time, outside street noise of construction distracted her (the stage door still remained open at her command), and at intermission she went to ask the construction workers to silence their equipment during her matinees.

Tracy's death had brought an overwhelming amount of sympathy her way. In the four years that had passed since then, Tracy and Hepburn had become a romantic legend. Louise had been turned into the unbending wife, and Kate, with dignity, had sacrificed a *normal* life for a *back-street* existence. Kate was now regarded as that exceptional woman who had been faithful to her personal standards and had made the world accept those standards as its own. Tracy would belong to her in death as he never had in life. Kate—the rich, the beautiful, the famous, the arrogant—had loved devotedly, selflessly, without any of the rewards a marriage would have brought and in the face of possible public censure. She had given, taken, suffered and survived, and had done so without any loss to her great and ebullient spirit. More than that, to her audiences, Kate, not unlike Judy Garland, had been a constant throughout their lives. For thirty-seven years, Katharine Hepburn had been making films and they had watched her grow from a beautiful young rich girl to a magnificent older woman.

The fine French actress Danielle Darrieux* replaced Kate in *Coco*. Darrieux could sing and dance and looked gloriously chic in Beaton's costumes. Even so, the show closed in less than two months after Kate left the cast.

During the run of the play, Kate had been nominated for a Tony as Best Actress in a musical. (She lost to her good friend Lauren Bacall for her performance in *Applause*, the musical adaptation of *All About Eve*.) For the televised award proceedings, she had filmed *Always Mademoiselle*, a moving production number from the show, and the clip remains as visual evidence of Kate's daring adventure in the musical theater. Directly after she left the cast, she made her debut as

---

* Danielle Darrieux (1917–   ). A major star of French and international films, her career began in 1931 as a romantic ingenue in *Le Bal*, and progressed through the decades to chic, women-of-the-world roles. *La Ronde* (1950), *Lady Chatterley's Lover* (1955), *The Young Girls of Rochefort* (1967). After World War II, she was accused of collaboration with the Nazis based on her participation in some shows before Nazi troops. Finally, exonerated after narrowly escaping execution, she resumed her career as successfully as before.

a recording artist when she re-created the role of Coco for the Paramount Records cast album.* Two weeks later, she departed for Spain to co-star with Vanessa Redgrave, Irene Papas and Genevieve Bujold† in *The Trojan Women* for Greek director Michael Cacoyannis.** Asked why she wanted to film the Euripides drama written in 415 B.C., Kate replied, "I've never done Greek Tragedy and before my time runs out I'd like to have done everything."

She and Phyllis had stopped in London to see Bryan Forbes for a weekend en route to Atienza, Spain, the location for *The Trojan Women*. On Sunday, Kate rang up the manager of the Drury Lane Theatre to ask if she could look around, her thought at the time being to bring *Coco* to London the following spring. The management was happy to oblige; but since *The Great Waltz*, their current attraction, was a smash hit, it seemed doubtful that *Coco* could be scheduled for a year, or even two, a great disappointment to Kate, who seemed unwilling to settle for any other theater.

Monday morning the two women flew to Paris so Kate could see Coco Chanel. For some reason the meeting was held in a park. "Do you know she never sits down when you talk to her?" Kate complained to an interviewer in Spain. "Finally, I was so tired I had to sit down on the ground like this." She demonstrated by squatting cross-legged on the floor of the small, spare house (overlooking a "vast, parched Spanish plain") that was to be her accommodation during the filming of *The Trojan Women*.

---

* On the album Hepburn sings "The World Belongs to the Young," "Mademoiselle Cliche de Paris," "On the Corner of the Rue Cambon," "The Money Rings Out Like Freedom," "Coco," "Ohrbach's, Bloomingdale's, Best and Saks," and "Always Mademoiselle."

† Vanessa Redgrave (1937–   ), English star of *Isadora* (1968), *Camelot* (1967), *Mary, Queen of Scots* (1971). She later won the Academy Award for Best Supporting Actress for *Julia* (1977). She is a member of the famous Redgrave family of actors.

Irene Papas (1926–   ), Greek star of *Antigone* (1954), *Electra* (1962) and *Zorba the Greek* (1964).

Genevieve Bujold (1942–   ). Born in Montreal, she starred in many French and American films and received an Academy Award nomination as Best Actress in 1969 for *Anne of the Thousand Days*.

** Michael Cacoyannis (1922–   ) had won high critical acclaim for his direction of *The Trojan Women* in the off-Broadway production in 1963, as well as popular recognition for his film direction of *Zorba the Greek*.

Seeing Kate in person, no one could possibly confuse her with the elegant Chanel. Off the set of *The Trojan Women* she wore her uniform—khaki trousers, a large black shirt with rolled up sleeves, a wide-brimmed straw hat to protect her from the strong rays of the sun, bare feet stuffed loosely into a pair of men's leather sandals. The rigor of appearing eight times a week for more than seven months in a monster musical had taken its toll. She was severely thin, and her skin was stretched tightly over her cheek and jaw bones. Her body looked surprisingly slight—almost frail—but the moment she began to talk, one could sense the toughness that constituted her character. For her role as Hecuba, the old queen of Troy, she wore one costume throughout most of the film—a torn black widow's dress streaked with dust. (The Greeks have conquered the city of Troy with the help of the wooden horse. Hecuba has been imprisoned in a wooden hut in an encampment outside the city walls. Her husband and sons are all dead, and she awaits the orders that will decide her fate.)

"As the old queen, I have to urge the captive women not to kill themselves, to say death is empty while life still has hope," she explained to a visitor. "[Hecuba] was a practical old dame." Reporters, photographers and visitors now found her quite amenable about being approached. The former belligerence toward such "invaders of her privacy" seemed to have vanished. Tracy's name invariably crept into the conversation, and she always had a quote or two that stoked fire to his legend of greatness as an actor and to the sanctity of their long liaison.

Kate and Cacoyannis never did make up differences that began during the first week of shooting. In the unenviable position of directing four such strong and individual actresses as Redgrave, Bujold, Papas and Hepburn, he apparently held to the belief that he must take the upper hand or lose control. His imperious attitude did not help. Kate bristled at it. To add to her discomfort, Kate was twenty to thirty-five years older than her three co-stars and very much aware of how the camera would pick this up. As usual, Kate was everywhere and into everything during the first week; and she had her own ideas on how her scenes should be played, filmed and cut. She and Cacoyannis drew swords instantly in an uneven match, for Cacoyannis not only was the director and the author of the screenplay but had directed *The Trojan Women* off-Broadway in 1963 to stunning reviews and had filmed the Greek tragedy *Electra* in 1961 with much success. He considered himself the master of the form and, as a Greek, more knowledgeable of the history of his native land than Kate could hope to be.

The Trojan Women never rose above the two major problems that were evident from the start: the staginess of the screenplay, which gave it the visual look of filmed theater, and the jarring, disparate accents of the four women in the cast. However, despite the film's lukewarm reception and the limited distribution it received, *The Trojan Women* contains some riveting moments. Kate was undoubtedly miscast, the arrogance she portrays setting the wrong tone for the grief-stricken, vengeful Hecuba. Yet in one short scene—when she hisses, "Kill her!" at the Greek king as he is deciding the fate of Helen of Troy—Kate sets the screen afire and Hecuba comes searingly, if only momentarily, alive.

Kate returned to New York by Christmas and went directly into rehearsals on *Coco* for a cross-country tour to commence in Cleveland at the Public Music Hall on January 11, 1972. Opening night proved to be dramatic. News reached Kate just before curtain that Coco Chanel had died the previous day in Paris. After her performance, for which she received a standing ovation, Kate stepped to the footlights, tears in her eyes, a catch in her voice, and announced Coco's death, adding, "Miss Chanel was a remarkable woman with a fine mind and a fine heart and the driving inspiration behind my performance. She is not with us anymore, but I hope that someplace she may be listening."*

The pace of the touring show was faster than in the New York production, which helped to point up the brittle laugh lines. Some of the choreography was redone and better executed, and some of the new cast members were more suited for their roles. All in all, the road show of *Coco* was a better production than the original Broadway show.

The late hours, the temporariness of hotel rooms and the tepid quality of room-service meals were not easy to bear.

---

* Chanel was buried the following day in Lausanne, Switzerland, but the show did not close in memorium.

But the enthusiasm of the audiences greatly compensated. For an actor, nothing can compare to the instant gratification of a well-received performance. Kate had hungered for this kind of acclaim ever since the success of *The Philadelphia Story* had piqued her appetite. In Cleveland, a reporter posed the question, "Why would Katharine Hepburn hit the road?" Her answer was simple. She had contracted to tour if the producer chose to do so. Kate, of course, retained a good percentage of the show which, because of its huge initial and running costs, had not yet earned back its investment for Paramount Pictures, who were now reconsidering exercising their film rights. Paramount's new young executives were doubtful that the current movie-going public would even have heard of Coco Chanel and had grave reservations that Katharine Hepburn, on her own, could carry a film that would have to be budgeted at between eighteen and twenty million dollars.

Kate's tour was to be a warm-up for a game that never was to be played. But for six months, as she crisscrossed the country, the Hepburn cult grew. To some of the young men and women who followed her from town to town, theater to theater, she represented the worldly older woman, totally independent of society's opinion of her; to others, the idealized lover-mother and mistress. Most saw her as the theater and film's grande dame, a staunch survivor of indomitable strength whose very presence inspired courage. Unlike the members of the Garland cult, few of Kate's followers ever dared to try to intrude upon her privacy. One fan (a youth in 1972) claims that, existing on peanut butter sandwiches, he hitchhiked to every city on Kate's *Coco* tour, did not miss one performance (he has the theater stubs to prove this), stood outside various theaters in the full blast of winter to catch a glimpse of her, and yet never had the temerity either to speak to Kate or to send her a note.

The high point of the tour was to be her appearance in Hartford at the Bushnell Auditorium, where she had last been seen in 1942 in *Without Love*. While in Hartford she stayed with her father's widow in the house on Bloomfield Avenue. Instead of the zenith, Hartford proved to be the nadir of the tour. Everything that could go wrong did—from the mechanical failure of Cecil Beaton's demon turntable to the worst February snowfall Hartford had experienced in several decades. The reviews were disastrous. ("They said I was quite talentless and should have stayed home," she is quoted as having commented.) And then there was the case of the assaulting chauffeur, fifty-five-year-old Luella G. West, a trained nurse by trade, whom Kate claims she had hired as a temporary maid-chauffeur and then fired for rudeness.

Late one night after an evening performance, Kate, Mrs. Hepburn, Phyllis, and Charles Newhill, Kate's former chauffeur, returned home. As they approached the front door, Kate noticed that a ground-floor window that had previously been shut was open. She insisted she lead the way to rout any intruder who might still be inside. The small group entered the darkness single file, Newhill behind Kate, Phyllis behind Newhill, and the seventy-year-old Madelaine Hepburn nervously bringing up the rear. Kate thought she heard sounds at the top of the front stairs and started doggedly up, the others following behind her. When she reached the top, Kate pulled open a closet door and out jumped the sizable Miss West, hammer in hand, ready to strike. She and Kate struggled and Kate went "over and over, down the stairs" as Newhill jumped into the fray. Madelaine Hepburn crouched back against the wall and Phyllis ran to telephone the police.

In the struggle, the woman had bitten the index finger of Kate's left hand through to the bone and then had disappeared out the front door. "The finger hung by a *thread*," Kate recalled of the bizarre encounter. "Phyllis got me to a doctor. I was in agony. Next day, I had to go on for a matinee in a splint. My brother Robert, who's a doctor, found a Dr. Watson, a wonderful man, who grafted it back on."*

In every city on the rest of the tour, Kate was seen by a hand specialist to make sure no infection set in, which could have cost her the finger. Yet not only did she refuse to sink the road tour, or even to interrupt it, she never missed a

---

* Hepburn's assailant had nearly severed the finger from Kate's left hand when Hepburn put her hand over the woman's chin and mouth in an effort to push her away. The incident occurred on February 21, 1971. Luella G. West was fined fifty dollars and given a suspended six-month jail sentence on September 11, 1971. Hepburn had not pressed charges, but Miss West's lawyer was quoted as saying, "Attacking Katharine Hepburn in Hartford is like attacking the judge before sentencing."

performance; and unless they had read about it, no members of the audience were aware of her pain or her inability to do much with her left hand.

The tour ended at the Ahmanson Theatre in Los Angeles in June. Kate had won over theater audiences (if not reviewers) across the country, but not the hardheaded executives at Paramount Pictures. *Coco* was not to be filmed.

Kate was exhausted and not at all sure of what she wanted to do next. For the second time, Fenwick and the activity of the growing Hepburn clan did not appeal to her. She felt lonely and belatedly bereaved. In California, Tracy's spirit hovered close by and everything seemed a reminder of their years together. George Cukor suggested she confront her loneliness. He offered her Tracy's bungalow for as long as she wanted it. Kate gratefully accepted.

Cukor had kept up the property, but it had remained unoccupied since Tracy's tenancy. A golden June sun blazed overhead and vibrant fuchsia covered one entire side of the small white house. Bowls of fresh-cut flowers—a welcome gift from her landlord—graced most of the rooms inside. Above the fireplace hung one of Tracy's few acquisitions—a model of an antique sailing ship—and on the walls, some of Kate's own landscapes, painted when she and Tracy had been in Cuba. Tracy's favorite big black-leather chair sat in a corner of the living room, commanding a view of the outdoor path to the front door. His bedroom door was closed; and Kate, Phyllis behind her, threw it open. Sun streamed in rivulets across the hardwood floors. The hospital equipment was gone. Otherwise, the room remained as it had been the day Tracy had died.

CHAPTER 26

While Kate was on the West Coast, Kate's old school friend Elizabeth Rhett (Murphy) lived in her house in Turtle Bay. Laura, now an elegant gray-haired lady with a vulnerable, cultured catch in her voice, came into New York from her farm in Holmdel, New Jersey (where she raised long-haired weimaraners), two days a week. She stayed at her own smart beige apartment on Beekman Place overlooking the East River, but she always stopped by Kate's house to make sure things were in order. Except for the acquisition of a television set, nothing much had changed. The gang—"a brace of Marienbadish chic people"—still wandered about the four-story brownstone with six-thirty drinks in their hands. If Kate had been there, perhaps iced tea would also have been served. But otherwise, the faces, the conversations, would have been the same. The gang (Luddy, Laura, Susan Seton and her husband, Florence Rich, and Elizabeth Rhett, among others) gathered in Kate's house much as she had once been drawn to her father's house and now felt toward Tracy's bungalow. The Turtle Bay house was a form of continuum for those who came there, for Kate's personality dominated the rooms even in her absence. Her desk looked as though she had just interrupted some work and was likely to return momentarily to complete it. And, despite Elizabeth Rhett's occupancy for a period of over a year, all of Kate's memorabilia was where she had left it. One wall in her bedroom remained dominated by a profile portrait of her mother, the picture centered and surrounded by dozens of framed photographs of the Hepburn clan. Her Oscar won for *Morning Glory* was on a shelf in the fourth-floor bedroom that she had turned into a small upstairs den. Her two more recent Oscars gleamed in the firelight of the living room from their positions on either side of the mantel, and a most treasured, inscribed photograph of Ethel Barrymore (whom she had gone to visit every day during the last months of her life) had been left on the table beside the couch.

The friends Kate had back East were the ones who truly mattered to her, the ones she considered *really* interested in her problems. In California, she had only "three or four people" whom she called true friends—Cukor, of course, and the Erskines. It helped that Phyllis was with her and that she could swim every day and take long walks. She seldom played golf anymore because she suffered from back problems and the game required a snap. She went to bed at eight-thirty and rose at five A.M. Her life was not glamorous, but Cukor had been right—living in Tracy's house had made her feel far less lonely. She longed to make a film in Hollywood, which she said would be the best of all possible worlds for her at that time. Cukor gave her a copy of Graham Greene's *Travels with My Aunt,* which he planned to film. At first, she did not see how the story—a collection of anecdotes revolving around a young man and his eccentric, vital aunt in her seventies—would make a screenplay. She read the book fifteen times and then finally, seeing a way it could be done, agreed to make the film.

One moment everything was falling into proper order, and the next, disintegrating all around her. In the fall of 1971, *McCall's* printed "excerpts from a soon-to-be-published book by Garson Kanin, *Tracy and Hepburn: An Intimate Memoir.*" Kate reeled with the blow. The memoir was not as intimate as the public might have wished. Mostly the book was a succession of anecdotes, a few with genuine insight, some warm or humorous or just curious. And in almost all instances, the narrator was present, and no revelations were actually made about Kate and Tracy's relationship.* Kanin's book treated their close friendship with extreme good taste and warmth. To Kate, however, its publication marked a public betrayal by Kanin, placing, as she said, "a great strain on our friendship." The situation between Kanin and Kate was made even more difficult due to the proximity of their homes.

The Christmas holidays reunited her with her family in Hartford and for the last time at her father's house. Madelaine had found the place too large for one person to live in and maintain. Dr. Hepburn's will had divided shares in the property to his widow, Kate and his son Robert. After some negotiation, Robert, his father's trustee, made an arrangement with the University of Hartford to buy Madelaine's share for eighty-two thousand dollars. He and Kate then signed quitclaim deeds to the property, giving the university their shares.†

"There was a lifetime of living in that house," Kate recalled, "and we had quite a job of cleaning it up. I was covered with filth, crawling around the floor, thinking the thousand thoughts you can imagine I might be thinking of this place where I had been brought up. Then, in comes my sister Marion with a strange man, both of them looking down at me and Marion saying, 'Oh, Katty, this is Dr. Woodruff, the Chancellor of Hartford University.' I was at a loss for words." Her father's house was finally turned over to the university on January 20, 1972.** Kate was by this time back in California, burrowed into Tracy's bungalow.

For months, she concentrated on her work on *Travels with My Aunt,* so much so that a good portion of the screenplay came from her pen. James Aubrey, then head of Metro, was

* *The New York Times* critic snidely commented that the book should have been titled *Tracy and Hepburn and Kanin.* Another suggested the name *We Three.*
† The house at 201 Bloomfield Avenue was valued at $100,000 in 1972, which made Kate and Dr. Robert Hepburn's shares worth $18,000. The trustees deed is dated January 17, 1972, and was recorded June 7, 1972, with the quitclaim deeds, in Volume 498 at Pages 865, 868 and 871 of the West Hartford Land Records.
** The house at 201 Bloomfield Avenue became a combination office/residence for Dr. Robert Vogel, executive director of the Greater Hartford Consortium for Higher Education.

stunned when he saw the script his company was scheduled to film. For him, the charm of the book had been lost. Also, he now thought Greene's aunt should be shown as a younger woman in flashbacks in the film; and seeing Kate, he knew this could no longer be possible.

"Well, you know I'm not going to be able to shoot that script," he told Kate in a telephone call that she claims she could tell was monitored. Then he said, carefully, "I think . . . and Metro thinks . . . and I agree with them, that we should put it aside for a time."

"You mean I'm fired?" Kate asked. Aubrey managed to get off the telephone without giving a direct reply.

The next day Kate's agents received word that she was being given notice because she had refused to work. "I would never refuse to work ten days before a picture was scheduled to start," Kate commented. "I would consider that an outrage. And I said, 'Go ahead and say I'm fired. It's all right with me.'" Well, anyway they hired Maggie Smith and within ten days they were shooting.

"I thought of suing them because I don't feel things like that should be allowed to happen. The script was practically all mine. Cut to hash, but practically all mine . . . but, then I thought it is a bore, trying to prove that you've been misused. I was never paid a sou for eight months work, sixteen hours a day. I would be curious to know why I was fired. I don't know whether it was Aubrey. . . . The only thing that he did that really offended me was to write me a letter to KathErine. I thought the least he could do when he fired me was to spell my name right."

Added to these setbacks, Kate had developed a painful arthritic condition in her hip and the first signs of the palsy condition that would continue to plague her ever after. Her head and hands shook slightly and her voice developed a quaver. Age and illness were two enemies she could and would gallantly battle. She worked hard to control her movements and to get the shake in her voice to work for her in underscoring and emphasizing words and phrases. Amazingly, she succeeded, but the effort was enormous.

She agreed to do a film, *Daisy Bates*, with her old friend Chester Erskine, who in the end could not get financing. In

February, 1972, producer David Susskind* made a special trip to California to try to convince her to appear in his planned television production of Tennessee Williams's *The Glass Menagerie* as the faded Southern beauty, Amanda Wingfield. He had started on what he calls "the longest wooing for a part in a lifetime of dealing with stars" back in 1965. "That part belongs to Laurette Taylor [who created it]," she told him then. He went back to her in 1967 and she repeated her refusal, adding, "I can't get the memory of Laurette Taylor out of my mind." Susskind was so certain that Kate should play Amanda, he put the property on a back burner, not submitting it elsewhere in the hope of one day persuading her to accept the role. Now he pointed out that Helen Hayes, Gertrude Lawrence, Shirley Booth and Maureen Stapleton had all played Amanda Wingfield and that two generations had never even *seen* Laurette Taylor.

"I'm too thin," she insisted.

"What do you mean, you're too thin?"

"I see her as buxom and rounded and I'm sharp and angular, and I'm too old to learn the new technique of [television] taping."

Susskind said the show could be shot like a film. She still refused but he felt she would eventually capitulate and returned to New York to put together a television package (star, director, scriptwriter).

When Susskind left, she went down to see John Ford in Palm Desert, a vacation and retirement community 140 miles from Los Angeles. Ford had terminal cancer and had been living a reclusive life for years. Although he had remained married to his wife, Mary, for more than forty-five years, his affair with Kate in 1937 had changed things in their marriage. Any pretense of monogamy had been given up and Mary had stood back, giving Ford free rein just so long as he kept his affairs from becoming public knowledge. Kate's visit to Palm Desert could have been awkward, but Mary Ford was a

---

* David Susskind (1920–   ), a talent agent who became a controversial television personality, hosting his own talk show while producing many high-quality productions for theater, television and films. His films include *A Raisin in the Sun* (1961), *Requiem for a Heavyweight* (1962) and *All Creatures Great and Small* (1974).

selfless woman who wanted her husband's last days to be as happy as possible. Also, she knew his real vice had always been alcohol, not women.

Appalled by his wasted appearance and deeply affected by his courage and remaining acerbic wit, Kate spent a week in Palm Desert talking with him for hours on end about old times. Ford tried to sustain these talks, but in the end he asked her to leave—and she understood that he no longer could keep up the façade.*

Kate spent the summer of 1972 at Fenwick. Ely Landau, the producer of *Long Day's Journey into Night* and *The Madwoman of Chaillot*, approached her with the idea of playing Agnes, the mother in Edward Albee's *A Delicate Balance*, which he planned to film in England for the American Film Theatre. Kate greatly respected Landau, but she had reservations about the role of Agnes, a character who is required to describe in some detail her husband's predilection for coitus interruptus, and who flirts with madness. Perhaps she would not have accepted Landau's offer had it not been that Joseph Cotten, her co-star in the stage version of *The Philadelphia Story*, would be appearing with her along with Paul Scofield. Also, Tony Richardson† was to direct.

Kate had first met Richardson when she appeared in the London production of *The Millionairess*. Richardson, only twenty-four at the time, had just come down from Oxford and he says he "thought she was sensational, and wrote to her with enormous enthusiasm and said in the letter, rather boldly . . . 'Do drop over and have tea.'" To his amazement, Kate appeared at his modest flat at Hammersmith. "I didn't have enough money to buy cakes," he admits, "so we had nothing to eat. She was absolutely sweet and charming." Kate and Richardson met again when he wanted to cast her in a Broadway revival of Tennessee Williams's *The Milk Train*

---

* Ford died on August 31, 1973.
† Tony Richardson (1928–   ) directed for stage and screen. His direction of John Osborne's *Look Back in Anger* both on stage (1956) and screen (1958) set the tone for the "Angry Young Men" movement. His other credits include the sensitive *The Loneliness of the Long Distance Runner* (1962), the dazzling *Tom Jones* (1963), for which he won an Oscar, and the misanthropic *The Loved One* (1965).

Doesn't Stop Here Anymore.* Tracy had been ill and Kate had not wanted to leave him.

Richardson's task of persuading her to undertake the role was not easy, for Kate loathed the character of Agnes. He found this odd because, as he says, "There's a lot of that same kind of inflexible, authoritarian quality in her. She suited the part terribly well, the obsession with the home—the New England background—all very 'Kate.' "

Kate claims she took the role to understand it. When filming began in a house just outside London, she recognized that Albee had written about self-protection. "I think we are all *enormously* self-protective. I identified with these people who resented the intruders in their privacy, and I think that's what made me, after not wanting to do it at all, finally decide to go ahead," Kate says. "I'm a very private person. Here were these people, miserable though they might be, and they wanted to keep their 'shell' intact. When two people came in and established a position in the household, they became threatening. The intruders expressed opinions. You don't want people to express opinions in your house. You only want your own opinion to be expressed. I think all of us banish people when they intrude in any sense. Yes, I grasped the play finally. But it wasn't easy."

The film company of *A Delicate Balance* ran immediately into problems. The location site proved a terrible handicap; the rooms in the house were not large enough to allow the cameras and equipment enough space to be moved around. The lighting was poor. Kim Stanley, who had been cast as Agnes's alcoholic sister, suffered a nervous collapse and had to withdraw from the film and be replaced by Kate Reid, who had not had the benefit of the two weeks' rehearsal time given the rest of the cast.† Richardson and Kate drew swords over every scene. Richardson treated *A Delicate Balance* more like theater than film and in the end it remained claustrophobic and static and, indeed, had the feeling of canned theater, an accusation that had been made toward others of Landau's films.

---

* The role in the revival of *The Milk Train Doesn't Stop Here Anymore* was played by Tallulah Bankhead.

† After a slow start, Reid turned in a stunning performance.

Kate very much enjoyed London. The memories were pleasant. She had come there as a young woman on her first true adventure, been acclaimed there as a stage performer, and shared some happy moments there with Tracy. When filming of *A Delicate Balance* had been completed, she decided to stay on and accept David Susskind's offer to film *The Glass Menagerie* in nearby Dulwich. Susskind had fulfilled her final request—that she have a director she could trust. When Susskind announced that he had hired Tony Harvey, who had directed her in *The Lion in Winter*, Kate agreed to make the film—her first for television.

The Glass Menagerie had always been one of Kate's favorite plays. She considered it a classic that said "more about what a lack of money can do to human beings than any play I know." Williams had put all his early suffering, his frustrations, into it, and Kate understood that Amanda Wingfield was the "most tenderly observed, the most accessible woman he ever created." In fact, Kate had a great and deep empathy for the character. After all, Dr. Hepburn had been a Southerner, a Virginian, and the Hepburn family was genteel and educated, but they had almost all known hard times and better days. Kate had had aunts and cousins to base the character upon. She worked hard on the Southern accent with some coaching, but relied mostly on memories of her father's family.

The Glass Menagerie had been filmed before, in 1950, with Gertrude Lawrence as Amanda. Those were the days when a big star simply did not play a frowsy, aging desperate creature. Then a star had to prove how eternally young, fascinating and beautiful she was. Filmed as middle-aged and still vital, Lawrence, in her performance, lost the sense of a woman who refused to accept the truth of having been reduced to humiliating and irrevocable circumstances. Kate played the role more as it had been created for the stage by Laurette Taylor and subsequently by Maureen Stapleton (who appeared in a revival) as older, more ravaged.

Susskind's *The Glass Menagerie* was not beset by the troubles Ely Landau had experienced on *A Delicate Balance*. Still, they both share the feeling of being artificially contained, of plays not fully transformed into movies. The great difference was in the basic material. Williams's talk floats, flowers, ascends and haunts; Albee's nettles, pontificates, puffs along and finally sinks.

After filming ended on *The Glass Menagerie*, Kate's feelings about television did a turnabout. She now decided the medium could be a tremendous challenge and that she might be able to attempt new and different roles, parts she might not be able to sustain on the stage and that a film company would no longer finance. To everyone's surprise, she accepted an invitation from talk-show host Dick Cavett.

Nervous about her first television appearance, she came early to the ABC sound stage where Cavett's show was to be taped.* Aside from Phyllis and some members of Cavett's staff, no studio audience was present. An amazed Cavett hurried from his office onto the set to greet her, alerting the director and camera crew first, thinking that, perhaps, she had confused the times. He found her wandering about in slacks, sandals, turtleneck shirt and a short jacket (not the usual attire for a female guest) and apparently made the decision to shoot the interview anyway just in case she did not return at the appointed hour. The cameras started turning as Kate, unaware she was already on camera, strode onto the set calling out orders to the stage and technical crew as they complained about her lack of makeup and the short time they had to prepare.

"Don't tell me what's wrong, just fix it," she ordered.

Cavett, in shirt sleeves and white tennis shoes, appeared even more nervous than his guest as he escorted her to her seat.

"Do you want to hear the story of my life?" she asked. "I presume that's why I'm here." She then launched into a narrative "brimming with no-nonsense practicality and thoroughly opinionated charm." As she told about her family and Hartford and her early stardom, she neatly inserted comments on such things as scene-stealing, which she explained to a chagrined Cavett was "like you wiggling that white foot while I'm trying to be fascinating." Asked about her ability to

---

* The Cavett show was filmed in one session but televised in two sections, on the nights of October 2 and 3, 1973.

sleep easily, she snapped back, "Clear conscience," adding, "I just think I'm an old bore—I do what I'm supposed to—I come on the program—if I'm supposed to talk, I talk. I go to bed to sleep. I have some food, I eat it. I'm uncomplicated." Cavett came off as the fledgling drama student who had to play a scene with a revered performer. Kate simply took the situation in hand and more or less interviewed herself.

Ostensibly, Kate's appearance on Cavett's show was to coincide with the opening of *A Delicate Balance*. But it kindled a fresh interest in her, and articles and interviews appeared at a stunning rate. The failure of *A Delicate Balance* (which did not get a major release) was offset by the excitement that had been drummed up over her soon-to-be-released first-ever television film, *The Glass Menagerie*. Members of the press seemed to be conducting a race to get there first with an exclusive interview or breathless review. The film was to be televised on Sunday evening, December 18. One film critic had managed to review the production laudatorily, four weeks earlier. On December 14, John J. O'Connor, *The New York Times* television critic, called the production lovely "but not flawless. Miss Hepburn's Amanda is a wonderfully effective blend of Southern gentility and fierce determination, but occasionally, only occasionally, she is overly dominated by another personality, that of a strong-willed, intensely mannered actress named Katharine Hepburn.

"When a temporarily stymied Amanda sits on a couch, puts her chin in her hands and turns in her feet, so that the weight of her legs is resting on her ankles, the portrait is pure Hepburn. The effect is hardly fatal, merely obtrusive. . . . Any reservations about this *Glass Menagerie* are relatively slight. It is a special TV event, demanding attention."*

During her Cavett interview, her host had asked Kate if she was not sorry she had never made a film with Olivier. "Well, neither one of us is dead yet," she retorted sharply enough for Cavett to stumble nervously on in a kind of apologia. Not long after that, George Cukor sent her a script by James

---

* Tennessee Williams comments on this production: "Thank God . . . they cut the narrations down. There was too much of them. And the play itself holds without much narration," adding, "The narrations are not up to the play."

Costigan, *Love Among the Ruins,* which he had agreed to make for ABC television and for which he hoped she might consent to play opposite Olivier. The osteoarthritis in Kate's hip had been giving her progressive trouble and she had recently submitted to a hip-replacement operation. But the project was too irresistible for Kate to decline. Six months after the surgery, she returned to London to make the film, which had a twenty-day shooting schedule.

Love Among the Ruins is an Edwardian comedy, and Kate plays Jessica Medicott, grande dame and former Shakespearean actress, being sued for breach of promise by a young man whose marriage proposal she had accepted in "one mad, impetuous moment." She seeks out a famous barrister, Sir Arthur Granville-Jones (Olivier), to represent her. Fifty years earlier, while touring as Portia in *The Merchant of Venice,* she had had an affair with a poor law student in Toronto. That young man had been Sir Arthur. But despite his attempt to jog her memory ("We made love continuously one weekend"), she fails to recall the man or the incident. Nonetheless, in the manner of romantic comedy, the now wealthy, glamorous pair, both "outrageously candid and addicted to sparkling conversation," fall in love.

Olivier claimed he had been dreading appearing with Kate all his life. Somehow he had assumed she would be very much the prima donna, temperamental, a star rather than an actress. Her professionalism astounded him, as did her stamina. They went back a long way in friendship. Kate had, after all, been a witness at his marriage to Vivien thirty-five years before,* and Olivier had been an admiring friend of Tracy's.

Working with Cukor again for the first time in twenty years (since *Pat and Mike*) was a great joy for Kate. Cukor was fastidious about every aspect of her appearance in the film. Her costumes were magnificent and marvelously flattering— high necks trimmed in soft lace, her hair femininely coiffed, sumptuous hats that cast kind shadows on her face and framed it becomingly. Carefully lighted in soft focus, Kate looked timelessly lovely. The sets were elegant and the final

---

* Olivier had married actress Joan Plowright after his divorce from Vivien Leigh.

film never has a sense of being hurriedly made. What *Love Among the Ruins* lacked was a strong story line and interesting peripheral characters. As long as Kate and Olivier are on screen, the film glitters, but it disintegrates into nothingness when they are gone.*

Cukor had engaged Susie Tracy as the unit's still photographer. She had had only one previous film assignment until then and was very nervous. She and Kate had met once before, in the summer of 1949, when Susie, a teenager at the time, had visited the set of *Adam's Rib*. Tracy had kept his family life and his relationship with Kate quite separate. Having Susie with her in London was a happy circumstance for Kate, who Susie Tracy says, "got a kick out of seeing me loaded down with my cameras." Kate kept a distance between herself and Tracy's daughter, but she did try to make her as comfortable as possible and to help in any way she could. "Miss Hepburn is very photogenic," Susie says. "It is a joy to work with someone like her. When she smiles, her face lights up and her hands are interesting—she uses them! She is warm, vital and humorous.

"I happened to be driving back to town with her one day when she had the driver stop at a charming nursery. She was walking around looking at the plants, dressed in her own casual way—slacks, a little hat tied on with a scarf, no makeup. Suddenly, a man walked in, came directly to her and inquired, 'Do you have any gooseberries?' He had mistaken her for a store employee.

"Miss Hepburn never skipped a beat. 'Gooseberries?' she said. 'Well, I'll have to see.'

"She walked away, found the woman in charge, returned and told him, 'No, sorry, no gooseberries.' He thanked her and left without the slightest idea who she was."

Kate stayed in the country near the studio and after a day's work would jump on her bicycle and pedal off down the nearest country lane, a car following her so that she could stop when she got tired—usually quite a distance on. Her recovery from her hip surgery had been close to miraculous.

Kate and Phyllis returned to New York for three weeks and

---

* Both Hepburn and Olivier won Emmy Awards for Best Actress and Actor in a single performance for their roles in *Love Among the Ruins*.

then left for California. Kate had agreed to co-star with John Wayne in *Rooster Cogburn,* a sequel to Wayne's Academy Award film of 1969, *True Grit.* Meeting him jolted her. "I was born to be your leading lady, Duke," she told him, "twenty-five years too late." Others in the room were aware of the tremendous chemistry that passed between them and made a mockery of their years.

CHAPTER 27

Kate wrote about Wayne, "From head to toe he is all of a piece. Big head. Wide blue eyes. Sandy hair. Rugged skin—lined by living and fun and character. Not by just rotting away. A nose not too big, not too small. Good teeth. A face alive with humor. Good humor, I should say, and a sharp wit. Dangerous when roused. His shoulders are broad—very. His chest massive—very. When I leaned against him (which I did as often as possible, I must confess—I am reduced to such innocent pleasures), thrilling. It was like leaning against a great tree. His hands so big. Mine, which are big too, seemed to disappear. Good legs. No seat. A man's body. Rare in these gay times."

A deep, abiding tenderness between Kate and the thrice-married Wayne was in evidence during the nine weeks they were on location in Oregon for the filming of *Rooster Cogburn*. Kate and the towering six-feet-four-inch Wayne were the same age* and made of the same tough fiber. Though they had not met before, they each shared a long,

---

* John Wayne (1907–1979), born Marion Michael Morrison, known as "Duke" from his football days at U.S.C. and originally as Duke Wayne when he entered films in 1928. He made more than 150 movies. The role of the Ringo Kid in *Stagecoach* (1939) made him a major star. A few of his best films were *The Spoilers* (1942), *She Wore a Yellow Ribbon* (1949), *The Quiet Man* (1952), *The Alamo* (1960) and *True Grit* (1969), for which he won the Academy Award.

close relationship with John Ford, who was Wayne's mentor and frequent drinking companion. From 1928 to 1939, Wayne portrayed the strong, silent hero who rode tall in the saddle in more than eighty movies. Then, Ford, who had been responsible for Wayne's first lead in director Raoul Walsh's *The Big Trail*, cast his friend in the role of the Ringo Kid in *Stagecoach*, and a hero who was to assume mythical proportions was born. To much of the world, Wayne embodied the American spirit—"the crusader of just causes and a leader of men . . . the ultra American, the superpatriot in the most rigid Old Guard style."

Politically, Wayne was a reactionary with the kind of superhawk, fundamentalist ideology that Kate had rejected all her life and that Mrs. Hepburn had loathed. Yet somehow, Kate had been able to rationalize his point of view so that she could accept it. "He was surrounded in his early years in the motion picture business by people like himself. Self-made. Hard working. Independent. Of the style of man who blazed the trails across our country. Who reached out into the unknown. People who were willing to live or die entirely on their own independent judgment. [John] Ford, the man who first brought Wayne into the movies, was cut from the same block of wood. Fiercely independent. They seem to have no patience and no understanding of the more timid and dependent type of person. . . . Pull your own freight. This is their slogan. Sometimes I don't think that they realize that their own load is attached to a very powerful engine. They don't need or want protection. They dish it out. They take it. Total personal responsibility."

Wayne had been the president of the Motion Picture Alliance for the Preservation of American Ideals, a group that was responsible for a great many broken lives and careers during the McCarthy era and against which Kate had once spoken out harshly. He had seemed to have taken on the Vietnam War as a personal crusade, feeling that America had every right to be involved. His craggy features, his huge body in western garb or officer's uniform, his thunderous voice driving men on to battle and possible death came to represent the ultimate macho American man and made Wayne one of the biggest box-office attractions in American films.

Unlike Tracy, Wayne never had any wish to cut Kate down

to size. Wayne's great appeal to women was the duality of his personality. "He's sweet, gentle, and he's a monster," Kate said. But seldom was he a monster with women on or off screen. Wayne was, in fact, almost schoolboyish in his abject respect for what he called "good women," a category Kate automatically fell into. Not only was Kate good, she was tough. "I love her," Wayne beamed to a visitor on the *Rooster Cogburn* location. "You should have seen her up on those mountain locations. She can't ride a hobby horse. But she climbed right up on those horses and gave 'em hell. We had a great girl stunt rider for her, but Kate said, 'She doesn't sit as straight in the saddle as I do.'

"And in one scene she jumped into a kayak and shoved off into a raging river. Yes, sir, she's tough. Christ! She wants to do everything! She can't ride worth a damn and I gotta keep reining my horse in so she can keep up. But I'd hate to think of what this goddamned picture would be without her."

Kate did all her own stunts. "I haven't waited all these years to do a cowboy picture with Wayne to give up a single moment now," she insisted.

"She's so feminine—she's a man's woman. Imagine how she must have been at age 25 or 30 . . . how lucky a man would have been to have found her," Wayne confided.

Less than a year had passed since Kate's hip surgery and she had not ridden a horse in decades. Wayne knew this, just as she knew that he had had a lung removed and was being monitored for any sign of the return of the cancer that had been cut away. Both hated pity or special privileges. But the combined powers of their personalities overwhelmed Stuart Millar,* their director.

Susie Tracy joined the company as still photographer and spent more time getting to know Kate. The Oregon terrain was rough, everything was shot outside and often in high wind and biting cold. Kate did not seem to mind the harsh conditions. Susie photographed her out canoeing with a ranger on Todd Lake and picking little earth-colored bou-

---

* Stuart Millar (1929–   ) gained his first credits as a producer and made some strong films with star performances—*Bird Man of Alcatraz* (1962) with Burt Lancaster, *I Could Go On Singing* (1963) with Judy Garland, *The Best Man* (1964) with Henry Fonda, and *Little Big Man* (1970) with Dustin Hoffman. *Rooster Cogburn* was his second directorial effort.

quets from among the rocks and ledges or in the open fields, which she would stick into whatever was handy, usually an old tin can.

The press was permitted on the set by Wayne, and Kate accepted the intrusion (which she did not like). On the last day of shooting, the presence of the press made her nervous and the final scene had to be reshot several times. When the cameras had stopped turning, Wayne shoved the eye patch he had worn for his role in the film up onto his forehead, took Kate in his arms, and kissed her soundly on the mouth. After he released her, Kate stood stunned for a moment looking around at the strangers on the set and then walked hurriedly away and disappeared. Wayne cleared his throat, lighted a cigar (defying doctor's orders) and spat on the sound-stage floor. His voice "a crash of boulders," he said, "Damn! There's a woman!" He puffed contentedly on his cigar until she returned a short time later, out of costume and in an attractive pantsuit, to share a toast with the cast and crew. Again, Wayne gave her a big bear hug.

"What a wonderful experience," she said, her eyes shining as she stared up at her co-star. Then, turning to the press, "He's one hell of an actor!" They were not to see each other more than a few times again. Kate went back to New York, and Wayne made only one more film before he began his courageous but losing three-year battle against death, undergoing open-heart surgery and then the removal of his stomach.*

One critic called *Rooster Cogburn* "Something of an *African Queen Goes West.*" The stories did bear a certain similarity. Kate is Eula Goodnight, a spinster whose clergyman father is murdered by outlaws. The Indian native village where father and daughter taught their faith is destroyed. Wayne, as Cogburn, is a hard-drinking marshal on the skids who reluctantly takes Eula with him to track down the murderers, and just as reluctantly finds a soft spot in his heart for her. Unlike Hepburn and Bogart in *The African Queen*, the two do not end up together.

Rooster Cogburn, released in October, 1975, was a tremen-

---

* Wayne's last film was *The Shootist* (1976). When he died, a congressional medal was awarded him posthumously.

dous commercial success. The critics all pointed out the second-time-around feeling of the plot and the pedestrian direction, but they were almost unanimous in their gratitude for a film "featuring two stars of the grand tradition who respond to each other with a verve that makes the years disappear."

In June, 1974, Kate returned to Hartford to narrate a film entitled *Resolved to Be Free,* produced by her brother-in-law, Ellsworth Grant, and sponsored by the Society for Savings (a banking concern) in conjunction with the State Bicentennial Commission. The film, a half-hour documentary on Connecticut's role in the War for Independence, was to be available, free of charge, to schools and other interested groups, following its premiere in early 1975. Kate is especially stirring when she repeats the famous lines, "Men, you are all marksmen—don't one of you fire until you see the whites of their eyes!"* Duke Wayne could not have done better.

The house in Turtle Bay had not undergone any changes, but one of Kate's neighbors was now Broadway composer Stephen Sondheim. During the winter of 1974–75, Sondheim was working through the nights on the film score for *A Little Night Music* and the piano kept Kate awake. One night, in a fury, she got up and, barefoot and clad only in thin pajamas, sloshed her way through the snow in her back garden, climbed the fence between the houses and made her way to the ground floor of Sondheim's music room. "I pressed my face against the window and looked in," she later admitted. "I must have looked like an old witch. He had another young man with him and they had drinks in their hands, and all of a sudden they both looked at me, and absolutely froze. I just stood there. Seconds passed. They just stared at me. I stared at them. I disappeared. Afterwards—*Silence.*"

She still kept very much to herself. The six-thirty group gathered several evenings a week. She had them to early dinner and dismissed them shortly after. Occasionally, she went to a friend's house for dinner or to a movie. One night she came out of a movie on Fifty-eighth Street to find her car hemmed in by a double-parked truck. Her only recourse, she

---

* Credited to William Prescott during the battle on Breed's Hill, June 17, 1775.

decided, was to drive her car deep onto the sidewalk and make a sharp turn out. The line of people waiting to get into the theater had recognized Kate, and they stood back to make room and to watch what she would do. "I gave it the gas," she explained, "aimed at the crowd—and turned amid cheers— 'That's it Katie, ride em!' It was thrilling."

She once had claimed that she had no pictures of the dead displayed. But a framed photograph of Dr. Hepburn now rested on the bureau in her third-floor bedroom and one of Tracy—youthful, handsome, wearing a polo helmet and flanked by some elegant polo ponies—occupied a major portion of her bedside table. Behind it rested a portrait of Tracy, seated, pensive, painted by her in the sixties. Elsewhere in the room was a small bronze bust, "that I did of him in wax in about ten minutes once . . . *that* profile, I think it's really caught him!" she boasted.

Not long after *Rooster Cogburn* was finished, Kate agreed to appear later in the year on Broadway for twelve weeks in Enid Bagnold's *A Matter of Gravity,* tour with it on the road for five or six weeks beforehand,* and for six months after the New York engagement. Kate had encountered Enid Bagnold thirty years before when R.K.O. purchased the English author's best-selling novel *National Velvet* for her.† Kate eventually decided the role (later played by Elizabeth Taylor and filmed by Metro) did not suit her.

Kate and Bagnold, who was eighty-six at the time, struck up a friendship. "Enid is quite extraordinary," Kate commented. "My God, imagine writing a play at her age!"

Presumably, Kate chose this play because of her admiration for the elderly playwright and author, because the role was strong, and because, as she said, "I always feel that if something is difficult—as the theater has always been for me—it must be good for me to do it." *A Matter of Gravity* was portentous and ponderous and the characters unlikely and disagreeable except for the eccentric Mrs. Basil, "the old lady of the mansion"—a thirty-room estate at Oxford in

---

* The show actually stayed on the road for twelve weeks before the Broadway opening.

† Enid Bagnold (1890–1981) was also the author of the novel *Serena Blandish* and the very successful play *The Chalk Garden.* In private life, she was Lady Jones, widow of the one-time Reuters Press Chairman Sir Roderick Jones.

which Mrs. Basil had chosen to live in only one room. A new cook-housekeeper named Dubois enters Mrs. Basil's world and the grandson she has doted on brings home four dubious friends. The woman who has feared change and death, who did not believe in God, nor the breaking down of class distinctions, suddenly witnesses a miracle. "She sees, with her own eyes, Dubois rise in the air as stately as a zeppelin, and bounce off the ceiling with plaster in her hair. Now she knows, as she says incomprehensibly: 'If only there were a mystery it would be the ladder to all mysteries.'"

The failings of the play were irrelevant. Audiences who came to see *A Matter of Gravity* came to see "Miss Hepburn play rather than the play Miss Hepburn is in." *A Matter of Gravity* opened in Philadelphia. Luddy had moved back to his family home a few years earlier and the two held a reunion after the show. The following morning Luddy met her at her hotel and they had breakfast in her suite. Luddy was now seventy-seven. Ill and aging, he still had the old natty look, the gallant manner, and his devotion to Kate had never wavered. From Philadelphia, the show went to Washington, New Haven, Boston and Toronto. By the end of the pre-Broadway tour, *A Matter of Gravity* had recouped its original investment. And the reason was Kate.

"I have rarely seen Miss Hepburn better even in the movies," Clive Barnes wrote in *The New York Times* on February 4, 1976, the morning after *A Matter of Gravity* opened on Broadway. ". . . her acting is now in the lambent heat of its Indian summer. Even her stylizations have become style in the certainty of their execution—so her startled and amused gentility, her crisp, ineffably unanswerable way with a cliché, all are unforgettable. Admirers of acting in that grand mannerism nowadays so easily lost, should see this performance and etch it on their memories. . . . *A Matter of Gravity* is not especially grave and there is probably too much matter, and too little art, but there is always Miss Hepburn, whose very presence could make a bonfire out of an old East Grinstead telephone directory."

Barnes returned to see the play a second time. Unable to contain his admiration for Kate within the boundaries of a review, he followed up on his daily review with a tribute in the Sunday drama section of *The Times* on February 15: "In

A Matter of Gravity Miss Hepburn . . . is acting better than she has ever before in her life. I'm allowing for some fine performances, particularly in films, and rather discounting the sheer loveliness that made gossamer of *The Philadelphia Story*. The loveliness is still with us, ostentatiously older, not as much older as proclaimed. But, there is something different here, now. It's as though the feathery bravura and the challenging nasality and a chin held so high that one scarcely dares question the authenticity behind so much panache had all dissolved at last, had been absorbed into simplicity, had come home to roost and rest, leaving only a clear intention in the eye, an economy of gesture (except for that walking stick the lady dropped twice on opening night, obviously because she had no conceivable use for it), and a directness of address—sometimes forceful, sometimes most quietly bemused—that together bespeak plainly the actress's sincerity. She isn't decorating, she *means* every bloody word of it. . . . In her tartness and her melting laughter, Miss Hepburn is integrity incarnate, piercingly authentic."

Again Barnes took aim at the writing of *A Matter of Gravity*, which he called, "at sixes and sevens as a play, willfully untidy, subject to dizzy spells, possessed by wanderlust, sometimes downright inexplicable. . . . Yet," he admits, "[Miss Bagnold] wrote the part Miss Hepburn is playing, and if she hadn't, in some mysterious way, written it honestly, Miss Hepburn would not have so much to be honest about. There's just no doubt that Miss Hepburn has got hold of something strong, tangible and real. Something apart from herself. And she had to find it somewhere." Kate had finally won over the New York critics and in the process redeemed Enid Bagnold's octogenarian effort single-handedly.

A Matter of Gravity could have had a long, successful run. But after twelve weeks, Kate insisted on stepping out of the play as originally planned, and it closed the first week in May. Two years earlier, a young director, Richard Colla, had sent her a script that she thought would be a wonderful escapade. Titled *Olly Olly Oxen Free*, the story was about an eccentric old junkyard proprietress who befriends two adventurous youngsters and helps them repair a hot-air balloon which accidentally takes the three of them aloft for the ride of their lifetimes. Kate had told Colla she would do it if he could find the money, "Because I've always wanted to fly a balloon." Colla now had financing and Kate did not go back on her verbal agreement, even though the budget was modest and the distribution unsure.

The film was made in California in the summer of 1976. Kate's role contained some dangerous stunts, and Colla had hired a double to do them for her. For one shot a stuntman, dressed as Kate, was readying himself for the moment when the cameras would start turning; as Kate's character, Miss Pudd, he was to grab on to a rope hanging from the rapidly escaping balloon. "That man doesn't look a thing like me at all," Kate snapped. Sweeping past him and into the shot, she grabbed hold of the rope as it dipped and then lifted her off the ground, holding her airborne for a few moments until crew members pulled her down.

The picture's finale was Kate and the two boys descending in the balloon on the Hollywood Bowl concert stage during a rendition of the "1812 Overture."* After the scene was shot, Kate climbed out of the balloon and announced to the many thousands of spectators who filled the Bowl, "This should prove to all of you that if you're silly enough you can do anything."

Kate was marvelous in the film, her two young co-stars engaging, and the balloon scenes spectacular. But the script never reached the same heights. Colla could not get a release, the fear being that Kate on her own could not carry the low-budget movie. Two years later the film played in mid-western theaters, but Kate's name had no marquee lure. Film and theater audiences obviously were very different groups. Finally, *Olly Olly Oxen Free* opened in New York in June, 1981, with no greater success; and after that it became known as Kate's lost film. *Olly Olly Oxen Free* contains some of her most enchanting latter-day footage, which makes its unrealized potential just that much more disappointing.

In October, 1976, she rejoined the company of *A Matter of Gravity* for a six-month tour, playing in Denver, Vancouver, San Francisco, Los Angeles, San Diego and Phoenix. A few

---

* For this shot, Hepburn, McKenzie and Dimster were held aloft over the stage until, on signal, the balloon was slowly pulled down by ropes as the orchestra darted out of its way.

days after the play opened at the Ahmanson Theatre in Los Angeles to excellent reviews, Kate stepped into a hole while gardening at the bungalow and fractured her ankle in three places. She continued in a wheelchair after missing two performances. During one show a woman photographer took a flash picture of her; and Kate, wheeling herself to the footlights, yelled out, "You're a pig. You have no consideration for the actors trying to concentrate during difficult scenes or for the people who paid good money to come here. Such a lack of consideration is an illness of our society." Then she pivoted and wheeled herself back to her original position and went on with the scene.

The transition from being Kate to becoming Mrs. Basil was not as jarring for an audience as one would suspect. The character she played was fiercely involved with issues that concerned Kate—"It's a me-me-me era," she said. "Right and wrong are mixed up. Integrity is not held in any great esteem. If we behave like mutts and roll around dissipating, being exhausted, what are we going to be? Mush!" And Mrs. Basil shares these opinions with equal passion.

The play closed in Phoenix in March, whereupon Kate joined her family at Fenwick. Aunt Kat's coming was much looked forward to by her nieces and nephews. The house—despite the March gale winds whipping around the corners, a pearlescent, depressing gray sea and bleak vistas seen through the many-windowed rooms—was always lively with Kate's arrival. Rooms were littered with reminders of her occupancy; canvas bags filled with scripts and books covered tabletops and were propped against furniture, scarves and old hats were balled up in the corners of chairs, glasses (misplaced constantly) could be found on ledges or windowsills and shoes kicked off might be in the way from one room to another. Kate loved to cook, and the big six-burner kitchen stove kept the windows steamed a good part of the day while countertops were covered with equipment and ingredients and the wastebasket was filled to overflowing. Her unmistakable voice filled Fenwick's large, comfortable rooms with enthusiastic conversation, her hardy laughter punctuating her speech. When the telephone rang more than she wished, she would pick it up and, if the caller was not a family member or close friend, say, "Katharine Hepburn? She's not here. This is her sister."

Marion and Peggy had matured into serious-minded women. But when Kate was with them, they regained their youthful spirit and sense of fun. Kate had always been and remained a strong-willed, opinionated woman, hard to win a point from in a heated discussion. She believed that standards must be passed from one generation to the next, and none of her nieces or nephews was spared her views. God "was a concept too vast for her mind to consider," but she believed in "the lessons of Jesus Christ" despite her feeling, shared with Marx, that "religion was a sop for the masses."

Late that summer she went to London as a guest of Enid Bagnold to discuss the possibility of presenting *A Matter of Gravity* in the West End. The older woman told Kate quite frankly that she should have a facelift, confessing that she had had one in 1956 "as a sort of celebration for the success of my play *The Chalk Garden*." Bagnold directed Kate to a Glasgow plastic surgeon, John Mustarde. Kate traveled incognito to Scotland with Bagnold and made immediate arrangements. Bagnold, in an unguarded interview that Kate did not appreciate, acknowledged that hers "was done by the late Sir Archibald McIndon, who took enough skin off my face to cover a handbag. Kate," she claimed, "didn't need anything like that. She only needed the skin beneath her eyes raised to correct a downward slant. . . . After the operation Kate said to the surgeon, 'I'll go home and go to bed.'

"But he said, 'Rubbish. Absolutely no need. Go and take some photographs of our beautiful Scottish coastline.'

"In the end it almost went wrong. Kate was staying at a hotel under some very carefully chosen alias, but her secretary [Phyllis] had forgotten to change the luggage labels which all said *Miss Katharine Hepburn*."

The possibility of a London production of *A Matter of Gravity* ended, and not long after the facelift Kate and Phyllis flew home. For several months Kate relaxed at Turtle Bay and at Fenwick, swimming whenever she could no matter how cold the water. In January, 1978, George Cukor came to visit her and to see if she would work with him one more time. Cukor, now almost eighty, did not feel he could stand the pressures of a major film—but, perhaps, another television production? Kate would have found it difficult to deny Cukor anything, and he suggested they collaborate on Emlyn Williams's *The Corn Is Green*. She got the play and read it. It had power and hope and was about ". . . someone moving forward, not falling backward, about someone at the wheel of their life instead of being dominated by excuses."

Agreeing straightaway, she immediately pressed for the play to be shot in its proper locale—Wales. Within a few weeks she and Cukor were in London and Wales searching for a cast and locations. Eight weeks later they had completed both tasks. "Walking from George's apartment," Kate recalled, "—I was living just down the way from him—I have to say a fleeting thought crossed my mind.

"What about those two young ones we'd just interviewed and cast [Ion Saynor and Toyah Wilson]? They are pretty attractive. Who's going to look at you, Kathy?

"Oh, hell, who cares. It's a great play . . . and it's life isn't it? You plow ahead and make a hit. And you plow on and someone passes you. Then someone passes them. Time levels."

Miss Moffat in the 1941 Broadway production of *The Corn Is Green* had been Ethel Barrymore's last great stage role.* Five years later, Bette Davis had given a memorable performance as Miss Moffat in the screen version.† As with *The Glass Menagerie*, Kate was taking on a role closely identified with other actresses.

Miss Moffat is a strong-minded English spinster and teacher who inherits a cottage in a Welsh mining village and dedicates her life to educating the young boys in the town who are forced at age ten to go down into the mines to work. She finds one extremely gifted student, Morgan Evans [Ion Saynor], and works diligently to help him win a scholarship for Oxford. Evans is seduced by a young woman [Toyah Wilson]. When he learns the girl is pregnant, he is ready to sacrifice his future to do his duty by her and the child she will

---

* Barrymore played the role of Miss Moffat in *The Corn Is Green* on Broadway and on tour for the next six years.
† Davis also starred in a musical version of *The Corn Is Green*, but it closed out of town.

bear. But Miss Moffat insists he leave and agrees to adopt and raise the child herself.

All the exteriors for *The Corn Is Green* were shot in Isybyty-Ifan, a small, bleak Welsh village. Nearby was a farm called Hafod Ifan—a stone house on the slope of a great hill with a group of long, beautiful stone cattle barns that housed Welsh Blacks. Hafod Ifan was to be Miss Moffat's home; the barns, her school. A short distance east of the town of Wexham was the Bersham Colliery, an old but still operative coal mine. In 1890, the period of the play, boys worked twelve-hour days in the Bersham, digging in places too small for a man to reach.

Kate insisted she go down in the mine with some of the film crew. "They put on coveralls, gloves, hard hats, boots. . . . I only needed a hat. My ordinary clothes were suitable, including my shoes," she wrote later. They descended thirteen hundred feet in the pitch dark in a two-level, open-cage elevator, each carrying a lamp, a gas detector and a gas mask. Kate and the men who accompanied her walked through a narrow tunnel over uneven ground to a darkish room where some miners were gathered drinking tea from thermos jugs. "There was a constant draft of wind," Kate remembered, "persistent and somehow exhausting. And . . . cold."

She talked to the curious men for a few minutes and then started back up. As she rose in the elevator she heard "a beautiful tenor voice . . . others gradually joined in. . . ." The experience was unforgettable for Kate, who reached ground level covered in coal dust—"thrilling."

Kate and Phyllis had a small three-hundred-year-old cottage at Capel Garmon, near Bettsw y Coed, with a great fireplace in the living room made of three big blocks of slate, quarried in the area. Capel Garmon also had several nearby woolen mills and Kate "spiffed up the room with big spools of wool. . . . Red, blue, white, blue-and-white mix."

Film work invigorated her as theater never did. Every day she did something different. She got up at five, devoured a huge breakfast—"Fruit, eggs, bacon, chicken livers, toast, marmalade, coffee" from a tray she had prepared and brought up to her room herself. For an hour she would study the script, then take a cold shower or bath and go out for a bike ride before the car arrived around seven to take her to the location. At night she had dinner on a tray "in front of the fire," she wrote. "Pretty. First thing I do when I get home is to wash my hair. I've always tended to that myself. Saves repeated nuisance. I do it every night. I pile it up wet. And it sort of dries before the fire while I'm eating."

Cukor and Kate had a lot of good-natured arguments. Cukor said, laughing, "Our relationship is give and take. I give and she takes."

One scene in the film called for Kate to ride an 1890 bicycle ("stiff and it weighed a ton") up to the top of a steep hill. For one of the few times in her life, Kate could not do what the script required. A young woman athlete who bore a fair resemblance to Kate (at least from a distance) shot the scene for her. "I was humiliated," she said. "Nearly had a stroke. But I just could not pump up that hill. Infuriating failure. I have always been able to do my own stuff. But my legs just could not push hard enough to keep that bike from a drunken wobble. They thought that I was silly to be so mad that she could and I couldn't. Yes, I suppose so. But, there it is. I still am mad. Damned old legs."

She left Capel Garmon with sadness—"the hills, valleys, skies, flowers, fields, stone farmhouses, barns, narrow roads lined with pink and purple foxgloves. Sheep roaming the hillsides—every possible view. The mountains of Snowdonia appearing and disappearing in the distance . . . were intoxicating. Lifted the soul." Somehow, cast and crew were never able to rekindle the wonder and spirit of it all once they were at work on a London sound stage.

The reviews of *The Corn Is Green* were not enthusiastic. Kate's performance was lauded; but in the years since Williams had written his semiautobiographical play, the story had become dated and Miss Moffat stereotyped. Kate had not brought new insight to the character as she had to Amanda Wingfield. The problem may have been that she felt too comfortable with the role, or that Cukor was not as strong as he should have been.

Cukor, in fact, was failing, and shortly after they both had returned to the States he confided to Kate that he had to sell his house and Tracy's old bungalow because he could no longer cope with such a large responsibility. He begged Kate to buy it, but she could not see herself making any more films in California and she knew if Cukor was not there, nothing would be the same anyway. Subsequently Cukor sold the place, and in March, 1979, the new owners asked Kate to please pack up her belongings and leave. An era had ended.

CHAPTER
28

A sign spelling out the name H-O-L-L-Y-W-O-O-D spreads across the stubby facade of the Hollywood Hills. But Hollywood, that fabled, glittering movieland of stars, dreams fulfilled and hopes dashed, never really existed.

The early studios were located there, but with sound new studios were built elsewhere—Warner Brothers, Universal and Republic over those hills and in the valley, Twentieth Century-Fox in the more verdant Beverly Hills, Metro-Goldwyn-Mayer and Selznick-International in nearby Culver City. Film stars always chose to live in the more select of Hollywood's neighboring towns—in the old days Beverly Hills, Brentwood, Bel Air, Santa Monica, Malibu and the canyons; more recently in the great expanses of the elite valley communities. Film circles in the thirties drove to Hollywood for premieres at Grauman's Chinese, a hot-fudge sundae at Brown's, lunch at Lucy's or Musso & Frank's or the Hollywood Brown Derby on Vine Street, an appearance on CBS or NBC or a chat with Louella Parsons on the radio show from the Hollywood Hotel.

The social life of the film community soon moved east to the new Chandler Pavilion in downtown Los Angeles and west to the restaurants and clubs frequented by the Rodeo Drive habitués. By the sixties, like the old *Movietone News*—

"they covered the world"—film production was moving to Europe and other, more exotic places. Never mind. In the beginning came the word and it appeared at the end of a movie's credits: "Made in Hollywood, U.S.A." To filmgoers Hollywood was a symbol for films and film stars—especially those great ones who had remained constant for decades.

When Kate moved her possessions from Tracy's bungalow, most of those fabled stars were either faded, retired or dead. With John Wayne's death in 1979, only two remained of the old personalities who could command star billing—Katharine Hepburn and Henry Fonda. And not only had they never played together, they had not yet met. (Kate said at the time: "I've never met *many* people, but I'm sure I must have said, 'How do you do?' to Henry Fonda at one time or another. I felt as though I knew him.")

On Golden Pond, the story that was to bring these two stars together, was written by Ernest Thompson, a playwright not yet thirty, and presented in the fall of 1978 off-Broadway at the Hudson Guild Theatre. Former screen star Greer Garson saw it and decided she would like to produce it for Broadway (just possibly she saw herself in the role of sixty-nine-year-old Ethel Thayer). Before it was brought to New York, the new production was tried out first in Wilmington, Delaware, and then at the Kennedy Center's Eisenhower Theatre in Washington, D.C.

The play is about a couple who have been married fifty years and come once again to their summer cottage in Maine on Golden Pond. Norman Thayer, at seventy-nine, suffers from a heart condition. His wife, Ethel, ten years his junior, is fighting to keep him alive and happy—not an easy task given her husband's disposition. But Ethel and Norman have an exceptional relationship, one that survives the unexpected arrival of their divorced daughter, their daughter's objectionable suitor, and his difficult thirteen-year-old son. The daughter has come to Golden Pond to confront the depth of her father's love for her before he dies. Kate had been sent the script by Greer Garson and her partner Arthur Cantor with a view to a film of the play and had been intrigued enough to go to Washington and sit through three performances.

No doubt had existed for Kate about the merits of the play. But Norman Thayer's role was the key to the story and had to be played by someone old enough to be real, and of equal status to her. Only one man fit that description—Henry Fonda. The script was sent to him and he "read it and got fired up." Fonda, who had been very ill, suffered from a heart condition and had worn a pacemaker for more than four years. A film that centered upon his character would not be easy to finance.

On Golden Pond opened on Broadway with Tom Aldredge and Frances Sternhagen in February, 1979, where it lasted a disappointing 128 performances, mainly because of the subject matter (old age) and the lack of star names. The producers transferred the show once again to a small off-Broadway theater for another 253 performances. Kate decided she would like to play Ethel Thayer in a film version. Fonda's enthusiasm grew after he had seen the stage performance several times. Still, no film company was willing to risk a seven-million-dollar investment on a story about "old folks." Then, Jane Fonda,* Henry's film-star daughter, asked to read the script.

"It's wonderful," she told her father. "I want to play the daughter." The part was small but her faith was strong enough to raise the money and co-produce the film, for which Thompson did his own screenplay—"the best I've ever read," Fonda said.

Kate met with Jane Fonda in New York and then flew out to California to meet Henry Fonda and the director, Mark Rydell.† The meeting was held in a conference room at Twentieth Century-Fox. Kate arrived last, walked straight over to Fonda, held out her hand and said, "Well, it's about time."

Rydell and co-producer Bruce Gilbert were concerned about Kate's health as well as about Fonda's. Her palsy had progressed, and her head shook involuntarily at more frequent intervals. They finally decided that Kate's palsy would give Ethel Thayer authenticity, and the starting date was set

---

* Jane Fonda (1937–   ) had just won an Oscar for Best Actress in *Coming Home* (1978). In 1971, she won the same award for *Klute*.
† Mark Rydell (1934–   ) made an auspicious debut as a director with *The Fox* (1968), following it the next year with *The Reivers*. He became a producer shortly afterward but returned to directing with *Harry and Walter Go to New York* (1976) and *The Rose* (1978).

for June, 1980. Late in April, Kate and a friend were playing tennis on an indoor New York court. As Kate raised her arm to serve, a searing pain cut through her shoulder and arm. She froze, unable to move. After being rushed to the hospital she underwent a rotator cuff operation on her shoulder, which had become severely dislocated. The doctors claimed she would need a full three months to convalesce and that even then a film would be out of the question.

"I knew the film was dependent on the Fonda part being lazy, and not working, and not wanting [or able] to do a lot of physical things," Kate recalled. "The wife, my part, had to carry all the luggage, do everything, and here I am with an arm that's really bad. Well, I tried to get out of the picture, but Fonda said, 'No, you'll be fine. You'll do it. We won't get anyone else.' He stuck to his guns and in July, 1980 [two weeks late], we found ourselves on location in New Hampshire."

The *On Golden Pond* company settled into the small town of Laconia, a summer place swarming in July with tourists who filled the cottages and lodges that bordered its four spring-fed lakes. One, Squam Lake, was the major location for the film.

"The first day," Fonda reported, "I was sitting in one of those high director's chairs with some of the company. We were between the cottage that was supposed to be our summer house and the lake. Shirlee [Mrs. Fonda] was there, the makeup people, the crew, a few members of the cast. And around the corner came Katharine Hepburn. Now, Hepburn is a presence wherever she is. In a room, she is the only one in it. In a big area, she doesn't do anything to dominate, she just does and is. But as people saw her, she was gesturing for them to move away, and they sort of just melted in front of her, just disappeared. By the time she got to me, I was alone. I was aware this was happening, but I wasn't quite sure why or how it happened. She came up to me holding her outstretched, cupped hands in front of her. Something crumpled was inside those hands but I didn't know what it was. She came right up to me and stood there."

"I want you to have this," she said. "This was Spencer's favorite hat."

Fonda was moved to tears and wore it in their first scene and then throughout the film.

The styles of Kate and Jane Fonda were less polarized than expected. Jane Fonda was an activist who spoke at rallies and listened to loud rock music. (A few days into the shooting she brought rock star Michael Jackson onto the set, a young man Kate found somewhat jarring in the beginning but eventually liked.) But Jane Fonda is also a woman of grit, a tough lady who can take it and deal it out, an independent, intelligent woman willing to back her controversial opinions.

Rydell feared that hostility would develop between the two women. "After all," he says, "Jane is the big star of the eighties and Katharine *was* the big star. You had the sense in the first few days of two lionesses prowling the same ground."

"I couldn't help fantasizing what would have happened if [Kate] and my dad had become lovers forty years ago, and Kate had been my mother," Jane Fonda said. "To work with her, and to work with my father, was a terrifying, waking-up-in-the-morning-wanting-to-throw-up kind of experience. But what happened was, when we went to rehearsals, I realized that she was as nervous as I was." Fonda paused and then added: "I had to get over the desperate need I once had for [Dad's] approval. We've never been intimate. My dad simply is not an intimate person. But that doesn't mean there isn't love."

During the filming Kate commented, "Henry Fonda's not one to make new friends and neither am I, but we got along okay. He has his own world. He likes to sit and fish, I like to walk through the woods alone. We are quite similar. He doesn't waste time. No small talk. And I hate to have idiotic conversations. We found we could work together just like *that*"—she snapped her fingers several times rapidly—"and we really did it.

"He had to do very, very, very uncomfortable things on cold evenings, in the wind, and sitting out in an open boat. He had to sit out in the bright sun, and he has skin like mine, can't take the sun at all. He never uttered a complaint."

"You want to hear about Katharine Hepburn?" Fonda replied. "She swam every morning and after work. She'd have her dinner, and go to sleep at eight o'clock, get up at

A REMARKABLE WOMAN

three or four and study her lines. . . . At the end of September, when it was bitter cold, they catapulted the fourteen-year-old boy* and me into the water. The company was more nervous than I. They thought, 'This old son-of-a-bitch is going to have a heart attack,' but I fooled 'em. I had a wet suit on under my wardrobe. Katharine had to dive into the water, too, but she didn't even wear a wet suit."

The summer was magic for both of them. "Their affection was palpable," recalls Mark Rydell. "One could feel it in the filming day to day. They approached this material bravely. Here you have Henry Fonda and Katharine Hepburn in their seventies, dealing with material that has to do with the final years of one's life, and how do you face death and how do you support one another . . . it was quite a resonant experience."

When the film was released in November, 1981, Henry Fonda received the lion's share of accolades. Fonda breathed such life into his character that he *was* Norman Thayer. Audiences were greatly moved by his performance of a dying man when they knew that his own health was deteriorating quickly and that *On Golden Pond* would be his last film. Speculators already had Fonda winning the Academy Award that next spring. Kate was cited as having made Ethel Thayer "an authentic human spirit," but she was faulted by what reviewers thought was an oversentimentalized performance. The condition of her eyes had grown steadily worse, and they teared throughout most of the film. So cleverly did she minimize the shake of her head that it looked as if her palsy could have been adopted for the role. Kate did not concern herself about the Awards or her chances of winning or losing. Ernest Thompson had given her another of his plays to read, *West Side Waltz*, and she had decided to accept still a new challenge. *West Side Waltz* was the story of an aging concert pianist, and Kate would have to give a realistic impression that she was playing the music being taped over the sound system in the theater.

Her shoulder had healed during the filming of *On Golden Pond*, but in the last few weeks of production she had walked into a glass door, miraculously without shattering it. The pain

* Doug McKeon (1966-   ). Best Juvenile Actor in Daytime Drama Award in 1976.

402

returned and Rydell had to shoot around her for several days. No serious damage to the shoulder had been incurred but two fingers on that hand had become numb. Playing the piano was marvelous therapy, but at the same time it was difficult, uncomfortable and frustrating. Kate liked Thompson's story, and though *West Side Waltz* dealt with the same theme—aging —as had *On Golden Pond,* it presented another, much different problem—that of aging alone.

Margaret Mary Elderdice, the widowed, seventyish former concert pianist, lives in a residential hotel on the West Side of Manhattan. She struggles fiercely to hold on to her independence, but as the play progresses she goes from a cane to a walker to a wheelchair and is finally forced to accept the offer of a somewhat vulgar middle-aged violinist to share the apartment. The two women are oddly matched, but their music bridges the wide gap that divides them and both find renewed spirit in the duets they begin to play together.

The role of Cara Varnum, the violinist, was almost of equal importance to Mrs. Elderdice; and the actress who played the part had to have a certain chemistry with Kate for the play to work. Kate had been to see the musical comedy star Dorothy Loudon* in *Ballroom,* in which she played a widow who meets a man her age at a public dance hall. Loudon was most moving in the role,† and Kate asked her to co-star with her in *West Side Waltz.* By now, Kate had brought in Noel Willman, the director, and Roger Stevens and Robert Whitehead, her producers on *A Matter of Gravity.*

Loudon and Kate rehearsed daily at Kate's house, practicing the piano and violin together as well. ("I don't think Vladimir Horowitz and Isaac Stern have anything to worry about," Loudon said at the time. "Actually, Kate is very good but I'm developing two chins from trying to balance the violin.") Onstage they were only to finger their instruments, synchronizing their movements to recordings of professional musicians. Kate had achieved a similar feat years before when

---

* Dorothy Loudon (1933–   ) was the original Miss Hannigan in *Annie* on Broadway.

† Maureen Stapleton had originated this role in an Emmy-winning performance on television. The play was then called *Stardust Ballroom.*

she made *A Song of Love*. Film, however, could be cut and intercut and the recorded music made to match the hand movements on screen. On the stage there would be no mechanical help. The women *had* to have their movements timed perfectly to the music and be careful not to touch their instruments.

Determinedly, Kate practiced three to four hours a day, regaining the mobility in her fingers, memorizing the intricacies of each piece, striving to achieve the appearance of a professional pianist at work. And Loudon matched her in her concentration.

The plan was to tour *West Side Waltz* in eight cities for almost a year before bringing it into New York. The play premiered in Los Angeles at the Ahmanson, in January, 1981, to praise for Kate and Loudon but less than enthusiastic reviews for the play. Thompson never stopped rewriting during the course of the tour, which ended in Philadelphia. The show opened in New York on November 18, 1981, coincidentally the same day *On Golden Pond* was placed in general release.

Walter Kerr in *The New York Times* wrote: "I'm not sure that author Ernest Thompson realizes . . . what multiple small miracles Katharine Hepburn is bestowing upon his play. . . . One mysterious thing she has learned to do is breathe unchallengeable life into lifeless lines. She does it, or seems to do it, by giving the most serious consideration to every syllable she utters. There may have been a time when she coasted on mannerisms, turned on her rhythms into a form of rapid transit. That time is long gone."

The limited three-month engagement was financially successful. Kate played to capacity houses as she had on the tour. When the show closed in February, 1982, it again took to the road, Kate with it, this time for a brief tour to begin in Washington, D.C. She had received her twelfth Academy nomination for *On Golden Pond*, but she was appearing at the Kennedy Center at the same time as the ceremonies. When asked by the film's publicist what she would like her representative to say, she replied, "A simple thank you will suffice," which is what Bruce Gilbert, *On Golden Pond*'s co-producer, repeated when he accepted her fourth Academy Award for Best Actress on her behalf. Fonda was awarded his

first for Best Actor.* Jane Fonda, tears in her eyes ("A Fonda
can cry at a good steak," Henry Fonda had once said)
accepted for him. Fonda was now confined to his bed. "My
father would say typically that this is just luck," she said as
she grasped the golden statuette and held it in front of her.
"But I will try to assure him that there's no *luck* to it." Three
weeks later Henry Fonda died.

Kate was now the last of the great film legends still able to
claim star billing. Although she was seventy-five, a good story
with something important to say still commanded her attention and dedication. One film script, *The Ultimate Solution of
Grace Quigley,* a black comedy about an elderly woman who
hires a professional "hit man" to help her put an end to the
lives of her aging compatriots who no longer care to live, had
consumed her interest for eleven years. Written by Martin
Zweiback, a relatively unknown scriptwriter, the screenplay
had literally been dumped on her back doorstep when she had
occupied the California bungalow. She had tried to get it
produced, but euthanasia was considered too controversial a
subject. Nonetheless, Kate pressed on, engaging Zweiback to
further develop the story.

When the tour of *West Side Waltz* ended in the summer of
1982, her interest in *The Ultimate Solution of Grace Quigley*
was reactivated, and she convinced Tony Harvey that he
should direct it and enlisted Nick Nolte* as her co-star. A
deal was being set for production.

Her plan was to spend the month of December with her
brother Dick and his family at Fenwick, where Phyllis joined
her. A record snowfall and freezing temperatures hit Fenwick
shortly after her arrival. Despite difficult road conditions
Kate would drive into town on errands, cautious but certain
she knew the roads well enough to navigate safely. On
December 13, with Phyllis beside her, Kate headed into
town. As they took a fairly sharp curve, the car skidded, spun

---

* Fonda had previously been nominated just once, for his portrayal of Tom Joad
in *The Grapes of Wrath*. In 1981, he had been presented an Oscar as a Life
Achievement Award.

* Nick Nolte (1941–   ) had made an auspicious debut in the television
adaptation of Irwin Shaw's *Rich Man, Poor Man* and had given a stunning
performance in 1977 in *Who'll Stop the Rain?* He has since become one of
Hollywood's most popular leading men.

and crashed headlong into a utility pole. The impact crumpled the front end of the car and a piece of steel nearly severed Kate's right foot. Phyllis had injured her hand and arm, but not seriously. When help came and Kate was extricated from the car and transferred to the ambulance, her foot "was hanging just from a tendon."

Kate insisted she be taken to Hartford Hospital, an hour's ride over icy roads, where the surgeon who had saved her finger was on the staff. He was alerted and immediately upon her arrival performed the intricate surgery to reattach the foot. The press was told only that she had an injury to her ankle. For several days after the surgery, it looked as though the operation might not have been successful. Nineteen days later, the day after New Year's, she left the hospital in a cast up to her hip and moved into her sister Marion's Hartford residence. The fear that she might lose the foot was past, but for the next eight months she spent equal time in and out of the hospital. After six more months of therapy (and the news that Luddy had just died), she decided to go back to work. By then, two Israeli producers, Menachem Golan and Yoram Globus, had agreed to finance *The Ultimate Solution of Grace Quigley* through their Cannon Films. The movie began shooting in New York in October, 1983. Golan and Globus were masters at bringing in small films under budget. The fact that they had Katharine Hepburn as their star did not affect their tightfisted attitude. *The Ultimate Solution of Grace Quigley* was strictly a no-frills production. And Golan and Globus were not informed of the seriousness of Kate's recent injury.

Her indomitability during the making of this film was awesome. She asked for no favors and received none. Nolte called her "a cranky old broad but a lot of fun." She did not have to do anything strenuous or physical (although she did tackle a scene without a double that called for her to ride a motorcycle with Nolte); but she had to, and did, appear spry, and she did brave the harsh conditions of shooting many exteriors in New York during an unseasonably cold fall. As always, she arrived on a set or location before her co-workers and had her hand into everything being done.

The Ultimate Solution of Grace Quigley was a great departure for Kate. Sophisticated comedy had always been her special forte; no one could deliver an acid one-liner better. Grace Quigley was a character in a black comedy that, if played wrong, since the topic was euthanasia, could easily have become distasteful. Kate never believed the story was offensive. "If people are offended by it, then I think they are wrong. If people can just learn to laugh instead of being terrified at what the future holds for them, they will be better off," she commented, adding that she personally had no fear of death. "What release! to sleep is the greatest joy there is. . . . If I were a burden to myself and I could leave my money to younger people who could really use it, I would feel it was my privilege to do what I could do. . . . There are no rules, except to know yourself."

"I'm not in a class with my parents," she countered when cited for her moral strength. "They were real reformers and noble people who set out to improve the state of man and woman—black, white, diseased, whatever. Why, I'm just ordinarily polite. They fought all the diseases of the day. I've fought for Planned Parenthood, abortion and how to laugh at life if I can."

Her work for Planned Parenthood had, in fact, been taking up a great deal of her time. Mailings carrying her name and soliciting funds had been sent out by the hundreds of thousands, and they had brought her a rush of unpleasant letters and numerous threats. "Things are getting worse," she told one interviewer. "Now they've even changed the rules about when a fetus is alive—although I've never seen a religious service for a miscarriage, have you?" To another writer, she confessed: "I was always a bit on the outside because I belonged to a small element of society who thought they were better than others because of their beliefs—they were out to help people who were victims of idiotic attitudes. When some local girl got pregnant, she would have the baby in our house if she had no place to go.

"I loved it at Bryn Mawr without any boys," she admitted, "and I cannot understand our current co-educational system! What do you expect young people to do when they're sleeping in the same corridor?"

With work completed on *The Ultimate Solution of Grace Quigley*, Kate returned to Hartford Hospital and submitted to surgery to fuse her anklebone. Afterward, she had to wear a knee-high plaster cast for months, a fact she accepted with more patience than anyone thought she could muster. *The Ultimate Solution of Grace Quigley* was shown in May, 1984, at the Cannes Film Festival and was poorly received. The American critics found that "The two actors [Hepburn and Nolte] exude endearing, though swarmy *[sic]* personas that impart a light-hearted and whimsical tone to otherwise unpleasant subject matter."

The critical and commercial failure of the film was a great disappointment. Kate thought the film was about "the abominable way we treat our elderly," not about euthanasia. "But," she said, "if my own mother had been desperately ill and attached to a lot of humiliating machines, I think I would have shot her."

In 1984, a national survey elicited answers from forty-five hundred teenagers as to whom they would name as their ten contemporary heroes. The survey-takers were stunned when Katharine Hepburn's name appeared in the number-seven slot, the only woman on a list that included such names as Michael Jackson, Clint Eastwood and the Pope. In fact, Kate was a notch above the Pope. Somehow she had broken down the barriers of age and sex. The Woman of the Year had become a kind of a guru. She had demystified old age, something the young feared and did not like to be reminded might some day befall them. Not only were they the *me-me-me* generation, they were the exponents of the *now-now-now* syndrome. Many teenagers had gone to see Jane Fonda in *On Golden Pond* and come away with unforgettable images of Katharine Hepburn, as unafraid of age as of the icy waters of Squam Lake, her eyes brimming yet refusing to give in to her deeply felt emotions when she knows her husband-lover-friend is about to die. In the past two years, they had seen her on television-interview programs (to which she had taken quite a fancy)—Barbara Walters, *60 Minutes, Good Morning America*—outspoken, radiating a tensile strength in her sure smile, the unique commanding voice, the comfortable trouser-clad body, the steady look in her eyes, the proud carriage of her head—a lioness who had marked off an entire jungle as her domain. Although she was seventy-seven, her face on the cover of a magazine could sell as many copies as those with photographs of Princess Di or Elizabeth Taylor.

To those past fifty she remained one of the last international figures who had been where they had been and survived it with them—the Depression, the golden days of cinema, World War II, McCarthyism, the civil-rights movement, the assassinations of Kennedy and Kennedy and King, Vietnam, Women's Lib, Nixon, the Iranian hostages, and the cutback of the Reagan administration's programs to the elderly, the poor, the minorities, and women. She had seen it all. She could have sung neighbor Stephen Sondheim's great song from *Follies*—"I'm Still Here." Kate represented continuum. She had come to symbolize qualities that they had been taught as children to recognize as heroic—integrity, strength, fearlessness, dedication to friends and family and to ideals; not an easy mark for cheats or deceivers.

A truly remarkable woman.

FILM CHRONOLOGY

A BILL OF DIVORCEMENT, R.K.O., 1932
Based on the play by Clemence Dane

CAST: Katharine Hepburn . . . . Sydney Fairfield
John Barrymore . . . . Hillary Fairfield
Billie Burke . . . . Margaret Fairfield
David Manners. . . . . Kit Humphrey
Henry Stephenson . . . . Doctor Alliot
Paul Cavanagh . . . . Gray Meredith
Elizabeth Patterson . . . . Aunt Hester
Gayle Evers. . . . . Bassett
Julie Haydon . . . . Party Guest

Executive Producer, David O. Selznick; *Directed by* George Cukor; *Assistant Director,* Dewey Starkey; *Technical Director,* Marion Balderstone; *Screenplay by* Howard Estabrook and Harry Wagstaff Gribble; *Photography by* Sid Hickox; *Art Direction by* Carroll Clark; *Music by* Max Steiner; *Piano Concerto by* W. Franke Harling; *Film Editor,* Arthur Roberts; *Costumes by* Josette De Lima; *Makeup by* Mel Burns.

CHRISTOPHER STRONG, R.K.O., 1933
Based on the novel by Gilbert Frankau

CAST: Katharine Hepburn . . . . Lady Cynthia Darrington
Colin Clive . . . . Sir Christopher Strong

Billie Burke	Lady Elaine Strong
Helen Chandler.	Monica Strong
Ralph Forbes	Harry Rawlinson
Irene Browne	Carrie Valentin
Jack La Rue.	Carlo
Desmond Roberts	Bryce Mercer
Gwendolyn Logan.	Bradford, the Maid
Agostino Borgato	Fortune Teller
Margaret Lindsay	Girl at Party
Donald Stewart.	Mechanic
Zena Savina.	Second Maid

Produced by David O. Selznick; *Associate Producer*, Pandro S. Berman; *Directed by* Dorothy Arzner; *Assistant Directors*, Edward Killy, Tommy Atkins; *Screenplay by* Zoë Akins; *Photography by* Bert Glennon; *Special Effects by* Vernon Walker; *Transitions by* Slavko Vorkapich; *Art Director*, Van Nest Polglase; *Associate Art Direction by* Charles Kirk; *Music by* Max Steiner; *Sound Recorder*, Hugh McDowell; *Film Editor*, Arthur Roberts; *Costumes by* Howard Greer; *Make-up by* Mel Burns.

MORNING GLORY, R.K.O., 1933
Based on the play by Zoë Akins

CAST: *Katharine Hepburn*	Eva Lovelace
Douglas Fairbanks, Jr.	Joseph Sheridan
Adolphe Menjou.	Louis Easton
Mary Duncan.	Rita Vernon
C. Aubrey Smith.	Robert Harley Hedges
Don Alvarado	Pepe Velez, the Gigolo
Fred Santley.	Will Seymour
Richard Carle.	Henry Lawrence
Tyler Brooke	Charles Van Dusen
Geneva Mitchell	Gwendolyn Hall
Helen Ware	Nellie Navarre
Theresa Harris	Maid

Produced by Pandro S. Berman; *Executive Producer*, Merian C. Cooper; *Directed by* Lowell Sherman; *Assistant Director*, Tommy Atkins; *Screenplay by* Howard J. Green; *Photography by* Bert Glennon; *Art Direction by* Van Nest Polglase; *Associate Art Director*, Charles Kirk; *Music by* Max Steiner;

Sound Recorder, Hugh McDowell; *Film Editor*, George Nicholls, Jr.; *Costumes by* Walter Plunkett; *Makeup by* Mel Burns.

LITTLE WOMEN, R.K.O., 1933
Based on the novel by Louisa May Alcott

CAST:
Katharine Hepburn	Jo
Joan Bennett	Amy
Paul Lukas	Professor Bhaer
Edna May Oliver	Aunt March
Jean Parker	Beth
Frances Dee	Meg
Henry Stephenson	Mr. Laurence
Douglass Montgomery	Laurie
John Davis Lodge	Brooke
Spring Byington	Marmee
Samuel S. Hinds	Mr. March
Mabel Colcord	Hannah
Marion Ballou	Mrs. Kirke
Nydia Westman	Mamie
Harry Beresford	Doctor Bangs
Marina Schubert	Flo King
Dorothy Gray, June Filmer	Girls at Boarding House
Olin Howland	Mr. Davis

Executive Producer, Merian C. Cooper; *Associate Producer*, Kenneth MacGowan; *Directed by* George Cukor; *Assistant Director*, Edward Killy; *Screenplay by* Sarah Y. Mason and Victor Heerman; *Photography by* Henry Gerrard; *Special Effects by* Harry Redmond; *Art Direction by* Van Nest Polglase; *Set Direction by* Hobe Erwin, *Music by* Max Steiner; *Sound Recorder*, Frank H. Harris, *Film Editor*, Jack Kitchin; *Costumes by* Walter Plunkett; *Makeup by* Mel Burns; *Production Associate*, Del Andrews.

SPITFIRE, R.K.O., 1934
Based on the play *Trigger* by Lula Vollmer

CAST:
Katharine Hepburn	Trigger Hicks
Robert Young	J. Stafford
Ralph Bellamy	G. Fleetwood

Martha Sleeper	Eleanor Stafford
Louis Mason	Bill Grayson
Sara Haden	Etta Dawson
Virginia Howell	Granny Raines
Sidney Toler	Mr. Sawyer
High Ghere	West Fry
Therese Wittler	Mrs. Sawyer
John Beck	Jake Hawkins

Executive Producer, Merian C. Cooper; *Associate Producer*, Pandro S. Berman; *Directed by* John Cromwell; *Assistant Director*, Dewey Starkey; *Screenplay by* Jane Murfin and Lula Vollmer; *Photography by* Edward Cronjager; *Art Direction by* Van Nest Polglase; *Associate Art Director*, Carroll Clark; *Music by* Max Steiner; *Sound Recorder*, Clem Portman; *Film Editor*, William H. Morgan; *Costumes by* Walter Plunkett; *Makeup by* Mel Burns.

THE LITTLE MINISTER, R.K.O., 1934
Based on the novel and play by J. M. Barrie

CAST:	*Katharine Hepburn*	Babbie
	John Beal	Gavin
	Alan Hale	Rob Dow
	Donald Crisp	Dr. McQueen
	Lumsden Hare	Thammas
	Andy Clyde	Wearyworld
	Beryl Mercer	Margaret
	Billy Watson	Micah Dow
	Dorothy Stickney	Jean
	Mary Gordon	Nanny
	Frank Conroy	Lord Rintoul
	Eily Malyon	Evalina
	Reginald Denny	Captain Halliwell
	Leonard Carey	Munn
	Herbert Bunston	Carfrae
	Harry Beresford	John Spens
	Barlowe Borland	Snecky
	May Beatty	Maid

Produced by Pandro S. Berman; *Directed by* Richard Wallace; *Assistant Director*, Edward Killy; *Screenplay by* Jane Murfin, Sarah Y. Mason, Victor Heerman; *Additional Scene·*

by Mortimer Offner, Jack Wagner; *Photography by* Henry Gerrard; *Special Effects by* Vernon Walker; *Technical Adviser,* Robert Watson, F.R.G.S.; *Set Direction by* Hobe Erwin; *Art Direction by* Van Nest Polglase; *Associate Art Director,* Carroll Clark; *Music by* Max Steiner; *Sound Recorder,* Clem Portman, *Film Editor,* William Hamilton; *Costumes by* Walter Plunkett; *Makeup by* Mel Burns.

BREAK OF HEARTS, R.K.O., 1935
Based on a story by Lester Cohen

CAST:

Katharine Hepburn	Constance Dane
Charles Boyer.	Franz Roberti
John Beal	Johnny Lawrence
Jean Hersholt	Prof. Talma
Sam Hardy	Marx
Inez Courtney.	Miss Wilson
Helene Millard	Sylvia
Ferdinand Gottschalk.	Pazzini
Susan Fleming	Elise
Lee Kohlmar	Schubert
Jean Howard	Didi Smith-Lennox
Anne Grey.	Phyllis
Inez Palange, Jason Robards, Egon Brecher, Dick Elliott	

Produced by Pandro S. Berman; *Directed by* Philip Moeller; *Assistant Director,* Edward Killy; *Screenplay by* Sarah Y. Mason, Victor Heerman, Anthony Veiller; *Photography by* Robert De Grasse; *Art Direction by* Van Nest Polglase; *Associate Art Director,* Carroll Clark; *Music by* Max Steiner; *Sound Recorder,* John Tribby; *Film Editor,* William Hamilton; *Associate Editor,* Jane Loring; *Costumes by* Bernard Newman; *Makeup by* Mel Burns.

ALICE ADAMS, R.K.O., 1935
Based on the novel by Booth Tarkington; adaptation by Jane Murfin

CAST:

Katharine Hepburn	Alice Adams
Fred MacMurray.	Arthur Russell
Fred Stone	Mr. Adams
Evelyn Venable.	Mildred Palmer

Frank Albertson	Walter Adams
Ann Shoemaker	Mrs. Adams
Charles Grapewin	Mr. Lamb
Grady Sutton	Frank Dowling
Hedda Hopper	Mrs. Palmer
Jonathan Hale	Mr. Palmer
Janet McLeod	Henrietta Lamb
Virginia Howell	Mrs. Dowling
Zeffie Tilbury	Mrs. Dresser
Ella McKenzie	Ella Dowling
Hattie McDaniel	Malena

Produced by Pandro S. Berman; *Directed by* George Stevens; *Assistant Director,* Edward Killy; *Screenplay by* Dorothy Yost, Mortimer Offner; *Photography by* Robert De Grasse; *Art Direction by* Van Nest Polglase; *Music by* Max Steiner; *Sound Recorder,* Denzil A. Cutler; *Film Editor,* Jane Loring; *Costumes by* Walter Plunkett; *Makeup by* Mel Burns. Song "I Can't Waltz Alone" by Max Steiner and Dorothy Fields.

SYLVIA SCARLETT, R.K.O., 1936
Based on the novel *The Early Life and Adventures of Sylvia Scarlett* by Compton Mackenzie

CAST:

Katharine Hepburn	Sylvia Scarlett
Cary Grant	Jimmy Monkley
Brian Aherne	Michael Fane
Edmund Gwenn	Henry Scarlett
Natalie Paley	Lily
Dennie Moore	Maudie Tilt
Lennox Pawle	Drunk
Harold Cheevers	Bobby
Lionel Pape	Sergeant Major
Robert (Bob) Adair	Turnkey
Peter Hobbes, Leonard Mudie,	
Jack Vanair	Stewards
Harold Entwistle	Conductor
Adrienne D'Ambricourt	Stewardess
Gaston Glass, Michael S.	
Visaroff	Pursers
Bunny Beatty	Maid

> *E. E. Clive, Edward Cooper,*
>   *Olaf Hytten.* . . . . Customs Inspectors
> *Dina Smirnova* . . . . Russian
> *George Nardelli* . . . . Frenchman
> *Daisy Belmore, Elspeth*
>   *Dudgeon, May Beatty,*
>   *Connie Lamont, Gwendolyn*
>   *Logan, Carmen Beretta*

Produced by Pandro S. Berman; *Directed by* George Cukor; *Assistant Director*, Argyle Nelson; *Screenplay by* Gladys Unger, John Collier, Mortimer Offner; *Photography by* Joseph August; *Art Direction by* Van Nest Polglase; *Associate Art Director*, Sturges Carne; *Music by* Roy Webb; *Sound Recorder*, George D. Ellis; *Music Recorded by* P. J. Faulkner, Jr.; *Film Editor*, Jane Loring; *Costumes by* Muriel King (for Miss Hepburn) and Bernard Newman (for Miss Paley); *Makeup by* Mel Burns.

MARY OF SCOTLAND, R.K.O., 1936
Based on the play by Maxwell Anderson

CAST:
Katharine Hepburn	Mary Stuart
Fredric March	Earl of Bothwell
Florence Eldridge	Elizabeth Tudor
Douglas Walton	Darnley
John Carradine	David Rizzio
Robert Barrat	Morton
Gavin Muir	Leicester
Ian Keith	James Stuart Moray
Moroni Olsen	John Knox
William Stack	Ruthven
Ralph Forbes	Randolph
Alan Mowbray	Throckmorton
Frieda Inescort	Mary Beaton
Donald Crisp	Huntley
David Torrence	Lindsay
Molly Lamont	Mary Livingston
Anita Colby	Mary Fleming
Jean Fenwick	Mary Seton
Lionel Pape	Burghley
Alec Craig	Donal

Mary Gordon	Nurse
Monte Blue	Messenger
Leonard Mudie	Maitland
Brandon Hurst	Arian
Wilfred Lucas	Lexington
D'Arcy Corrigan	Kirkcaldy
Frank Baker	Douglas
Cyril McLaglen	Faudoncide
Lionel Belmore	English Fisherman
Doris Lloyd	His Wife
Bobby Watson	His Son
Robert Warwick	Sir Francis Knellys
Ivan Simpson, Murray Kinnell, Lawrence Grant, Nigel de Brulier, Barlowe Borland . . .	Judges
Walter Byron	Sir Francis Walsingham
Wyndham Standing	Sergeant
Earle Foxe	Duke of Kent
Paul McAllister	Du Croche
Gaston Glass	Chatelard
Neil Fitzgerald	Nobleman
Jean Kircher and *Judith Kircher*	Prince James

Produced by Pandro S. Berman; *Directed by* John Ford; *Assistant Director,* Edward Donahue; *Screenplay by* Dudley Nichols; *Photography by* Joseph H. August; *Special Effects by* Vernon L. Walker; *Art Direction by* Van Nest Polglase; *Associate Art Director,* Carroll Clark; *Music by* Nathaniel Shilkret; *Orchestrator,* Maurice De Packh; *Sound Recorder,* Hugh McDowell, Jr.; *Film Editor,* Jane Loring; *Costumes by* Walter Plunkett; *Makeup by* Mel Burns; *Miss Hepburn's Hairdresser,* Louise Sloan.

A WOMAN REBELS, R.K.O., 1936
Based on the novel *Portrait of a Rebel* by Netta Syrett

CAST: *Katharine Hepburn*	Pamela Thistlewaite
Herbert Marshall	Thomas Lane
Elizabeth Allan	Flora Thistlewaite
Donald Crisp	Judge Thistlewaite
Doris Dudley	Young Flora

A REMARKABLE WOMAN

David Manners	Alan
Lucile Watson	Betty Bumble
Van Heflin	Gerald
Eily Malyon	Piper
Margaret Seddon	Aunt Serena
Molly Lamont	Young Girl
Lionel Pape	Mr. White
Constance Lupino	Lady Gaythorne
Lillian Kemble-Cooper	Lady Rinlake
Nick Thompson	Signor Grassi
Inez Palange	Signora Grassi
Tony Romero	Italian Boy
Joe Mack	Italian Bit
Marilyn Knowlden	Flora, Age 10
Bonnie June McNamara	Flora, Age 5
Marilyn French	Flora, Infant

Produced by Pandro S. Berman; *Directed by* Mark Sandrich; *Assistant Director*, Dewey Starkey; *Screenplay by* Anthony Veiller and Ernest Vajda; *Photography by* Robert De Grasse; *Art Direction by* Van Nest Polglase; *Associate Art Director*, Perry Ferguson; *Set Decorator*, Darrell Silvera; *Music by* Roy Webb; *Music Recorded by* Clem Portman; *Orchestrator*, Maurice De Packh; *Musical Director*, Nathaniel Shilkret; *Sound Recorder*, George D. Ellis; *Film Editor*, Jane Loring; *Costumes by* Walter Plunkett; *Makeup by* Mel Burns; *Ballroom Dances by* Hermes Pan.

QUALITY STREET, R.K.O., 1937
Based on the play by Sir James M. Barrie

CAST: *Katharine Hepburn*	Phoebe Throssel
Franchot Tone	Dr. Valentine Brown
Fay Bainter	Susan Throssel
Eric Blore	Sergeant
Cora Witherspoon	Patty
Estelle Winwood	Mary Willoughby
Florence Lake	Henrietta Turnbull
Helena Grant	Fanny Willoughby
Bonita Granville	Isabella
Clifford Severn	Arthur
Sherwood Bailey	William Smith

Roland Varno	Ensign Blades
Joan Fontaine	Charlotte Parratt
William Bakewell	Lieutenant Spicer
York Sherwood	Postman
Carmencita Johnson	Student

Produced by Pandro S. Berman; *Directed by* George Stevens; *Assistant Director,* Argyle Nelson; *Screenplay by* Mortimer Offner and Allan Scott; *Photography by* Robert De Grasse; *Art Direction by* Van Nest Polglase; *Set Decorator,* Darrell Silvera; *Music by* Roy Webb; *Sound Recorder,* Clem Portman; *Orchestrator,* Maurice De Packh; *Film Editor,* Henry Berman; *Costumes by* Walter Plunkett; *Makeup by* Mel Burns.

STAGE DOOR, R.K.O., 1937
Based on the play by Edna Ferber and George S. Kaufman

CAST:	*Katharine Hepburn*	Terry Randall
	Ginger Rogers	Jean Maitland
	Adolphe Menjou	Anthony Powell
	Gail Patrick	Linda Shaw
	Constance Collier	Catherine Luther
	Andrea Leeds	Kaye Hamilton
	Samuel S. Hinds	Henry Sims
	Lucille Ball	Judy Canfield
	Pierre Watkin	Richard Carmichael
	Franklin Pangborn	Harcourt
	Elizabeth Dunne	Mrs. Orcutt
	Phyllis Kennedy	Hattie
	Grady Sutton	Butcher
	Jack Carson	Milbank
	Fred Santley	Dukenfield
	William Corson	Bill
	Frank Reicher	Stage Director
	Eve Arden	Eve
	Ann Miller	Annie
	Jane Rhodes	Ann Braddock
	Margaret Early	Mary
	Jean Rouverol	Dizzy
	Norma Drury	Olga Brent
	Peggy O'Donnell	Susan

Harriett Brandon . . . . Madeline
Katherine Alexander, Ralph
    Forbes, Mary Forbes, Huntley
    Gordon . . . . Cast of Play
Lynton Brent . . . . Aide
Theodore Von Eltz . . . . Elsworth
Jack Rice. . . . . Playwright
Harry Strang . . . . Chauffeur
Bob Perry . . . . Baggageman
Larry Steers . . . . Theater Patron
Mary Bovard, Frances Gifford. Actresses
Whitey the Cat . . . . Eve's Cat

Produced by Pandro S. Berman; *Directed by* Gregory La
Cava; *Assistant Director,* James Anderson; *Screenplay by*
Morrie Ryskind and Anthony Veiller; *Photography by* Robert De Grasse; *Art Direction by* Van Nest Polglase; *Associate
Art Director,* Carroll Clark; *Set Decorator,* Darrell Silvera;
Music by Roy Webb; *Sound Recorder,* John L. Cass; *Film
Editor,* William Hamilton; *Costumes by* Muriel King; *Makeup by* Mel Burns.

BRINGING UP BABY, R.K.O., 1938
Based on a story by Hagar Wilde

CAST: Katharine Hepburn . . . . Susan Vance
Cary Grant . . . . David Huxley
Charles Ruggles . . . . Major Horace Applegate
May Robson . . . . Aunt Elizabeth
Walter Catlett . . . . Constable Slocum
Barry Fitzgerald . . . . Gogarty
Fritz Feld. . . . . Dr. Fritz Lehmann
Leona Roberts . . . . Mrs. Gogarty (Hannah)
George Irving. . . . . Alexander Peabody
Tala Birell . . . . Mrs. Lehmann
Virginia Walker. . . . . Alice Swallow
John Kelly . . . . Elmer
George Humbert . . . . Louis, the Headwaiter
Ernest Cossart . . . . Joe, the Bartender
Brooks Benedict . . . . David's Caddy
Jack Carson . . . . Roustabout
Richard Lane . . . . Circus Manager
Ward Bond . . . . Motor Cop

Nissa . . . . Baby, the Leopard

Asta . . . . George, the Dog

Produced by Howard Hawks; *Associate Producer,* Cliff Reid; *Directed by* Howard Hawks; *Assistant Director,* Edward Donahue; *Screenplay by* Dudley Nichols and Hagar Wilde; *Photography by* Russell Metty; *Special Effects by* Vernon L. Walker; *Art Direction by* Van Nest Polglase; *Associate Art Director,* Perry Ferguson; *Set Decorator,* Darrell Silvera; *Music by* Roy Webb; *Sound Recorder,* John L. Cass; *Film Editor,* George Hively; *Costumes by* Howard Greer; *Makeup by* Mel Burns.

HOLIDAY,* Columbia, 1938
Based on the play by Philip Barry

CAST: Katharine Hepburn . . . . Linda Seton

Cary Grant . . . . Johnny Case

Doris Nolan. . . . . Julia Seton

Lew Ayres . . . . Ned Seton

Edward Everett Horton . . . Nick Potter

Henry Kolker . . . . Edward Seton

Binnie Barnes. . . . . Laura Cram

Jean Dixon . . . . Susan Potter

Henry Daniell. . . . . Seton Cram

Charles Trowbridge . . . . Banker

George Pauncefort. . . . . Henry

Charles Richman. . . . . Thayer

Mitchell Harris . . . . Jennings

Neil Fitzgerald . . . . Edgar

Marion Ballou . . . . Grandmother

Howard Hickman . . . . Man in Church

Hilda Plowright . . . . Woman in Church

Mabel Colcord . . . . Cook

Bess Flowers . . . . Woman on Staircase

Harry Allen, Edward Cooper . Scotchmen

Margaret McWade. . . . . Farmer's Wife

Frank Shannon. . . . . Farmer

Aileen Carlyle. . . . . Farm Girl

Matt McHugh. . . . . Taxi Driver

Maurice Brierre . . . . Steward

---

* Released as FREE TO LIVE in Great Britain

Esther Peck . . . . Mrs. Jennings
Lillian West . . . . Mrs. Thayer
Luke Cosgrave . . . . Grandfather

Associate Producer, Everett Riskin; *Directed by* George Cukor; *Assistant Director*, Clifford Broughton; *Screenplay by* Donald Ogden Stewart and Sidney Buchman; *Photography by* Franz Planer; *Art Direction by* Stephen Goosson; *Associate Art Director*, Lionel Banks; *Set Decorator*, Babs Johnstone; *Music by* Sidney Cutner; *Musical Director*, Morris Stoloff; *Sound Recorder*, Lodge Cunningham; *Film Editors*, Otto Meyer and Al Clark; *Costumes by* Kalloch; *Jewelry by* Paul Flato.

THE PHILADELPHIA STORY, Metro-Goldwyn-Mayer, 1940

Based on the play by Philip Barry; as produced on the stage by The Theatre Guild, Inc.

CAST:
Katharine Hepburn . . . . Tracy Lord
Cary Grant . . . . C. K. Dexter Haven
James Stewart . . . . Mike Connor
Ruth Hussey . . . . Liz Imbrie
John Howard . . . . George Kittredge
Roland Young . . . . Uncle Willie
John Halliday . . . . Seth Lord
Virginia Weidler . . . . Dinah Lord
Mary Nash . . . . Margaret Lord
Henry Daniell . . . . Sidney Kidd
Lionel Pape . . . . Edward
Rex Evans . . . . Thomas
Russ Clark . . . . John
Hilda Plowright . . . . Librarian
Lita Chevret . . . . Manicurist
Lee Phelps . . . . Bartender
David Clyde . . . . Mac
Claude King . . . . Willie's Butler
Robert De Bruce . . . . Dr. Parsons
Veda Buckland . . . . Elsie
Dorothy Fay . . . . First Mainliner
Florine McKinney . . . . Second Mainliner
Helene Whitney . . . . Third Mainliner

Hillary Brooke . . . . Fourth Mainliner

Produced by Joseph L. Mankiewicz; *Directed by* George Cukor; *Assistant Director,* Edward Woehler; *Screenplay by* Donald Ogden Stewart; *Photography by* Joseph Ruttenberg; *Art Direction by* Cedric Gibbons; *Associate Art Director,* Wade B. Rubottom; *Set Decorator,* Edwin B. Willis; *Music by* Franz Waxman; *Sound Recorder,* Douglas Shearer; *Film Editor,* Frank Sullivan; *Costumes by* Adrian; *Makeup by* Jack Dawn; *Hairstyles by* Sydney Guilaroff.

WOMAN OF THE YEAR, Metro-Goldwyn-Mayer, 1942

CAST:
Katharine Hepburn	Tess Harding
Spencer Tracy.	Sam Craig
Fay Bainter	Ellen Whitcomb
Reginald Owen	Clayton
Minor Watson.	William Harding
William Bendix.	Pinkie Peters
Gladys Blake	Flo Peters
Dan Tobin.	Gerald
Roscoe Karns	Phil Whittaker
William Tannen.	Ellis
Ludwig Stossel	Dr. Martin Lubbeck
Sara Haden	Matron at Refugee Home
Edith Evanson	Alma
George Kezas.	Chris
Jimmy Conlin.	Reporter
Henry Roquemore.	Justice of the Peace
Cyril Ring	Harding's Chauffeur
Ben Lessy	Punchy
Johnny Berkes	Pal
Ray Teal	Reporter
Duke York.	Football Player
Edward McWade.	Adolph
Joe Yule	Building Superintendent
Winifred Harris	Chairlady
William Holmes	Man at Banquet

Produced by Joseph L. Mankiewicz; *Directed by* George Stevens; *Assistant Director,* Robert Golden; *Original Screenplay by* Ring Lardner, Jr., and Michael Kanin; *Photography by* Joseph Ruttenberg; *Art Direction by* Cedric Gibbons; *Associate Art Director,* Randall Duell; *Set Decorator,* Edwin

B. Willis; *Music by* Franz Waxman; *Sound Recorder,* Douglas Shearer; *Film Editor,* Frank Sullivan; *Costumes by* Adrian; *Makeup by* Jack Dawn; *Hairstyles by* Sydney Guilaroff.

KEEPER OF THE FLAME, Metro-Goldwyn-Mayer, 1942
Based on the novel by I.A.R. Wylie

CAST:
Katharine Hepburn	Christine Forrest
Spencer Tracy	Steven O'Malley
Richard Whorf	Clive Kerndon
Margaret Wycherly	Mrs. Forrest
Donald Meek	Mr. Arbuthnot
Horace (Stephen) McNally	Freddie Ridges
Audrey Christie	Jane Harding
Frank Craven	Dr. Fielding
Forrest Tucker	Geoffrey Midford
Percy Kilbride	Orion
Howard da Silva	Jason Rickards
Darryl Hickman	Jeb Rickards
William Newell	Piggot
Rex Evans	John
Blanche Yurka	Anna
Mary McLeod	Janet
Clifford Brooke	William
Craufurd Kent	Ambassador
Mickey Martin	Messenger Boy
Manart Kippen, Donald Gallaher, Cliff Danielson	Reporters
Major Sam Harris, Art Howard, Harold Miller	Men
Jay Ward	Pete
Rita Quigley	Susan

Produced by Victor Saville; *Associate Producer,* Leon Gordon; *Directed by* George Cukor; *Assistant Director,* Edward Woehler; *Screenplay by* Donald Ogden Stewart; *Photography by* William Daniels; *Special Effects by* Warren Newcombe; *Art Direction by* Cedric Gibbons; *Associate Art Director,* Lyle Wheeler; *Set Decorator,* Edwin B. Willis; *Associate Set Decorator,* Jack Moore; *Music by* Bronislau Kaper; *Sound Recorder,* Douglas Shearer; *Film Editor,* James E. Newcom; *Costumes by* Adrian; *Makeup by* Jack Dawn.

STAGE DOOR CANTEEN, United Artists, 1943

CAST: *Katharine Hepburn* . . . . Herself
Cheryl Walker. . . . . Eileen
William Terry. . . . . Ed "Dakota" Smith
Marjorie Riordan . . . . Jean
Lon McCallister . . . . "California"
Margaret Early. . . . . Ella Sue
Michael Harrison . . . . "Texas"
Dorothea Kent . . . . Mamie
Fred Brady . . . . "Jersey"
Marion Shockley. . . . . Lillian
Patrick O'Moore. . . . . the Australian
Ruth Roman . . . . Girl
*Judith Anderson, Henry Armetta, Benny Baker, Kenny
Baker, Tallulah Bankhead, Ralph Bellamy, Edgar Bergen
and Charlie McCarthy, Ray Bolger, Helen Broderick, Ina
Claire, Katharine Cornell, Lloyd Corrigan, Jane Cowl,
Jane Darwell, William Demarest, Virginia Field, Dorothy
Fields, Gracie Fields, Lynn Fontanne, Arlene Francis,
Vinton Freedley, Billy Gilbert, Lucile Gleason, Vera Gor-
don, Virginia Grey, Helen Hayes, Hugh Herbert, Jean
Hersholt, Sam Jaffe, Allen Jenkins, George Jessel, Roscoe
Karns, Virginia Kaye, Tom Kennedy, Otto Kruger, June
Lang, Betty Lawford, Gertrude Lawrence, Gypsy Rose
Lee, Alfred Lunt, Bert Lytell, Harpo Marx, Aline MacMa-
hon, Elsa Maxwell, Helen Menken, Yehudi Menuhin, Ethel
Merman, Ralph Morgan, Alan Mowbray, Paul Muni,
Elliott Nugent, Merle Oberon, Franklin Pangborn, Helen
Parrish, Brock Pemberton, George Raft, Lanny Ross,
Selena Royle, Martha Scott, Cornelia Otis Skinner, Ned
Sparks, Bill Stern, Ethel Waters, Johnny Weissmuller,
Arleen Whelan, Dame May Whitty, Ed Wynn*

With: Count Basie and His Band; Xavier Cugat and His
Orchestra, with Lina Romay; Benny Goodman and His
Orchestra, with Peggy Lee; Kay Kyser and His Band; Freddy
Martin and His Orchestra; Guy Lombardo and His Orches-
tra.

SONGS: "She's a Bombshell from Brooklyn," Sol Lesser, Al
Dubin, Jimmy Monaco; "The Girl I Love to Leave
Behind," Lorenz Hart, Richard Rodgers; "We

Mustn't Say Goodbye," "The Machine Gun Song," "American Boy," "Don't Worry Island," "Quick Sands," "A Rookie and His Rhythm," "Sleep Baby Sleep in Your Jeep," "We Meet in the Funniest Places," "You're Pretty Terrific Yourself," Al Dubin, Jimmy Monaco; "Why Don't You Do Right?," Joe McCoy; "Bugle Call Rag," Elmer Schoebel, Billy Meyers, Jack Pittis; "Ave Maria," Franz Schubert; "Flight of the Bumble Bee," Rimsky-Korsakov.

Produced by Sol Lesser; *Associate Producer,* Barnett Briskin; *Directed by* Frank Borzage; *Assistant Directors,* Lew Borzage and Virgil Hart; *Original Screenplay by* Delmer Daves; *Photography by* Harry Wild; *Art Direction by* Hans Peters; *Set Decorator,* Victor Gangelin; *Production Designer,* Harry Horner; *Assistant Production Designer,* Clem Beauchamp; *Talent Coordinator,* Radie Harris; *Film Editor,* Hal Kern; *Music by* Freddie Rich; *Sound Recorder,* Hugh McDowell; *Musical Director,* C. Bakaleinikoff; *Costumes by* Albert Deano.

DRAGON SEED, Metro-Goldwyn-Mayer, 1944
Based on the novel by Pearl S. Buck

CAST:

Katharine Hepburn	Jade
Walter Huston	Ling Tan
Aline MacMahon	Mrs. Ling Tan
Akim Tamiroff	Wu Lien
Turhan Bey	Lao Er
Hurd Hatfield	Lao San
Frances Rafferty	Orchid
Agnes Moorehead	Third Cousin's Wife
Henry Travers	Third Cousin
Robert Lewis	Captain Sato
J. Carrol Naish	Japanese Kitchen Overseer
Robert Bice	Lao Ta
Jacqueline De Wit	Mrs. Wu Lien
Clarence Lung	Fourth Cousin
Paul E. Burns	Neighbor Shen
Anna Demetrio	Wu Sao
Ted Hecht	Major Yohagi
Abner Biberman	Captain Yasuda
Leonard Mudie	Old Peddler

Charles Lung	Japanese Diplomat
Benson Fong	Student
Philip Van Zandt.	Japanese Guard
Al Hill	Japanese Officer
J. Alex Havier	Japanese Soldier
Philip Ahn.	Leader of City People
Roland Got	Speaker with Movies
Robert Lee	Young Farmer
Frank Puglia	Old Clerk
Claire Du Brey.	Hysterical Woman
Lee Tung Foo.	Innkeeper
Jay Novello	Japanese Soldier
Leonard Strong.	Japanese Official
Lionel Barrymore	Narrator

Produced by Pandro S. Berman; *Directed by* Jack Conway and Harold S. Bucquet; *Assistant Director*, Al Shenberg; *Technical Director*, Wei F. Hsueh; *Screenplay by* Marguerite Roberts and Jane Murfin; *Photography by* Sidney Wagner; *Special Effects by* Warren Newcombe; *Art Direction by* Cedric Gibbons; *Associate Art Director*, Lyle R. Wheeler; *Set Decorator*, Edwin B. Willis; *Associate Set Decorator*, Hugh Hunt; *Music by* Herbert Stothart; *Sound Recorder*, Douglas Shearer; *Film Editor*, Harold F. Kress; *Costumes by* Valles; *Costume Supervisor*, Irene; *Makeup by* Jack Dawn.

WITHOUT LOVE, Metro-Goldwyn-Mayer, 1945
Based on the play by Philip Barry; as produced on the stage by The Theatre Guild, Inc.

CAST:	*Katharine Hepburn*	Jamie Rowan
	Spencer Tracy.	Pat Jamieson
	Lucille Ball	Kitty Trimble
	Keenan Wynn.	Quentin Ladd
	Carl Esmond	Paul Carrell
	Patricia Morison	Edwina Collins
	Felix Bressart	Professor Grinza
	Emily Massey.	Anna
	Gloria Grahame	Flower Girl
	George Davis	Caretaker
	George Chandler.	Elevator Boy

Clancy Cooper	Sergeant
Wallis Clark	Professor Thompson
Donald Curtis	Professor Ellis
Charles Arnt	Colonel Braden
Eddie Acuff	Driver
Clarence Muse	Porter
Franco Corsaro	Headwaiter
Ralph Brooks	Pageboy
William Forrest	Doctor
Garry Owen	Soldier
Joe Devlin	Soldier
William Newell	Soldier
James Flavin	Sergeant
Hazel Brooks	Girl on Elevator

Produced by Lawrence A. Weingarten; *Directed by* Harold S. Bucquet; *Assistant Director*, Earl McEvoy; *Screenplay by* Donald Ogden Stewart; *Photography by* Karl Freund; *Special Effects by* A. Arnold Gillespie and Danny Hall; *Art Director*, Cedric Gibbons; *Associate Art Director*, Harry McAfee; *Set Decorator*, Edwin B. Willis; *Associate Set Decorator*, McLean Nisbet; *Music by* Bronislau Kaper; *Sound Recorder*, Douglas Shearer; *Film Editor*, Frank Sullivan; *Costume Supervision*, Irene; *Associate Costumer*, Marion Herwood Keyes; *Makeup by* Jack Dawn; *Montage*, Peter Ballbusch.

UNDERCURRENT, Metro-Goldwyn-Mayer, 1946
Based on a story by Thelma Strabel

CAST:		
	Katharine Hepburn	Ann Hamilton
	Robert Taylor	Alan Garroway
	Robert Mitchum	Michael Garroway
	Edmund Gwenn	Prof. "Dink" Hamilton
	Marjorie Main	Lucy
	Jayne Meadows	Sylvia Lea Burton
	Clinton Sundberg	Mr. Warmsley
	Dan Tobin	Prof. Joseph Bangs
	Kathryn Card	Mrs. Foster
	Leigh Whipper	George
	Charles Trowbridge	Justice Putnam
	James Westerfield	Henry Gilson
	Billy McLain	Uncle Ben

Bess Flowers . . . . Julia Donnegan
Sarah Edwards . . . . Cora
Betty Blythe . . . . Saleslady

Produced by Pandro S. Berman; *Directed by* Vincente Minnelli; *Assistant Director*, Normal Elzer; *Screenplay by* Edward Chodorov; *Photography by* Karl Freund; *Art Direction by* Cedric Gibbons; *Associate Art Director*, Randall Duell; *Set Decorator*, Edwin B. Willis; *Associate Set Decorator*, Jack D. Moore; *Music by* Herbert Stothart; *Sound Recorder*, Douglas Shearer; *Film Editor*, Ferris Webster; *Costumes by* Irene; *Makeup by* Jack Dawn; *Hairstyles by* Sydney Guilaroff.

In 1946, Katharine Hepburn and Spencer Tracy made a short trailer for the Cancer Society.

THE SEA OF GRASS, Metro-Goldwyn-Mayer, 1947
Based on the novel by Conrad Richter

CAST: Katharine Hepburn . . . . Lutie Cameron
Spencer Tracy . . . . Colonel James Brewton
Melvyn Douglas . . . . Brice Chamberlain
Phyllis Thaxter . . . . Sara Beth Brewton
Robert Walker . . . . Brock Brewton
Edgar Buchanan . . . . Jeff
Harry Carey . . . . Doc Reid
Ruth Nelson . . . . Selena Hall
William "Bill" Phillips . . . . . Banty
James Bell . . . . Sam Hall
Robert Barrat . . . . Judge White
Charles Trowbridge . . . . George Cameron
Russell Hicks . . . . Major Harney
Robert Armstrong . . . . Floyd McCurtin
Trevor Bardette . . . . Andy Boggs
Morris Ankrum . . . . Crane
Nora Cecil . . . . Nurse

Produced by Pandro S. Berman; *Directed by* Elia Kazan; *Assistant Director*, Sid Sidman; *Screenplay by* Marguerite Roberts and Vincent Lawrence; *Photography by* Harry Stradling; *Art Direction by* Cedric Gibbons; *Associate Art Director*, Paul Groesse; *Set Decorator*, Edwin B. Willis; *Music by* Herbert Stothart; *Sound Recorder*, Douglas Shearer; *Film Editor,* Robert J. Kern; *Costumes by* Walter Plunkett; *Makeup by* Jack Dawn.

SONG OF LOVE, Metro-Goldwyn-Mayer, 1947
Based on the play by Bernard Schubert and Mario Silva

CAST:
Katharine Hepburn	Cara Wieck Schumann
Paul Henreid	Robert Schumann
Robert Walker	Johannes Brahms
Henry Daniell.	Franz Liszt
Leo G. Carroll	Professor Wieck
Else Janssen	Bertha
Gigi Perreau.	Julie
"Tinker" Furlong	Felix
Ann Carter	Marie
Janine Perreau.	Eugenie
Jimmie Hunt	Ludwig
Anthony Sydes	Ferdinand
Eilene Janssen	Elsie
Roman Bohnen.	Dr. Hoffman
Ludwig Stossel	Haslinger
Tala Birell	Princess Valerie Hohenfels
Kurk Katch	Judge
Henry Stephenson	King Albert
Konstantin Shayne.	Reinecke
Byron Foulger	Court Officer
Josephine Whittell	Lady in Box

Produced by Clarence Brown; *Directed by* Clarence Brown; *Assistant Director,* Al Raboch; *Screenplay by* Ivan Tors, Irmgard Von Cube, Allen Vincent and Robert Ardrey; *Photography by* Harry Stradling; *Special Effects by* Warren Newcombe; *Art Direction by* Cedric Gibbons; *Associate Art Director,* Hans Peters; *Set Decorator,* Edwin B. Willis; *Music by* Bronislau Kaper; *Sound Recorder,* Douglas Shearer; *Piano Recordings,* Arthur Rubinstein; *Orchestra,* M.G.M. Symphony Orchestra; *Conductor,* William Steinberg; *Chorus,* St. Luke's Boys Choir; *Music Adviser,* Laura Dubman; *Film Editor,* Robert J. Kern; *Women's Costumes by* Walter Plunkett; *Men's Costumes by* Valles; *Costume Supervision by* Irene; *Makeup by* Jack Dawn; *Hairstyles by* Sydney Guilaroff.

STATE OF THE UNION,* Metro-Goldwyn-Mayer, 1948 (a Liberty Film Production)
Based on the play by Howard Lindsay and Russel Crouse

CAST:		
Katharine Hepburn	. . . .	Mary Matthews
Spencer Tracy	. . . .	Grant Matthews
Van Johnson	. . . .	Spike McManus
Angela Lansbury	. . . .	Kay Thorndyke
Adolphe Menjou	. . . .	Jim Conover
Lewis Stone	. . . .	Sam Thorndyke
Howard Smith	. . . .	Sam Parrish
Maidel Turner	. . . .	Lulubelle Alexander
Raymond Walburn	. . . .	Judge Alexander
Charles Dingle	. . . .	Bill Hardy
Florence Auer	. . . .	Grace Orval Draper
Pierre Watkin	. . . .	Senator Lauterback
Margaret Hamilton	. . . .	Norah
Irving Bacon	. . . .	Buck
Patti Brady	. . . .	Joyce
George Nokes	. . . .	Grant, Jr.
Carl Switzer	. . . .	Bellboy
Tom Pedi	. . . .	Barber
Tom Fadden	. . . .	Waiter
Charles Lane	. . . .	Blink Moran
Art Baker	. . . .	Leith
Rhea Mitchell	. . . .	Jenny
Arthur O'Connell	. . . .	First Reporter
Marion Martin	. . . .	Blonde Girl
Tor Johnson	. . . .	Wrestler
Stanley Andrews	. . . .	Senator
Dave Willock	. . . .	Pilot
Russell Meeker	. . . .	Politician
Frank L. Clarke	. . . .	Joe Crandall
David Clarke	. . . .	Rusty Miller
Dell Henderson	. . . .	Broder
Edwin Cooper	. . . .	Bradbury
Davison Clark	. . . .	Crump
Francis Pierlot	. . . .	Josephs
Brandon Beach	. . . .	Editor

* Released as THE WORLD AND HIS WIFE in Great Britain

A REMARKABLE WOMAN

Produced by Frank Capra; *Associate Producer*, Anthony Veiller; *Directed by* Frank Capra; *Assistant Director*, Arthur S. Black, Jr.; *Screenplay by* Anthony Veiller and Myles Connelly; *Photography by* George J. Folsey; *Special Effects by* A. Arnold Gillespie; *Art Direction by* Cedric Gibbons; *Associate Art Director*, Urie McCleary; *Set Decorator*, Emile Kuri; *Music by* Victor Young; *Sound Recorder*, Douglas Shearer; *Film Editor*, William Hornbeck; *Costumes by* Irene.

ADAM'S RIB, Metro-Goldwyn-Mayer, 1949
Based on an original story by Ruth Gordon and Garson Kanin

CAST: *Katharine Hepburn* . . . . Amanda Bonner
Spencer Tracy. . . . . Adam Bonner
Judy Holliday. . . . . Doris Attinger
Tom Ewell. . . . . Warren Attinger
David Wayne . . . . Kip Lurie
Jean Hagen . . . . Beryl Caighn
Hope Emerson . . . . Olympia La Pere
Eve March. . . . . Grace
Clarence Kolb . . . . Judge Reiser
Emerson Treacy . . . . Jules Frikke
Polly Moran. . . . . Mrs. McGrath
Will Wright . . . . Judge Marcasson
Elizabeth Flournoy . . . . Dr. Margaret Brodeigh
Janna Da Loos. . . . . Mary, the Maid
James Nolan. . . . . Dave
David Clarke . . . . Roy
John Maxwell Sholes . . . . . . Court Clerk
Marvin Kaplan . . . . Court Stenographer
Gracille La Vinder . . . . Police Matron
William Self. . . . . Benjamin Klausner
Paula Raymond . . . . Emerald
Ray Walker . . . . Photographer
Tommy Noonan . . . . Reporter
De Forrest Lawrence,
  John Fell . . . . Adam's Assistants
Sid Dubin . . . . Amanda's Assistant
Joe Bernard. . . . . Mr. Bonner
Madge Blake . . . . Mrs. Bonner
Marjorie Wood . . . . Mrs. Marcasson

Lester Luther . . . . Judge Poynter
Anna Q. Nilsson . . . . Mrs. Poynter
Roger David . . . . Hurlock
Louis Mason . . . . Elderly Elevator Operator
Rex Evans . . . . Fat Man
Charles Bastin . . . . Young District Attorney
E. Bradley Coleman . . . . . . Subway Rider

Produced by Lawrence Weingarten; *Directed by* George Cukor; *Assistant Director,* Jack Greenwood; *Screenplay by* Ruth Gordon and Garson Kanin; *Photography by* George J. Folsey; *Special Effects by* A. Arnold Gillespie; *Art Direction by* Cedric Gibbons; *Associate Art Director,* William Ferrari; *Set Decorator,* Edwin B. Willis; *Associate Set Decorator,* Henry Grace; *Music by* Miklos Rozsa; *Sound Recorder,* Douglas Shearer; *Film Editor,* George Boemler; *Costumes by* Walter Plunkett.
Song "Farewell, Amanda" by Cole Porter.

THE AFRICAN QUEEN, United Artists, 1951
Based on the novel by C. S. Forester

CAST: Katharine Hepburn . . . . Rose Sayer
Humphrey Bogart . . . . Charlie Allnut
Robert Morley . . . . Reverend Samuel Sayer
Peter Bull . . . . Captain of *Louisa*
Theodore Bikel . . . . First Officer
Walter Gotell . . . . Second Officer
Gerald Onn . . . . Petty Officer
Peter Swanick . . . . First Officer of *Shona*
Richard Marner . . . . Second Officer of *Shona*

Produced by S. P. Eagle; *Directed by* John Huston; *Assistant Director,* Guy Hamilton; *Screenplay by* James Agee and John Huston; *Photography by* Jack Cardiff; *Special Effects by* Cliff Richardson; *Second Unit Photography by* Ted Scaife; *Music by* Alan Gray; *Sound Recorder,* John Mitchell; *Film Editor,* Ralph Kemplen; *Production Managers,* Leigh Aman, T. S. Lyndon-Haynes, Wilfred Shingleton and John Hoesli; *Sound Editor,* Eric Wood; *Costumer for Miss Hepburn,* Doris Langley Moore; *Film Costumes by* Connie De Pinna; *Wardrobe Mistress,* Vi Murray; *Makeup by* George Frost; *Camera Operator,* Ted Moore; *Continuity,* Angela Allen.

A REMARKABLE WOMAN

PAT AND MIKE, Metro-Goldwyn-Mayer, 1952
Based on an original story by Ruth Gordon and Garson Kanin

CAST:
Katharine Hepburn	Pat Pemberton
Spencer Tracy.	Mike Conovan
Aldo Ray.	Davie Hucko
William Ching	Collier Weld
Sammy White.	Barney Grau
George Mathews	Spec Cauley
Loring Smith	Mr. Beminger
Phyllis Povah	Mrs. Beminger
Charles Buchinski (Bronson). .	Hank Tasling
Frank Richards.	Sam Garsell
Jim Backus	Charles Barry
Chuck Connors.	Police Captain
Joseph E. Bernard.	Gibby
Owen McGiveney	Harry MacWade
Lou Lubin.	Waiter
Carl Switzer.	Bus Boy
William Self.	Pat's Caddy
Billy McLean, Frankie Darro, Paul Brinegar, "Tiny" Jimmie Kelly	Caddies
Mae Clarke, Helen Eby-Rock, Elizabeth Holmes	Women Golfers
Hank Weaver	Commentator
Tom Harmon	Sportscaster
Charlie Murray.	Line Judge, Tennis Court
Gussie Moran, Babe Didrickson Zaharias, Don Budge, Alice Marble, Frank Parker, Betty Hicks, Beverly Hanson, Helen Dettweiler . .	Themselves

Produced by Lawrence Weingarten; *Directed by* George Cukor; *Assistant Director,* Jack Greenwood; *Screenplay by* Ruth Gordon and Garson Kanin; *Photography by* William Daniels; *Special Effects by* Warren Newcombe; *Art Direction by* Cedric Gibbons; *Associate Art Director,* Urie McCleary; *Set Decorator,* Edwin B. Willis; *Associate Set Decorator,* Hugh Hunt; *Music by* David Raskin· *Sound Recorder.*

Douglas Shearer; *Film Editor*, George Boemler; *Miss Hepburn's Costumes* by Orry-Kelly; *Makeup* by William Tuttle; *Montage* by Peter Ballbusch.

SUMMERTIME,* United Artists, 1955 (A Lopert Film Production)
Based on the play *The Time of the Cuckoo* by Arthur Laurents

CAST: *Katharine Hepburn* . . . . Jane Hudson
      Rossano Brazzi . . . . Renato di Rossi
      Isa Miranda . . . . Signora Fiorini
      Darren McGavin . . . . Eddie Jaeger
      Mari Aldon . . . . Phyl Jaeger
      Jane Rose . . . . Mrs. McIlhenny
      MacDonald Parke . . . . Mr. McIlhenny
      Gaitano Audiero . . . . Mauro
      André Morell . . . . Englishman
      Jeremy Spenser . . . . Vito di Rossi
      Virginia Simeon . . . . Giovanna

Produced by Ilya Lopert; *Associate Producer*, Norman Spencer; *Assistant to the Producer*, Robert Kingsley; *Directed by* David Lean; *Screenplay by* David Lean and H. E. Bates; *Photography by* Jack Hildyard; *Art Direction by* Vincent Korda; *Associate Art Directors*, W. Hutchinson and Ferdinand Bellan; *Music by* Alessandro Cicognini; *Sound Recorder*, Peter Handford; *Film Editor*, Peter Taylor; *Sound Editor*, Winston Ryder; *Hairstyles by* Grazia de Rossi; *Makeup by* Cesare Gamberelli; *Production Managers*, Raymond Anzarut and Franco Magli; *Camera Operator*, Peter Newbrook; *Continuity*, Margaret Shipway.

THE RAINMAKER, Paramount, 1956
Based on the play by N. Richard Nash

CAST: *Katharine Hepburn* . . . . Lizzie Curry
      Burt Lancaster . . . . Starbuck
      Wendell Corey . . . . File
      Lloyd Bridges . . . . Noah Curry
      Earl Holliman . . . . Jim Curry

* Released as SUMMER MADNESS in Great Britain

Cameron Prud'homme	H. C. Curry
Wallace Ford	Sheriff Thomas
Yvonne Lime	Snookie
Dottie Bee Baker	Belinda
Dan White	Deputy
Stan Jones, John Benson, James Stone, Tony Merrill, Joe Brown	Townsmen
Ken Becker	Phil Mackey

Produced by Hal B. Wallis; *Associate Producer*, Paul Nathan; *Directed by* Joseph Anthony; *Assistant Director*, C. C. Coleman, Jr.; *Screenplay by* N. Richard Nash; *Photography by* Charles Lang, Jr.; *Special Effects by* John P. Fulton; *Art Direction by* Hal Pereira; *Associate Art Director*, Walter Tyler; *Set Decorator*, Sam Comer; *Associate Set Decorator*, Arthur Krams; *Music by* Alex North; *Sound Recorders*, Harold Lewis and Winston Leverett; *Film Editor*, Warren Low; *Costumes by* Edith Head; *Makeup by* Wally Westmore; *Hairstyles by* Nellie Manley; *Technicolor Color Consultant*, Richard Mueller.

THE IRON PETTICOAT, Metro-Goldwyn-Mayer, 1956 (A Benhar Production)

Based on an original story by Harry Saltzman

CAST:	*Katharine Hepburn*	Vinka Kovelenko
	Bob Hope	Chuck Lockwood
	James Robertson Justice	Colonel Sklarnoff
	Robert Helpmann	Ivan Kropotkin
	David Kossoff	Dubratz
	Alan Gifford	Colonel Tarbell
	Paul Carpenter	Lewis
	Noelle Middleton	Connie
	Nicholas Phipps	Tony Mallard
	Sidney James	Paul
	Alexander Gauge	Senator
	Doris Goddard	Maria
	Tutte Lemkow	Sutsiyawa
	Sandra Dorne	Tityana
	Richard Wattis	Lingerie Clerk
	Maria Antippas	Sklarnoff's Secretary

Martin Boddey . . . . Grisha

Produced by Betty E. Box; *Directed by* Ralph Thomas; *Assistant Director,* James H. Ware; *Screenplay by* Ben Hecht (name removed from credits); *Photography by* Ernest Steward; *Art Direction by* Carmen Dillon; *Set Decorator,* Vernon Dixon; *Music by* Benjamin Frankel; *Sound Recorders,* John W. Mitchell and Gordon K. McCallum; *Sound Editor,* Roger Cherrill; *Film Editor,* Frederick Wilson; *Costumes by* Yvonne Caffin; *Makeup by* W. T. Partleton; *Production Manager,* R. Denis Holt; *Camera Operator,* H.A.R. Thompson; *Continuity,* Joan Davis.

THE DESK SET,* Twentieth Century-Fox, 1957
Based on the play by William Marchant; as produced on the stage by Robert Fryer and Lawrence Carr

CAST: | | |
|---|---|
| Katharine Hepburn | Bunny Watson |
| Spencer Tracy | Richard Sumner |
| Gig Young | Mike Cutler |
| Joan Blondell | Peg Costello |
| Dina Merrill | Sylvia |
| Sue Randall | Ruthie |
| Neva Patterson | Miss Warringer |
| Harry Ellerbe | Smithers |
| Nicholas Joy | Azae |
| Diane Jergens | Alice |
| Merry Anders | Cathy |
| Ida Moore | Old Lady |
| Rachel Stephens | Receptionist |
| Sammy Ogg | Kenny |

Produced by Henry Ephron; *Directed by* Walter Lang; *Assistant Director,* Hal Herman; *Screenplay by* Phoebe and Henry Ephron; *Photography by* Leon Shamroy; *Special Effects by* Ray Kellogg; *Art Direction by* Lyle Wheeler; *Associate Art Director,* Maurice Ransford; *Set Decorator,* Walter M. Scott; *Associate Set Decorator,* Paul S. Fox; *Music by* Cyril J. Mockridge; *Musical Director,* Lionel Newman; *Orchestrator,* Edward B. Powell; *Sound Recorders,* E. Clayton Ward and Harry M. Leonard; *Film Editor,* Robert Simpson; *Costumes*

---

* Released as HIS OTHER WOMAN in Great Britain

by Charles le Maire; *Makeup by* Ben Nye; *Hairstyles by* Helen Turpin; *Color Consultant,* Leonard Doss; *Cinema- 'cope Lenses by* Bausch & Lomb.

SUDDENLY LAST SUMMER, Columbia Pictures, 1959 (A Horizon [G.B.] Limited Production in association with Academy Pictures and Camp Films)
Based on the short play by Tennessee Williams

CAST: *Katharine Hepburn* . . . . Mrs. Venable
Elizabeth Taylor . . . . Catherine Holly
Montgomery Clift . . . . Dr. Cukrowicz
Albert Dekker . . . . Dr. Hockstader
Mercedes McCambridge . . . . . Mrs. Holly
Gary Raymond . . . . George Holly
Mavis Villiers . . . . Miss Foxhill
Patricia Marmont . . . . Nurse Benson
Joan Young . . . . Sister Felicity
Maria Britneva . . . . Lucy
Sheila Robbins . . . . Dr. Hockstader's Secretary
David Cameron . . . . Young Blond Intern
Roberta Woolley . . . . A Patient

Produced by Sam Spiegel; *Directed by* Joseph L. Mankiewicz; *Assistant Director,* Bluey Hill; *Screenplay by* Gore Vidal and Tennessee Williams; *Photography by* Jack Hildyard; *Special Effects by* Tom Howard; *Production Supervisor,* Bill Kirby; *Production Designer,* Oliver Messel; *Art Direction by* William Kellner; *Set Decorator,* Scott Slimon; *Music by* Buxton Orr and Malcolm Arnold; *Sound Recorders,* A. G. Ambler and John Cox; *Film Editor,* Thomas G. Stanford; *Editorial Consultant,* William W. Hornbeck; *Assembly Editor,* John Jympson; *Costumes for Miss Hepburn by* Norman Hartnell; *Costumes for Miss Taylor by* Jean Louis; *Associate Costumer,* Joan Ellacott; *Makeup by* David Aylott; *Hairstyles by* Joan White; *Camera Operator,* Gerry Fisher; *Construction Manager,* Dewey Dukelow; *Continuity,* Elaine Schreyeck.

LONG DAY'S JOURNEY INTO NIGHT, Embassy, 1962
Based on the play by Eugene O'Neill

CAST: *Katharine Hepburn* . . . . Mary Tyrone
Ralph Richardson . . . . James Tyrone, Sr.

Jason Robards, Jr.. . . . . James Tyrone, Jr.
Dean Stockwell. . . . . Edmund Tyrone
Jeanne Barr . . . . Cathleen

Co-Producers, Ely Landau and Jack J. Dreyfus, Jr.; *Directed by* Sidney Lumet; *Screenplay by* Eugene O'Neill; *Photography by* Boris Kaufman; *Music by* André Previn; *Film Editor,* Ralph Rosenblum; *Production Designer,* Richard Sylbert; *In Charge of Production,* George Justin; *Costumes by* Motley.

GUESS WHO'S COMING TO DINNER, Columbia, 1967
(A Stanley Kramer Production)

CAST: Katharine Hepburn . . . . Christina Drayton
Spencer Tracy. . . . . Matt Drayton
Sidney Poitier. . . . . John Prentice
Katharine Houghton . . . . Joey Drayton
Cecil Kellaway . . . . Monsignor Ryan
Roy E. Glenn, Sr.. . . . . Mr. Prentice
Beah Richards . . . . Mrs. Prentice
Isabel Sanford . . . . Tillie
Virginia Christine . . . . Hilary St. George
Alexandra Hay. . . . . Car Hop
Barbara Randolph. . . . . Dorothy
D'Urville Martin. . . . . Frankie
Tom Heaton. . . . . Peter
Grace Gaynor . . . . Judith
Skip Martin. . . . . Delivery Boy
John Hudkins. . . . . Cab Driver

Produced by Stanley Kramer; *Associate Producer,* George Glass; *Directed by* Stanley Kramer; *Assistant Director,* Ray Gosnell; *Original Screenplay by* William Rose; *Photography by* Sam Leavitt; *Special Effects by* Geza Gaspar; *Process Photography by* Larry Butler; *Production Designer,* Robert Clatworthy; *Set Decorator,* Frank Tuttle; *Music by* Frank de Vol; *Sound Recorders,* Charles J. Rice, Robert Martin; *Film Editor,* Robert C. Jones; *Costumes by* Joe King; *Wardrobe Supervisor,* Jean Louis; Song "Glory of Love" by Billy Hill, sung by Jacqueline Fontaine.

THE LION IN WINTER, Avco Embassy, 1968 (A Martin Poll Production)

Based on the play by James Goldman

CAST:
Katharine Hepburn	Eleanor of Aquitaine
Peter O'Toole	Henry II
Jane Merrow	Princess Alais
John Castle	Prince Geoffrey
Timothy Dalton	King Philip
Anthony Hopkins	Prince Richard, the Lion-Hearted
Nigel Stock	William Marshall
Nigel Terry	Prince John
Kenneth Griffith, O.Z. Whitehead	

Produced by Martin Poll; *Executive Producer,* Joseph E. Levine; *Associate Producer,* Jane C. Nusbaum; *Directed by* Anthony Harvey; *Assistant Director,* Kip Gowans; *Screenplay by* James Goldman; *Photography by* Douglas Slocombe; *Art Direction by* Peter Murton; *Set Decorator,* Peter James; *Music by* John Barry; *Sound Recorder,* Simon Kaye; *Film Editor,* John Bloom; *Production Supervisor,* John Quested; *Production Manager,* Basil Appleby; *Costumes by* Margaret Furse; *Makeup by* William Lodge; *Hairstyles by* A. G. Scott.

THE MADWOMAN OF CHAILLOT, Warner Brothers-Seven Arts, 1969 (An Ely Landau–Bryan Forbes Production, a Commonwealth United Corporation Film)

Based on the play by Jean Giraudoux, as translated into English by Maurice Valency

CAST:
Katharine Hepburn	Aurelia, the Madwoman of Chaillot
Charles Boyer	Broker
Claude Dauphin	Dr. Jadin
Edith Evans	Josephine, the Madwoman of La Concorde
John Gavin	Reverend
Paul Henreid	General
Oscar Homolka	Commissar
Margaret Leighton	Constance, the Madwoman of Passy

Giulietta Masina	Gabrielle, the Madwoman of Sulpice
Nanette Newman	Irma
Richard Chamberlain	Roderick
Yul Brynner	Chairman
Donald Pleasence	Prospector
Danny Kaye	Ragpicker
Fernand Gravey	Police Sergeant
Gordon Heath	The Folksinger
Gerald Sim	Julis
Jacques Marin, Joellina Smadja, Henry Virjoleux, Giles Segal, Gaston Palmer, Harriett Ariel, Catherine Berg	

Produced by Ely Landau; *Executive Producer*, Henry T. Weinstein; *Associate Producer*, Anthony B. Ungar; *Directed by* Bryan Forbes; *Assistant Director*, Louis-Alain Pitzeie; *Screenplay by* Edward Anhalt; *Photography by* Claude Renoir and Burnett Guffey; *Production Designer*, Ray Simm; *Art Direction by* Georges Petitot; *Set Decorator*, Dario Simoni; *Music by* Michael J. Lewis; *Orchestrator*, Wally Scott; *Sound Recorder*, Janet Davidson; *Sound Mixer*, Bill Daniels; *Film Editor*, Roger Dwyre; *Wardrobe Designed by* Rosine Delamare; *Makeup by* Monique Archambault; *Hairstyles by* Alex Archambault; *Production Manager*, Henri Jacquillard; Song "The Lonely Ones" by Michael J. Lewis and Gil King.

TROJAN WOMEN, Cinerama Releasing, 1971, based on the tragedy by Euripides

CAST:	*Katharine Hepburn*	Hecuba
	Vanessa Redgrave	Andromache
	Genevieve Bujold	Cassandra
	Irene Papas	Helen
	Brian Blessed	Talthybius
	Patrick Magee	Menelaus
	Alberto Sanz	Astyanax

Produced by Michael Cacoyannis and Anis Nohra; *Executive Producer*, Josef Shaftel; *Director*, Michael Cacoyannis; *Assistant Directors*, Stavros Konstantarakos, Jose Maria Ochoa and Roberto Cirla; *Screenplay by* Michael Cacoyannis; *Photography by* Alfio Contini; *Production Supervisor,* Carlo Lastricati; *Production Assistant,* Derek Horne; *Location Manager,* Paco Lara; *Special Effects,* Basilio Cortijo; *Art Direction by* Nicholas Georgiadis; *Assistant Art Directors,* Alistair Livingstone, Roman Calatayud; *Music,* Mikis Theodorakis; *Sound,* Mikes Damalas; *Sound Mixer,* Gordon McCallum; *Sound Editor,* Alfred Cox, G.B.F.E.; *Assembly Editor,* Russell Woolnough; *Coordinator,* Yannoulla Wakefield; *Continuity,* Margarita Pardo; *Camera Operator,* Maurizio Scanzani; *Makeup by* Francesco Freda; *Hairstyles by* Adalgisa Favella; *Wardrobe by* Annalisa Nasalli Rocca.

ROOSTER COGBURN, Universal Pictures, 1975
Based on a character from the novel *True Grit* by Charles Portis

CAST:
Katharine Hepburn	Eula Goodnight
John Wayne	Rooster Cogburn
Anthony Zerbe	Breed
Richard Jordan	Hawk
John McIntire	Judge Parker
Strother Martin	McCoy
Paul Koslo, Lane Smith, Jack Colvin, Jerry Gatlin, Mickey Gilbert, Chuck Hayward, Gary McLarty	Hawk's Gang
Richard Romancito	Wolf
Warren Vanders	Bagby
Tommy Lee	Chen Lee
Jon Lormer	Rev. Goodnight

Produced by Hal B. Wallis; *Directed by* Stuart Millar; *Assistant Director,* Pepi Lenzi; *Screenplay by* Martin Julien; *Photography by* Harry Stradling, Jr.; *Editor,* Robert Swink; *Music by* Laurence Rosenthal; *Art Direction by* Preston Ames; *Set Decoration by* George Robert Nelson; *Sound by* Leonard S. Peterson and John Carter; *Second Unit Director,* Michael Moore; *Stunt Coordinator,* Jerry Gatlin.

OLLY OLLY OXEN FREE, Sanrio Film Distribution release of a Rico Lion production, 1978

Based on a story by Maria L. de Ossio, Eugene Poinc and Richard A. Colla

CAST: *Katharine Hepburn* . . . . Miss Pudd
      Kevin McKenzie . . . . Alby
      Dennis Dimster. . . . . Chris
      Peter Kilman . . . . Mailman

Produced by Richard A. Colla; *Executive Producer,* Don Henderson; *Directed by* Richard A. Colla; *Executive in charge of production,* James M. Colla; *Screenplay by* Eugene Poinc; *Photography by* Gayne Rescher; *Editor,* Lee Burch; *Production Design by* Peter Wooley; *Music by* Bob Alcivar; *Costumes by* Edith Head.

ON GOLDEN POND, Universal, 1981
Based on the play by Ernest Thompson

CAST: *Katharine Hepburn* . . . . Ethel Thayer
      Henry Fonda . . . . Norman Thayer, Jr.
      Jane Fonda . . . . Chelsea Thayer Wayne
      Doug McKeon . . . . Billy Ray
      Dabney Coleman . . . . Bill Ray
      William Lanteau . . . . Charlie Martin
      Chris Rydell. . . . . Sumner Todd

Produced by Bruce Gilbert; *Directed by* Mark Rydell; *Screenplay by* Ernest Thompson; *Production Designer,* Stephen Grimes; *Set Decorator,* Jane Bogart; *Cinematographer,* Billy Williams; *Production Mixer,* David Ronne; *Sound Editor,* Victoria Rose Sampson; *Music by* Dave Grusin; *Film Editor,* Robert L. Wolfe; *Costumes by* Dorothy Jeakins; *Rerecording Mixer,* Richard Portman.

THE ULTIMATE SOLUTION OF GRACE QUIGLEY, MGM/UA and Cannon Films release of a Golan-Globus production for Northbrook Films, 1984

CAST: *Katharine Hepburn* . . . . Grace Quigley
      Nick Nolte . . . . Seymour Flint
      Elizabeth Wilson. . . . . Emily Watkins
      Chip Zien . . . . Dr. Herman
      Kit Le Fever. . . . . Muriel
      William Duell. . . . . Mr. Jenkins

Walter Abel	Homer Watkins
Francis Pole	Sarah Hodgkins
Truman Gaige	Sam Pincus
Paula Trueman	Dorothy Truger
Christopher Murney	Max Putnam
William Cain	George Quigley
Howard Sherman	Alan
Jill Eikenberry	Faith
Michael Charters	Todd
Christopher Charters	Trevor
Harris Laskawy	Mr. Argo

Produced by Menachem Golan and Yoram Globus; *Executive Producers,* A. Martin Zweiback and Adrienne Zweiback; *Directed by* Anthony Harvey; *Screenplay by* A. Martin Zweiback; *Camera (M.G.M. color),* Larry Pizer; *Editor,* Bob Raetano; *Music by* John Addison; *Costumes by* Ruth Morley; *Associate Producer,* Christopher Pearce.

NARRATIONS:

WOMEN IN DEFENSE, released by the Office of War Information, distributed by the War Activities Committee of the Motion Picture Industry; Copyright 1941. 11 minutes, sound, black and white, 16mm

CREDITS: Commentary . . . . Eleanor Roosevelt
          Narrator . . . . Katharine Hepburn

RESOLVED TO BE FREE, documentary sponsored by the Society for Savings in conjunction with the State Bicentennial Committee, produced by Ellsworth Grant, June, 1974. 30 minutes

CREDITS: Narrator . . . . Katharine Hepburn

THEATER CHRONOLOGY

SUMMER STOCK: The Edwin H. Knopf Stock Company, Baltimore, Maryland, 1928. Also in company—Mary Boland, Kenneth MacKenna, Alison Skipworth, Dudley Digges, Violet Heming and Robert Montgomery.

THE CZARINA by Melchior Lengyel and Lajos Biro

> *Katharine Hepburn* . . . . A Lady-in-Waiting to *Mary Boland* as Catherine the Great

THE CRADLE SNATCHERS by Russell Medcraft and Norma Mitchell

> *Katharine Hepburn* . . . . A Flapper

THE BIG POND by George Middleton and A. E. Thomas

> CAST: *Katharine Hepburn* . . . . Barbara*

---

* Miss Hepburn was fired after one performance of the pre-Broadway tryout at Great Neck, Long Island, New York, due to her inexperience and headstrong attitude. Barbara was played by Lucille Nikolas when the play opened on Broadway in August, 1928.

A REMARKABLE WOMAN

Marius Rogati	Francesco
Reed Brown, Jr.	Ronny Davis
Marie Curtis	Mrs. Billings
Doris Rankin	Mrs. Livermore
Kenneth MacKenna	Pierre de Mirande
Harlan Briggs	Henry Billings
Virginia Russell	Sarah
Penelope Rowland	Molly Perkins

Produced by Edwin H. Knopf and William P. Farnsworth;
Staged by Edwin H. Knopf.

THESE DAYS by Katharine Clugston
Opened: November 12, 1928, Cort Theatre, New York

CAST:

Katharine Hepburn	Veronica Sims*
Mary Hall	Rosilla Dow
Mildred McCoy	Virginia MacRae
Gertrude Moran	Pansy Larue Mott
Gladys Hopeton	Miss Guadaloupe Gorham
Bruce Evans	"Chippy" Davis
William Johnstone	Dwight Elbridge
Edwin Phillips	Stephen MacRae
Elaine Koch	Frannie MacRae
May Buckley	Mrs. MacRae
George MacQuarrie	Mr. MacRae
Marie Bruce	Miss Dorothea Utterback
Ruth Reed	Stephanie Bliss
Helen Freeman	Miss Signhild Valdimir Van Alystyne
Ada Potter	Miss Cleo Almeda Young
Suzanne Freeman	Winifred Black
Mary Hubbard	Miss Wilda Hall
Nellie Malcolm	Miss Serena Lash
Marian Lee	Dolly
Ruth Wilton	Marjory
Francis Corbin Burke	Richard
Willard S. Robertson	Guy

---

* After eight performances *These Days*, Miss Hepburn's Broadway debut,
closed. In 1934, R.K.O. filmed the play, retitled *Finishing School*, with Frances
Dee and Ginger Rogers.

Henri Lase	Philip
Ruth Wilcox	Puss

Produced by Arthur Hopkins; *Staged by* Arthur Hopkins; *Settings by* Robert Edmond Jones.

HOLIDAY by Philip Barry
Opened: November 26, 1928, Plymouth Theatre, New York

CAST:	*Hope Williams*	Linda Seton*
	Ben Smith	Johnny Case
	Dorothy Tree	Julia Seton
	Monroe Owsley	Ned Seton
	Barbara White	Susan Potter
	Donald Ogden Stewart	Nick Potter
	Walter Walker	Edward Seton
	Rosalie Norman	Laura Cram
	Thaddeus Clancy	Seton Cram
	Cameron Clemens	Henry
	J. Ascher Smith	Charles
	Beatrice Ames	Delia

Produced by Arthur Hopkins; *Staged by* Arthur Hopkins.

DEATH TAKES A HOLIDAY by Alberto Casella, adapted by Walter Ferris
Opened: October, 1929, Adelphi Theatre, Philadelphia

CAST:	*Katharine Hepburn*	Grazia†
	Florence Golden	Cora
	Thomas Bate	Fedele
	James Dale	Duke Lambert
	Ann Orr	Alda
	Olga Birkbeck	Stephanie

---

* Miss Hepburn understudied Hope Williams for six months, beginning in late December, 1928, but never appeared in the role. The play closed in June, 1929. She did play one performance when *Holiday* reopened at the Riviera Theatre on Seventy-seventh Street in July, 1929.
† Miss Hepburn played Grazia for five weeks, but was fired at Philadelphia's Adelphi Theatre during the week of November 25 after many fights with director Lawrence Marston. Rose Hobart played Grazia when the play opened on Broadway on December 26, 1929.

Viva Cirkett	Princess of San Luca
Wallace Erskine	Baron Cesarea
Lorna Lawrence	Rhoda Fenton
Roland Bottomley	Eric Fenton
Martin Burton	Corrado
Philip Merivale	His Serene Highness, Prince Sirki of Vitalba Alexandri
Frank Greene	Major Whitbread

Produced by Lee Shubert; *Staged by* Lawrence Marston; *Settings by* Rollo Wayne.

A MONTH IN THE COUNTRY by Ivan Turgenev
Translated by M. S. Mandell
Opened: March 17, 1930, Guild Theatre, New York

CAST:	*Charles Kraus*	Herr Shaaf
	Minna Phillips	Anna Semenova
	Alla Nazimova	Natalia Petrovna
	Elliot Cabot	Mikhail Aleksandrovich Rakitin
	Eda Heinemann	Lizaveta Bogdanovna
	Eddie Wragge	Kolia
	Alexander Kirkland	Aleksei Nikolaevich Bieliaev
	Louis Veda	Matviei
	Dudley Digges	Ignati Ilich Spigelski
	Eunice Stoddard	Viera Aleksandrovna*
	John T. Doyle	Arkadi Sergieich Islaev
	Hortense Alden	Katia†
	Henry Travers	Afanasi Ivanych Bolshintsov

Produced by The Theatre Guild, Inc.; *Acting Version and Direction by* Rouben Mamoulian; *Settings and Costumes by* M. S. Dobuzinsky; *Executed by* Raymond Sovey.

SUMMER STOCK: The Berkshire Playhouse, Stockbridge, Massachusetts, June–July 1930

---

* Miss Hepburn was Miss Stoddard's understudy.
† In the second month of production, Miss Hepburn replaced Miss Alden.

THE ADMIRABLE CRICHTON by Sir James M. Barrie

CAST:
Geoffrey Kerr	Hon. Ernest Woolley
Richard Hale	Mr. Crichton
Katharine Hepburn	Lady Agatha Lasenby
Laura Harding	Lady Catherine Lasenby
Phyllis Connard	Lady Mary Lasenby
Frothingham Lysons	Rev. John Treherne
Robert Greig	The Earl of Loam
George Coulouris	Lord Brocklehurst
June Walker	Tweeny
Minna Phillips	Lady Brocklehurst
Lora Hayes	Perkins
Karl Swenson	Fleury
Harold Lefkovits	Rolleston
Frederick Voight	Tompsett
Marie Lavezzo	Fisher
Jane Wyatt	Simmons
Niela Goodelle	Jeanne
Robert Sosman	Thomas
Walter Simmons	John
William Tracy	Page boy
Russell Rhodes	Naval Officer

Produced by Alexander Kirkland and F. Cowles Strickland.

THE ROMANTIC YOUNG LADY by Martinez Sierra (Don Gregorio Sierra and Marie Lejárrago)

CAST:
Edith Barrett	Rosario
Richard Hale	Luis Felipe de Cordoba
Minna Phillips	Dona Barbarita
Margaret Love	Maria Pepa
Earl MacDonald	Emilio
Leo Carroll	Don Juan
Frederick Voight	Mario
Maren Evensen	Irene
Frothingham Lysons	Guillermo
Katharine Hepburn	Amalia
Karl Swenson	Pepe

ROMEO AND JULIET by William Shakespeare

CAST: Alexander Kirkland . . . . Romeo
Edith Barrett . . . . Juliet
Richard Hale . . . . Mercutio
Minna Phillips . . . . Nurse
Katharine Hepburn . . . . Kinswoman to the Capulets

ART AND MRS. BOTTLE (or THE RETURN OF THE PURITAN) by Benn W. Levy
Opened: November 18, 1930, Maxine Elliott Theatre, New York

CAST: Katharine Hepburn . . . . Judy Bottle
G. P. Huntley, Jr. . . . . Michael Bottle
Joyce Carey . . . . Sonia Tippet
Elise Breton . . . . Parlor Maid
Walter Kingsford . . . . George Bottle
Jane Cowl . . . . Celia Bottle
Lewis Martin . . . . Charles Dawes
Leon Quartermaine . . . . Max Lightly

SUMMER STOCK: Ivoryton, Connecticut, 1931

Katharine Hepburn had supporting roles in three plays: JUST MARRIED by Adelaide Matthews and Anne Nichols, THE CAT AND THE CANARY by John Willard and THE MAN WHO CAME BACK by Jules Eckcert Goodman.

THE ANIMAL KINGDOM by Philip Barry

CAST: Katharine Hepburn . . . . Daisy Sage*
G. Albert Smith . . . . Owen Arthur
Frederick Forrester . . . . Rufus Collier
Lora Baxter . . . . Cecelia Henry
William Gargan . . . . Richard Regan
Leslie Howard . . . . Tom Collier
Betty Lynne . . . . Franc Schmidt
Harvey Stephens . . . . Joe Fisk

* After the Pittsburgh opening, Miss Hepburn was fired and Frances Fuller replaced her.

Ilka Chase. . . . . Grace Macomber
Produced by Gilbert Miller and Leslie Howard; *Staged by*
Gilbert Miller.

THE WARRIOR'S HUSBAND by Julian Thompson
Opened: March 11, 1932, Morosco Theatre, New York

CAST: Katharine Hepburn . . . . Antiope
Paula Bauersmith . . . . First Sergeant
Virginia Volland . . . . Buria
Edna Holland. . . . . Second Sergeant
Frances Newbaker. . . . . First Sentry
Avalon Plummer. . . . . Second Sentry
Rita Rheinfrank . . . . Third Sentry
Bertha Belmore . . . . Caustica
Dorothy Walters . . . . Heroica
Jane Wheatley. . . . . Pomposia
Irby Marshal . . . . Hippolyta
Romney Brent . . . . Sapiens
Arthur Bowyer . . . . Sapiens Major
Helene Fontaine . . . . Captain of Archers
Colin Keith-Johnston . . . . Theseus
Don Beddoe. . . . . Homer
Thelma Hardwick . . . . Runner
Al Ochs . . . . Hercules
Porter Hall . . . . Gaganius, the Herald
Alan Campbell . . . . Achilles
Randolph Leymen. . . . . Ajax
Eleanor Goodrich, Nina
    Romano, Agnes George, Eve
    Bailey, Clara Waring,
    Dorothy Gillam, Rose
    Dresser . . . . Amazon Sentries and
                                     Guards
Theodosia Dusanne, Mary
    Stuart, Miriam Schiller,
    Barbara Dugan . . . . Amazon Huntresses
Thaddeus Clancy, Walter Levin,
    Arthur Brady, Jerry Feigan. . Greek Warriors
Produced by Harry Moses; *Staged by* Burk Symon; *Combats
staged by* Randolph Leymen; *Incidental Music by* Richard

A REMARKABLE WOMAN

Malaby; *Lighting Effects by* Leo Hartman; *Settings and Costumes by* Woodman Thompson.

SUMMER STOCK: Ossining, New York, July, 1932.

THE BRIDE THE SUN SHINES ON by Will Cotton

CAST: *Katharine Hepburn* . . . . Psyche Marbury
Henry Hull . . . . Hubert Burnet
Katharine Hawley, Catherine
    Locke . . . . Bridesmaids
Charlotte Wynters, Roy
    Gordon, William Lawson,
    Lili Zehner, Margaret
    Hatfield
Directed by Ralph Macbane; *Scenes by* Charles Friedman

THE LAKE by Dorothy Massingham and Murray Mac-Donald
Opened: December 26, 1933, Martin Beck Theatre, New York

CAST: *Katharine Hepburn* . . . . Stella Surrege
Frances Starr . . . . Mildred Surrege
J. P. Wilson . . . . Williams
Blanche Bates . . . . Lena Surrege
Lionel Pape . . . . Henry Surrege
Roberta Beatty . . . . Marjorie Hervey
Esther Mitchell . . . . Ethel
Geoffrey Wardwell . . . . Cecil Hervey
Colin Clive . . . . John Clayne
Mary Heberden . . . . Maude
Edward Broadley . . . . Stoker
Philip Tonge . . . . Stephen Braite
Wendy Atkin . . . . Dotty Braite
Audrey Ridgwell . . . . Jean Templeton
Vera Fuller-Mellish . . . . Anna George
Rosalind Ivan . . . . Mrs. George
Florence Britton . . . . Miss Kurn
Eva Leonard-Boyne . . . . Mrs. Hemingway
O. Z. Whitehead . . . . Dennis Gourlay
Reginald Carrington . . . . Lady Stanway

James Grainger. . . . . Captain Hamilton
Lucy Beaumont . . . . Miss White
Elliott Mason. . . . . Lady Kerton

Produced by Jed Harris; *Staged by* Jed Harris; *Assisted by* Geoffrey Kerr; *Settings by* Jo Mielziner.

JANE EYRE by Charlotte Brontë, dramatized by Helen Jerome
On tour from December, 1936, to April, 1937

CAST: Katharine Hepburn . . . . Jane Eyre
Viola Roache . . . . Mrs. Fairfax
Phyllis Connard . . . . Leah
Denis Hoey . . . . Mr. Rochester
Patricia Peardon . . . . Adele Varens
Irving Morrow . . . . Mason
Teresa Dale . . . . Grace Poole
Sandra Ellsworth . . . . Blanche Ingram
Teresa Guerini . . . . The Maniac
Katharine Stewart . . . . Lady Ingram
Reginald Carrington . . . . . . Lord Ingram
Wilfred Seagram . . . . Briggs
Reginald Malcolm. . . . . Rev. Wood
Barbara O'Neil. . . . . Diana Rivers
Marga Ann Dieghton. . . . . . Hannah
Stephen Ker Appleby. . . . . . St. John Rivers

Produced by The Theatre Guild, Inc.; *Staged by* Worthington Miner; *Production Supervised by* Theresa Helburn and Lawrence Langner; *Settings and Costumes Designed by* Lee Simonson.

THE PHILADELPHIA STORY by Philip Barry
Opened: March 28, 1939, Shubert Theatre, New York

CAST: Katharine Hepburn . . . . Tracy Lord
Lenore Lonergan . . . . Dinah Lord
Vera Allen. . . . . Margaret Lord
Dan Tobin. . . . . Alexander Lord
Owen Coll. . . . . Thomas
Forrest Orr . . . . William Tracy
Shirley Booth . . . . Elizabeth Imbrie
Van Heflin . . . . Macaulay Connor

A REMARKABLE WOMAN

Frank Fenton	George Kittredge
Joseph Cotten	C. K. Dexter Haven
Philip Foster.	Edward
Nicholas Joy.	Seth Lord
Myrtle Tannahill	May
Lorraine Bate.	Elsie
Hayden Rorke	Mac

Produced by The Theatre Guild, Inc.; *Staged by* Robert B. Sinclair; *Scenery and Lighting by* Robert Edmond Jones; *Supervised by* Theresa Helburn and Lawrence Langner.

WITHOUT LOVE by Philip Barry
Opened: November 10, 1942, St. James Theatre, New York

CAST:		
Katharine Hepburn	Jamie Coe Rowan
Elliott Nugent.	Patrick Jamieson
Tony Bickley	Quentin Ladd
Emily Massey.	Anna
Ellen Morgan.	Martha Ladd
Audrey Christie	Kitty Trimble
Robert Shayne	Peter Baillie
Sterling Oliver	Paul Carrel
Robert Chisholm.	Richard Hood
Neil Fitzgerald	Robert Emmet Riordan
Royal Beal.	Grant Vincent

Produced by The Theatre Guild, Inc.; *Staged by* Robert B. Sinclair; *Scenery and Lighting by* Robert Edmond Jones; *Supervised by* Theresa Helburn and Lawrence Langner; *Miss Hepburn's Costumes by* Valentina.

AS YOU LIKE IT by William Shakespeare
Opened: January 26, 1950, Cort Theatre, New York, and on tour

CAST:		
Katharine Hepburn	Rosalind
William Prince	Orlando
Burton Mallory.	Adam
Ernest Graves.	Oliver
Robert Foster	Dennis
Michael Everett.	Charles
Cloris Leachman.	Celia
Bill Owen	Touchstone

Jay Robinson	Le Beau
Dayton Lummis	Frederick
Jan Sherwood	Lady-in-Waiting
Aubrey Mather	Duke
Frank Rogier	Amiens
Everett Gamnon	Lord
Whitford Kane	Corin
Robert Quarry	Silvius
Judy Parrish	Phebe
Ernest Thesiger	Jaques
Patricia Englund	Audrey
Jay Robinson	Sir Oliver Martext
Robert Foster	William
Craig Timberlake	Rowland
Jan Sherwood, Marilyn Nowell, Margaret Wright	Ladies-in-Waiting and Shepherdesses
Kenneth Cantril, Charles Herndon, William Sutherland, Richard Hepburn, Robert Wark, John Weaver, Craig Timberlake	Lords, Attendants and Shepherds

Produced by The Theatre Guild, Inc.; *Staged by* Michael Benthall; *Scenery and Costumes by* James Bailey; *Incidental Music Written and Arranged by* Robert Irving; *Technical Assistant,* Emeline Roche; *Supervised by* Theresa Helburn and Lawrence Langner.

THE MILLIONAIRESS by George Bernard Shaw
Opened: October 17, 1952, Shubert Theatre, New York
June 27, 1952, New Theatre, London

CAST:
Katharine Hepburn	Epifania, the Lady
Campbell Cotts	Julius Sagamore
Peter Dyneley	Alastair Fitzfassenden
Genine Graham	Patricia Smith
Cyril Ritchard	Adrain Blenderbland
Robert Helpmann	The Doctor
Bertram Shuttleworth	The Man
Nora Nicholson	The Woman

A REMARKABLE WOMAN

Vernon Greeves. . . . . The Manager
Produced by The Theatre Guild, Inc.; *Staged by* Michael Benthall; *Settings by* James Bailey; *Miss Hepburn's Costumes by* Pierre Balmain.

SUMMER TOUR: Australia, May 2 through November 2, 1955. Sydney, Melbourne, Brisbaine, Adelaide and Perth. Appeared with Cecil Hardwick and Robert Helpmann in THE TAMING OF THE SHREW (as Katharine), MEASURE FOR MEASURE (as Isabella) and THE MERCHANT OF VENICE (as Portia).

THE MERCHANT OF VENICE by William Shakespeare
Opened: July 10, 1957, American Shakespeare Festival Theatre, Stratford, Connecticut

CAST: *Katharine Hepburn* . . . . Portia
Richard Waring. . . . . Antonio
John Frid. . . . . Salerio
Kendall Clark. . . . . Solanio
Donald Harron. . . . . Bassanio
Richard Lupino . . . . Lorenzo
John Colicos . . . . Gratiano
Lois Nettleton. . . . . Nerissa
Michael Kennedy . . . . Balthazar
Morris Carnovsky. . . . . Shylock
Richard Easton. . . . . Lancelot Gobbo
William Cottrell . . . . Old Gobbo
Earle Hyman . . . . Prince of Morocco
Dina Doronne . . . . Jessica
Stanley Bell . . . . Prince of Arragon
Jack Bittner . . . . Tubal
Russell Oberlin. . . . . Stephano
Larry Gates . . . . Duke of Venice
Conrad Bromberg, James
Cahill, Richard Cavett,
Harley Clements, Tamara
Daniel, Michael Kasdan,
Simm Landres, Michele La
Bombarda, Michael
Lindsay-Hogg, Susan Lloyd,

456

William Long, Jr., Michael
Miller, David Milton, Vivian
Paszamont, Ira Rubin, D. J.
Sullivan, Peter Trytler, Gain
Warner . . . . Attendants, Citizens and
                                                    Dignitaries
Staged by Jack Landau; *Scenery by* Rouben Ter-Arutunian; *Costumes by* Motley; *Production and Lighting by* Jean Rosenthal; *Music by* Virgil Thomson.

MUCH ADO ABOUT NOTHING by William Shakespeare
Opened: August 3, 1957, American Shakespeare Festival Theatre, Stratford, Connecticut

CAST: Katharine Hepburn . . . . Beatrice
Jack Bittner . . . . Borachio
Morris Carnovsky . . . . Antonio
Russell Oberlin . . . . Balthasar
Sada Thompson . . . . Margaret
Jacqueline Brookes . . . . Ursula
Larry Gates . . . . Dogberry
Donald Harron . . . . Verges
Richard Lupino . . . . First Watchman
William Cottrell . . . . Second Watchman
Kendall Clark . . . . Friar Francis
John Frid . . . . Sexton
John Colicos . . . . Leonato
Donald Harron . . . . Messenger
Lois Nettleton . . . . Hero
Stanley Bell . . . . Don Pedro
Alfred Drake . . . . Benedick
Richard Easton . . . . Claudio
Richard Waring . . . . Don John
Mitchell Agruss . . . . Conrade
Michael Borden, Benita
  Deutsch, Michael Kasdan,
  Michael Miller, David
  Milton, Joe Myers, Dino
  Narizzano, Ira Rubin, Judith
  Steffan, Peter Trytler, Jack
  Waltzer, William Woodman . Soldiers and Servants

A REMARKABLE WOMAN

Staged by John Houseman and Jack Landau; *Scenery and Costumes by* Rouben Ter-Arutunian; *Production Supervised by* Jean Rosenthal; *Lighting by* Tharon Musser; *Dances Arranged by* John Butler; *Music by* Virgil Thomson.

TWELFTH NIGHT by William Shakespeare
Opened: June 3, 1960, American Shakespeare Festival Theatre, Stratford, Connecticut

CAST:
Katharine Hepburn	Viola
Donald Davis	Orsino, Duke of Illyria
Stephen Strimpell	Curio
John Harkins	Valentine
Will Geer	A Sea Captain
Loring Smith	Sir Toby Belch
Sada Thompson	Maria
O. Z. Whitehead	Sir Andrew Aguecheek
Morris Carnovsky	Feste
Margaret Phillips	Olivia
Richard Waring	Malvolio
David Gress	A Boy
William Hickey	Fabian
Clifton James	Antonio
Clayton Corzatte	Sebastian
Claude Woolman	A Guardsman
Patrick Hines	Priest
Constance Bollinger, Lorna Gilbert, Donald Hatch, Charles Herrick, Alfred Lavorato, George Parrish, Donald Pomes, Howard Poyrow, Robert Reilly, Lou Robb, Sandra Saget, George Sampson, Wisner Washam, Beverly Whitcombe	Sailors, Fishermen, Guardsmen and Ladies

Staged by Jack Landau; *Production Designed by* Rouben Ter-Arutunian; *Lighting by* Tharon Musser; *Music and Songs by* Herman Chessid.

458

ANTONY AND CLEOPATRA by William Shakespeare

Opened: July 22, 1960, American Shakespeare Festival Theatre, Stratford, Connecticut

CAST:

Katharine Hepburn	Cleopatra
Robert Ryan	Antony
Douglas Watson	Canidius
John Harkins	Scarus
Donald Davis	Enobarbus
Patrick Hines	Mardian
Earle Hyman	Alexas
Rae Allen	Charmian
Anne Fielding	Iras
John Ragin	Octavius Caesar
Morris Carnovsky	Lepidus
Will Geer	Agrippa
John Myhers	Thidius
Stephen Strimpell	Dolabella
Clifton James	Pompey
Claude Woolman	Menas
Sada Thompson	Octavia
Richard Waring	A Soothsayer
Ted Van Griethuysen	Egyptian Messenger
Clayton Corzatte	Eros

John Abbey, Stephen Carnovsky, David Clayborne, Jack Gardner, David Groh, Donald Hatch, Charles Herrick, Lloyd Hezekiah, Joseph Kleinowski, Alfred Lavorato, Christopher Lloyd, Robert Packer, Christian Parker, George Parrish, Don Pomes, Howard Poyrow, Robert Reilly, Lou Robb, George Sampson, Frank Spencer, Richard Thayer, Herman Tucker, Wisner Washam . . . . Officers, Soldiers and Attendants

Staged by Jack Landau; *Production Designed by* Rouben

A REMARKABLE WOMAN

Ter-Arutunian; *Lighting by* Tharon Musser; *Music by* Norman Dello Joio.

COCO by Alan Jay Lerner (book and lyrics)
Opened: December 18, 1969, Mark Hellinger Theatre, New York

CAST: Katharine Hepburn . . . . Coco
Maggie Task. . . . . Helene
Jeanne Arnold . . . . Pignol
Al DeSio . . . . Armand
Nancy Killmer . . . . A Seamstress
Jack Beaber . . . . Albert
Richard Marr . . . . A Lawyer
George Rose . . . . Louis Greff
Eve March . . . . Docaton
David Holliday . . . . Georges
Gene Varrone . . . . Loublaye
Shirley Potter . . . . Varne
Lynn Winn . . . . Marie
Rita O'Connor . . . . Jeanine
Graciela Daniele . . . . Claire
Margot Travers . . . . Juliette
Carolyn Kirsch . . . . Madelaine
Diane Phillips . . . . Lucille
Charlene Ryan . . . . Simone
Suzanne Rogers . . . . Solange
Gale Dixon . . . . Noelle
Rene Auberjonois . . . . Sebastian Baye
Richard Woods . . . . Dr. Petitjean
David Thomas . . . . Claude
Will B. Able . . . . Dwight Berkwit
Robert Fitch . . . . Eugene Bernstone
Chad Block . . . . Ronny Ginsborn
Dan Siretta . . . . Phil Rosenberry
Gene Varrone . . . . Lapidus
Leslie Daniel . . . . Nadine
Jack Dabdoub . . . . Grand Duke
Michael Allinson . . . . Charles
Paul Dumont . . . . Julian Lesage
John Cypher . . . . Papa

Produced by Frederick Brisson; *Sets and Costumes by* Cecil Beaton; *Music by* André Previn; *Lighting by* Thomas Skelton; *Orchestrations by* Hershy Kay; *Dance Music Continuity by* Harold Wheeler; *Music Direction by* Robert Emmett Dolan; *Music Numbers and Fashion Sequences Staged by* Michael Bennett; *Staged by* Michael Benthall.

A MATTER OF GRAVITY by Enid Bagnold
Opened: February 3, 1976, Broadhurst Theatre, New York

CAST: *Katharine Hepburn* . . . . Mrs. Basil
    Charlotte Jones . . . . Dubois
    Robert Moberly . . . . Estate Agent
    Christopher Reeve . . . . Nicky
    Elizabeth Lawrence . . . . Shatov
    Paul Harding . . . . Herbert
    Wanda Bimson . . . . Elizabeth
    Daniel Tamm . . . . Tom

Presented by Robert Whitehead, Roger L. Stevens, Konrad Matthael; *Directed by* Noel Willman; *Setting by* Ben Edwards; *Costumes by* Jane Greenwood; *Lighting by* Thomas Skelton; *Production Stage Manager,* Ben Strobach.

WEST SIDE WALTZ by Ernest Thompson
Opened: November 19, 1981, Ethel Barrymore Theatre, New York

CAST: *Katharine Hepburn* . . . . Margaret Mary Elderdice
    Dorothy Loudon . . . . Cara Varnum
    David Margulies . . . . Serge Barrescu
    Regina Baff . . . . Robin Bird
    Don Howard . . . . Glenn Dabrinsky

Presented by Robert Whitehead and Roger L. Stevens, in association with the Center Theater Group; *Directed by* Noel Willman; *Settings by* Ben Edwards; *Costumes by* Jane Greenwood; *Lighting by* Thomas Skelton; *Music Supervision by* David Krane; *General Manager,* Oscar E. Olesen; *Publicity,* Seymour Krawitz and Patricia Krawitz; *Stage Managers,* Ben Strobach, Valentine Mayer, Sally Lapiduss.

TELEVISION

THE GLASS MENAGERIE, ABC, December 16, 1973

CAST: *Katharine Hepburn* . . . . Amanda Wingfield
   Joanna Miles . . . . Laura Wingfield
   Sam Waterston . . . . Tom Wingfield
   Michael Moriarty . . . . Gentleman Caller
Produced by David Susskind; *Directed by* Anthony Harvey; *Written by* Tennessee Williams; *Music by* John Barry.

A DELICATE BALANCE, Filmed 1973; Released 1974, Cable TV

CAST: *Katharine Hepburn* . . . . Agnes
   Paul Scofield . . . . Tobias
   Lee Remick . . . . Julia –
   Kate Reid . . . . Claire
   Joseph Cotten. . . . . Harry
   Betsy Blair. . . . . Edna
Producer, Ely A. Landau; *Director,* Tony Richardson; *Author,* Edward Albee; *Screen Adaptation,* Edward Albee; *Executive Producer,* Neil Hartley, *For The American Film Theatre,* Henry Weinstein; *Production Manager,* Zelda Barron; *Production Associate,* Neil Landau; *Assistant Director,* Andrew Grieve; *Director of Photography,* David Watkin;

Editor, John Victor Smith; *Camera Operator,* Freddie Cooper; *Art Director,* David Brockhurst; *Costumes,* Margaret Furse; *Makeup,* Bill Lodge.

LOVE AMONG THE RUINS, ABC, March 6, 1975

CAST: Katharine Hepburn . . . . Jessica Medlicott
      Laurence Olivier . . . . Sir Arthur Granville-Jones, K.C.
      Colin Blakely . . . . J. F. Devine, K. C.
      Richard Pearson . . . . Druce
      Joan Sims . . . . Fanny Pratt
      Leigh Lawson . . . . Alfred Pratt
      Gwen Nelson . . . . Hermione Davis
      Robert Harris . . . . The Judge

Produced by Allan Davis; *Directed by* George Cukor; *Written by* James Costigan; *Director of Photography,* Douglas Slocombe, B.S.C.; *Art Direction,* Carmen Dillon; *Editor,* John F. Burnett, A.C.E.; *Costumes by* Margaret Furse; *Miss Hepburn's Gowns Executed by* Germinal Rangel; *Production Supervised by* Herb Jellinek; *Production Executives,* Marty Katz, Dennis L. Judd, II; *Music by* John Barry.

THE CORN IS GREEN, CBS, January 29, 1979
Based on Emlyn Williams's play *The Corn Is Green*

CAST: Katharine Hepburn . . . . Miss Moffat
      Ian Saynor . . . . Morgan Evans
      Bill Fraser . . . . The squire
      Patricia Hayes . . . . Mrs. Watty
      Anna Massey . . . . Miss Ronberry
      Artro Morris . . . . John Goronwy Jones
      Dorothea Phillips . . . . Sarah Pugh
      Toyah Wilcox . . . . Bessie Watty
      Huw Richards . . . . Idwal
      Bryn Fon . . . . Robbart
      Dyfan Roberts . . . . Gwyn
      Robin John . . . . Ivor

Produced by Neil Hartley; *Directed by* George Cukor; *Director of Photography,* Ted Scaife, B.S.C.; *Written for Television*

A REMARKABLE WOMAN

by Ivan Davis; *Music by* John Barry; *Associate Producer,* Eric Rattray; *Production Designer,* Carmen Dillon; *Film Editors,* Richard Marden, John Wright; *Costume Consultant,* David Walker; *Makeup,* Ann Brodie; *Hairstylist,* Ramon Gow; *Sound Mixer,* Peter Handford; *Music Editor,* Kenneth Hall.

TELEVISION INTERVIEWS

Dick Cavett, ABC, October 2 and 3, 1973
60 Minutes, CBS, August 26, 1979
Barbara Walters, ABC, July, 1981, and August, 1981
Good Morning America, ABC, November 5–8, 1984
Today, NBC, May 14, 1985

RADIO

ROMEO AND JULIET, Radio Hall of Fame, 1936
Katharine Hepburn read the balcony scene only

FAREWELL TO ARMS, Mercury Theatre, 1938

CAST: Katharine Hepburn
    Joseph Cotten

THE PHILADELPHIA STORY, Lux Radio Theatre, July 20, 1942

CAST: Katharine Hepburn
    Cary Grant
    Lt. James Stewart
    Virginia Weidler

THE PHILADELPHIA STORY, Theatre Guild of the Air, June 18, 1947

CAST: Katharine Hepburn
    Cary Grant
    Joseph Cotten

LITTLE WOMEN, Theatre Guild of the Air, 1947

CAST: Katharine Hepburn
Elliot Reid
John Lodge
Oscar Homolka

LITTLE WOMEN, Theatre Guild of the Air, December 21, 1947

CAST: Katharine Hepburn
Paul Lukas

WOMAN OF THE YEAR, Theatre Guild of the Air, 1948

CAST: Katharine Hepburn
Spencer Tracy

THE GAME OF LOVE AND DEATH, by Romain Rolland, Theatre Guild of the Air, January 2, 1949

CAST: Katharine Hepburn
Paul Henreid
Claude Rains

KATHARINE HEPBURN'S ACADEMY AWARDS AND NOMINATIONS FOR BEST ACTRESS OF THE YEAR
(Asterisk [*] Denotes Winner)

1932/33   Katharine Hepburn (MORNING GLORY)*
May Robson (LADY FOR A DAY)
Diana Wynyard (CAVALCADE)

1935   Elisabeth Bergner (ESCAPE ME NEVER)
Claudette Colbert (PRIVATE WORLDS)
Bette Davis (DANGEROUS)*
Katharine Hepburn (ALICE ADAMS)
Miriam Hopkins (BECKY SHARP)
Merle Oberon (THE DARK ANGEL)

1940   Bette Davis (THE LETTER)
Joan Fontaine (REBECCA)
Katharine Hepburn (THE PHILADELPHIA
STORY)
Ginger Rogers (KITTY FOYLE)*
Martha Scott (OUR TOWN)

1942   Bette Davis (NOW, VOYAGER)
Greer Garson (MRS. MINIVER)*
Katharine Hepburn (WOMAN OF THE YEAR)
Rosalind Russell (MY SISTER EILEEN)
Teresa Wright (THE PRIDE OF THE
    YANKEES)

1951   Katharine Hepburn (THE AFRICAN QUEEN)
Vivien Leigh (A STREETCAR NAMED
    DESIRE)*
Eleanor Parker (DETECTIVE STORY)
Shelley Winters (A PLACE IN THE SUN)
Jane Wyman (THE BLUE VEIL)

1955   Susan Hayward (I'LL CRY TOMORROW)
Katharine Hepburn (SUMMERTIME)
Jennifer Jones (LOVE IS A
    MANY-SPLENDORED THING)
Anna Magnani (THE ROSE TATTOO)*
Eleanor Parker (INTERRUPTED MELODY)

1956   Carroll Baker (BABY DOLL)
Ingrid Bergman (ANASTASIA)*
Katharine Hepburn (THE RAINMAKER)
Nancy Kelly (THE BAD SEED)
Deborah Kerr (THE KING AND I)

1959   Doris Day (PILLOW TALK)
Audrey Hepburn (THE NUN'S STORY)
Katharine Hepburn (SUDDENLY LAST
    SUMMER)
Simone Signoret (ROOM AT THE TOP)*
Elizabeth Taylor (SUDDENLY LAST SUMMER)

1962   Anne Bancroft (THE MIRACLE WORKER)*
Bette Davis (WHATEVER HAPPENED TO
    BABY JANE?)
Katharine Hepburn (LONG DAY'S JOURNEY
    INTO NIGHT)
Geraldine Page (SWEET BIRD OF YOUTH)
Lee Remick (DAYS OF WINE AND ROSES)

1967 Anne Bancroft (THE GRADUATE)
Faye Dunaway (BONNIE AND CLYDE)
Dame Edith Evans (THE WHISPERERS)
Audrey Hepburn (WAIT UNTIL DARK)
Katharine Hepburn (GUESS WHO'S COMING
 TO DINNER)*

1968 Katharine Hepburn (THE LION IN WINTER)*
Patricia Neal (THE SUBJECT WAS ROSES)
Vanessa Redgrave (ISADORA)
Barbra Streisand (FUNNY GIRL)*
Joanne Woodward (RACHEL, RACHEL)
(Two awards for Best Actress were given this
year.)

1981 Katharine Hepburn (ON GOLDEN POND)*
Diane Keaton (REDS)
Marsha Mason (ONLY WHEN I LAUGH)
Susan Sarandon (ATLANTIC CITY)
Meryl Streep (THE FRENCH LIEUTENANT'S
 WOMAN)

MAIN REPOSITORIES FOR
HEPBURN MATERIAL

The American Film Institute, Beverly Hills, California
Lincoln Center Library for the Performing Arts, New York, New York
Academy of Motion Picture Arts and Sciences, Beverly Hills, California
British Film Institute, London
University of Wisconsin, Film Archives, Madison, Wisconsin
Directors Guild Archives, California State University, North Ridge, California
Screen Actors Guild, Los Angeles, California
University of Southern California Film Archives, Los Angeles, California
University of Hartford, Hartford, Connecticut
Kingswood-Oxford School, Hartford, Connecticut
Hartford Hospital, Hartford, Connecticut (Dr. Thomas N. Hepburn)
Stowe-Day Foundation, Hartford, Connecticut
Camera Press, London Photographic Archives
Time/Life Magazines Photographic Archives, New York, New York
Stockbridge Library, Stockbridge, Massachusetts
Bryn Mawr Alumni Archives, Bryn Mawr, Pennsylvania

ACKNOWLEDGMENTS

A biography requires much research. In the case of this book, less time was spent in libraries than in pursuit of co-workers, friends, and acquaintances of Katharine Hepburn who are scattered over two continents. A tremendous and admirable bond of loyalty exists between Miss Hepburn and her closest associates. To those who have spoken with me, I express my most deep-felt appreciation and hope this book will justify your trust in my sense of responsibility. I have withheld your names as you have requested. But your firsthand accounts have helped me immeasurably.

I am immensely grateful for the help given me at the various libraries and institutions listed under Main Repositories for Hepburn Material, to Fiona Lindsay, who did special research for me in Europe, and to Steven Rossen, who engaged in the same task in California. I must also single out the continuing assistance given me by Anthony Slide at the Academy of Motion Picture Arts and Sciences and Dorothy Swerdlove at the Library of the Performing Arts at Lincoln Center in New York. To my secretary, Barbara Howland, I owe a special debt of gratitude. She is a meticulous and uncomplaining researcher on her own and an indefatigable typist. And to Judy Horgen of the New Milford Public Library and Randee Marullo, my fine copy editor, my additional appreciation.

Acknowledgments

Since I have lived for so many years with a foot on two continents, I have been most fortunate in having found two marvelous editors—in America, Harvey Ginsberg, and in England, Ion Trewin—and two wonderfully supportive agents—Mitch Douglas and Hilary Rubenstein. My love, my admiration and my gratitude to my husband, Stephen Citron, who gave—as he always has given—his unstinting encouragement and sound counsel.

My grateful acknowledgment as well to the following for their help: Robert F. Burke; Ben Carbonetto; Edward Chodorov; Gail Chumley; Patricia De Chiara Lubar; Homer Dickens; Geraldine Duclow; Carol Epstein; Maxine Fleckner; Joan Fontaine; Donald Fowle; Joseph Fullum; William Handley; Ginette Harris; Mary Haselton; Lieutenant Colonel Joseph P. Hollis, Jr.; Courty Andrews Hoyt; Mrs. Clyde Hudson; Richard John; Michael Korda; Rob Kyff; Paul Lerner; Steven R. Lytle; Don Madison; Lynn Masters; Mark Meader; Barbara S. Melone; Russel Meret; Betty J. Mullendore; Mary Lou Nesbitt; Steven Ourada; Bernard F. Pasqualini; Pauline Pierce; Martin Poll; Diana Royce; Elizabeth Shentor; David R. Smith; James Spada; Larry Swindell; J. C. Trewin; Harriet Louise Taylor Watts; Charlotte White; and Mildred Wright.

—ANNE EDWARDS

Blandings Way
February, 1985

Notes

NOTES

The following abbreviations are used in the note section:

AFI: American Film Institute
BS: Baltimore Sun
LAHT: Los Angeles Herald Tribune
LAT: Los Angeles Times
LCLHA: Lincoln Center Library, Hepburn Archives
LHJ: Ladies' Home Journal
NYDN: New York Daily News
NYHT: New York Herald Tribune
NYP: New York Post
NYS: New York Sun
NYT: New York Times
NYWT: New York World-Telegram
PI: Personal Interview
SEP: Saturday Evening Post
WP: Washington Post

Page   CHAPTER 1

3 "just what she deserved": J. Bryan III and Lupton A.
   Wilkerson, "The Hepburn Story," SEP, December 27,
   1941

5 "our dear sweet ex": Oliver O. Jenson, "The Hepburns,"
    Life, 1939.
  "The Doctor": Ibid.
6 "How do you stand": Ibid.
  "How dull": Ibid.
  "anybody doing": Ibid.
7 "I find it droll": Kanin, p. 36.
  "beguiling": Ibid.
  "to remold": Ibid.
10 "My God . . .": Ibid, p. 142.
   "undistressed": Bryan.
11 "Motion pictures": *NYHT*, September 9, 1938.
   "one of the best acted": Ibid.
12 "Let's go on the pier": Higham, *Kate*, p. 390.
   "The most precarious": Bryan.

CHAPTER 2

19 "That's the one": Ibid.
   "I'd marry him": Ibid.
   "The best thing": Ibid.
   "How can you say": Ibid.
20 "hold her up": Ibid.
   "thick with rambler roses": Bryan.
21 "Mother was outraged": Kanin, pp. 115–116.
22 "perhaps all": Ralph G. Martin, "KH, My Life and Loves
      LHJ, August, 1975.
   "If I haven't": Bryan.
23 "silly isn't it": Ibid.
   "Would look": Ibid.
25 "being cuffed": Kanin, p. 139.
   "I mean a real": Ibid., pp. 59–60.
26 "There are men": Ibid.
   "Here I go!": Bryan.
   "That gave me": Ibid.
   "Here comes 3405": Bryan.
   "whip-snapped": Ibid.
   "Sir, your little girl": Ibid.

CHAPTER 3

27 "scientifically and": Oliver Jensen, *Life.*
   "Oh": Ibid.
   "Some day": *Look,* July 11, 1967.
   "I want to tell": Ibid.
28 "in the English tradition": *Kingswood, Fifty Years, 1916–1966,*
   p. 14.
   (fn) "to the middle-class": Brendan Gill, *TV Guide,* October
   30, 1982.
   "Oh she was so": *The Kingswood-Oxford Today* magazine,
   Commemorative Issue, 1909–1984, p. 68.
29 "I was never a member": Bryan.
   "Niles to Woodland": Ibid.
   "straight out": Ibid.
   "I still remember": *Kingswood-Oxford Today,* p. 68.
30 "I wouldn't play Eva": Bryan.
32 "faithful picturization": *NYT,* April 1, 1920
33 "My son was normal": *NYT,* April 4, 1920
34 "I am now convinced": *NYT,* April 5, 1920.
   "Whenever I needed them": Ralph G. Martin, *LHJ,* August,
   1975.

CHAPTER 4

37 "Oh, with what": *NYT,* June 18, 1967.
   "your beaux": Bryan.
38 "Ah! Conscious beauty": Ibid.
   "exhaustingly intense": Ibid.
   "If I had a patient": Ibid.
39 "a very nice man": *Vogue,* November, 1981.
   "What are you": Ibid.
40 "sometime sullen": *May Day Revels and Plays* (program),
   Bryn Mawr College, May 4 and 5, 1928.
   "You can take them": Ibid.
41 "Her forehead": Ibid.
   "You see I've": Ibid.
42 "You want to be": Ibid.
   "I don't want": Ibid.
   "All right": Ibid.

CHAPTER 5

46 "never seen anyone": Bryan.

"I won": Bryan.

49 "I want to be": Miss Frances Robinson-Duff interview, *Night Life*, April, 1939.

"Sometimes we have": Ibid.

50 "Darling": Ibid.

"You hold your hands": Ibid.

"I thought": Higham, *Kate.*

51 "You won't wear": Ibid.

"she was carelessly groomed": Helburn, p. 136.

52 "that Park Avenue amateur": Bryan.

"Aren't you proud": Ibid.

"You don't mean": Bryan.

"I'd have": Ibid.

54 "I'm getting married": Ibid.

"If you want": *LA Herald Examiner*, April 14, 1968.

(fn) "We've had some nuts": *NYT*, June 18, 1967.

(fn) "I wasn't fit to be married": Ibid.

55 "What am I doing?": Ibid.

CHAPTER 6

57 "Resign hell!": Dickens, p. 6.

"They're absolutely right": *NYT*, June 18, 1967.

58 "I tried to put her": Higham, *Kate*, p. 11.

"However, if I": Ibid., p. 11.

"Cheryl, I want you": Ibid.

60 "skinny red-haired girl": Higham, *Kate*, p. 14.

"she played": Bryan.

61 "You're a fool": Ibid.

"Well, I like that": *NYT*, June 18, 1967.

"Miss Hepburn, you": Bryan.

62 "I asked for decent," Lee Israel, "Last of the Honest to God Ladies," *Esquire.*

"disruptive perverseness": Bryan.

63 "I just don't like": Ralph Martin, "KH, My Life and Loves," *LHJ.*

64 "What does she use": Bryan.

"Didn't I ask you": Bryan.

"promise of": Ibid.

"I don't think": Ibid.

65 "outrageous posturings": Higham, *Kate*, p. 16.

66 "The Hepburn house": "The Hepburns," *Life*, December, 1939.

"pink, arty and Godless": Ibid.

"high-class broad": Kanin, p. 36.

"la-de-da": Ibid., p. 66.

67 "a fish wife tirade": Ibid.

"I think Leslie Howard": Lee Israel, *Esquire*, November, 1967.

"bounded down": Ibid.

68 "They didn't like me": Ibid.

"Hello, everybody!": Bryan.

69 "Kate had some little": Bryan.

"I'm just sort of making": Ibid.

70 "sort of a John Held": Israel.

71 "She had this very": Lambert, p. 60.

"She's too marvelous": St. John.

"Take my word for it": Ibid.

72 "Not bad for": Gottfried.

CHAPTER 7

75 "the very rich": F. Scott Fitzgerald, "The Rich Boy" from *All the Sad Young Men*, 1926.

77 "This is what": Dickens, p. 9.

78 "haphazard impediments": Cecil Beaton, p. 61.

"As long as I live": St. John.

79 "I'm sure Miss": Lambert.

81 "I also hit the": Higham, *Kate*, p. 25.

"You!": Bryan.

82 "Something about her": Barrymore interview (undated), AFI.

83 "I learned a": *Look*, July 11, 1967.

"You're not much": Ibid.

"Then I stopped": Barrymore interview.

"She just stood": Ibid.

84 "a creature": Ibid.

"Just because": Lambert, p. 99.

"the cold": Ibid.

85 "made for the screen": Ibid., p. 101.

"odd awkwardness": Ibid.

86 "It's your job": Burke, p. 31.

"practically naked": *TV Guide*, December 16, 1973.

"So I did it": Ibid.

87 "Everybody was": Memo from David O. Selznick.

88 "There's no reason": Higham, *Kate*, p. 37.

90 (fn) "God, what a": Ibid., p. 33.

91 "No, no!": Bryan.

"didn't emerge": Higham, *Kate*, p. 33.

"I could look over": *NYT*, December 9, 1973.

92 "If my feet": Ibid.

"Everybody watches": F. Scott Fitzgerald, "Crazy Sunday."

CHAPTER 8

94 "I think men": Ralph Martin, *LHJ*, August, 1975.

97 "She resembles": *NYS*, Jack S. Cohen, Jr., March 10, 1933.

"a woman of breeding": Lambert.

"right up there with": Hayward, p. 317.

"A certain look": Ibid.

98 "an air both": Ibid.

"The wives of the moguls": Ibid.

99 "I thought": *LAHT*, January 19, 1976.

"This is what I'd": Ibid.

"your friend": Lambert, p. 99.

(fn) "one of the most": Bankhead, p. 305.

"Suddenly, the front door": Higham, *Kate*, p. 45.

100 (fn) "Sherman was gifted": Sarris, p. 136.

101 "Miss Hepburn shines": *NYT*, July, 1933.

"I can remember": *NYT*, December 9, 1973.

"the jitters": *NYT*, 1937.

"The way she walks": Ibid.

102 "a story that": Lambert, p. 75.

"admirable New England": Ibid.

103 "a spell of magic": Ibid., p. 77.

"no obvious effects": Ibid.

"Once, I actually hit": Lambert p. 99.

104 "Kate [who had not . . .]": Lambert, p. 101.

"Again she weaves": Advertisement, AFI.
"The radiant Star": Newspaper advertisement, AFI.

105 "a genius for": Gottfried, p. 6.
"he had the grin": Ibid., p. 90.
"his athletic use": Ibid.

106 "her parents had": PI.

107 ". . . with a free and": Dickens, p. 56.
"her artistry": *The New Yorker* (undated), LCLHA.

108 "You make other": Bryan.
"Bow-Gaynor-", *LAT*, November, 1933.

109 "kind of off-beat": Hayward, p. 166.
"when in New York": *Colliers*, March 17, 1934.

CHAPTER 9

111 "a play with": *NYT* (undated), LCLHA.

112 "I could see": Higham, *Kate*, pp. 56–57.
"If she turned her head": Bryan.

113 "I could have loved": Higham, *Kate*, p. 56.
"I never thought": Ibid.
". . . she was totally": Ibid.
"an agent": Bryan.

114 "staccato": *WP*, December 18, 1933.
"There was never": Ibid.

115 "My dear": Bryan.
"Miss Hepburn began": *NYT*, December 27, 1933.
"Don't let it get": Bryan.

116 "She ran the gamut": Dorothy Parker, *Journal-American*,
December 27, 1933.
"100 years from now": *NYT*, January, 1934.
"Ridiculous!": Ibid.

117 "With twelve million": Ibid.
STAR'S MOTHER: Ibid.
"the women's rights": Ibid.
"Mrs. Thomas N. Hepburn": Ibid.
"I have ceased": Ibid.
"the suicide": Ibid.
"Nonsense!": Ibid.

119 "The pictures will be": UP, March 19, 1934.
"Miss Hepburn sought": UP, March 26, 1934.

"official spokesman": UP, March 27, 1934.

"Kate has no": Ibid.

"Miss Suzanne Steele": Ibid.

120 "don't be a mug!": *NYT,* April 4, 1934.

"I'm not": Ibid.

"Well—": Ibid.

"I never meant": Ibid.

"I just needed": Ibid.

"going to Key West": Baker, p. 314.

"need not wait": Ibid.

121 "Deep disagreement": AP, April 27, 1934.

122 "Miss Hepburn has no": *Miami Herald,* April 30, 1934.

"You pay a terrible price": International News Service, May 3, 1934.

"Mother has accomplished": Ibid.

CHAPTER 10

125 "criticism was a": F. Scott Fitzgerald, *Tender Is the Night.*

126 "too young and too": *Time,* January, 1934.

127 "Louis B. said only": Helburn, p. 276.

(fn) "About Mourning Becomes Electra": Ibid., p. 277.

128 "I really didn't want": Carey, p. 73.

129 "unconquerable gift": *NYHT,* Richard Watts, 1934.

130 "When I'm asked": *NYHT,* LCLHA, 1934.

"For the independent": Ibid.

"join them in Paris": Ibid.

"How she got on": Ibid.

"News gatherers": Ibid.

131 "labored and palpably": *NYWT,* LCLHA, 1935.

"Miss Hepburn makes": *Time,* February, 1935.

133 "It's ridiculous!": Bryan.

134 "The Power Behind Katharine Hepburn": *Screenplay,* March, 1935.

"to stop living": Higham, *Kate,* p. 64.

". . . it became clear": Ibid.

135 HEPBURN DARES DEATH: *NYWT,* December, 1934.

"I was in a blind": Bryan.

"swinging the basket": Ibid.

"Not at all": Ibid.
136 "What does it matter": Ibid.

CHAPTER 11

137 "What about your"; Edwin C. Hill, syndicated, 1935.
140 "We got John Collier": Lambert, p. 92.
"This picture": Robinson.
141 "Oh Kate": Robinson.
(fn) "Up to then": Lambert, p. 96.
"Pandro, scrap": Lambert, p. 97.
142 "The dynamic Miss Hepburn": Richard Watts, Jr., *NYHT*,
January, 1936.
"Sylvia Scarlett reveals": *Time*, January, 1936.
"And [Sylvia Scarlett]", *NYP*, January, 1936.
143 "She was this slip": Wansell, p. 106.
144 "a soft-focused": Sarris, p. 48.
"fought, bickered": Ford, p. 98.
145 "Mary of Scotland": Ibid.
147 "Kate was confused": Higham, *Kate*, p. 77.
148 "Eureka!": PI.
"I don't think": Higham, *Kate*, p. 77.
"a little lost boy": PI.
149 "[I don't know]": Carey, p. 87.
"Her Phoebe Throssel": Frank Nugent, *NYT*, October, 1936.
"Mr. Marshall": Graham Greene, *The Spectator*, November,
1936.
150 "clawing, scratching": Ibid.

CHAPTER 12

151 "In my relationships": Ralph Martin, *LHJ*, August, 1975.
152 "Well, I'll never": Ibid.
"I'm like the girl": Ibid.
"getting up at 4:30": Ibid.
154 "You must be hungry": PI.
155 "her not too exacting": *Boston Globe*, January 12, 1937.
"thoroughly delightful": *Cleveland Plain Dealer*, January 21,
1937.

"Charlotte Brontë's": *Baltimore Sun*, March 2, 1937.

"applauded her the more": *Washington Post*, March 19, 1937.

"Kate . . . knew": Helburn, p. 304.

157 "You'd be lucky": Bryan.

"The situation for today": *Screenplay*, August, 1937.

158 "Ginger is strictly": Ibid.

"If it is real": Ibid.

159 "To both of its female": *Life*, August, 1937.

"She is completely": Bryan.

"Moreover, when the": Ibid.

160 "To win her": interview, *Movie Mirror*, LCLHA.

HEPBURN HURLS BOLT: *NYT*, LCLHA, 1937.

161 "If Miss Hepburn": Dickens, p. 95.

"bullet-speed direction": *NYWT*, February, 1938.

"a man is measured": Sarris, p. 53.

"She has an amazing": Dickens, p. 95.

162 "For *Bringing Up Baby*": *Time*, February, 1938.

163 "Willie Wyler tells": Bob Thomas, *King Cohn*, p. 117.

165 "the quality of the": Selznick.

"You know what": Bryan.

166 "I accept": Deschner, p. 47.

"Mrs. Tracy": Ibid.

"everyone present got an": Ibid.

167 "went down, smiling": Kanin, p. 155.

"If you must drink": Ibid.

CHAPTER 13

168 "the belle of": Lesley, p. 259.

169 "Every time Kate looks": PI.

170 "handsome and attractive": Kanin, p. 113.

"It seems to me": Ibid.

(fn) "There were Shubert": Kanin, p. 113.

171 "All you New England": "The Hepburns," *Life*, December, 1939.

"Health is youth": Kanin, p. 89.

"she use[d] cold baths": Ibid.

172 (fn) "I think we should": Selznick, p. 180

173 (fn) "Not for anybody's": Ibid., p. 175.

174 "For God's sake": Helburn, p. 307.

174 "the bloom would": Helburn, p. 307.
"Do anything you want": Ibid.
175 "so keen it was": *Newsweek,* November 10, 1969.
"This is Indianapolis": Ibid.
176 "I still grin": Helburn, p. 304.
177 "I'd find Kate": Lee Israel, *McCall's,* LCLHA.
"still boyishly awkward": Ibid.
"which emphasized the droop": Ibid.
"Louis B. Mayer": *Look,* July, 1967.
178 "scrupulous honesty": Ibid.
"reasonable script supervision": Ibid.
180 "I got too much sun": Kanin, p. 142.
181 "When I started": Bryan.

CHAPTER 14

185 "she is the woman": Mary Roberts Rinehart, *Pictorial
Review,* January, 1935.
"No other individual": Ibid.
186 "It's magnificent": Bryan.
"Swell!": Ibid.
187 "Who wrote it—": Ibid.
188 "with generations of": Speech by Spencer Tracy at Ripon
College, June, 1941.
"I wanted to help": Swindell, p. 97.
189 "never passed up": Tracy's speech at Ripon College, June,
1941.
"itch to travel": Ibid.
"ruffians from the": Ibid.
"You know how it": Kanin.
190 "a silly idea": Deschner, p. 35.
"two steep, shady": O'Brien, p. 63.
"one flickering": Ibid.
"when the gray wind": Ibid.
"out of Egypt": Ibid.
191 "Kid, you're the best": Swindell, p. 103.
"Spencer Tracy had a contract": Geist, p. 78.
192 "Christ, he used up": Ibid.
"his masterful technique": Ibid.
"almost the best": Kanin, p. 49.

"The thing about": Ibid.
"The only thing": Ibid.
193 "I've learned more": Ibid.
"a damn fine actress": Ibid.
"Tracy likes it": Bryan.
"put down—literally—": Kanin, p. 1.
"He began": *Look*, July 11, 1967.
194 "I'm afraid I'm": Ibid.
195 "Not me, boy": Ibid.
"and two clattering typists": Kanin, p. 82.
"always with enthusiasm": Ibid.
"gourmet stuff": Ibid.
"were too stiff": Ibid.
"Kate, I will give you": Ibid.
196 "It's all right": Bryan.

CHAPTER 15

199 "big-bear, Midwestern": McDowall, *Look*, July 11, 1967.
200 "I accidentally": Higham, *Kate*, p. 105.
"From the beginning": Ibid., p. 107.
201 "He's a sort": Kanin, p. 49.
"She was the rarer": Higham, *Kate*, p. 106.
202 "I'm alive, alert": Wayne Ober Park, *WP*, November 2, 1941.
204 "The average": *Geist*, p. 106.
"completely fucked it up": Ibid.
"the worst bunch": Ibid.
"The title part": *NYWT*, LCLHA, 1941.
205 "his face all": Kanin, p. 3.
206 "like an animal": Ibid., p. 5.
"On the conscious level": Ibid.
207 "Actors Tracy and Hepburn": Agee, *Time*, January, 1942.
"each complements": Donald Kirkley, *BS*, January, 1942.

CHAPTER 16

208 "Size 17": Bacon, p. 186.
209 "He could be a mean": Ibid.
"Kate and I": Ibid., p. 183.

"every name": Ibid.
210 "a shot or two": Harris, p. 53.
"Why?": Bacon, p. 262.
211 "The play never jelled": Langner, p. 219.
212 "a nice speech": *Life*, May 3, 1942.
"Its Broadway opening": LCLHA.
213 "girls, all sorts": *Daily Express*, London, April, 1950.
"Where were you?": Kanin, p. 108.
214 "a big put on": Carey, p. 129.
"the simple and pure": *Newsweek*, January, 1963.
215 "The story was": Lambert, p. 169.
216 "a wax work": Ibid.
"marvelous as the": Ibid.
"as a piece of": Ibid.
(fn) "The film is . . .": Ibid., p. 170.
217 "romantic glamor": Ibid.
218 "like an old bum": Earl Wilson, *Journal American*, June 15, 1943.
"wonderful English": Ibid.
219 "I get my hands": Ibid.
"Really deep consideration": *LAT*, March 12, 1943.
220 "I will fight": Ibid.
221 "he was intense": Signe Hasso, Deschner, p. 185.
222 "Peck and Peckish": James Agee, *Time*, April, 1944.
"twangy New England": Ibid.
"a rather wondrous": Barnes, *NYHT* April, 1944.
223 "People always said": Higham, *Kate*, p. 120.

CHAPTER 17

225 "spark off each other": Beaton, p. 100.
"dispense with all": Ibid.
226 "like a couple of": Ibid.
"their extravagances": Ibid.
"The Hepburns all love": Kanin, p. 114.
"First time I got": Capra, pp. 391–392.
228 "Most of all": Kanin, p. 96.
"I could be good": Ibid.
229 (fn) "Tracy quit": The Burns Mantle Theatre annual, 1945.
"Damn place": Kanin, p. 98.

"gave a performance": George Jean Nathan, *NYT*, November 11, 1945.

"I had tried to convey": Kanin, p. 99.

230 "too dumb to quit": Carey, p. 146.

"a lot of high-flown": Ibid., p. 147.

231 "everything you own": Kanin, p. 109.

"You already have": *Good Morning America* interview, November 5, 1984.

"where in the bedroom": Kanin, p. 54.

232 "no-nonsense": PI.

"considerate": PI.

"unprotected": PI.

"Fear is no builder": PI.

233 "I'm sure we'll": Minnelli, p. 176.

"getting the right": Ibid. p. 181.

234 "Can you see": Ibid.

"You know young man": Ibid.

235 "the proper techniques": Dickens, p. 138.

"with skill and feeling": *Time*, February, 1947.

"[he] plays Brahms": John McCarken, *The New Yorker*, February, 1947.

"vast, flat New Mexico": John McManus, *PM*, February, 1947.

CHAPTER 18

237 "At first I was": Carey, p. 151

"J. Parnell Thomas": *NYT*, May 22, 1947.

(fn) "Before every free": Edwards, *Judy Garland*, p. 117.

238 "very special": Carey, p. 152.

(fn) "the triumph of honesty": Katz, pp. 203–204.

239 "Waal, come to": Capra, p. 389.

"There are women": Capra, p. 389.

240 "Scratch a do-gooder": Carey, p. 154.

"You scratch some": Capra, p. 389.

"wisecracking, witty": PI.

"go off the deep end": PI.

242 "the happiest when": Edwards, *Vivien Leigh*, p. 154.

243 "Hepburn's antics": Lambert, p. 200.

245 "followed or appeased": *NYT*, June 9, 1949.

"the product of liars": Ibid.

"refused to dignify": Ibid.

246 "Kate definitely": Helburn, p. 308.

247 "I was so happy": *NYT*, January 22, 1950.

248 "There is too much": Brooks Atkinson, *NYT*, January 22, 1950.

CHAPTER 19

250 "I don't want": Earl Wilson, *Journal-American,* September 27, 1950.

"any woman": Ibid.

"We would have": UP, November 11, 1950.

252 "a gin-swilling": Dickens, p. 149.

253 "It is difficult": David Lewin, *Daily Express,* April 17, 1951.

254 "The thing about life": Ibid.

255 "I'm tall, skinny": Ibid.

"Katie starts out": Ibid.

"I'd say I": Ibid.

(fn) "She has the air of": Ibid.

(fn) "She wore her": *Sunday Express*, April 22, 1951.

(fn) "There was a press": Bacall, p. 181.

256 "a battery of press": Ibid.

"get on board": Ibid.

257 "natives dancing in": Ibid.

258 "The natives didn't": Ibid., p. 185.

"I hope you're not": David Robinson, LCLHA.

"Now you know": Ibid.

"Well, what is it": Ibid.

259 "I thought you said": Huston, p. 200.

260 "Upon meeting": Alistair Cooke, p. 129.

"dark haired juvenile": Ibid.

"the cryptic Hemingway": Ibid.

261 "The big joke": David Lewin, *Daily Express,* June 27, 1952.

"soft and sleek": McDowell, p. 23.

262 "with my Bdingo": Bacall, p. 187.

(fn) "he got the meat": Huston, p. 196.

263 "You *seem* to be": Ibid., p. 201.

"Presently we entered": Ibid.

264 "Stop Katie": Ibid.
"sit in camp": Ibid.
"all at once": Ibid.
265 "The water was": Behlmer, *America's Favorite Movies*,
p. 245.
266 "the many nights": Huston, p. 202.
"That's what they all": PI.

CHAPTER 20

269 "a smooth, fast-talking": Dickens, p. 152.
"in one frame": Kanin, p. 187.
"She can swing": Bosley Crowther, *NYT*, November, 1952.
270 "I am finishing": *Saturday Review*, November 1, 1952.
271 "Is she a good": Ibid.
272 "with such a furious": London *Times*, June 27, 1952.
"so vivid": Ibid.
273 "hit London with such": A. A. Darlington, London critic,
NYT, July 6, 1952.
"exhibition of personality": *NYT*, July 6, 1952.
"This millionairess": Ibid.
274 "a shade more edge": *NYT*, October 12, 1952.
"Drive on": *Daily Express*, September 25, 1952.
275 "indeterminate": Lesley, p. 317.
"fat little": Ibid., p. 318.
"Miss Hepburn had": Brooks Atkinson, *NYT*, October 18,
1952.
276 "beautifully conceived": Kanin, p. 166.
"to forego reimbursement": Ibid.

CHAPTER 21

278 "how old and gaunt": Korda, p. 388.
279 "no bare arms": Ibid.
280 "If you think": Ibid.
"vind machines": Ibid.
"It tastes lousy": Ibid.
281 "Nobody asked me": Thomas Wiseman, *Evening Standard*,
September 14, 1954.

Notes

"the sad mouth": *Saturday Review*, April, 1955.

"the greatest calcium": A. A. Darlington, The London *Times*, June 5, 1955.

282 "was to make": Lesley, p. 338.

"the best loosener-upper": Ibid.

284 "I have no idea": *The Melbourne Sun-Times*, June, 1955.

"The great shallow": Edwards, *Vivien Leigh*, p. 200.

285 "secretary-companion": Kanin, p. 196.

"gentle-gentlewoman": Ibid.

"he would often": Ibid.

286 "Mind you": Selznick.

289 "local people": Baker, p. 598.

"browned to a colour": Ibid., p. 601.

291 "blow-torched out": Dickens, p. 166.

"I used to get by": Thomas Wiseman, *Evening Standard*, January, 1956.

"She never lost": Higham, *Kate*, p. 159.

"to the cheap tricks": Dickens, p. 165.

292 "too fat and rich": Baker, p. 627.

"hoped to get through": Ibid.

"about the milder terrors": Dickens, p. 170.

"it almost burst": Ibid.

"they lope through": *NYT*, May, 1957.

294 "Goodbye, Spence": Carey, p. 187.

"Bogie's going": Ibid.

"getting on": *Films in Review*, May, 1957.

"People kept coming": *Newsweek*, May, 1957.

"getting drenched": Houseman, *Final Dress*, p. 80.

295 "If there was a": John Gassner, *NYT*, June 11, 1957.

"Miss Hepburn": Walter Kerr, *NYT*, June 14, 1957.

296 "I am sure that": Houseman, *Final Dress*, p. 86.

"unfeminine and": Ibid.

(fn) "watched a very young": Houseman, *Run-Through*, p. 79.

297 "weary but": Houseman, *Final Dress*, p. 86.

"I reminded him": Ibid.

". . . at the knee of": Ibid. p. 87.

"not only shrewd": Atkinson, *NYT*, August 8, 1957.

298 "always with a mingling": Houseman, *Run-Through*, p. 81.

"she joyfully": Ibid.

493

"Finally, during": Ibid.
"traveled with trunkloads": Helen Dudar, *NYDN*, 1967.
"they were such": Selznick, pp. 369–370.
299 "I've joked about": Swindell, p. 239.

CHAPTER 22

302 "the most talked about": Tischler.
"an oedipal relationship": Geist, p. 293.
"was somewhat damaged": Dickens, p. 173.
"starving Spanish": Geist, p. 293.
303 "to disguise": Ibid. p. 296.
(fn) "his own homosexual": Ibid.
(fn) "whose sensibilities": Ibid.
304 "Kate wanted very much": Ibid.
"gilded, ornately carved": Ibid.
"with a great": Ibid.
"haughty eccentricity"; Ibid.
"If you only": Ibid.
"That's the play": Ibid.
"worked diligently": Bosworth, p. 339.
"a crazy drunk": Ibid.
(fn) "a rare psychological": Katz, p. 246.
305 "added strength": Bosworth, p. 247.
306 "to get rid": Ibid., p. 339.
"he washed down": Ibid.
"He used to have": Ibid.
"none of my arguments": Ibid.
"I had all sorts": Geist, p. 294.
"was in": Ibid.
"in limousines": Ibid.
307 "When [Mrs. Venable]": Ibid., p. 297.
"Hepburn wanted": Ibid., p. 298.
"Are you absolutely": Ibid.
308 "To the best": Ibid., p. 298.
"When I disapprove": *McCall's*, February, 1979.
"[He] has little": Patrick Gabbi, *London Daily Telegraph*,
December 23, 1959.
"Kate is a playwright's": Tennessee Williams to *NYT*,
October, 1959.

(fn) "I didn't spit": Dick Cavett interview on ABC, October 2, 1973.

310 "who maintained her": *McCall's*, February, 1970.
(fn) "refrained from including": PI.

311 "a half-naked": *Saturday Review*, August, 1960.

312 "Miss Hepburn has": *NYHT*, June 4, 1960.
"You'd have to": KH to Calvin Tomkins, *Newsweek*, September, 1960.
"Tennessee Williams": Ibid.

313 "he was much too": Deschner, p. 15.
"breeze in ready": Ibid.

314 "if a makeup": Ibid.
"It's his concentration": Swindell, p. 248.
"Tracy had no": Deschner, p. 16.
"Tracy didn't want": Ibid.
"I finally stepped": Swindell, p. 248.
"I was afraid," Deschner, p. 14.

315 "thought and listened": Ibid.
"Nobody at Metro": Swindell, p. 250.
"the greatest actor": Ibid.

316 "Tracy was on": Ibid.
"he would twinkle": Ibid.
"still photographers": Deschner, p. 15.
"pretended that he": Ibid.
"Spence, these are": Swindell, p. 250.
"no matter what": Deschner, p. 14.

317 "casually picked up": Dudar, *NYDN*, July, 1969.

318 "he was literally": Deschner, p. 16.
"As the presiding": Larry Tubelle, *Hollywood Daily Variety*, 1962.

319 "It was extraordinary": Higham, *Kate*, p. 181.

321 "Her transformations": Arthur Knight, *The Saturday Review*, May, 1962.
"From being perhaps": Kael, pp. 298–299.
"that terrible smile": Dwight McDonald, *Esquire*, May, 1962.

322 "Dad had a": Leland Hayward Collection, LCLHA, January, 1963.
"dimly remembered": Arthur Knight, *Saturday Review*, May, 1962.

CHAPTER 23

325 "long, slow-paced": Swindell, p. 262.
326 "Mr. Tracy": Deschner, p. 17.
"During the filming": Ibid.
328 "as soon as a visitor": Carey, p. 206.
329 "all dowdied up": *NYT*, April, 1966.
330 "In case my niece": Ibid.
"I'm the best": Ibid.
"I'll give you": Ibid.
"[Kate] and I had": Higham, *Kate*, p. 191.
331 "She had to run": Ibid.
"he had finished": Carey, p. 211.
"I had the part": *Look*, July 11, 1967.
332 "the publicity guys": Higham, *Kate*, p. 189.
"She had declared": Jack Hamilton, *Look*, July 11, 1967.
333 "You know, I read": Carey, p. 212.
334 "Do you intend": Kanin, p. 269.
"Did you hear": Ibid., p. 250.
"To Spencer Tracy": Ibid.
335 "People said I": Kramer, p. 277.
"Mr. Tracy": Brendan Gill, *The New Yorker*, December, 1966.
336 "while either": Penelope Mortimer, London *Observer*, January, 1967.

CHAPTER 24

342 "a remarkable legacy": *LAT*, June 12, 1967.
343 "Oh *no*": *NYT*, December 9, 1973.
"in order to better": Ibid.
344 "When she came": Frook.
345 "talk-singing": Ibid.
"She's remarkably musical": Ibid.
"I sang for them": Ibid.
"working with": Carey, p. 219.
"She must have been": Frook.
346 "about the stage": Ibid.
"If we'd had a camera": Ibid.

"Look at this!": *Daily Express,* November 20, 1967.

"Peter, stop towering": Ibid.

"to a shadow": Ibid.

347 "Why on earth": Ibid.

"Triumphant in her": Judith Crist, *NYT,* November, 1968.

348 "her way through": Alexander Walker, *Standard,* May 21, 1968.

"It's true": Ibid.

"like a machine gun": Ibid.

"Deaf people": Ibid.

"Hide the ladder": Ibid.

350 "Well, I suspect": Ibid.

"I had twenty-five years": Ibid.

"I'm enormously": Motion Picture Academy of Arts and Sciences, Hepburn Archives.

(fn) "It was delightful": Kanin, p. 27.

351 "Much of what": Swindell, p. 250.

CHAPTER 25

352 "to end her": *Sunday Express,* July 27, 1969.

"I'm rich, fat": Ibid.

354 "I think": Israel Shenker, *NYT,* April 28, 1968.

"I was scared": *NYT,* December 9, 1973.

355 (fn) "Has anyone": Tennessee Williams, *Memoirs,* p. 170.

356 "from simplifying": *Newsweek,* November 10, 1969.

357 "She's Man": Ibid.

358 "I've felt all along": Ibid.

"Now that I've": Ibid.

359 "a disastrous party": *Time,* December 19, 1969.

"[Miss Hepburn's] voice": Clive Barnes, *NYT,* December 19, 1969.

360 "It's obviously": Hepburn speech, last Coco performance, August 1, 1970.

361 "The show has": Walter Kerr, *NYT,* December 21, 1969.

363 "I've never done": *Evening Standard,* September 11, 1970.

"Do you know": Ibid.

364 "As the old queen": Ibid.

365 "Miss Chanel": *Cleveland Plain Dealer,* January 12, 1971.

366 "Why would Katharine Hepburn": Ibid.

367 "They said I was: Higham, *Kate*, p. 212.
   "over and over": Ibid., p. 211.
   "The finger hung": Ibid.
   (fn) "Attacking Katharine Hepburn": *NYT*, November 11,
   1971.

CHAPTER 26

370 "three or four people": *LHJ*, August, 1975.
371 "a great strain": *TV Guide*, December 15, 1973.
   "There was a lifetime": *LHJ*, August, 1975.
372 "Well you know": *TV Guide*, December 15, 1973.
373 "the longest wooing": Ibid.
   "That part belongs": Ibid.
   "I can't get the": Ibid.
   "I'm too thin": Ibid.
374 "thought she was": Higham, *Kate*, p. 214.
   "I didn't have": Ibid.
375 "There's a lot of": Ibid.
   "I think we are": *NYT*, December 9, 1973.
376 "more about what": Higham, *Kate*, pp. 15–16.
377 "Don't tell me": Cavett interview on ABC, October 2 and 3,
   1973.
   "Do you want to hear": Ibid.
378 "Well, neither": Ibid.
379 "one mad": *NYT*, March 6, 1975.
   "We made love": Ibid.
   "outrageously candid": Ibid.
   (fn) "Thank God": Tennessee Williams, *Memoirs*, p. 84.
380 "got a kick out of": *LHJ*, October, 1975.
   "Miss Hepburn is": Ibid.
381 "I was born": UPI, October, 1975.

CHAPTER 27

382 "From head to toe": *TV Guide*, September 17, 1977.
383 "the crusader of just": Katz, p. 1214.
   "He was surrounded": *TV Guide*, September 17, 1977.
384 "He's sweet": UPI, September, 1977.

"I love her": Ibid.

"I haven't waited": Spada, p. 191.

"She's so feminine": Ibid.

385 "a crash of boulders": UPI, September, 1977.

"Damn!": Ibid.

"what a wonderful": Ibid.

"Something of an": Spada, p. 91.

386 "featuring two stars": Ibid.

"I pressed my face": *LHJ*, August, 1975.

387 "I gave it": Ibid.

"that I did": Ibid.

"Enid is": Clive Barnes, *NYT*, February 4, 1976.

"I always feel": Ibid.

"the old lady": Ibid.

388 "she sees": Ibid.

"Miss Hepburn play": Ibid.

390 "Because I've always": Spada, p. 194.

"That man": Ibid.

"This should prove": Spada, p. 194.

391 "You're a pig": *Time*, November 29, 1976.

"It's a me-": Carey, p. 247.

392 "was a concept": Ibid.

"religion was a sop": Ibid.

"as a sort": Bagnold, *Daily Express*, August 29, 1977.

"was done by": Ibid.

393 "someone moving": *TV Guide*, January 27, 1979.

"Walking from George's": Ibid.

394 "They put on": Ibid.

"a beautiful tenor": Ibid.

"thrilling": Ibid.

"spiffed up": Ibid.

"Fruit, eggs": Ibid.

395 "in front of": Ibid.

"Our relationship": Spada, p. 197.

"stiff and": *TV Guide*, January 27, 1979.

"the hills, valleys": Ibid.

CHAPTER 28

398 "I've never met": Teichman, *Fonda*, p. 344.
399 "read it and got": Ibid.
   "It's wonderful": Ibid.
   "Well, it's": Ibid.
400 "I knew the film": Ibid.
   "The first day": Ibid., p. 345.
401 "After all": Ibid.
   "I couldn't help": Ibid.
   "Henry Fonda's": Ibid., p. 348.
   "You want to hear": Ibid.
402 "Their affection": Spada, p. 208.
   "an authentic": Ibid.
403 "I don't think": *Hollywood Reporter*, August, 1980.
404 "I'm not sure": Walter Kerr, *NYT*, February 4, 1976.
405 "A Fonda can": Teichman, *Fonda*, p. 349.
406 "was hanging": *NYT*, December 14, 1976.
   "a cranky old": *Newsweek*, November 7, 1983.
407 "If people are": *McCall's*, November, 1984.
   "I'm not in a": Ibid.
   "Things are getting": *LHJ*, February, 1985.
   "I was always": *McCall's*, November, 1984.
408 "The two actors": *Variety*, May 16, 1984.
   "the abominable": *LHJ*, February, 1985.

Bibliography

BIBLIOGRAPHY

Agee, James. *Agee on Film*. Vol. II, New York: Perigee Books, 1983.

Bacall, Lauren. *By Myself*. New York: Alfred A. Knopf, 1979.

Bacheller, Martin A., ed. *The Hammond Almanac*. Maplewood, N.J.: Hammond Inc., 1982.

Bacon, James. *Hollywood Is a Four-Letter Town*. Chicago: Henry Regnery Co., 1976.

Bainbridge, John. *Garbo*. New York: Holt, Rinehart and Winston, 1971.

Baker, Carlos. *Ernest Hemingway: A Life Story*. London: Collins, 1969.

Bankhead, Tallulah. *Tallulah*. New York: Harper & Brothers, 1952.

Barker, Felix. *The Oliviers: A Biography*. London: Hamish Hamilton, 1953.

Barlett, Donald L. and James B. Steele. *Empire, The Life, Legend and Madness of Howard Hughes*. New York: W. W. Norton & Co., 1979.

Beaton, Cecil. *Photobiography*. London: Odhams Press Limited, 1951.

Behlmer, Rudy. *America's Favorite Movies: Behind the Scenes*. New York: Frederick Ungar Publishing Co., 1982.

Behlmer, Rudy, ed. *Memo from: David O. Selznick*. New York: Viking Press, 1972.

Bibliography

Billquist, Fritiof. *Garbo: A Biography.* New York: G. P. Putnam's Sons, 1960.

Boatner, Mark M. *The Civil War Dictionary.* New York: David McKay Co., Inc.

Bosworth, Patricia. *Montgomery Clift, A Biography.* New York: Harcourt Brace Jovanovich, 1978.

Burke, Billie. *With a Feather on My Nose.*

Capote, Truman. *The Muses Are Heard.* New York: Random House, 1956.

Capra, Frank. *The Name Above the Title: An Autobiography.* New York: Macmillan, 1971.

Carey, Gary. *Katharine Hepburn: A Hollywood Yankee.* New York: St. Martin's Press, 1983.

Carson, Julia M. H. *Mary Cassatt.* New York: David McKay Co., Inc., 1966.

Cavett, Dick. *Cavett.* New York: Harcourt Brace Jovanovich, 1974.

Collier, Christopher, with Bonnie B. Collier. *The Connecticut Scholar: The Literature of Connecticut History.* Middletown, Conn.: Connecticut Humanities Council, 1983.

Cooke, Alistair. *Six Men.* New York: Alfred A. Knopf, 1977.

Coward, Noël. *The Lyrics of Noël Coward.* Woodstock, N.Y.: Overlook Press, 1983.

Crofut, Florence S.M. *Guide to the History and Historic Sites of Connecticut.* Vol. II. New Haven, Conn.: Yale University Press, 1937.

Delury, George E., ed. *The World Almanac and Book of Facts.* New York: Newspaper Enterprise Assn., 1975.

Deschner, Donald. *The Films of Spencer Tracy.* Secaucus, N.J.: Citadel Press, 1971.

Dickens, Homer. *The Films of Katharine Hepburn.* Secaucus, N.J.: Citadel Press, 1971.

Edwards, Anne. *Judy Garland: A Biography.* New York: Simon and Schuster, 1975.

Edwards, Anne. *Road to Tara: The Life of Margaret Mitchell.* New Haven, Conn.: Ticknor & Fields, 1983.

Edwards, Anne. *Vivien Leigh: A Biography.* New York: Simon and Schuster, 1977.

Flanner, Janet. *Janet Flanner's World: Uncollected Writings, 1932–1975.* ed. Irving Drutman. London: Secker & Warburg, 1979.

Fonda, Henry. *Fonda: My Life,* as told to Howard Teichmann. New York: NAL Books, 1981.

Ford, Dan. *Pappy: The Life of John Ford.* Englewood Cliffs, N.J.: Prentice-Hall, Inc., 1979.

Fredrik, Nathalie. *Hollywood and the Academy Awards.* Beverly Hills, Cal.: Hollywood Awards Publications, 1969.

French, Philip. *The Movie Moguls.* London: Weidenfeld and Nicolson, 1969.

Frook, John. "Ageless Queen Full of Beans," *Life,* Lincoln Center Library, Hepburn Archives, undated.

Funke, Lewis and John E. Booth, ed. *Actors Talk About Acting.* New York: Avon Books, 1961.

Geist, Kenneth L. *Pictures Will Talk: The Life & Films of Joseph L. Mankiewicz.* New York: Da Capo Press, Inc., 1978.

Gerber, Albert B. *Bashful Billionaire: An Unauthorized Biography.* Secaucus, N.J.: Lyle Stuart, Inc., 1967.

Gottfried, Martin. *Jed Harris: The Curse of Genius.* Boston: Little, Brown and Co., 1984.

Hall, William H. *West Hartford,* West Hartford, Conn.: The West Hartford Chamber of Commerce, 1930.

Halliwell, Leslie. *Halliwell's Filmgoer's Companion.* 7th ed. New York: Charles Scribner's Sons, 1983.

Harris, Warren G. *Gable & Lombard.* New York: Simon and Schuster, 1974.

Harwell, Richard, ed. *Margaret Mitchell's Gone With the Wind Letters, 1936–1949.* New York: Macmillan, 1976.

Hayward, Brooke. *Haywire.* New York: Alfred A. Knopf, 1977.

Helburn, Theresa. *A Wayward Quest.* Boston: Little, Brown and Co., 1960.

Higham, Charles. *Kate: The Life of Katharine Hepburn.* New York: W. W. Norton & Co., 1975.

Higham, Charles and Joel Greenberg. *Hollywood in the Forties.* Hollywood, Cal.: Tantivy Press in association with A. Zwemmer Ltd. and A. S. Barnes & Co., Inc., 1968.

Houseman, John. *Final Dress.* New York: Simon and Schuster, 1983.

Houseman, John. *Front and Center.* New York: Simon and Schuster, 1979.

Houseman, John. *Run-Through.* New York: Simon and Schuster, 1973.

Huston, John. *An Open Book.* New York: Ballantine Books, 1981.

Bibliography

Johnson, Doris and Ellen Leventhal, eds. *The Letters of Nunnally Johnson*. New York: Alfred A. Knopf, 1981.

Kael, Pauline. *Kiss Kiss Bang Bang*. Boston: Little, Brown & Co., 1968.

Kanin, Garson. *Tracy and Hepburn*. New York: Viking Press, 1971.

Katz, Ephraim. *The Film Encyclopedia*. New York: Putnam Publishing Group, 1979.

Keats, John, *Howard Hughes*. New York: Random House, 1966.

Kelley, Kitty. *Elizabeth Taylor: The Last Star*. New York: Simon and Schuster, 1981.

Keylin, Arleen and Christine Bent, eds. *The New York Times at the Movies*. New York: Arno Press, 1979.

Koozarski, Richard. *Hollywood Directors 1914–1940*. New York: Oxford University Press, 1976.

Korda, Michael. *Charmed Lives*. New York: Random House, 1980.

LaGuardia, Robert. *Monty: A Biography of Montgomery Clift*. New York: Arbor House, 1977.

Lahr, John. *Coward, The Playwright*. London: Methuen London Ltd., 1982.

Lambert, Gavin. *On Cukor*. New York: G. P. Putnam's Sons, 1972.

Langner, Lawrence. *The Magic Curtain*. New York: E. P. Dutton & Co., 1951.

Lardner, Ring, Jr. *The Lardners: My Family Remembered*. New York: Harper & Row, 1976.

Lesley, Cole. *Remembered Laughter: The Life of Noel Coward*. New York: Alfred A. Knopf, 1976.

Love, William De Loss. *The Colonial History of Hartford*. U.S. Bicentennial Edition, Chester Conn.: Centinel Hill Press, in association with The Pequot Press, Inc., 1974.

MacGowan, Kenneth, ed. *Famous American Plays of the 1920's*. New York: Dell Publishing Co., 1959.

Marill, Alvin H. *Katharine Hepburn*. Pyramid Illustrated History of the Movies, Elmhurst, N.Y.: Pyramid Press, 1973.

Mathison, Richard. *His Weird and Wanton Ways: The Secret Life of Howard Hughes*. New York: William Morrow & Co., 1977.

McClintick, David. *Indecent Exposure*. New York: William Morrow and Co., 1982.

McDowell, Roddy. *Double Exposure*. New York: Delacorte Press, 1966.

Michael, Paul. *The Academy Awards: A Pictorial History*. New York: Crown Publishers, 1972.

Mills, Lewis Sprague, M. A. *The Story of Connecticut*. W. Rindge, N.H.: Richard R. Smith Publisher, Inc., 1958.

Minnelli, Vincente. *I Remember It Well*. New York: Berkley Publishing Group, 1974.

Moore, Terry. *The Beauty and the Billionaire*. New York: Pocket Books, 1984.

Mordden, Ethan. *Movie Star: A Look at the Women Who Made Hollywood*. New York: St. Martin's Press, 1983.

O'Brien, Pat. *The Wind at My Back*. Garden City, N.Y.: Doubleday & Co., 1964.

Parker, John. *Who's Who in the Theatre*, 13th ed., ed. Freda Gaye. New York: Pitman Publishing Corp., 1961.

Phelan, James. *Howard Hughes: The Hidden Years*. New York: Random House, 1976.

Pratt, William. *Scarlett Fever*. New York: Macmillan, 1977.

Rhoden, Harold. *High Stakes: The Gamble for the Howard Hughes Will*. New York: Crown, 1980.

Robinson, David. "The Hepburn Years," Lincoln Center Library, Hepburn Archives, undated.

St. John, Adela Rogers. *The Honeycomb*. Garden City, N.Y.. Doubleday & Co., 1969.

Sanders, Marion K. *Dorothy Thompson: A Legend in Her Time*. Boston: Houghton Mifflin Co., 1973.

Sarris, Andrew. *The American Cinema, Directors and Directions 1929–1968*. New York: E. P. Dutton & Co., 1968.

Sellers, Helen Earle. *Connecticut Town Origins*. Stonington, Conn.: Pequot Press, 1942.

Selznick, Irene Mayer. *A Private View*. New York: Alfred A. Knopf, 1983.

Shipman, David. *The Great Movie Stars: The Golden Years*. New York: Hill and Wang, 1970.

Signoret, Simone. *Nostalgia Isn't What It Used to Be*. New York: Harper & Row, 1978.

Simon, John. *Singularities*. New York: Random House, 1975.

Sobel, Bernard, ed. *The Theatre Handbook*. New York: Lothrop, Lee and Shepard, 1943.

Bibliography

Spada, James. *Hepburn: Her Life in Pictures*. Garden City, N.Y.: Doubleday & Co., 1984.

Spoto, Donald. *Stanley Kramer Film Maker*, New York: G. P. Putnam's Sons, 1978.

Swindell, Larry. *Spencer Tracy: A Biography*. Mountain View, Cal.: World Publishing Co., 1969.

Taylor, John Russell. *The Penguin Dictionary of Theatre*. New York: Penguin Books, 1981.

Thomas, Bob. *Astaire, The Man, the Dancer*. New York: St. Martin's Press, 1984.

Thomas, Bob. *King Cohn*. New York: Bantam Books, 1968.

Time-Life Books. *This Fabulous Century, 1950–1960*. New York: Time-Life Books, 1970.

Tischler, Nancy. *Tennessee Williams: Rebellious Puritan*. Secaucus, N.J.: Citadel Press, 1965.

Todd, Charles Burr. *In Olde Connecticut*. New York: Grafton Press, 1906.

Vermilye, Jerry. *The Films of the Thirties*. Secaucus, N.J.: Citadel Press, 1982.

Wansell, Geoffrey. *Haunted Idol: The Story of the Real Cary Grant*. New York: William Morrow and Co., 1984.

Warner, Charles. *Contemporary Man of Letters Series*, ed. William Aspenwall Bradley. New York: McClure, Phillips & Co., 1904.

Warner, Charles Dudley. *My Summer in a Garden*. Boston: Houghton Mifflin Co., 1871.

Williams, Neville. *Chronology of the Modern World, 1763–1965*. New York: Penguin Books, 1975.

Williams, Tennessee. *Memoirs*. Garden City, N.Y.: Doubleday & Co., 1975.

Wilson, Edmund. *The Forties*. New York: Farrar, Straus & Giroux, 1984.

Wilson, Edmund. *The Thirties*. New York: Farrar, Straus & Giroux, 1980.

Yardley, Jonathan. *Ring: A Biography of Ring Lardner*. New York: Random House, 1977.

Index

INDEX

511

She was called "Katharine of Arrogance," a stranger to compromise who blasted McCarthyites and male chauvinists, who ridiculed the press, defied convention and the Hollywood system to become one of the greatest stars of our time. Here is the Hepburn who paraded in her underwear on a movie set when the studio took away her worn-out dungarees . . . whose father managed her money and refused to buy her a dress (she was forty years old) . . . the fearless Hepburn who never dined in restaurants because she was terrified of people watching her eat . . . who enjoyed breaking into strangers' houses and using their pools . . . who adored Spencer Tracy, the only man who could really "smash her down."

"By far the most interesting material in the book concerns Hepburn's long-standing affair with Spencer Tracy . . . the attachment that impressed Hollywood with its taste and discretion is meticulously detailed."
—Cosmopolitan

"*A REMARKABLE WOMAN* captures the singularity that has made this Yankee icon seemingly invulnerable to fashion."
—The New York Times Book Review

"Veteran biographer Anne Edwards offers a remarkably open portrait of Hepburn. . . . Nearly every page is footnoted with fascinating mini-biographies and Hollywood minutiae. Edwards has also gotten Hepburn's friends to talk about the actress's relationships with Spencer Tracy and Howard Hughes . . . A TOP-NOTCH EFFORT."
—Library Journal

Books by Anne Edwards

A Remarkable Woman: A Biography
    of Katharine Hepburn
Vivien Leigh: A Biography

Published by POCKET BOOKS